SCREENWRITERS ADVICE

The Guerilla Filmmakers Handbooks
Series Editors:
Andrew Zinnes, Genevieve Jolliffe, and Chris Jones

Also Published in the Series

The Guerilla Film Makers Handbook, 3rd edition (UK Edition)
Chris Jones and Genevieve Jolliffe

The Guerilla Film Makers Handbook (US Edition)
Genevieve Jolliffe and Chris Jones

The Guerilla Film Makers Movie Blueprint
Chris Jones

The Guerilla Film Makers Pocketbook: The Ultimate Guide to Digital Film Making
Chris Jones, Andrew Zinnes & Genevieve Jolliffe

The Documentary Filmmakers Handbook (2nd Edition)
Genevieve Jolliffe and Andrew Zinnes

SCREENWRITERS ADVICE

FROM POPULAR AND AWARD-WINNING FILM, TV, AND STREAMING SHOWS

ANDREW ZINNES & GENEVIEVE JOLLIFFE

BLOOMSBURY ACADEMIC
NEW YORK • LONDON • OXFORD • NEW DELHI • SYDNEY

BLOOMSBURY ACADEMIC
Bloomsbury Publishing Inc
1385 Broadway, New York, NY 10018, USA
50 Bedford Square, London, WC1B 3DP, UK
29 Earlsfort Terrace, Dublin 2, Ireland

BLOOMSBURY, BLOOMSBURY ACADEMIC and the Diana logo are trademarks of Bloomsbury Publishing Plc

First published in the United States of America 2024

Copyright © Andrew Zinnes and Genevieve Jolliffe, 2024

For legal purposes the Acknowledgments on p. 9 constitute an extension of this copyright page.

Cover design: Andrew Zinnes & Genevieve Jolliffe
Cover image © Antti Heikkinen / iStockPhoto / Getty Images
Photo Credit of Bill Nicholson: Finn Beales

All rights reserved. No part of this publication may be reproduced or transmitted in any form or by any means, electronic or mechanical, including photocopying, recording, or any information storage or retrieval system, without prior permission in writing from the publishers.

Bloomsbury Publishing Inc does not have any control over, or responsibility for, any third-party websites referred to or in this book. All internet addresses given in this book were correct at the time of going to press. The author and publisher regret any inconvenience caused if addresses have changed or sites have ceased to exist, but can accept no responsibility for any such changes.

A catalog record for this book is available from the Library of Congress.

ISBN: HB: 978-1-5013-6328-3
       PB: 978-1-5013-6327-6
       ePDF: 978-1-5013-6330-6
       eBook: 978-1-5013-6331-3

Series: The Guerilla Filmmaker's Handbooks

Typeset by Andrew Zinnes
Printed and bound in Great Britain

To find out more about our authors and books visit www.bloomsbury.com and sign up for our newsletters.

TABLE OF CONTENTS

Introduction to Screenwriters Advice	8
Acknowledgments/Legal Disclaimer	9
Contributors	10
Chapter 1: **The Idea**	15
Chapter 2: **Pitching**	33
Chapter 3: **Breaking Story**	53
Chapter 4: **Character**	83
Chapter 5: **Dialogue**	109
Chapter 6: **Rules?**	123
Chapter 7: **Finding Your Voice**	133
Chapter 8: **Screenwriting Competitions**	139
Chapter 9: **Writing Teams**	147
Chapter 10: **The Writers Room & Writing On Set**	157
Chapter 11: **Rewriting**	183
Chapter 12: **Action & Thriller**	195
Chapter 13: **Horror & Sci-Fi**	207
Chapter 14: **Horror Comedy**	223
Chapter 15: **Telenovelas**	229
Chapter 16: **Comedy**	237
Chapter 17: **Romantic Comedy**	247
Chapter 18: **Drama & Adaptation**	259
Chapter 19: **Animation & Family**	275
Chapter 20: **The Business**	291
Chapter 21: **Perspective**	315
Chapter 22: **Inspiration**	331
Writing Exercises & References	351
Index	356

LIST OF TIPS

High Concept/Low Concept	20
Spec Screenplays	24
Short Film Screenplays	27
Types of Pitches	35
Online Pitching	37
IP/Public Domain	39
Bake Off	41
Narrative Transport	43
Pitching Tips	45
Tone	46
TV Series Bible vs. Pitch Deck	51
The Hero's Journey	55
Open World vs. Closed World	56
The Call To Adventure	61
Story Structure	63
Jed Mercurio's Critical Mass Theory	65
Screenwriting Books	67
Writer's Block	75
Development Documents	76
Motivation	85
Flat Characters vs. Dynamic Characters	87
Anti-Heroes	97
Supporting Characters	100
Character Identity	104
Dialogue Tips	117
Screenwriting Podcasts, Websites & Blogs	128
Screenwriting Courses	136

LIST OF TIPS

Screenwriting Competitions	141
The Black List	143
Screenwriting Software	151
Mini & Alternative Rooms	163
TV & Streaming Producer Credits (USA)	177
Killing Your Darlings	186
Development Terms	188
The First 10 Pages	190
WGA Credit Arbitration	294
Writing Step Terms	297
Development Hell/Turnaround	298
Copyrighting Your Screenplay	301
Options & Shopping Agreements	302

INTRODUCTION TO SCREENWRITERS ADVICE

All narrative filmed content, no matter if it's a feature film, series or a short, starts with a screenplay. Without one, a project can get chaotic, which usually results in a lot of time and money wasted. Over the years, we at *The Guerilla Film Makers Handbook* have interviewed a screenwriter or two in order to shed light on what a filmmaker needs to know about the craft. However, given screenwriting's importance to the process, plus the developing need for new and more diverse stories, we feel it needs greater exploration. So, as with all our books, we asked professional screenwriters from across all formats and genres, their opinions on topics related to their craft via our staple Q&A style. However, there are a couple of points we want to make to help orient the read.

Only interviewing screenwriters presents an interesting challenge. In our other books, we speak to one expert from each area of the industry who answers 10-15 pertinent questions on that craft. We don't have such variety this time around, so we altered the approach to a "roundtable" or "panel" format. In each chapter, you will see the questions we asked in bold followed by multiple answers from screenwriters. We feel this promotes a richer discussion of the topics and allows our readers to compare and contrast the information to a greater extent.

There are a myriad of books on screenwriting available these days that employ a "how-to" approach from the POV of the author. You can view a list of them on page 67. While these are useful and we wholeheartedly encourage reading as many as possible, we are not trying to be Syd Field or Robert McKee. We fundamentally believe that humans learn best from hearing a wide variety of stories and experiences of others in their own voices. So while we give tips on story theory, we are not positioning ourselves or the book as "gurus" or some other sage-like term. For us, it has always been about democratizing information for you to use as you see fit.

So it is with great pleasure that we introduce, *Screenwriters Advice*. We hope it will enlighten, inspire, and entertain a new generation of screenwriters who will have their work on all screens big and small.

Andrew and Genevieve, 1.39 am, May 4, 2023

ACKNOWLEDGMENTS

Making a book like this is never a solitary endeavor. So we would like to thank...

All of our contributors who gave up their valuable time to share their hard earned knowledge with the hope that others may learn from their experience. We know that they are all extremely busy individuals but even so, they managed to find time out of their hectic lifestyles to sit down and share with us (and you) their advice.

Jennifer Champagne, Gloria Fan, Lizzie Francke, Hilary Galanoy, Alex Goldstone, Chris Jones, Dan MacRae, Ryan Saul, Jane Steventon, John Tomko, Jeanette Volturno, and Karen Walton for introducing us to some of our contributors.

To Casey Mae, Caleb, and Cash who make life wonderful.

To Chris and Jo Jolliffe, Lynn and Stan Morris, and Allen Zinnes for their never ending patience with our exploits.

We dedicate this book to Ilse Stoll Zinnes.

LEGAL DISCLAIMER
PLEASE READ FIRST!

Nothing in this book should be considered as legal advice. The information provided and any samples or examples contained within are not a substitute for consulting with an experienced entertainment lawyer and receiving counsel based on the facts and circumstances of a particular transaction. Furthermore, case law and statues for the United States, United Kingdom, European and other international law and industry practice are subject to change, and differ from country to country.

The authors of this book and the publishers cannot be held responsible for any losses or claims arising from any use of the information contained within.

CONTRIBUTORS

SCOTT BECK
65
A QUIET PLACE

BRIANA BELSER
GINNY AND GEORGIA
ALL RISE

MICHAEL BRANDT
CHICAGO FIRE
WANTED

ELI CRAIG
LITTLE EVIL
TUCKER & DALE VS EVIL

CHRIS CULLARI
THE AVIARY
12 DEADLY DAYS

HILARY GALANOY
FALLING INN LOVE
LOVE, GUARANTEED

JOSH GREENBERG
LAST MAN STANDING
THE MCCARTHYS

MARSHA GREENE
THE PORTER
CORONER

ELIZABETH HACKETT
FALLING INN LOVE
LOVE, GUARANTEED

DEBORAH HAYWOOD
PIN CUSHION
BEAK

LAUREN IUNGERICH
ON MY BLOCK
AWKWARD

TONY JORDAN
DEATH IN PARADISE
DICKENSIAN

CONTRIBUTORS

EMMA KO
1899
DANI'S HOUSE

PAUL KING
WONKA
PADDINGTON

MEG LEFAUVE
INSIDE OUT
MY FATHER'S DRAGON

RON LESHEM
EUPHORIA
VALLEY OF TEARS

ALEX LITVAK
THE THREE MUSKETEERS
PREDATORS

SCOTT LOBDELL
HAPPY DEATH DAY
MAN OF THE HOUSE

MOHAMAD EL MASRI
SEVERENCE
OCTOBER FACTION

DAN MAZER
BORAT
DIRTY GRANDPA

JED MERCURIO
LINE OF DUTY
TRIGGER POINT

BILL NICHOLSON
THIRTEEN LIVES
GLADIATOR

JOSH OLSON
A HISTORY OF VIOLENCE
TRIGGER WARNING

BEN PHILIPPE
ONLY MURDERS IN THE BUILDING
INTERVIEW WITH THE VAMPIRE

CONTRIBUTORS

JENNIFER RAITE
THE AVIARY
12 DEADLY DAYS

DAVE REYNOLDS
GARFIELD
FINDING NEMO

CAROLINA RIVERA
THE WAR NEXT DOOR
JANE THE VIRGIN

BARBARA STEPANSKY
OUTLANDER
TOTENFRAU

DANNY STRONG
DOPESICK
THE HUNGER GAMES:
MOCKINGJAY

BECCA TOPOL
MIRA, ROYAL DETECTIVE
ELENA OF AVALOR

KAREN WALTON
ORPHAN BLACK
GINGER SNAPS

JULIE SHERMAN WOLFE
A HOLIDAY SPECTACULAR
A DICKENS OF A HOLIDAY!

BRYAN WOODS
65
A QUIET PLACE

MOÍSES ZAMORA
SELENA: THE SERIES
STAR

GET AN IDEA

WRITE IT DOWN

REWRITE

CHAPTER 1

THE IDEA

The most important part of screenwriting is sometimes the most difficult to discuss. But our panel of screenwriters is up to the challenge of explaining how they generate their concepts and how they figure out if they are worth pursuing. Should it be a feature film? Should it go to a streamer? Will it pigeonhole me into a certain genre? It's all part of the mental calculus used when figuring out what makes a good story.

Q: How do you come up with your ideas?

Tony Jordan - You don't. Life comes up with ideas. Life comes up with interesting things that inspire you in some way. As a writer, you just observe. That can be something as obvious as a story on the TV that leads to something. It could be a book. It could be a conversation with a friend. It could be a story that you hear from someone else. "You will never believe what just happened to me!" It's things that get you excited. The idea of a writer sitting in a dark room waiting for that light bulb to appear over his head with a bright idea, I think is a bit nonsensical.

Alex Litvak - I write what appeals to me. I start with what appeals to my head and what appeals to my heart. Where do I get engaged intellectually so that I want to spend time solving the creative math problems within that story? Also, where can I break off a piece of myself and put it into that character or that scene?

Scott Lobdell - Allen Ginsberg once said, *"Writers notice what they notice."* And it's true. After it's rained, everybody sees the earthworm on the sidewalk. People walk over it and don't notice it's been squished. A writer does. A writer is the person who is able to present a detail that triggers a response in the reader.

Bill Nicholson - I think my ideas come from my life. Serendipity. The brain of a writer is like a strip of flypaper - that sticky stuff they used to hang from ceilings to catch flies. Your brain is like that and things stick to it. Anything that sticks to it that begins with some dim idea, begins to grow. You become extremely receptive. I'm now on my twenty-first completed movie and almost without exception, somebody has come to me and said, "We want to make this film. Will you write it for us?" That means they are already semi-committed to it. Whereas, when I send them something out of the blue, quite often all of their instincts say, "Oh, this isn't part of our plan. We're thinking no." Sadly, I think a lot of my time has consisted of responding to ideas that I receive. However, when I receive them, I transform them like every writer.

Hilary Galanoy - My writing partner and I get ideas from all around us. It can be a dating or a romance experience of our own; a romantic story we heard from a friend; an article we read that inspires us. Sometimes, we option ideas from IP, like a book. Much of the time, though, the best ideas come from us brainstorming situations like, "Wouldn't it be funny if X happened?"

Moisés Zamora - I think my ideas come from my identity. Who I am. My experience. Things that I truly believe could change the world or at least the mindset about something. It goes back to what you are passionate about, what you love. So if I love an idea, it could be from art, personal experience, reading another book, or another artist, anything; I pay attention to whether, after a while, that idea lingers in my head. I also think the process for me now is in crafting. How do I package it? How do I structure it? How do I develop those storylines that have commercial appeal? I know commercial sounds like a dirty word, but Shakespeare was commercial and popular. What that tells you is that people have got to love your art. I'm not interested in creating art that is not accessible. So I'm not going to take on a project in which I don't believe, in some way or another, at a core level.

Lauren Iungerich - Usually, my ideas are based on themes I am working on or working through as a person or related to some kind of storytelling that I was inspired by as I was coming up and don't see in the entertainment landscape anymore. So I'm inspired to fill that gap.

Jed Mercurio - I think the first thing to do is to pursue a cognitive process where you are seeking ideas rather than expecting ideas to land on you. The word "inspiration" can sometimes be misleading, creating the idea that there is a magical process and if you make yourself receptive to that magic, it will happen. Actually, it's all about the creative labor of following what's happening in the news; seeing what's going on in the world; watching TV; reading books and just absorbing events and incidents from the world around you. Also, think about the kinds of things that you're personally interested in. If you can find a happy juxtaposition or a happy synergy between what you are interested in and ideas that come from the outside world, then that's a good starting point for an idea. But as we know, ideas are cheap and you should have lots and lots of ideas. It's more about how you shape them than the idea itself.

Ron Leshem - As writers, we always tend to forget that we are going to spend five years with a project. We have to love this world if we're going to be living in it for five years. I'll be crying about how long it takes to produce something - to green-light something. *Euphoria* in the U.S. took us six and half years of everyone saying no. *Valley of Tears* took us ten years. Aaron Sorkin, I think he wrote the *Chicago 7* or was fighting for it for something like fifteen to twenty years. My friend, Matthew Winer, wrote the pilot for *Mad Men* in 1994 and it was produced in 2007. So you are going to live and fight for this world for so long. We tend to choose something that sounds exciting or is sellable, but we often forget where our passion lies.

Eli Craig - Usually, it's an "a-ha" moment. Then, 90% of those get scrapped after having thought they were the most genius idea anybody has ever thought up. When those moments hit, you have to write it down - the general thought. I keep a long list of ideas. Sometimes, they go away and come back later. But to nail down the idea and distill it and understand the genre and where it's coming from, I try to geolocate it into a group of movies. So when I was looking at *Tucker and Dale,* the movies I was watching were *The Texas Chainsaw Massacre* and *The Evil Dead.* Then, I watched the *Wrong Turn* series and *Dumb and Dumber.* My thought was, what if I take all these movies and stick them together? What would it look like?

Becca Topol - I spend a lot of time reading to come up with inspiration for new ideas. Most of my original ideas come from themes I want to explore. Other times, production companies or studios will approach me with an idea and then I'll need to find a way in. To me, this means coming up with a way to connect with the idea, flesh it out and make it my own.

Scott Lobdell - *Happy Death Day* started out with me wanting to upend the horror movie expectation where the bad girl dies in the beginning. She's the first kill. The last kill is usually the good girl, running around in her underwear trying to keep the dead killer, dead. Are people going to want to follow a bad girl for an entire movie? Probably not. Are they going to cheer as the good girl gets killed? How do I make a movie where the bad girl is the hero? Well, maybe she starts out bad, but then she becomes a better person through this horrible experience. But if the horrible experience is getting killed, then she would have to get better each time. Yes, that is a *Groundhog Day* mechanism, but I didn't start out to make a *Groundhog Day* horror movie. It was, "How do I make a horror movie where the bad girl lives to the end?"

Marsha Greene - My ideas come from all over the place. One show came from watching a makeover reality show where a woman who was training to be a priest wanted to date. I had all these questions. Does she have a Tinder profile? Does she say she's a minister? Another show came from thinking about the decisions you make when you are young. A twenty-year-old woman has a baby girl and gives it up for adoption, assuming she has all the time in the world to get married and have a baby. She's now thirty-nine and it's never happened. Then, the daughter comes back into her life. I have never gone through that, but I didn't become a screenwriter until I was in my early 30s. I had a serious boyfriend and I faced a choice: I could marry this guy, live in a certain place, and have this whole life ahead of me; or, I could start all over again with my career. I don't regret my decision, but then again, I didn't get married or have children. So it was more about: would I have made that decision if I had known what I know now? So my question became the show. My ideas often start with a thought and then develop into what I think that would be like for a person.

Dan Mazer - Sometimes, I will have an idea for a funny scene or idea or a ridiculous notion. I will store those up and think about how they will fit into a particular movie that I'm writing. I will try to engineer the plot to try and include five or six of those. They are the things that people will come away from the movie talking about. For example, in *I Give It A Year*, every Christmas, the charade scene in that goes around as a meme. Friends get in touch with me and ask if I've seen it. People may not have seen the movie, but they really like the funny scene. I sort of take great pride in the fact that those comedy moments live on, rather than being a pleasant meander through a vague plot with ten jokes in there. I like comedies to be properly laugh-out-loud funny. So the naked fight in *Borat* or the cage fight in *Brüno* or the charade scene in *I Give It A Year,* for example. It's important to create memorable set pieces.

Barbara Stepansky - My ideas come from everywhere. Images, characters, newspaper articles, even travel destinations. I'm a big history buff so a lot of my ideas come from reading history books and thinking about how certain events could be fictionalized.

Scott Lobdell - I was at a funeral in New York and at the wake the night before, I went out to get some air. Outside, there was this elderly couple and me. While we were about to pass the parking lot, a man came out and asked us to stop for a minute to let a hearse leave because it had to pick up a body. I said, "That's interesting. You ask us wait for the one person who is not in a hurry." I said it not to be funny, just as an observation. The older man next to me says, "Most heart transplants take place at 2 a.m.? Do you know why that is?" I had no idea and he told me that the time between the airport and the hospital has to be the shortest amount of time and that would be in the dead of night. No traffic. I wondered how he knew that and he said he was a heart surgeon. They walked on and I was left standing there thinking that was the coolest idea for a movie. I then found out that a bypass machine can only circulate blood for 102 minutes. And what's the average script length? 102 pages. It was right there! This is my way to do *Speed*. And it would be in real-time. I knew that the movie would open with a woman going under because a donor heart would be landing at the local airport and she would have to be prepped for surgery. It's now a movie that's in production called *Bypass*. A story about a transplanted heart that has to get from the airport to the hospital and the bad guys attack. It's up to these two EMTs to get it there. That idea came from stopping in the parking lot and speaking to that doctor while we waited.

Q: Does life experience shape you as a writer?

Tony Jordan - Completely. I discovered the power of that during my *EastEnders* days, a hundred years ago. We had some domestic scenes that were, potentially, quite close to me. I remember the character, Frank Butcher's daughter, Janine, went missing when she was a kid, so we had a missing child story. I have six kids. The only way I could write that scene properly was to put myself in that place and imagine. So I had to choose a child that went missing in my head. It was kind of like *Sophie's Choice,* but Tony's Choice. Then, when I am writing dialogue for Frank, I'm literally pouring out my heart. It's what I am feeling at that moment. I remember writing that scene and sobbing with snot bubbles. You have to use that stuff.

I didn't start writing until I was thirty-five. Thrown out of school at fourteen. I've worked about a hundred different jobs. I was a market trader for years. I've done things that, perhaps, I shouldn't have done. I've been married a hundred times. Divorced. I've got six kids. I've had a life. So not using any of that seems a bit daft. It's like having a Ferrari and not putting any petrol in it. Just have it sitting in the garage and playing with the radio.

> ## HIGH CONCEPT/LOW CONCEPT
>
> When producers or financiers are considering your projects, they will often sort them into high concept and low concept ideas.
>
> **High concept** stories have a central premise so clear that you can see the story unfold from a very short logline. The concept usually has a very specific goal. Many genre films (comedy, action, etc.) are high concept.
>
> Example: Three friends must retrace their steps following a debaucherous stag night in Las Vegas in order to find the missing groom and get him to his wedding on time. (*The Hangover*)
>
> **Low concept** stories tend to be more nebulous; the concept isn't the central driver. You may get a subject matter or character and you may know the time period, but the plot could go in any direction. Most dramas tend to be low concept.
>
> Example: In New England, a repairman reluctantly returns to his hometown to take care of his nephew following his brother's death. (*Manchester By The Sea*)

Meg LeFauve - Life experience makes you who you are. At the end of the day, it's the base that's creating the writing. Personally, I'm always driving towards how I see and experience the world. My POV of the world. Emotionally, especially. When I am teaching writing, I always ask, "What's personal about this?" I'm not talking about memoirs. I'm saying emotionally and psychologically. To me, that's the difference between craft and art. Don't get me wrong, you certainly have to have craft as a screenwriter; that is a huge part of it. To elevate it to art and great storytelling, it has to be threads of your own vulnerability and perspective on the world. That comes from your life experience.

Briana Belser - Oh my God, I am so American. Like denim jeans and apple pie! When you grow up in a Black town in a Black city, there's a contrast between "mainstream" or "being White" or "half Black in a Black community." There are so many divisions. I thought, "I'm so special!" No. I did a semester in Spain and I didn't know that Spain had a regime! I didn't know that they had gone through a dictatorship! They could tell me about the Obamas and this and that. It was humbling. Also, the students that I lived with told me about the Spanish grading scale, 1 through 10. 10 is equivalent to an A and maybe 3 and below would be an F. I'm trying to get 10s on everything and the Spaniards are like, "I got a 6, that's enough. Let's go hang. Let's go play." They were so perplexed by my drive to wring out every point. They were like, "For what? You will graduate with all 10s and I'll graduate with all 6s and we'll have the same degree." It questioned and challenged this notion of working hard for the sake of perfectionism. I was letting perfection be the enemy of the good. It taught me character-building and to a certain extent, world-building, by getting out of my head. To avoid getting bogged down in detail and minutiae almost to the point that you might never finish a script. I have a couple of writing friends who have been writing the same script for five or ten years. I think about that when I write. This is going to get revised. Get to the next draft. That's what life experience brought me.

Carolina Rivera - Something I get from my students a lot is, "Do I have to live this to be able to write about it?" They are twenty years old and they want to write a character that's fifty. Am I going to be able to write this or not? Yes, you are just going to write it differently than if you were someone sixty years old writing someone who is fifty. From my own experience, my characters are of all ages. Of course, I might write them wrong, but that's why you have a writers room, it helps. If you are writing a feature by yourself, you had better do some research. Is this how kids talk now? I better go ask my kids!

Ron Leshem - There's a reason why it's rare to see someone young in a showrunner role. You have to spend endless years with a show. You need maturity and life experience and enormous patience. A twenty-five-year-old might be brilliant at creating a film, but not when creating a series. You have to be able to say a lot about life. For me, being a journalist was the best gift ever. I was a news writer, but I was also a news editor and could listen to hundreds of stories a day or a week and look for the nuances as to what makes this story unique. What would make somebody listen to this story? What makes it different from the other stories that were told tons of times? And you have to do all of this in a ticking clock environment. In Israel, a guy would write a story about his very funny childhood in the kibbutz and then his very sad childhood in the kibbutz. What's going to be his third film if he didn't get the tools to write other voices? "Now, I want to be a girl in Japan. How do I do that?" If you are attracted to the story of a girl in Japan, you just need the tools of a journalist to be there and try to empty yourself of all your language and vocabulary and try to think like someone else.

Eli Craig - As a writer, I think you go through different stages in life of what you are doing and I don't think they are necessarily better or worse. Some people write incredible things when they are teenagers. Sometimes, you will have a dry spell and then you will find the thing that's really cooking on all cylinders. I do believe that stories are things that are out there that you are trying to discover. Not to sound too far out, but it's like the movie exists somewhere and you're just trying to find it. It's not so much that you are creating it. It's like sculpting… you're just getting rid of all the pieces that don't work.

Jed Mercurio - There are plenty of writers who have little life experience and seem to have been involved in creative endeavors their entire adult life who have done very well. And then some people come to it late with quite a rich background of primary experience. So I don't think you can say one rules over the other. I think it's what works for the individual writer. If you can exploit your primary experience and add authenticity and verisimilitude to your work that makes it distinctive, I think that's incredibly helpful to you as an individual. But if that's not what you are about - you are writing entirely escapist things, then that's no barrier.

Dave Reynolds - My first job was as a staff writer on *Late Night with Conan O'Brien*. I was one of the original writers on that show. Our challenge was to mount a talk show with someone who had never been on camera. Conan O'Brien was, and still is, a fantastically gifted and hilarious writer and personality - our job was to figure out how to get that out to the public via a talk show. Robert Smigel was our head writer and he and Conan had the idea of doing things like sketches and fake guests. And to do this was a challenge. We were all huge fans of David Letterman's show, so we worked hard not to do anything that would step on his legacy. If Dave did a specific bit outside of the studio, say in the hallway near the elevators, we couldn't have Conan do anything similar. We had to learn to write differently.

Robert Smigel was an amazing head writer who was schooled at *SNL* and taught us all how to mine the best line or idea for a sketch. For example, if we needed one line to button a sketch, he might ask you to write ten different versions of that line. He would look over your list and say that he liked line number two and number six. So I knew to write ten more versions of line two and ten more versions of number six. This would continue as we would whittle it down until he said, "That's the joke." And it was. You learned to keep honing in to find the best version of your initial idea. Tossing good ideas aside in the process as you keep trying new angles. The other fifty versions of the one line get thrown in the bin. You can't go, "Wait, what about all of those?" They are done. They were good, maybe great, but they were not the right one. I think that skill is key to any writer. To be willing to toss out good ideas to get to the best.

What I learned on late night television was the ability to adapt, the ability to toss something out without regret. I always said the movie is the hero, not you. If you do your job well and it gets a laugh or it's a dramatic moment, then the movie works. That's the win.

Q: Do you research your ideas/stories?

Barbara Stepansky - Yes. For the Lifetime movie, *Flint*, I went to Flint, Michigan to do research and set up interviews with the residents. I set up at least two interviews per day. I spoke to the ACLU (American Civil Liberties Union) and I talked to whomever I could about the subject. One day I drove with plumbers to every household where they were putting in filters for the lead, like old people's homes and areas with people who were struggling. There were people who felt a certain way about the media and didn't want to talk to me but I wanted to be as factually accurate as to what was happening and capture the spirit of these activists that were ringing the alarm bell.

Emma Ko - I like to write from a place of knowledge. I don't like to make too many things up. Ultimately, if there's something where you are writing the State of the Nation or Parliament or the House of Commons, I would really want to get the nuances of what that world is like. Ditto, police procedures. I would use a consultant; to the extent that I would want them to talk me through the layout of the office. I need to see it. I need to be able to know how they talk to each other in the office. Do they sit across a desk from each other? Or do they have to get up and physically go somewhere? That all lends itself to the action that takes place as you write. Personally, for me, research is definitely important.

Becca Topol - When I start a new project, I spend a lot of time researching. When I wrote *Ramen Girl*, I researched how ramen was made, as well as the history of ramen. I lived in Japan and many of the scenes were inspired by personal experiences, so it was a matter of doing a lot of inner work as well. When I started working with Disney on *Mira, Royal Detective*, I was very worried that I had never written a detective show before, so I made time to watch every single detective show, both for adults and kids. One of the episodes in Season 2 was inspired by *Rear Window*. Mira sprains her ankle and has to solve the mystery in a chair by the window. She ends up doing it with the help of her friends. Now, I had seen *Rear Window* before, but then it's: What are all the detective shows that I like? What can I pull out of them that I can apply?

Ron Leshem - When my partner and I were writing about ISIS for *No Man's Land,* research helped a lot. It was very challenging, but because I am so fascinated by this part of history and toxic religious ideas, I had enough tools in my suitcase to write in an authentic way to understand what fuels them; where their hatred comes from. And this is not the obvious stuff - they are angry at the West, it's a social-economic thing, or...they are brainwashed. These are not good enough answers. You must find the deeper answer or else it's not relevant. I always ask myself about the guy who runs the grocery store downstairs. If I ask him how to write a certain character without doing research and digging into it, he would give me a basic answer. This guy is going to fall in love with a girl. Or he's doing this because he's angry at that. If I write like this, then I am a failure because I haven't brought anything new to the table.

Marsha Greene - Research is important because you have to understand the context of the world; what the lives your characters are or were living. When you write the story, hopefully your mind will be infused with all of that so you can just write. On *The Porter*, we'd do the research, break the story and then we would then ask the historian who was hired on the show whether there was anything historically inaccurate?

Q: What do you think makes a good story?

Danny Strong - I think that's different for every audience member. The great thing about story is that there are different genres. There's something for everyone's taste. If you like comedies, romantic comedies, horror films, dramas - so much of the story, I think, is dictated by the genre. The genre sets the rules or the template of the kind of story you are telling. From there, you are trying to achieve a different experience for the audience member depending on the genre you are doing. If you are doing a horror film, you are trying to scare them. If you are doing a comedy, you are trying to make them laugh. Ultimately, all good stories benefit from having a foundation of stakes; interesting characters that are trying to achieve goals, and sources of antagonism that get in the way of those goals. Then, you can combine those principles with a strong theme and dovetail them all in the tone of your genre.

Barbara Stepansky - Any story that posts challenges to a character and causes them to change, can work. I'm a big believer in "The Hero's Journey" and putting the lead character through as much emotional and physical pain as I can muster so the ending feels deserved.

Tony Jordan - It has to be that whomever the story is aimed at, whoever is watching, listening, or reading the story, can find some way of putting themselves, to some degree, in the protagonist's shoes. Unless you are some kind of sociopathic serial killer, in which case, you want to put yourself in the antagonist's shoes. You need to care about the outcome.

> ## SPEC SCREENPLAYS
>
> If you have not been paid to write a screenplay, but rather you are writing with the hope of selling it when it's completed, then you are writing "on spec." This means it's speculative. While the vast majority of these scripts never get made, they can be used as writing samples or "calling cards" which can open doors to getting work on projects financiers do want to make.
>
> If you have representation, they will get your work into the hands of producers and financiers in order to get you meetings with them. If you don't have representation, then you will need to find an alternative way to get noticed such as entering your work into screenplay competitions, using pitching entities like **Roadmap Writers** (www.roadmapwriters.com), or working in development or production and becoming friends with those who would be willing to read your work.
>
> You own all rights to your specs. Others can only exploit them if they option the script from you in some way. Any notes you implement on behalf of a producer or financier that haven't been paid for, are owned by you.
>
> TV/Streaming specs come in two varieties: original pilots and sample episodes. The first is a pilot script based on your own idea. The second is an episode of an existing show to prove to showrunners that you can write in the voice of someone else.

It can be as simple as in *Snow White* where you want her to meet the prince. I don't know how Disney does it because you know she's going to in the first moment, but you still want to see it. You want it to happen. That is the real trick of storytelling. You have to care. The audience has to have empathy with the characters within it. They must put themselves in the character's shoes or at least, ask themselves what they would do in that situation. How would I have handled that? In its basest form, it's in our souls. We want to live in a world where there is order. Where everyone gets what they want. Where everybody is fed. Where everyone is happy. Where everyone finds love. Storytelling gives us that order, albeit, fictional, so that we can be surrounded by wars and pestilence and floods and earthquakes and then sit in front of a screen that promises, and delivers order.

Marsha Greene - It has to feel real. It has to be grounded in human emotion or experience. That doesn't mean, for example, that it can't be sci-fi, but I need to understand why a person is making the decisions that they are making. What would I do if I was them? When I am watching it, I should get it. I don't have to agree with them, but I have to get their point of view. I don't mind things that are a little bit heightened, but I am most attracted to stories that are grounded emotionally. My friends joke around and they say my favorite thing is to watch two people talking to each other forever. I find people interesting, so when I don't have that connection to a person and cannot understand them, it's not a good story for me.

Paul King - The stories that work best for me tend to be the ones that speak to something deep inside, a hope or fear or anxiety. With *Paddington*, it was the fear of being all alone in a world that you don't understand without your parents or loved ones to look after you.

That evacuee-like image of a young bear with nothing but a small suitcase and a luggage table around his neck saying "Please Look After This Bear" speaks to a universal fear for all children. That is probably the key to the success of story and the reason Paddington, as a character, has resonated with audiences for such a long time. It makes your brain fire in a way that can take you to the highs and lows of emotion.

Dave Reynolds - A good story is a story that you can relate to. *Star Wars* is set in outer space, which isn't relatable. But if you take out all the sci-fi elements, you see it's about a guy whose family is killed and he decides to fight against the villains who did it. That's understandable. You strip the story down to the basics, and then ask yourself: What if our hero can do this, but can't do that? What if he can't save the world and can't get home? Or in a more relatable world, say a workplace idea, what if he doesn't get the promotion? So what? There are a lot of people out of work. Why do I care about his situation? Oh wait, the promotion for him is everything. It means he can bring his family over from another country. Oh! It's life-saving! All of those feelings are relatable to your audience. Audiences need something to root for and if you don't have a character that you care about, you're not going to care about the story.

Q: Do you consider the commissioning landscape when you generate ideas?

Tony Jordan - No, because that way lays madness. Commissioner briefs are usually born of a meeting somewhere, which is almost certainly some kind of corporate meeting where someone has seen how other things in a genre have done. Then, they see that the algorithms say yes, so let's make some more of that, please. I don't recognize that as a creative trigger. It doesn't make any sense to me.

I've always said that on a personal level as a writer, and then with our production company, Red Planet, can we please swim upstream? A teen romance film comes out, and it takes £50 squillion at the box office. The next day, 400 meetings all over Hollywood happen demanding scripts of teen romance. Then, all those execs will have meetings all that day and the next week talking to writers and agents saying all they want are teen romances. So then all the writers go off and write teen romances. Then, three months later, all those scripts are delivered and on that exec's desk. This huge pile. On the other side of the exec's desk is the one writer who is a bit pissy. He didn't want to write teen romance and wanted to write something else - *Citizen Kane* or something about a newspaper editor. That's what he wanted to write. So to me, it makes sense to be the pile of one, instead of the pile of many.

Emma Ko - To a certain degree, I do, yes. There are certain projects where I know they would be able to be placed on BBC 1 or ITV 1 - big viewership, mainstream. They tend to be a little less risky. If I wanted something crazy like aliens in dinosaur time, I wouldn't take it there. When I start developing something, I take it to a few producers or production companies with a couple of lines and say, "What do you think of this?" Then, I develop it the way I want to. One of my first questions to production companies or producers is: To whom do you think this would go? If it's Netflix, I feel like anything goes. If it's Channel 4, it has to push the envelope; it has to be more subversive. I can probably do more risky things. If it's ITV 1, then really mainstream - probably a procedural. If it's BBC 1, then something like that, but they may be riskier. So to a certain degree, yes, but, for me, it's always project first.

Moisés Zamora - As a professional screenwriter, I have to pay attention to the market before I set out to spend months on a piece of writing. Sometimes, a manager or an agent will be able to guide you, especially because they see what type of stories are in the marketplace - what gets sold and what doesn't. For example, TV writers tend to be inspired by headlines, or there's an idea in the zeitgeist. What ends up happening is that many people write about the same thing, which floods the marketplace with similar scripts. Some stories are not producible, especially if you're creating a TV show on Mars. I want to reach audiences, so I do take a look at the genres that do well commercially and I try to keep them in mind when I write, because I want to be able to sell it to the studios. The execution however needs to be compelling, no matter what. For emerging writers, however, that's not a mandate. Emerging writers need to be risky and dangerous with their writing to make an impression.

Q: What makes you realize an idea works for television rather than feature film or vice versa?

Lauren Iungerich - Usually, it's an idea that is less plot driven and more character driven. If there is something complicated about a character to work out, it usually screams to make it a series.

Emma Ko - That's a really tricky question to answer because in the right hands, two people sitting on a bench or in a car, can make good television. Ryan Reynolds stuck in a box underground for ninety minutes could be a compelling film. It comes back down to the intent of the storyteller. If it's Ryan Reynolds in a box underground, ultimately what makes it a great film? Yes, we want to know why he is there, but it's the characterization of Ryan Reynolds and the character who put him there.

Lots of things can start out as a film. Shorts become features. Features become TV series. I think it's down to how much there is to give up from the characters that are introduced. If there is more within the space of the lives of the characters that is worth telling stories about, and it's past a feature film time length, then TV. If not, then a feature film is the perfect time length for those characters. It comes from the intent of the storyteller. Why am I telling this story and what am I trying to say? Could *The Notebook*, which is a perfect feature film, be a TV series? Sure, if you make the family compelling enough. If you make it, *This Is Us*.

Danny Strong - Usually, something feels more like a feature if it's a self-contained story that you think should end pretty quickly. That's a movie because I don't think that can go on for more than two hours. The form that I just worked in with *Dopesick*, which is a limited series, is a hybrid of a TV show and a movie. It's an elongated movie that's structured like

> ## SHORT FILM SCREENPLAYS
>
> One way to make a name for yourself as a screenwriter is to get your work made. If you're having trouble getting into the series or feature film sectors, you might want to explore short films as a way to get some notice. With YouTube and Vimeo, you have a simple way to get your work out to the masses. However, it's challenging to adapt to shorter time frames when you're used to working in 30-120 minute chunks. Here are some tips that can help you make that transition easier.
>
> - Shorts are still stories, so they need a beginning, a middle, and an end. Characters need to be fully fleshed out just like their long form cousins.
>
> - Shorts work best when they are trying to capture a moment in time like when a child chooses to hang out with their friends over their parents for the first time. Or, if doing an action or thriller short, perhaps one long set piece where the stakes continually rise.
>
> - Comedy works best in short form, so satire and ironic explorations of controversial topics are great ways to go.
>
> - Keep your locations and characters to a minimum to make production easier.
>
> - Dialogue takes up a lot of page space. Show instead of tell.
>
> - If your subject has a social aspect to it like civil rights, human rights, or a medical condition like autism, try to engage with organizations related to it. They can give you information to help make your story authentic, as well as provide a built-in audience once the film is made.

a TV show. But it ends in six, eight, or ten episodes and I love that. It's very much a writer's form because you are building to a conclusion, but you are doing it over many hours. You can really dive deep into the characters and have a journey with them that's much longer than a film. In a movie, sometimes, they can replace the writer or the director can do a pass. There's a whole bunch of people who can step in on a ninety-minute movie. Many writers can come in and take a stab at it. You can't really do that on a limited series. You can have a writers room and there are multiple writers working on it, but there's usually someone in charge of that process and it's usually a writer. You are not going to bring in all these different writers to do rewrites of every episode. I guess you could, but that sounds like a real nightmare.

As far as process goes, if the director is not a real writer, but maybe has some cool instincts and can do a polish on a screenplay, that's very different from rewriting eight episodes of television.

Q: Can you be pigeonholed into a particular genre?

Meg LeFauve - Many writers are worried about this. They want to break into the business with many different genres of scripts because they are afraid of being pigeonholed. The problem with that is that when you are first starting out, the business wants to know: Who are you? How is an agent going to sell you? You almost have to have a brand. If you were your own agent and you were calling the studio, what are you saying? This writer can really do what? The easiest thing is a genre. It just is. The easiest thing for everyone to understand is, "She can knock horror out of the park. She can scare you in ways that you have never been scared before. I was up for five days and I cried. How weird is that?" They have to have enthusiasm about the brand so they know how to sell you.

Eventually, your brand can evolve. So if you came in through a certain door and you got good at that, now you can expand. I know people think of me for emotional characters. Now that's not a genre. That's a piece of the storytelling and of the artistry that I can bring to any genre. It can expand to, "Nobody does dialogue like this guy." Or, "This guy is so funny!" So you can expand within the craft, but to get in - pigeonhole yourself. This is your voice. If you get pigeonholed into something you don't like, then, yes, you would have to re-brand yourself. Take a piece of whatever you got branded with and rethink it.

Becca Topol - I was reading in *The New Yorker* about the writer of *Strangers On A Train* and *The Talented Mr. Ripley,* Patricia Highsmith. She was upset because she wrote the book *Carol* but felt that her publisher wasn't taking it seriously. She felt very pigeonholed because she had proven success as a mystery writer but she was passionate about writing a different type of book. In Hollywood, writers complain that they are pigeonholed and this happens a lot. I feel fortunate that I have written for different genres and continue to do so. The key is to make sure you continue to write original material in the genre of your choice, either to be produced, or as samples.

Mohamad El Masri - Pigeonholing does happen, but a lot of it is in your control, as well. Either way, it's only a co-incidence. For example, that I've written a lot of thrillers. Though I love them, genre doesn't necessarily drive what I write - story does. In this way, I avoid being pigeonholed by the industry, but also pigeonholing myself. If there's a story or character I'm dying to bring to life, that's what I spend time on. The genre often emerges from that creative conversation. Most of the time, I see a character and have a big idea orbiting them, which I've been wanting to service in some way. Everything tends to come out of that. In general, everything made today tends to blend multiple genres and tones - so creative versatility and nimbleness have been key. In short, the story's the thing. The genre comes after that.

Ron Leshem - I was an intelligence officer in the military, and the tragic thing is that every time I step into an executive's office at the streamers or networks, they would say, "Bring us your next *Homeland*, or your next espionage story." I don't want to forever be writing about espionage. I want to reinvent myself all the time. That is why I created *Euphoria*.

Barbara Stepansky - I think people pigeonhole you on the specs that you present. So if you have a writing sample of a certain genre that's really strong, then that's probably the genre people will hire you for. I had a lot of thriller genre specs. Thriller, drama, and period come kind of easy for me and you want to be working in something you are strong in. I couldn't do a comedy show to save my life because I'm not good coming up with jokes on the spot. There's humor in my scripts, but it's not ha ha laugh out loud funny. That is such a skill, which I really admire. So I think you should do what you are passionate about.

Alex Litvak - I don't think it's about getting pigeonholed. It's about what stories you want to tell and what stories can you tell, well. Find the best story you have at this moment in time and tell it the best way you can. You will have many stories over the course of your career. A long time ago, Simon Kinberg (screenwriter of *Mr. and Mrs. Smith, The Martian*) told me, "If you only have one story, you're in trouble." What story should I do first? Pick one. There will be some that are better and some that are worse. There are some that will make your career and some that will fall through the cracks. All true. I can tell you from experience when I recently rewrote myself from years ago, there were some times when I was like, "Wow, that's so clever and fun. This guy really knew what he was doing." And then other times, I go, "Wow, what an idiot." I say this with no hubris or humility, it's just who you are now is different from then. So just pick the best story you have now and tell it the best way you can. And know that the only time the writer has control is when he or she is writing something. Make those words as juicy, as delicious, as delightful, and as eye-catching as you can, because that is when you are preparing the dish. Once it goes out to the customer, they might say they love it and that it is the most delightful meal they've ever had. Or they might say it needs more ketchup. Trust me, it needs more ketchup.

Emma Ko - I think with certain writers, it's not so much that they are pigeonholed, but they end up writing the same thing. I love writing what I watch and I watch so much. I love a really great thriller. I love a fantastic zombie comedy. I just like smart drama. The only thing I probably can't write is straight-up drama, which is what I think most people write here in the UK. My agent said to me recently, "You're very genre-based." It turns out that anything that isn't genre-based is drama. So I don't pigeonhole myself. I always write what I want to write. My sitcom, *Hello, Mrs. Chan,* was born out of rage about what was happening in diversity and equality-wise and the only way that I could do it with the rage that I felt, was to make it funny. Otherwise, it would have been a boring public service announcement.

Scott Beck - Certainly in Hollywood, you can get known for something, but it can become your asset. The work begets the work. To a certain extent, you have to have some business acumen if you want to work in the industry for a while. My writing partner, Bryan Woods, and I understand that there's a brand that maybe *A Quiet Place* has put us into, but that doesn't mean that we are going to write ten more films that are just about aliens and people on farms. We wrote that film because there was a passion that we were chasing. That's the number one thing that any screenwriter, director, or filmmaker should make sure that they are chasing. What is keeping you passionate? That is what has led to doors opening. Even when we haven't set up the scripts that we were passionate about, it felt like it moved us forward in a more interesting direction. We are always making sure to listen to that instinct.

Eli Craig - There's this old saying: "Bruce Lee is not afraid of the man who practices 10,000 kicks one time. He's afraid of the man who practices one kick, 10,000 times." So there is something to honing in on what your genre is and just doing that well. I don't feel like I've exhausted that yet, though I am eager to expand my range. There's also so much room to explore the horror-comedy genre that I'm in, possibly because it's seen as a bastard child. I want to prove them wrong. I love the misfits of the world, so I make misfit movies. I've always had a propensity to watch the movies that weren't the top number one movie of the month. I don't want to watch *Spiderman*, I want to watch *Evil Dead*, again.

Dave Reynolds - When I came out to Los Angeles after *Late Night*, I was known as a joke guy. Then, years later when I left Disney Animation, I was known as a story guy! And from my time at Pixar, I was a story structure guy. You try to tell everyone that you can do all three but sometimes they see you the way they think you are. So after six years I left Feature Animation. I thought this was my chance to do something different. I could go do romantic comedies, action movies, maybe even a romantic action movie. The bottom line was I was finally going to do live action. My very first meeting was with this executive at Universal Studios. As I walk in, she reaches out her hand and says, "Dave Reynolds! How would you like to write some animation for us?" I immediately said, "I'm your guy. What do you need?" I literally sold myself out in forty seconds.

Q: What tips would you give on writing a sequel?

Paul King - Before writing *Paddington 2*, I watched pretty much every sequel I could get my hands on. There weren't many where I went, "Oh, so that's how you do it," but I did learn a lot about what not to do.

It always annoyed me when the first film had ended with the characters all happy and their flaws fixed - and then film two started with them in a completely different emotional place. They have to say something like, "You know why I've never really been happy...? Oh, and did I mention I am terrified of water?" Obviously, the writers want to give the characters a new flaw or a starting point for their journey, but as the audience, you feel cheated. It's like "Hang on! You can't do that. They were definitely happy - and they loved swimming!"

The first *Paddington* film tied everything up very neatly. So I knew where I left the characters, but I needed to find a way to take them emotionally into a new scenario in a way which felt organic and earned. We wanted to find a way for the story to start really small and then snowball into a movie with stakes and scale where Paddington and the rest of the characters learn something they didn't realize they needed to learn.

Simon Farnaby, my co-writer, told this story about when he was little and he went away from home to camp. He had been given £10 and he bought his parents a mug. It was the first time he used his own money to get them a present. It was one of those light bulb moments where you get an insight into a child. Hey, guess what? Children want their parents to know how loved they are, even if they can't express it. And they want to make them proud. It's so obvious in retrospect, but it was the key to the whole story. We realized pretty much every single human on the planet must have had that worry, that anxiety, and we had found a universal emotional truth to dig into. So we thought, maybe he wants to get a present for Aunt Lucy so she'll be proud of him and his new life in London. Maybe a hundredth birthday present. And that could start our snowball rolling.

CHAPTER REVIEW: IDEAS

- Think about your life experiences. Do any of them stand out?

- Look around you wherever you are. Who are the people? What are their stories? Issues?

- Books, articles, images, mixing film ideas are all good for idea generation.

- Talk to people and hear their stories or eavesdrop. What makes them tick could lead somewhere.

- Do you have a passion? That's always a good place to start.

- Travel exposes you to new concepts and ideas.

- Wouldn't it be funny if? Irony and humor work if you find out the root of the reasons.

- What if? This works as a jumping off place, but you always need to go deeper.

- Keep an idea notebook.

- Research. Necessary, but beware of rabbit holes.

- Don't restrict your genre - write what you're passionate about.

- Pay attention to the market around you but don't force your idea into that market.

- Think of the best format for your idea. Is it a feature, series, short, or news piece?

- Write from the heart. Write for you.

- Keep doing it. Never stop looking for ideas.

CHAPTER 2

PITCHING

Film and TV are collaborative processes, so at some point, you need to sell your ideas to other people. However, when and to whom you pitch can change your strategy. Our panelists give their top tips on how to prepare and give a pitch so it will go as smoothly as possible. They also have thoughts on what to do when a pitch starts tanking.

Q: What makes a good or a bad pitch?

Barbara Stepansky - Let me start with length. Pitches are bad when they go on forever. A good pitch is when you are able to succinctly tell what the show or movie is; what is the opening image? What is going to happen? How does it pique your interest? Then, you get to a place of what it's going to be about. It's the journey of this woman learning how to love again, or whatever the story is. So before you get into the second act or third act minutiae, you need a strong setup. Next, what's the arc? What's the hook? If it's a TV show, what's the driving force that keeps me watching from one week to the next? The rest can be figured out at a later point.

Sometimes, people get bogged down in all the minutiae. If you're reading out a half-hour pitch, nobody is listening anymore. Instead they're looking at how many papers you're holding in your hands. Five pages?! Talking about your project is different from reading it out loud, and you have to be aware of your audience. You need to keep the interest alive all the way through. I whittle my pitches down to the bare minimum and then afterward see what the questions are. It's not that I've haven't figured everything out, but I want to get across the most powerful stuff first. Then, when the person has questions, I can say, "That is a great question. I've thought about it and this is what I'm thinking..." So I am trying to keep the engagement as high as I can, especially now that we do it over Zoom, where it's so easy to zone out.

Eli Craig - It's funny because sometimes you think you kill it on a pitch and you get a pass. Or you think that was a boring one and you get interest. Ultimately, you want to make the executives think you've thought out the nuts and bolts of the story. What is the engine of the story? What is the drive? For me, everything comes down to the obstacle of the main character. What is the want? What is the intention? You have to build those stakes so they are compelling to an audience. You want to make somebody feel like you have a grasp on the structure and a lead character that you can imagine a star actor playing. If I'm going to pitch a project that I am going to direct and it's early on, then I won't always use visuals. As I move forward, I definitely start to build visuals for what my shooting style will be. I take visuals from other films and I lay out whom the cast is going to be; locations, too. Early on, it can just be a pitch where you are talking about what the structure is going to be and the genre it's going to fit into. You have to be very clear about that.

I find that studio executives are often smarter than you think. They're all educated graduates, so you want to have a larger theme - they really enjoy it when you talk about these grandiose themes even when you are talking about a movie as absurdist as *Tucker and Dale*. "This is about the social tribalism that our culture goes through. The tribalism between the educated class and the less uneducated." You mention a few words like tribalism and they like it. So it helps to sound smart. But all of that can add up to nothing as well because, ultimately, they want to think that this is a project that can make them money. Some of it has to do with the attachments. For better or worse, Hollywood is still a game of image. Sometimes, it's who the producers are that you come in with. Sometimes, it's the actors that are attached. Sometimes, it doesn't even matter what the project is that's pitched. If you come in with a major star attached, they are still going to make your movie.

Emma Ko - To me, a good pitch is a belief in the story that you're pitching. If I'm having a general meeting, I usually ask the producer what they are watching right now. "What do you love? What are you really not liking so much and why?" This gives me a sense of their taste so I know which one of my projects to pitch. There's no point trying to sell something to someone who doesn't want or like it. I always prepare. If it was on the fly or I had something that is tucked away and I don't really know what it is, that leads to bad pitches. You don't really believe in it. I can't really bullshit. I'm one of those people who has to say why it's really important and why I want to make it. When I don't do that, it fizzles out and you can see it in their faces. Then, I have to say, "It needs work." If you leave a pitch with "It needs work," that's not a great pitch.

Mohamad El Masri - Presenting, pitching, articulating, explaining, captivating, and

---

TYPES OF PITCHES

Elevator Pitch
A quick, thirty seconds to a minute sum up of your project to get someone to solicit your screenplay. The idea is that you could get on an elevator with someone and tell them your idea before you reach their floor. This one's harder than it looks. You really need to know your project inside and out to get to its essence.

Cocktail Party Pitch
Two to five minutes, or about as long as it takes a bartender to make a drink. This allows you to get a bit more detail into the premise, your characters, and the plot. Again, the goal is to get your script solicited. Don't waffle. Gin and tonics don't take that long to make.

In the Room Pitch
The end goal of the Elevator and Cocktail Party pitches. Your script has been read and someone wants to talk to you about it, seriously. Fifteen minutes for your pitch but expect an hour in the room. After some chit-chat, there will be a deep discussion on the pros and cons of every aspect of your script. That includes you, yourself. Do they want to work with you? Are you reasonable? Can you fix problems? Can they put you in front of decision-makers and you won't embarrass them? So drink the bottle of water and be open to their needs.

capturing attention - it's all about aspects of performance and public speaking. A lot of meetings are one-person shows; like a stand-up routine. The challenge is captivating an audience quickly and in a condensed period of time. Also, delivering complex ideas in a digestible and universal way in a sterile situation either over video conference or in a conference room to people who are busy, stressed, and overworked. A big part of it is having enthusiasm, collaborative spirit, and presence, things that do not involve actual writing. These are vital. Then, of course, you have to deliver on that enthusiasm by actually writing. The sizzle and the steak, as they say. But it all starts with you in the room, being an accessible person with people - exuberance and spirit is infectious. Everyone in the business is waiting to be inspired. The fun is in being the one to inspire them with a good pitch that does all the above.

Alex Litvak - I used to be a development/production executive, so I sat through A LOT of bad pitches - and a few very good ones. There are all sorts of tricks but it comes down to this: audience engagement. Tell a good story and tell it well. Get them hooked early and end before you start boring them. No one wants to hear every single detail. Save it for the script. Think of a pitch as a professional date: you are sitting across from your audience and have limited time to engage them. Make them laugh, make them feel something, make them care. Even if they won't buy the pitch, selling them now is incredibly difficult, they'll like how you told the story. That's a win.

Bryan Woods - The most important thing in a good pitch is making your audience lean in. Obviously, a pitch is about story, character, and all these elements, but if you are not entertaining the person on the other side of the table, then you've really got nothing. That's what you should think about first and foremost - is it engaging, exciting, and entertaining?

Scott Beck - There are many forms of pitches that have been heard, so a good pitch can be your story offering a new world that hasn't been seen on film before. You can tell a story about someone trapped in space that you've seen a million times, or you can tell a story that's nuanced about auto mechanics in their day-to-day. It's a world that you haven't necessarily seen on film or on television. There's something captivating about diving into that process that feels like the every day, but it feels extraordinary because it is not something that has been represented on screen. That's another window in. There are other pitches where it's genre or more character-based. They can be equally captivating depending on what the content is.

Bryan Woods - Something Scott and I say for every pitch is: What is our personal window into this story? What's a personal anecdote? What's a thing we experienced when we were kids? What happened to that person we went to high school with, that relates? We lead with why we connect to a particular story that we want to talk about.

Q: How do you make your ideas stand out in a pitch?

Moisés Zamora - People remember how you make them feel and after thirty minutes of

ONLINE PITCHING

Screenwriters need to be prepared for working and pitching online. While you still need to know your ideas inside and out, there are some other items you need to consider in order to make your Zoom (Google Meet? FaceTime? WhatsApp?) go smoothly.

- It sucks talking to a black screen; there's no energy to feed off. Get as many people to put on their cameras. And put on yours, too.

- When you aren't speaking, mute your microphone. Background noise from sirens to keyboard typing is distracting. Hopefully, everyone else will do the same.

- Use the Share Your Screen or similar function to show images, video, and other documents. This engages the viewers by giving a place to focus their attention.

- Use the Chat function if someone doesn't have a microphone or use to share links or documents that you want others to have.

- As long as you get consent from everyone, record the meeting. It's a fantastic resource for recalling information, as well as to do a post mortem on pitches that went wrong.

- Good lighting is always helpful.

- Warn everyone about pets, children, and any other distractions that may be around. People are pretty good about these things - they may even welcome them!

- Take a good look behind you. Make sure you have nothing embarrassing in the background. Most of these platforms have an artificial background you can choose instead of your real one if need be.

talk, talk, talk, they are going to catch on to two or three things that are exciting to hear. They may not know the details of everything else that you said, but if I drop something like, "When I was a kid, my Dad was a doctor and he delivered a lot of babies in our house where he had a practice. My job was to bury the placentas in the backyard." Most people react and are going to remember that about me for the rest of their lives. You might forget all the wise words that I just spoke about, but you will remember that. You want to drop that and especially those elements that are part of your vision. Those little kernels are impactful images of what you are trying to pitch. If an exec, after all the hundreds of pitches they've heard this year, can remember a couple of nuggets from yours, you're in good shape. You're an entertainer. You're in entertainment. If you can't entertain three people on a Zoom call, what are you doing? Go into real estate and sell houses. Well, actually, you have to sell people there, too. You have to pitch them that a house is the best. Never mind.

Dan Mazer - With pitching in general, to a certain extent, you are pitching yourself, as well as the idea. You've got to give the people in the room confidence in yourself, as much as you have to give them confidence in your nascent idea. If you haven't written the script and are just going in with an idea, it's so tricky to convey what you want and what it will be. I always use the analogy of going out and buying a red dress. I love the idea of a red dress. But your idea of how the red dress looks may be different from the idea of the red dress that I'm thinking about. So somehow you have to educate the person so that when the red dress arrives on their desk in the post, they are not incredibly disappointed. In order to do that, they have to have faith in your taste and sensibilities. Ergo, I think, if you are pitching a comedy, it helps to be funny when you go into the room.

Be entertaining, loquacious, and garrulous. Mischievous. Iconoclastic, to a certain degree. It's important to make your pitch funny, but it's also important for you to come across as funny or at least as having a sense of humor. Don't go in with a whole stand-up routine because people will see through that. Speaking from my point of view, and I've been pitched to, as well as having had to pitch, I place as much value on the chat beforehand and the chat afterward, as I do on the idea. Ideas are all about execution. It can be the most brilliant one-line idea that is executed abysmally and vice versa. You just have to convince the people in the room that you will execute whatever it is in a way that will be funny, witty, and entertaining.

The Hollywood pitch is a really difficult thing. Often you will go around with your producer and there may be as many as five or six of you who go to each pitch. If I am going over to pitch from England for a week, they will line up eight different pitches in three days. You will have to do the same pitch. It's a schtick. Wisened Hollywood types are very happy to go in and do exactly the same thing every time and make it seem impromptu. I get mortified by doing that in front of the five or six people that I am with. Making it sound like an ad-lib is something I find humiliating. So I go in and I'm loose and rely on hopefully being funny and engaging around the idea and not too rigidly prepared with a schtick.

Now within the pitch itself, if it's a comedy, you have jokes and you make them laugh. It can't come across as a dry drama. Have funny lines that you have prepared for the characters that they might say. Be specific about funny set pieces and try to convey those like you are telling an anecdote down the pub that is designed to make people laugh. Rehearse that and be aware that your goal is to be funny and entertaining. You have to be the best ambassador for your idea that you can be. That may seem incredibly obvious, but perversely a lot of the comedy writers that I know are not the funniest or most charming people in a room! But if you are awkward and nervous, then lean into it. Make it part of your persona. A pitch is a performance and there are lots of performers and comedians who go on stage as heightened versions of themselves.

Marsha Greene - When I pitch, the number one thing that I think about, is to try to make it interesting. I know that sounds obvious but writers have the tendency to get mired in the details. I write my pitch out and then read it aloud. If I find myself getting bored as I am going through saying what each character is like, then I know it isn't the right way to pitch. People need to be interested in listening to you talk for probably twenty minutes. That's a very long time. There can be details that you leave out. There's questions and answers afterwards and they can ask you anything then. Or maybe you don't do all the characters one by one if you have eight of them. You do four and then come back to the others later. It's important for you to have a pitch that gives all the information about the show, but not

IP & PUBLIC DOMAIN

Intellectual Property (IP) means creations of the mind that are owned by a person - usually the creator, themselves. This could mean a novel, comic book, graphic novel, poem, stage play, documentary film, or any kind of journalistic article.

Basing a project on IP, sometimes called the "underlying" property, is a favorite of funding bodies, as it means someone has already taken a chance on the idea. It could also mean that there will be a built-in audience for your movie or series - those that enjoyed the IP the first time around.

If you choose to base your project on IP, you will need to contact the copyright owner and negotiate for the right to convert the property into a film or TV series. There are many points to consider with the two biggest being the length of term and the price. A rule of thumb for length is eighteen (18) months with an option to extend for another eighteen (18) months. Price can be free to tens of thousands of dollars or more.

Sometimes, it helps to team up with an experienced producer when approaching someone for their rights. You should have a vision as to what you will do with the property. And, as always, it's always best to contact a lawyer to get advice on avoiding pitfalls.

Creative materials not covered by intellectual property laws (copyright, trademark, patent, etc.) are said to be in the public domain. That means anyone can use them for the basis of a story without getting permission, but no one can ever own them. If you can't afford an option or license on a piece of intellectual property, this may be a way to create a project that satisfies the "someone else gave it a chance" stamp. This is why Shakespeare's plays, Viking sagas, Chinese tales, and Greek myths are often used as the basis for projects.

When something falls into the public domain, it is tricky, as each country has its own rules. In the USA, it's 70 years after the death of the author or creator. If there are multiple owners, then it's 70 years from when the last person dies. Copyrights can be renewed, authors can voluntarily put things into the public domain, and some works aren't always covered by the laws, so check with your country's copyright office before you start working on the property.

---

compromising it being interesting. It's a sales pitch. You're selling this thing. You want people to be excited. Some people are very articulate and can do the song and dance. I have a friend who is an actor and writer so she does the whole thing.

Something I do before I pitch is watch TED Talks. TED Talks is not an actor's performance. It's an expert explaining something to you in a way that's interesting for you to retain information. That's the neighborhood that I want to be in. Not trying to be all funny. Not trying to act it all out. If you're a performer, maybe go that way. But if you aren't, maybe you want some visuals, as maybe you don't want people staring at you the whole time. Visuals can keep it going. If you are not a person who is comfortable speaking to a lot of people, try to find a way to make it interesting. Just reading it off a piece of paper is going to be even worse. When we pitched *The Porter*, we did more of the "why now?" People will always ask why this show should be on the air now? So we talked about it historically and where we are today; why we felt the world needed a show like that. Then, we talked about the characters - who they were, what was their goal, what they were fighting for, and what were they up against.

I once did a pitch that was a family show and there was a lot of material to get through. I started with a personal story about myself and then went into what the show was about. Then, I went backwards. Ten years ago, this happened and then, I moved to the present where the pilot starts. Now, everybody is this, this, and this. I do think you have to tailor it for the show, but you always want to be saying the logline because someone else is going to be telling another person about this great pitch that they heard. It would be nice if they had a handy way to sum it up. You always want to have a description of your series. You always want to have a description of your main characters. Then, a series arc that you can kind of change. As for tone, sometimes you can talk about it but sometimes the pitch is in the tone of the show. So for a comedy, you will be making it funny, so you don't have to mention tone.

Q: What are the differences between pitching your own original idea and pitching someone else's idea, like IP?

Josh Olson - It's kind of the same thing. *A History of Violence* is a perfect example. It had a cool title. I read the back of the book and it's this really interesting setup. Just from reading the back of the book, I immediately saw a three-act movie - beginning, middle, and end. I really wanted to see what this author did with it. It was such a tantalizing setup. A guy with a past who has managed to bury it, is now being forced to address the consequences of that in an interesting way. There were so many ways it could have gone. I ended up pitching the version of the story I would have written if I'd come up with that great title and central idea, and it turned out the studio preferred that to the book's approach.

Alex Litvak - The main difference is that with an original idea you control the rights and the creative direction - at least at the outset. You are truly the captain of your own ship, which is a major pro. The con is it's harder to sell an original in the current market. With IP you have the value of the brand working in your favor. But that also means it's likely work for hire, and you may be one of several writers pitching on this to the studio/the rights holders. Fundamentally, you are less of a captain and more a navigator pitching the course to the passengers who may or may not approve the direction you want to head in or hire you for the job.

Personally, I would always bet on the original. Unless you truly feel a connection to the IP and feel like you have a real shot of landing the gig, you are better off developing your own ideas, despite the challenges of selling them.

Q: Do you enjoy pitching?

Becca Topol - I actually love pitching. It's fun. It's as close as I will ever get to acting. I get super excited. I love to tell people about my themes. I think it's really my passion. It's also a game of whether I can win these people over or not. I like that challenge.

Eli Craig - I don't think I do until I do. It's never fun preparing or going into it. It's sort of fun to do. Part of writing is pitching. It's part of life. This was my message in my film, *The Tao of Pong*. There is no point where you are 100% ready for this. You kind of have to talk yourself into it. Go through a series of mental exercises to just be confident and open to what's going on and not shut down. And be connected as a human being.

When you are nervous, locked up and reading, or you are looking down at cards, those are the ones that don't work. My wife once told me these little things that I would do. I would go into the bathroom and I would do the dorky *Saturday Night Live* thing where I would say to myself, "You're a good person. You're amazing!" I did that because walking into meetings, you see people hunched over with their shoulders down. No! Raise your arms. There's a reason why when people win, they put their arms up!

Marsha Greene - I get nervous, but what calms me down is just going in and having a good time. There's this poem that someone sent me years ago and at the end of the poem, there is this stanza that says, "Stop asking if I am good enough. Ask only if I am showing up with love." I say that to myself. I am going in there and being myself and really excited. I can't control what's going on the other side.

One show, I did nine pitches in three days. By day two, how nervous can you be? It's the first one or two where the nerves hit. Then, it gets way easier because you've done it and you know it better. Maybe you tweak it a little bit depending on the feedback. That's the good thing about setting up a lot of meetings. You can get into a rhythm. I recorded myself pitching and I don't recommend it. I was terrible. I hate my voice. It was such a bad idea. But what is a good idea is that I pitched it to some friends over Zoom. Then, I pitched it

BAKE OFF

The entertainment industry loves taking old concepts and repackaging them new. For many years, when a studio, network or broadcaster had an idea they wanted to produce, they asked many writers to come in and pitch their version or "take" on the story. If the financiers liked one, they bought it and engaged the writer to write the script. The others…better luck next time.

Thanks to the popularity of a cooking competition show, *The Great British Bake Off*, these pitching events have a new (at the publishing of this book) moniker: "bake offs." They are time-consuming and very stressful for the writer, as they take a lot of preparation and you don't get paid for it. But, if you want the job, and it's often a BIG job, it's part of the process.

to the producers before we went out with it. So you get a little bit of practice before you're sitting in a meeting.

Barbara Stepansky - Open writing assignments on the studio level are sometimes these weird "bake-offs." So my first question to my agent when they want me to pitch on a project is: How many writers are they hearing pitches from and do I want to be in that mix? If it's three, maybe. If it's ten, fuck no. It's two weeks out of my life trying to break story because I have to pitch it in a way that people will get it, which means a lot of practice. I have to bother my friends to listen to me for half an hour and give me notes. I do that three or four times until I feel confident enough that I can do it for the executive in question. That's a lot of work that often doesn't lead to anything so it can sometimes be frustrating.

Q: How has pitching changed with Zoom?

Barbara Stepansky - I think there will still be personal meetings for the bigger pitches. But for general meetings, probably neither I nor the executives want to do a general in person ever again. I'd rather not drive an hour to Santa Monica to talk about my life story and then drive back for another hour. That's four hours out of my life! I should clarify that a general meeting means there is no job offer. They just want to meet you, talk about your experience, and what you are working on. So when Zoom general meetings happened, I thought, "This is great!" They don't have to put in a big effort to make me comfortable. I don't have to drive anywhere. For generals, I hope Zoom is here to stay.

For pitching an original idea or project, I also like Zoom because I can do a mood board that I can share on-screen when I am talking. It's more interactive. When I used to go to pitch meetings in person, I would have a giant visual packet of what the project is going to look like and I had a clicker where I would click through the images on my computer screen. Over Zoom people aren't confused about whether to look at me or the screen. For writers rooms, however, I do miss the dynamics of being with people together in one place. That's much harder to replicate over Zoom.

Eli Craig - The only problem with presenting your pitch on a screen is that they are looking at that and hearing your voice instead of looking at you. It's always better to pitch in person. There's no doubt. But Zoom is a really good alternative. I was getting a lot of jobs during the pandemic. Part of it is that you are on your home turf. Let's say you go to Steven Spielberg's Amblin' Entertainment to pitch and there are twelve people in the room. They have all the *E.T.* posters outside and all of a sudden you just feel yourself sweating. I didn't think I would be nervous, but the *E.T.* poster is out there. None of these execs worked on *E.T.*, but they still have the poster out there. But when you are at home and you see the executive at home and his apartment looks like crap - this guy's broke! I'm not intimidated by him. He's got a little apartment in Studio City and can't do his own laundry!

Josh Greenberg - I really hope that writers rooms will go back to everybody pitching in a room together *(Ed. Note: This interview was conducted in the middle of the COVID-19 pandemic)*. It's such a different dynamic. There are writers rooms that are Zoom only. You

> **NARRATIVE TRANSPORT**
>
> In *Experiencing Narrative Worlds* (1993), author and cognitive psychologist, Richard Gerrig, draws an analogy between a reader or viewer who has been immersed in a fictional character's journey, with a real person who has a literal travel experience and where both return to their regular world, transformed
>
> Academics Melanie Green and Timothy Brock in *Journal of Personality and Social Psychology* (2000), explored this concept in greater detail and named this effect of immersive storytelling, "narrative transport." They discovered there are many factors that go into why this happens, but chief among them are low distractions in the storytelling environment, prior knowledge of story topics, and a person's need for cognition and sensation seeking.
>
> In our humble opinion, this is the goal screenwriters should be aiming for when pitching or writing their projects.

lose something by doing that. You lose subtleties, especially when you pitch jokes over Zoom as something gets lost. It works, but it's tricky. The show that I am on now has such a great, rigorous COVID testing protocol that we are now meeting in a room together. It's way easier to pitch jokes and stories that way.

Hilary Galanoy - There are pros and cons to each. There's more energy in person, and it's nice to get out of the house. But sometimes it's easier to be relaxed over Zoom, and you can also wear your yoga pants!

Marsha Greene - One thing that is true for doing a pitch over Zoom or in person is that, as well as doing your pitch, you need to be present. On Zoom, if something is going wrong, you need to acknowledge that. When I did nine pitches consecutively, on one of them, I got close to the end and then, weirdly, a radio or some music turned on. So I acknowledged it by saying that we were getting close to the big ending and everyone appreciated that. You are still in a room on Zoom and you still want to make eye contact. You look directly into the camera. If people are freezing, then you laugh about it. It just makes it feel more real to people.

Q: How many people are generally on a Zoom call?

Barbara Stepansky - In a face-to-face meeting, it would usually be with just with one person. Now with Zoom, there are more people because everyone can listen in, which muddies the waters a little bit. I prefer gallery view as I have to have everyone in front of me. I did a pitch a week ago for a show and one of the producers didn't even switch on his camera. I could hear his voice but I couldn't tell what he was thinking. So there's a part of Zoom that doesn't work, but it allows more people to be present in the meeting.

Q: How do you prepare for a pitch?

Eli Craig - Sometimes, I bring in visuals. I find it helps because it keeps the attention of the executive going and it can also keep me on track if I have a visual. The best pitches, for me, are memorized, but you can't do that off the bat. You need to have some performance to be able to talk naturally. If you are reading off a page, forget it. People just unplug and even more so, when you are Zoom-ing. You want it to be free-flowing, but at the same time, I know myself well enough that I can end up going into the stratosphere. So if I can have an image, too, I can be like, "Oh, yeah, the cornfield. We are going to be shooting Act 3 in this beautiful cornfield." So on both fronts, I think visuals are really helpful in keeping attention.

Barbara Stepansky - There are pitch documents now that you can follow. Warner Brothers has a pitch template that I like to use. CAA has a good TV pitch template, too. Keeping it simple is the most important part. I like conversational introductions and making the project personal to you. Then, into the logline, theme, the tone of the world, and the characters. I keep the pilot short and the possibility of other episodes as well. Go into the series arc and then wrap it up.

Hilary Galanoy - Every writer has a different pitching process. As a team, we write out the pitch in its entirety. It should feel like a campfire story; an engaging, impossible-to-check-your-phone-during-it experience that makes the executive, producer, director, or talent feel like they're seeing the movie in their head. Once we have a locked document, we practice, practice, practice. By the time of the pitch meeting, we have the entire pitch mostly memorized. This way we can be as "off book" as possible. We do bring a pitch document with us, and it's not frowned upon to refer to those pages while pitching. Before the pandemic, pitch decks, which are a visual slideshow to accompany the pitch, weren't the norm. When everything pivoted to Zoom, pitch decks became a great tool for breaking up the monotony of back-to-back online meetings. If the executives can see examples of locations, environments, moods, cast photos, even stock photos that convey the energy of something like a car chase or romantic moment, the pitch becomes so much more real for them.

Scott Beck - The pitching process has evolved for us over the years. Usually, what we do first and foremost is write everything out, sometimes into a ten-page document. That covers how to grab somebody's attention. Then, teasing who the characters are, and what are their main issues. Then, starting to tease out the plot. You don't pitch everything. You pitch a solid first act. You tease a bit about the second and the third act, and you bring it home. Other times, we've left the third act a bit of a mystery. We've already got the script written, we're just pitching you the general idea. Make them want to read the script to find out what happened. Leave a little mystery there if it feels like they are engaged. In terms of visuals, they are a huge component for us. We usually take a lot of time to prep a visual story that can accompany what we are pitching in real time. We put together slides made in Photoshop that are meticulously curated to fit the tone of the movies, as well as certain set pieces or visuals that really get you in the feel of what the movie will be. It promises that this is a movie that deserves to be put on screen. That can vary from us putting those slides together to even playing clips in the background with no audio as we go through the pitch in the room with the executives or the producers.

PITCHING TIPS

- Keep the pitch as short as possible. 10-15 minutes max.

- Pitch context first. Why is the story meaningful to you and the larger world?

- Use the genre to your advantage. If it's a comedy, make it funny. If it's a thriller, make it thrilling.

- Maintain eye contact. Don't read directly from a script or cards, as it breaks your connection with your audience. Magic gone!

- Have an open body posture. Don't cross your arms, slouch, or look down at the floor.

- Consider to whom you are pitching. If an actor, you should focus on what the characters are doing and the motivations behind these actions. If it's a financier, make them see how many people would want to watch the movie or show.

- Talk with them, not at them.

- You are aiming for Narrative Transport (see the box out on page 43).

- Good hygiene is always a plus!

Q: Is there a time limit for a pitch?

Eli Craig - Oh, for sure. You don't want it to be more than fifteen minutes. It can go to twenty. But if anyone is doing a half-hour pitch, it's just too long. A pitch could be ten minutes with open questions. I find that if you get the executives interested and you are just talking on a level like we are right now, it maintains their interest more. So sometimes I will do ten minutes and then open it up to discussion and then we will just go back and forth. It gets harder to do that as more people get into a room. And if you are on Zoom, all of a sudden you have twelve people on there. Or you will walk into a room with twelve people in it and you are setting up a screen because it really helps to have visuals at that point, so you don't have twelve people just staring at you.

Barbara Stepansky - Anything over fifteen minutes and people's eyes start to glaze over.

Q: How do you involve your characters in your pitch?

Eli Craig - Usually, when you are pitching the movie, they are interested in the beats of

TONE

This is one of the more esoteric aspects of writing screenplays. The tone is often described as the mood, attitude, or manner of how a story is told. Think of it like an atmosphere in which your story resides. Like most atmospheres, the more even and uniform it is, the more often things within it thrive. Tone is set up from the very beginning of your script and should be carried all the way through. Not doing so, will often lead to a note from a reader stating the tone is uneven or confusing.

As an example, if you are writing a romantic comedy, such as *When Harry Met Sally*, you would see characters discussing romance right from the start. There would be playful banter between them which would inform the audience as to what they are about to watch. If later in the script, the comedy starts to become very over the top, broad, or gross such as *The Hangover*, the audience may tune out because that is not what they signed up for. It may be funny, but it's likely inappropriate.

An even greater breach of tone involves switching genres in the story. If in a romantic comedy, you start killing people ala a horror film like *The Descent*, the audience will almost certainly switch off. If you want to have such swings in your story, you need to take a hybrid approach such as a horror comedy like *Shaun of the Dead*. Using comedy, the film sets up both a romantic comedy played against the backdrop of a zombie apocalypse from the first moments. This allows the writers to swing back and forth between tones, but never too far in one direction or the other.

---

the story, and then maybe you will do a carve-out of who these characters are. It's better if you can tell the characters' outlines while you are telling the story, especially when you are pitching TV. You can break out each character and talk about them individually as people you can follow for multiple seasons; what is it that makes them so interesting? There are two things in every character: a want and a need. They are not the same. The want is what the individual thinks they need to get. The need makes them a better person. The need often gets them to overcome their want. The want isn't important. What's important is the journey that gets them their need. An example is *Tucker and Dale*. Dale wants to save the girl. What he needs is self-confidence. Those are basic things. It should be really basic. What you want is love. What you need is to believe in yourself. The love doesn't matter or the love comes naturally. So those character things are really interesting to break out as well as how they fit into the beats of the story.

Q: What are some of your worst and best pitching experiences?

Barbara Stepansky - One of my best pitching experiences was very early in my career, when I walked into the room and said "This is a story about a girl and her horse." The executive across from me responded, "Say no more. I love it." As things go, however, that script never got made as the executive moved to a different company with different project slates. One of the worst pitching experiences I had was over Zoom was when I was pitching an adaptation for a book and the executive stopped me and said, "That's just like the book." It was humbling to realize that they wanted a very different spin on the material and here I was, basically just recounting the book for them.

Eli Craig - I think one of my worst ones was early in my career. I was raising my hands in the air in triumph after having a good pitch. I was feeling really good about myself. Then, I walked out of the room and realized there was a piece of toilet paper on my shoe. That didn't go well. But you learn the most from the bad ones. Early on, I wasn't pitching as many visual signposts in order to get me through the story, and sometimes I would have faith that I knew the story well enough to just go in there and talk it out. I would just end up rambling and then I would find myself making stuff up on the fly. I would walk out thinking that I had just made up some good stuff in there, but they would totally call you on it. They could totally see that you were just making it up.

Lauren Iungerich - My best experiences have been selling the show or the feature in the room. My worst includes having an exec interrupt my pitch to tell their own story and oh, seeing an exec fall asleep.

Q: What happens in the room when you realize your pitch isn't working?

Eli Craig - You can see in someone's body language when it's not working. I think now instead of plowing forward, I will stop and say, "What do you think? I have more to go, but what are you thinking so far?" I will force a response from them early on. A lot of the time you lose them because they are thinking or are caught up on something. If you are just plowing forward, they are sitting there going, "Wait a minute, how is this first act going to work? He mentioned Joe and Suzanne, but I can't remember what happened to Joe. And now, it's Suzanne's story."

Executives are always going to think: Whose story is this? What's their journey? When you're losing somebody, they are usually hung up on something you said earlier. So if you ask them what they are thinking, sometimes you can clear it up. "Oh, good question. Okay, actually, what happens here is..." Then, they are just relieved that you thought of it. And if you haven't thought of it, at least it gives you insight into what you do need to think about.

Tony Jordan - On multiple occasions, I have been halfway through a pitch and I've looked into the commissioner's eyes, and I know they are never in a hundred years going to make this show. They just fundamentally don't like it or they are bored by it. I'm halfway through that pitch and I've said a lot, and I say, "You know what? I'm listening to this myself and I'm not buying it. I'm really sorry. I don't think it's for you." Then, I will ask if I can talk about something else or ask them how their kids are. The beauty of that is that it's kept me in good stead over the years. If I come in to pitch to you and I'm passionate, you feel that and you know that's true. If you're a commissioner and you know me as a writer, you know that I am quite liable of going, "You know the more I'm talking about this, the more shit it is." That takes all the pressure off them. It works in your favor as well.

Hilary Galanoy - Honestly, it's difficult to read the room. We've pitched to cold rooms where no one cracked a smile, and they bought the pitch. And we've pitched to warm rooms where the executives laughed the entire time, enjoying the story, and then they passed. Instead of trying to judge how it's going in the moment, do your pitch, keep it professional, and keep it short. Also, be prepared to answer questions at the end. If you don't know the answer, just wing it. We've winged answers to questions we weren't expecting that turned out better than if we had tried to work them out in advanced. If you know your material well enough, these answers will come to you.

Bryan Woods - There is always that moment when their eyes glaze over and you realize, "This is not going well."

Scott Beck - Or these days, you are on Zoom and you literally see somebody pick up their phone and answer an email.

Bryan Woods - You can leave the pitch room and you're like, "Well, we didn't sell that one. That was a total disaster." Then you get the phone call that you did sell it in the room. So you never really know. You just have to do your best. Reading the room is a big part of pitching. As you are going through your process, you want to have one part of your mind focused on the story and what you are presenting, but another part focused on the people that you are engaging and detecting if they are bored. If you can sense boredom, it's good to push through or skip over elements, as long as you are not going to get tripped up. Just feel the energy in the room, it's important. You want to respond. It should feel like a conversation. The worst pitches are when it feels like you are monologuing. You are just going on and on about all these details. If you can make it feel like a spontaneous conversation and both parties are leaning in and there's participation on the other side of the table where they are asking questions, that's a home run.

Scott Beck - It takes a lot of energy to pitch. Physical energy. Mental energy. You have to prepare yourself to be a performer. For Bryan and I, we are naturally introverts. It's very difficult for us to get in front of people and be excited about what we are pitching. Usually, our excitement translates on the page and we are more comfortable handing over a finished script. But for those next twenty minutes, you have to put on the energy that will help you mentally get through that process. If you feel like you are losing the energy, you just have to make the mental shift. I have to reinvigorate the room for a moment. I have to shift my posture. You try to make it authentic, but you do need to engage everybody there. It's really difficult if you are starting to drain the energy. It becomes contagious in the room.

Barbara Stepansky - If a pitch in the writers room isn't working, the showrunner or one of the EPs will quickly shut it down. You lick your wounds, quietly, and you never speak of it again.

Q: What is a table read and how is that experience?

Eli Craig - A table read is when you read the script through to hear how it flows. I think it's really fun, but it's hard when you have just your friends read through it to hear it. As far as having a studio setting up a table read to see if they want to buy it, I haven't done one like that, but I believe they happen. I've always done it when we have financing and we're going to shoot. It's usually a very exciting experience because you have your cast together. I, personally, haven't been through a bad table read. Though with Amazon and *Zombieland,* they had a lot of notes after the end of the table read and we were going to shoot two days later. It was really fun to watch the writers Rhett Reese and Paul Warnick in the meeting with Amazon. They look at each other and are like, "Oh, come on, guys. Let's just shoot. We've been working on this thing forever." The Amazon guys said this is the way we do it; we need a new draft. I saw them the next morning drinking coffee, all grim. They made it through the script and it was impressive to see that they affected the spirit of the notes. They did do the changes that they were asking for without really changing anything. Then the executives were like, "Oh, fantastic! Great work, guys." It was impressive to me because I can get a little more stubborn. They were stubborn, too, but they did it. I would have been, "Fine! Let's just throw out the script. You hate the script!" I'm way too sensitive.

Josh Greenberg - We do a few drafts really trying to sharpen the show and get it as good as we can get it. Then we will bring in the cast, who in the old days would sit at a long table and read the script almost like a radio show. Now, because of COVID, they do it over Zoom, which is really challenging. You lose a lot of the subtlety. Zoom is not a perfect medium for comedy. It has really hurt laughter and feedback for a table read. With some shows, you don't mute your speakers so you can hear the laughter, which gives it a kind of energy, but that laughter can also cut off the person who is speaking. That has really been frustrating. The table read points out the weaknesses of the script. You can see when a character drops out of a scene when you really need to beef up their presence in a scene. You can also see where the story starts to drag a little bit. It's a really useful tool.

Elizabeth Hackett - I would say the more you can hear your writing out loud, the better. Even if you just have a group of actor friends or non-actor friends. It's a script, so you see it in your mind and you perfect it on the page, and then someone says it out loud and it's awful! Or you have a great line and you don't get a great actor and it's awful. We have a friend that teaches an acting class and he helps us workshop scenes. It's really interesting to see different actors cycle through and read your work and you get a sense of "Oh, that could be better." Or, "Oh, I didn't think that could work."

Q: What happens when a producer or a commissioning editor likes your idea?

Emma Ko - You are expected to write up one to one and a half pages of something to send within an email - either in the email body or as an attachment - saying this is what it is. That might be off the back of a general meeting or it might be sending a few lines to producers or production companies who you have experience with and asking them what they think. My outlines can be between six to twenty-five pages. That includes a first episode breakdown, overview, and detailed episode ideas. I do ask when we start the process what they expect me to deliver. It's usually that in some form. The fee will be discussed, which is some percentage of the ultimate fee. Then you bandy that back and forth a few times. Ultimately, you get to a point where everyone thinks this is it. Next, it goes off to be made into a very sexy pitch deck that the production company makes.

Julie Sherman Wolfe - I'll write up a paragraph and a one-pager and if they like that, then they will put it into development. Then it's official at that point. They then send my agent a contract and off we go. So that's for when I have had the idea. Many times, a producer will come to me with an idea that they've sold to Hallmark, but still need someone to write the outline and the screenplay. Generally, the ideas they bring to me are also one-page or less, and it's my job to flesh out the story and characters. I do rewrites sometimes. To be honest, I don't love doing them, but if I really like the idea, or it's a producer/executive who I know and love, I'll do it. Rewrites are a lot harder, though, because you're taking someone else's work and trying to salvage as much as you can, but still fixing what the network has notes on. It's a totally different skill set to do these rewrites. I'd say a lot of them end up being page-one rewrites, so you're kind of just starting over, but you don't have an outline. At this point, after twenty of these movies, the structure of a Hallmark movie is ingrained in my head. You instinctively know where you're supposed to be story-wise, on whatever page you're on. And you know if the story is heading in the right direction.

Q: What is in a television bible?

Marsha Greene - The bible is a document that can be anywhere between five to fifty pages depending on the showrunner. It explains what the show is. It will typically start with an overview of the series. Character descriptions. What the tone of the show is. What the world of the show is. If you are doing sci-fi, the world can be a huge part of it. It's a different world with all these rules. Or it could be a *Sex And The City* type show that's set in New York. It has a tone and a feel to it so you explain that. Depending on what kind of show you are doing, you might do sample episodes. If you are doing a medical procedural show, you might write some examples of the kinds of cases you might see in the show. If it's a serialized show, you might write a document that's a Season 1 arc - what the journey is. Often you do a bible to sell the project. That's really why it exists. Sometimes, you don't have a bible because you sold the show from a pitch or script and you don't want to go back and write a bible. It is helpful though, for other people involved in the show, like the director, other writers, or the other departments. They can read it and get a sense of how you picture the series and where it is going instead of just relying on the scripts, themselves.

Emma Ko - For me, it's an overview of the project essentially. That starts with the title, what it is - 6 x 60 minutes, etc. I like to do some sort of thematic quote. Then, I do a little paragraph of the absolute overview and then I go into the synopsis of the series. After that, I do character breakdowns - a paragraph each. I do suggested episodes. Currently, I'm doing an adaptation of a book and in that one, it was 10 x 30 minutes, so I did an outline for all ten episodes. I always do a paragraph on theme and style because that is almost like a writer's statement where you get to say why it's meaningful and important. I have also been asked to do writer's statements, which is interesting. One of the projects I'm currently working on is loosely based on my childhood, so there, I'll go into why it's important to me, who I am and why I'm writing it. It's quite important these days to say "Why this writer?"

Q: Are bibles the same across all platforms?

Emma Ko - I think that it can be unclear what broadcasters want. I've been told by one production company that you can only get something going with Netflix with a script. Then I've been told by another company that has a different relationship with Netflix, that if you get a script to them and they are not invested in it, they are likely to say no. I think everything is predicated on the relationship that the production company has with the broadcaster or streamer. I trust that the producers and the production companies that I am working with, know what they are doing. So whatever they need to sell it, I will try and give them what they need.

TV SERIES BIBLE VS. PITCH DECK

When you work at a large company, employees can come and go frequently. In order to get new employees up to speed, they receive training manuals and guides that provide best practices to help orient and integrate them into the workplace.

Series bibles essentially do the same thing. The creator makes a document that delineates the essence and ethos of the show. This will include: where the show takes place, who the main characters are as well as their main motivations, the characters' backstories, the tone of the show/story, where the plot will go in the first season/series, where it may go in future series, the themes the show will explore. From this, a new writer can enter a writers room and get into the flow of breaking story much faster.

Bibles aren't just for production, these days. They have become vital sales pitch documents and are frequently required by financiers. Often, they will be in digital form and use the medium to their advantage by embedding video, audio, and hyperlinks to examples or data that help paint a robust picture of the show.

Pitch decks are similar to bibles, but tend to be more visual and used by directors to convey the overall look and tone they wish to achieve. Due to this, they tend to be associated more with feature films.

Creating a bible or a pitch deck forces a writer to understand their world on a deep level. These documents will expose most flaws in your project, giving you a chance to fix them before pitching anyone.

CHAPTER REVIEW: PITCHING

- Know your theme and message.

- Be clear about your tone.

- Have a strong set up and a strong hook they can remember.

- State who the main characters are.

- What's the main character's goal/want?

- Make sure the stakes, threat, antagonistic forces are clear.

- Believe in your pitch/story.

- Don't get bogged down in plot details unless they ask.

- Ask execs what they like and why.

- Have confidence in yourself and be enthusiastic when pitching.

- Make them feel something, make them care.

- Sell the genre. If it's a comedy, tell them a funny scene. If it's a horror, tell them a scary sequence.

- Give a personal anecdote of why you relate to the story. Your passion helps sell your pitch.

- Be open to collaboration.

- Watch their body language to give you clues as to whether your are engaging them or not. If not, pause and see if they have any questions or ask what they are thinking about it. They may be confused on a story point and need redirecting.

- Expect to answer questions at the end - or throughout. Make it feel like a conversation.

- Don't read your pitch. Know it by heart, so you can maintain eye contact with your audience.

- Table reads are a good way to hear your writing out loud.

CHAPTER 3

BREAKING STORY

―――――

You've got your concept. Fantastic! Now you have to start pounding it into a full-fledged screenplay. That means wrangling the story. Do you start with the plot? Or do you look at the characters first? What kind of structure do you use? Do you have to know the ending when you first begin? The panelists give us their thoughts on those issues and so much more as the hard work begins.

Q: How do you begin?

Josh Olson - I figure out most of the important stuff in advance and my outlines are pretty spare. *A History of Violence* was like a page and a quarter. There was a beginning, middle, and end. Outlines are pretty slim. It's the beats. When John Brancato (*The Game, Terminator 3: Rise of the Machines*) and I write together, our outlines are really spare. If you broke into our computers and stole an outline for one of our scripts, you wouldn't know what to do with it. We will leave entire chunks of plot or character development out and just write short statements such as, "Drives an E," because we both know what that means.

Barbara Stepansky - I take a week for an outline, which is five to ten pages. Once I move into script, I try to write five pages a day. That way I am usually done with a feature script in six weeks unless I get stuck somewhere along the way.

Deborah Haywood - I do an outline in bullets. I usually know what the ending is. Then when I get that signed off, I go back and write it in beats. Once I've written my script, then I go back before I write another draft and write all the story points. Then, I play with the story points and move them around and add things. Then, I rewrite the script. I keep doing that over and over again. I can't keep reading a script and keep it in my head. When you have dialogue in it, you can't see the mechanics of the script. So I always write my outlines in bullets or brief sentences.

Moisés Zamora - It depends on where the idea comes from first. For pilots and screenplays, I do beat sheets. Not so much outlines anymore. Outlines are more for the business. The beat sheet gives me more or less an emotional journey; more than an outline. I want to know the journey of the emotion through the scenes that I am putting together. Then I put notes of things that need to be planted. A watch needs to be planted here. Little payoffs that you need to track do start off in that way. I am not the kind of writer that writes organically and freely about their characters first. I start with the concept, then I go to structure, then I find my character or they are usually in my head as to who they are. I don't tend to write prose about them or the story, like a treatment. I hate treatments.

If I am writing a horror story, then I am actually following the conventions of horror to some degree. *Save the Cat* by Blake Snyder uses some of the formulas and some of the rules that I'm still using. Not necessarily the pacing. Not - on page 15, you have to have the catalyst - but something like that. There are examples of the catalyst happening on page

> ## THE HERO'S JOURNEY
>
> The Hero's Journey is Joseph Campbell's monomyth theory that describes how many of the world's stories and lore have similar characteristics and structures. It is the basis for much of the underlying theory of how humans tell stories. It's definitely worth reading, but right now, we will give you a quick summary:
>
> A hero goes on an adventure out of their ordinary/common world and into the unknown/supernatural world where they meet a myriad of entities who help or hinder them defeat a crisis and return home changed or transformed.
>
> Campbell proposes various stages of the journey, which line up with many of the current ways of thinking about plot and character development. They are...
>
> The Call to Adventure
> Supernatural Aid
> Crossing the Threshold
> Meeting the Mentor
> Abyss (Death and Rebirth)
> Transformation
> Atonement
> Return (with the Elixir)
>
> The Hero's Journey also has several archetypal characters that populate stories from across cultures like the Hero, the Mentor, and the Shadow. For a fun discussion of many of the character portions of The Hero's Journey (with puppets!) check out the *Glove and Boots* YouTube Channel.
>
> To learn more, read Campbell's seminal work *The Hero With A Thousand Faces*. Also, look at Christopher Vogler's *The Writer's Journey*, which takes Campbell's theory and places it squarely on screenwriting.

40, but if you do that, you have to justify it. So that's where the organic beat sheet process comes in. For example, I am on the third draft of a co-write with a friend of mine. It's horror inspired by a Latin American myth with a monster. If you're from Latin America, you know it, but if not, you need some extra context, so we are taking a little bit longer to contextualize this monster before we get to the catalyst and all these other things that need to happen in order to get into the story and savor it.

Jed Mercurio - I do outlining and that's particularly because in writing episodic TV or in writing movies, people will expect to read those if you're being commissioned to write the script. If you are writing a spec, then it's entirely up to the writer. I think most writers would recommend doing an outline so you can have an overview of the story, which will then guide you through the drafting process. I think that is very useful. But there is also room for discovery as you are drafting. This happens to every writer. You realize that there's something better and available to you than what's been outlined or you have

> ## OPEN WORLD VS. CLOSED WORLD
>
> **Open World:** A story concept that is ever-expanding in its plot, characters, locations, and possibly, time. Stories of this kind work best as a series.
>
> **Closed World:** A story concept whose plot is finite and contained to a limited number of characters, locations, and time. Closed worlds are best for feature films and limited series.
>
> An intriguing mix of these two styles comes in a serialized feature film franchise such as the Marvel Cinematic Universe (MCU). Here, each film (*Iron Man*, *Black Panther*, etc.) has a distinct, fully resolved plot, but fits into a much larger, never-ending story.

that unfortunate encounter with a logic problem. Or some other continuity problem, which means that you've got to rethink your outline strategy.

Bill Nicholson - I'm very character-based, so I create a central character with whom the audience identifies with and loves. Storytelling is really the same thing as character. It's all linked. The story is: What does my main character want? You start off by really thinking about that because it may not be obvious. It may be that your character wants to make a lot of money, but when you think about it a little bit more, you realize that your character wants respect. Therefore, you may have a story structure where the character makes the money, but it doesn't deliver what they want and they move on to the next stage. So think about: who is this character? What does this character want? Why do I love this character? Find your character and identify with them. And then start to work out the obstacles.

Julie Sherman Wolfe - There's no waiting for your muse to arrive. There's no time for luxuries like writer's block. You're being paid to write, you've signed your contract - you have to start! With these movies, you can go from having all the time in the world, to... "We need it in three days!" For me, the hard part is the outline, because that's where you find out if you have a story that can sustain itself for nine acts, or if you really have nothing to fill the middle of the script. So in feature language, you don't have an Act 2. I've had moments where I don't have anything for the middle. That's the stressful part. Usually, it means I'm missing something. It's on me to add an element to the story, or to the main characters' lives, to give the plot something to hang on to. The outline can sometimes take me longer than the actual draft because the outline is about fifteen to twenty pages for a full-length TV movie. By the time I get to draft, the heavy lifting is done because, for me, the easy part is putting the dialogue on the page. That's fun. That being said, once I get to draft, a lot of changes may happen from the outline because you start to find the voices of your characters. I start figuring out the world that they're in, and suddenly something I loved in the outline doesn't make sense for these characters anymore. As long as the general story stays the same, I can go with the flow, and discover who these characters are even more as I write.

For me, a normal pace for an outline might be two or three weeks. And four-ish weeks for a first draft - if it's going well. But of course, life can get in the way sometimes. It's definitely faster paced than the feature writing lifestyle. I know feature writers who are very, very excited if they get three pages done a day. For me, that would be a terrible writing day. If I'm writing new stuff, I try to do a minimum of five pages a day on a draft, then I go back and edit. One thing that I'll sometimes do is a vomit draft. That, to me, works the best because I get the gist of each scene on the page - often with placeholder dialogue, and then I go back in later and really focus on the characters' banter, voice, jokes, etc. That's the fun part. The vomit part is almost painful. Hence, its name.

Meg LeFauve - It's different depending on what the project is. If it's IP, then it's breaking down the IP and deciding what can I use and what I can't - just in terms of the form. A book and a movie are two different things. Sometimes, it's with research. Mostly, I start with: Can I have an idea - a word - just a word of what this is about? Something that's thematic. Then, I try to figure out where the characters start and finish. It can be very hazy, honestly. What's the main relationship going on? I like to have some broad ideas of the engine of the piece. Tonally, what do I think I am going for? Again, it can be a bit wavy and it can change as I am thinking about those things. Do I really want it to be that funny? Or this is getting super-serious as I think about the pieces. So I ask myself a lot of questions to get an engine or a concept.

Then I do a puke draft where I forget all of that and I start writing. I don't worry about page count. I don't worry that this doesn't line up. If I get to a point where I don't know what is happening, I type, "I don't know what is happening here," into the document. I write my questions into the document. It's not for anyone else, but me. I just keep going because you can't really know what your movie is until you get to the end. You can't know what Act 1 is until you've seen the third act. If you are spending six months in Act 1, I hate to tell you, but you have no idea what's going on. And the third act, in that great writerly experience, it's a dream. You don't know what it is. Your intellect doesn't know what it is. I'll look at that massive lump and I will go in and start carving...I thought this person was going to be the main character, but it's not about them, it's about this other character... I start seeing what could be the movie.

If you have a writing partner, that's harder to do, so I might do that in a quick treatment or story-ment, as they call it, just to get it up and out. Sometimes, you are doing that together in a room, verbally, or on a board. Now, if you are doing a TV series, it's very different. You have to start charting episodes. There are other things that come in to change that process, but I do think that right brain experience is very important for the process.

Eli Craig - Executives want you to start with an outline, as that's where everything will be ironed out. Then you write. But the discovery process is where fresh things happen and where it finds its life. So once I'm into the script, although I have the outline there, a lot of it goes out the window, but it does help me kind of know where I'm going. Then I will start writing and rewriting and rewriting. I usually have a destination in mind. I have a general idea of what's going to happen. He's going to save the kid, but I don't know exactly how. Part of my discovery is getting there and figuring it out.

Dan Mazer - Because it's specifically comedy that I write, what I do when I start writing is to think: What are the really funny set pieces? What are the really funny ideas and how can

I use those as the tentpoles of this script? Yes, the plot has to work and it has to engage, but I always think what are those hilarious things that will stay with you forever, long after you've seen the movie? In *Bridesmaids*, it's the puking in the waiting room. With all the *Airplane*, Mel Brooks, and Richard Pryor movies, there was always a thing that you went into school and talked about. Like the movie, *There's Something About Mary* - there are just some things that live independently and are sublime.

Marsha Greene - As a creator, I would say it's more common to focus on the big idea and know where you are going. I think it's important for two reasons. When you are doing a show, it is a collaborative experience, but you are following the vision of the creator and the showrunner. Once you are in the writers room, people are looking to you to know what's right or where you want to go. When you haven't done any of that work, then you don't know and they don't know how to do their work. It's really important for you to have a clear vision, not necessarily of everything that is going to happen, but who they are and what feels real and authentic to the characters and the world. That way, when you hear ideas, it will go through that filter and you can say, "Yeah, that's a good idea, but it doesn't feel right for this character." Or maybe you tweak the idea in a certain way to make it fit that character better.

Scott Lobdell - I write a treatment. Ninety-nine times out of a hundred, my treatment is just slug lines of every single scene in the movie - even establishing shots. I may even go so far as to do a slug line for when a character has a conversation, then gets up to get a glass of water in the kitchen and comes back to the conversation in the living room. I'll write a slug line for that. I need to know what every single scene is before I start. My writing partner on *Man of The House*, John McLaughlin (screenwriter of *Black Swan*, *Hitchcock*), needs to have a piece of paper that he writes notes on, and then he starts. For the life of him, he hates it when I give him an eighty-three page script and say I have to get to page 110. He has to start from the beginning. Once I have the treatment, I write within the treatment to get to the script.

Mohamad El Masri - It depends on the story I'm telling. It's case by case. Sometimes, it's just a few beats on a piece of paper, sometimes it's an elaborate series bible. Occasionally, I'll start with a specific structure that story lends itself to and write to that. Sometimes, it's just a character profile. Sometimes, it's a one page sketch. It really depends on the story I'm telling. Everything should be in process of the specific piece you're embarking on. I don't usually lock myself into one overarching process.

Q: Should a writer know the ending before they start writing?

Jed Mercurio - I wouldn't say always, but I think it's incredibly helpful to know the ending if you are doing a closed piece of work like a feature film, a novel, or a play. I think if you are working in episodic TV, then endings have a different character, which is that, often, an ending is just part of an ending if it's the end of an episode. It might round off that particular installment, but it also needs to have the promise of forwarding the story, so that it carries you into the next episode.

Scott Lobdell - When you are building a mystery especially, you need to know the end.

Bill Nicholson - Some writers are much more excited by not knowing where they are going. I respect that. It's not my way, at all. I have the whole trajectory in place before I start writing. It doesn't mean it might not change, but I think you need to know where you are going. I am not a fan of open-ended television. To start with, it's all fine, but once they get into Series 2 and Series 3, they have to keep the story going, but they've run out of ways that the character can surprise us. They might start giving us five more episodes of plot, but now we don't really believe it. I think you should write knowing where you are going and maybe limit it to only three series so you are heading somewhere and you have a climax. With that, you can build your character and their choices instead of this slightly sinking feeling of what can we do next, which breaks the faith with the audience.

Marsha Greene - Not always, to be honest, but it's actually quite popular in today's world for you to go to a pitch and for people to ask you what happens in Season 5. My personal opinion is that the show is a thing that is growing and changing. You go into it with some ideas, but sometimes as you start to work on it, it goes in a different way. Or an actor comes into it and brings something different to it, and it starts to veer. With *The Porter*, we did know what we wanted the ending to be because we envisioned it as three seasons. Partially, that was because it's a historical series. We knew the first season would be the lead-up to starting this Black union. The second season would be the trials and tribulations of that. The third would be where it ended. As to the story itself, they started the union in 1917 but signed the first contracts in 1945. It took many, many years. We had an idea of how we could do three seasons, but we could have done two and slowed it down. So I feel it's important to be loose and allow the show to go in the direction it wants to go. But sometimes you have an idea and you just know the ending.

Josh Olson - You have to have an ending. Without that, there's no point in sitting down with your characters. It can change, but you need to have one there. You may find a better one.

Moisés Zamora - Usually, I know how things are going to end. I try to put in those pillars to hit - those events, those set pieces. But sometimes the story or the character plays tricks on me and forces me to change the ending. That's when you're deeply intuitive and instinctual - almost as if that character is living with you. People refer to that. That they know them and they are so real. And when you get to that point, you may realize that it wouldn't make sense to end their story a certain way. It's important to have that flexibility. To me, those little discoveries feel like you've solved the world's problems. Like you have the formula for world peace. That wonderful feeling is my happy place. I happen to love the writing process. I know some writers find it painful and frustrating. And it can be frustrating and painful, but I think the frustration and pain come from the rejection of this world in this industry.

Tony Jordan - I always have two things: I have an endpoint and a first image. I think the first image tells you a lot. It tells you what the story is. Tells you what the world is. This is where we are and this is what is going on. That's my "once upon a time" moment. And

I always kind of know the last scene. If not the content - the feeling, image, or taste of what the scene is. I might be willing to accept that could be because of my *EastEnders* background. Obviously, I was always starting from a cliffhanger. You always knew what the cliffhanger was. I know where I am and where I'm going, but the rest of it is a bit jazzy. I like to think about it like this…I might be in London and I know I'm going to Birmingham. To get there, I might take the M1, which would be quicker. Or I might go for a little toddle and head through the Cotswolds and have a cream tea. Or I could go, fuck it, I'm going to go via Norwich. It's unheard of, but I quite like it. It's funky. That's how I am in the middle bit.

Scott Lobdell - I will say that in the script I am working on right now, I know how it ends and who is responsible for X, Y, and Z. As I started to break down the draft, I realized, shit, this is boring. It's a claustrophobic on-the-plane movie, not *Non-Stop*, but that type of movie. I have to make the audience believe that it's the pilot who's at fault. I have to make sure that the woman with the tattoo on her arm is a red herring. When the script is done, you have to make sure that there are four or five people who the audience is 100% sure that it's them, but it's not.

Eli Craig - I think that it is kind of essential to know how it's going to end and how it fits into its genre. Is it going to have a happy ending? I write horror comedy and the reason it's a horror comedy is that almost always they have a somewhat happy ending. They have a joyful ending. Whereas, a horror movie doesn't necessarily end like that.

Paul King - We had the ending of *Paddington 2* mapped out pretty early. I think it was maybe the second or third day. I knew he was happy with the Brown family and perhaps the obvious thing would have been to drive a wedge between them, but I felt the Browns had all learned to love Paddington in the first film and unpicking that would just be frustrating for the audience. But beyond Mr. Curry, we hadn't said much about the wider community of Windsor Gardens.

We had this notion of Paddington wanting to get a present for his Aunt Lucy but ending up in prison and the neighbors turning on him. Ultimately, we thought they should come round, and then we thought it would be a lovely twist if he never got her his present, but got something better - to see her. I can remember how I felt when we first said it, and I knew it could work.

Personally, I have to know an ending in order to chart out the emotional journey of the movie, but of course things change radically from draft to draft. The middle of that movie changed all the time. We knew we wanted Paddington in prison for *Paddington 2* – that was going to be our comic motor – but people were anxious about that. "Oh, don't have him in prison too long!" So we wrote a messy first version where he escapes and went on the run and then we wrote a good second draft where we thought if this is going to be a Paddington in prison movie, it should be a prison movie. Then the stakes are, how can I get out of prison? We tend to throw too much into it and then have to strip it back.

Michael Brandt - I can't imagine taking on a project and not knowing the ending. A simple way I think about this is when you're tucking your kids in bed and they ask you to tell them a story about, let's say, a frog. So you start with the frog jumping around trying to find food.

THE CALL TO ADVENTURE

Joseph Campbell's first major plot point in The Hero's Journey has been renamed many times over the years. Whether it's the Inciting Incident (Syd Field), the Disruption (Tzvetan Todorov), or the Catalyst (Blake Snyder), it all means the same thing...

- **An external event or problem happens to the lead character (or group of characters) of such import, that they cannot ignore it. This forces them to react to the event by going on a journey to deal with the issue thereby beginning an internal transformation of their character.**

Without this opening moment, the story cannot move forward. So if at the beginning of your script, you feel that your characters are waiting around for something to happen - make something happen! There's no hard and fast rule as to when it occurs, but halfway through Act 1 is a good rule of thumb.

In your mind, you know that the frog will get the food to feed his family in the end. But to get the food, the frog realizes that it has to cross a dangerous road because the flies it eats live on the other side. So now I know he has to get across the road because he has to feed his family. Knowing the end helps dictate the story you tell.

Starting a story where you don't know the end, that's not for me. Maybe other people can work that way, but I don't. *Arthur the King* is an adventure racing movie and a dog is a big part of it. I knew, in the end, what was going to happen to the dog. I can't imagine not knowing. In a world where you're given IP, you know what's going to happen in the end. I do have some original stories I'm working on, but even then, I one hundred percent know what's going to happen before I put pen to paper.

Q: Do you think character or plot first?

Eli Craig - Plot and character go hand in hand, right? The character has to fit into the plot, but the plot and the beats of it and the nuts and bolts of the story have to fit the characters. If I asked my son to describe the new *Spiderman* movie, I want to know in five sentences what the story is. You have to be able to tell the story in a few sentences. Or just one sentence, preferably. That's the logline. It's important for that to be an anchor. And then it's important to have the wants and needs of the character and the beats of the story in an outline. Once I have that, I am not one to stick tooth and nail to it, I start experimenting and I find so much when I write through the dialogue and character. Sometimes, characters that I didn't think would matter at all, are way more interesting and way more valuable characters. So the relationships build, as I fall in love with them as I write. So I need that time with the script.

Meg LeFauve - I think emotional thematic first, which is experienced through the main character, and therefore the plot would come out of that. I do know great writers who work completely the opposite, so there is no one way. It's how your brain works. I learned storytelling from actor/director, Jodie Foster. If you wanted to pitch her a script that you had read, she would ask me, *"What's the big, beautiful idea in here?"* It's always: What is this about? Not just intellectually but emotionally because as an actor, she is going to take that journey emotionally, so she wants to know what she, as an actor, is going to hold onto emotionally. Where do I start and where do I finish? So I start with that.

Now, this is also something that evolves over the many drafts that you do, and it's the hardest thing to get to. It's usually sitting in your subconscious as a writer. It's not an intellectual thing; it's an emotional thing. So I often start with a word, like guilt or redemption. Then I try to get to a sentence. What am I trying to say about guilt or redemption? That can take many, many drafts. Then you can realize that after draft six, shit! It's not about redemption at all. It's about this other thing. That's normal that your rudder for the story changes. When I worked at Pixar, the rudder is: What is this about?

Briana Belser - Personally, I find that it is easier for me to generate a story when I have a very specific character. And then I can put that person in a world that I know very well. From there, many things can occur and I have a semblance of a plot. If I want a certain person to have a breakup, I can get myself there. Where I find structure is so critical, and where I have learned to stop free writing and create a beat sheet, is when the plot takes into account the experience of the story and how it unfolds. It's where the intrigue is, and how the audience, the directors, the actors, and the editor might move your words from a place of just script and page to reality. The structure keeps you honest. If your movie is boring and I'm twenty pages in, I don't care how beautifully it's written, pace matters.

In Western media, there's plot armor where we believe the hero will win and the villain will be vanquished. I have found that in some forms of East Asian television and media, they are not so pressed about a happy ending - those sorts of things can be an opportunity for your story, to misdirect. So if you know that the midpoint is going to be a narrative inversion of what the ending is, you can abide by that formula. The character is on a high and the ending will be lower. Or vice versa, the hero will be at a low at the midpoint and then win in the end. You can invert those and create misdirects. I think it is a more economical use of time to beat out and understand where your plot is in a loose structure. Even by page 10, some things need to be popping. The first scene needs to be my main character doing an awesome thing that shows you who they are. I do subscribe to those things when I get in. I'll play a little bit, but for commercial work, it's so helpful to have that structure.

Bill Nicholson - The big failure is when the plot drives the character. Suppose you set up a plot where the protagonist has to go into a room and confront the villain. The protagonist could pull a gun on the villain but then it would be game over. He's got a gun, the villain hasn't. If you decide in your plot that all you want is for the villain to fail to react, you've served the plot, but you haven't served the character. So instead, you must think of what the villain could do in this situation that would demonstrate something really clever. This adds to the sense that they are a legitimate villain. So why not have the antagonist say, "I'm so glad you've come. I'm tired. Do it. Do it, now." Now the protagonist has to think, "Is this something I want to do? Am I going to kill this guy in cold blood?" Now you've started to create a relationship between the two. If you drive all your plot decisions through character; you still have to invent tricks. You still have to think: Where are they? Are they in a car? In a house? On a cliff? You set the location of a scene, which sets the rules of a scene. Let's

STORY STRUCTURE

Story structure refers to how the plot points and character development moments are arranged. The format you're working in (feature film, TV sitcom, etc.) will dictate many of the structural choices you make. There are some basic rules that apply to all formats and others that are specific to them.

Feature films
The most common way to structure long form content is via the three act structure. Act 1 aka "the beginning" orients the audience to the world, the genre, the tone, and introduces the main characters and the main problems they will face. This lasts approximately 1/4 the length of the screenplay. Act 2 aka "the middle" where the main characters try to solve the problems they are faced with in Act 1. This is roughly 1/2 the length of the screenplay. They interact with new characters and learn new information. They confront obstacles put in their way by various forces of antagonism. Act 3 aka "the end" brings the story to a close via some sort of resolution in both character and plot that answers the problem introduced at the beginning. Like Act 1, this is about 1/4 the length of the screenplay.

There are many theories on how to manipulate the three act structure. Two of the more popular are the **Syd Field Paradigm (SFP)** and **Blake Snyder's Save the Cat Beat Sheet (SCBS)**. They roughly mirror each other and line up a lot with Joseph Campbell's Hero's Journey. In each of these theories, there are a few important points that appear, which all screenplays seem to contain.

Inciting Incident (SFP)/Catalyst (SCBS) - sometimes called the "disruption" or "the Call to Adventure." This is the first major plot point in a story. Usually, an external force brings information or a problem to the main characters and they must decide to solve it. This typically happens halfway through Act 1 (around page 15).

Plot Point 1 (SFP)/Break into 2 (SCBS) - this is the end of Act 1 and the beginning of Act 2's journey. Typically, this happens when the lead characters actively decide to solve the problem created by the inciting incident/catalyst. In a two hour feature screenplay, this occurs around page 30.

Midpoint (SFP/SCBS) - as it states, this is the halfway point of the script. The lead characters have been working on the problem brought to them by the inciting incident/catalyst and have gathered enough information to make a realization of some sort. This leads to a new way to solve the inciting incident/catalyst. This usually brings the protagonists and antagonists into direct opposition thereby raising the tension in the story. In a two hour feature screenplay, this happens around page 60.

Plot Point 2 (SFP)/Break into 3 (SCBS) - this is often referred to the "all is lost" moments for the lead characters. This is the point where they are the furthest away from achieving their internal and external goals. In a two hour feature screenplay, this happens around page 90.

STORY STRUCTURE CONTINUED

Climax (SFP)/Finale (SCBS) - Act 3 is about resolution and this point is when most of that happens. The lead characters must use everything they've learned through the story to overcome the problem set up by the inciting incident/catalyst - win or lose. Most, if not all, plot and character arcs are tied up. This happens halfway through Act 3 to the end of the story, so about pages 100-120 in a feature.

Some writers think the three act structure isn't exact enough and think in terms of five, seven, or even nine acts. In truth, no matter how many acts you decide upon, you are still breaking the story up at roughly the same places and just calling them something different.

Series
Dramas and comedies that must stop for advertisements have similar plot points as the feature film model. However, these usually happen right before a commercial break and become cliffhangers in order to retain the viewing audience. Sitcoms typically have two acts with optional "tags" that happen either before the opening credits or as the final credits run. Dramas can have anywhere between five to nine acts depending on how each network/broadcaster break up their shows. Also, these will often have multiple storylines (see non-linear structures).

For those platforms that don't require ad breaks, the only real difference is a shorter page count. You can estimate where your plots points would go.

Non-linear structures
The three act structure doesn't have to be applied to one character moving forward in linear time. You may break time using flash forwards or flashbacks to either create foreshadowing or to fill in backstory. Even though you are going backwards and forwards, the superstructure of the story usually remains consistent to the three act structure. So a flashback may reveal plot information at the climax.

TV series, especially dramas, often have multiple story lines that could be concurrent, previous, or subsequent to the main character's storyline. In this case, you will find yourself bouncing between timelines. Often, the switch happens at one of the major points listed in the three act structure and can cause a cliffhanger. *21st Century Screenplay* by Linda Aronson's (listed on page 67) focuses on non-linear storytelling.

Micro and Macro structure
An interesting occurrence with the three act structure is that the pattern appears on small and large scales. Each Act can be broken down into a beginning, middle, and end. Each scene can be done in the same way, too. In a serialized drama series, the three act structure can appear over the course of a season (or series) where the first few episodes are like Act 1, the last few are like Act 3. It can also appear over the course of the life of a series where Season 1 is like Act 1, Season 2 is Act 2 and Season 3 wraps up everything. It's like story DNA!

say the rule of a clifftop scene is that if you get too close to the cliff, you will die. So if your character gets to the cliff and he falls over it but there's a tree that catches him, you've slightly cheated the audience because you've previously set that up as really dangerous. Don't do that. Do it through character. Work out a way that, as a character, he can avoid falling over the edge. Otherwise, all you are doing is mechanical.

Jed Mercurio - I try to do the two things at the same time. I think that one feeds off the other. It's a very natural, virtuous circle between character design and plot design. As you start to identify who your character is, you start to get a clearer idea of what would be the optimum plot for that character to be in. And vice versa, as you devise the plot, you start to refine the idea of the character who would be best suited to that plot.

Ron Leshem - It depends on the story. I am always trying to find something that will capture my attention and be solid enough. Often, you do have an idea for a plot or character, but a lot of times you don't. You just know you want to live in this world at this time. You start your research and find voices that you fall in love with. It really depends. Every story would be different for me.

Tony Jordan - I don't know if you can have a story in your head without a character. I'm not sure you can have a character in your head without a story or a backstory - something to make them a character.

Scott Lobdell - I need to know enough about the character going in because story feeds

---

JED MERCURIO'S CRITICAL MASS THEORY

Jed has an interesting analogy in the way he thinks about getting a story moving. In physics, when enough nuclear material comes together to start a chain reaction and sustain it, that is called the **critical mass**.

Jed feels that no single story element can get a story rolling in Act 1. However, if he can bring together the right amount of them together, the story will move forward with lots of energy. Some of the story elements are:

- The antagonistic elements
- The allied elements
- The various goals and objectives
- The character designs
- The plot and its structure, which promises a premise

If you're interested in learning more from Jed himself about writing drama for TV, check out his **BBC Maestro** course. Lots of videos and other resources to get your creative juices flowing. There are other writing courses on the platform as of the printing of this book, such as comedy and novel writing. There is a fee.
bbcmaestro.com

character, character feeds story. I don't believe that they are independent of each other. You kind of find your way.

Josh Greenberg - I always think character first. If you look at so many examples of successful sitcoms like *Frasier* or *Friends* or *Everybody Loves Raymond* - they're filled with jokes, but the reason people keep coming back is because of the characters. They love these characters and they want to spend time with them every week. You can have a really wacky or unique or cool premise, but it's always about finding a character that people would want to spend time with, possibly for years.

Q: Do you use a three-act structure?

Bryan Woods - Yes and no. Yes, in the sense that every story has a beginning, a middle, and an end. Three acts. It has a logic to it. No, in the sense that it doesn't really matter. We all have movies that we love that throw all the rules out the window. Maybe they have a single scene. It's not acts at all. Great writers like Aaron Sorkin or William Goldman would say sometimes that they write in five acts. I don't even know what that means, but it works for them. When you are pitching and attempting to sell something to a studio and it's not an art project, it's just a transactional piece of business. The business loves three acts. They love the idea of setting up a character, putting them through a situation, and then watching them get out of that difficult situation.

Scott Beck - For instance, if we were pitching *Inglorious Bastards*, it would be: you have to assemble this team to infiltrate Adolph Hitler and go to this screening. The second act is trying to get into Germany and then in the third act, everything goes wrong and you find your way to the end of the film. But there is so much nuance in the journey of that. I know for us, from a pitching standpoint, you want to be a little more defined of where your edges are. But in the writing process, it's fun to take more liberties. You understand the principles of what the three acts are getting at, but you can paint outside the lines. Usually, that creates interesting diversions you otherwise wouldn't anticipate. So always giving yourself a little bit of leeway results in something a little more fresh rather than telling a tale that has been told many times over.

Deborah Haywood - I wouldn't be able to tell you where my acts end and begin, but I do know that you need a beginning, a middle, and an end. And things need to get worse before they can get resolved. I also know that if the ending isn't working, then probably the setup isn't working. I find the setup the hardest thing.

Bill Nicholson - I have to preface this by saying I have no training. I came into the business without any theory about it. I haven't been to film school. I wasn't much of a film watcher. I was wanting to be a novelist. It kind of happened by accident and sideways. I don't know what the three-act structure means. I'm not remotely interested in it. I think people that try to build their screenplays like they are building a house have got the wrong idea entirely. Some films are such a mess structurally, but they still work. For me, it may be that when I look back on my work, it all follows the rules unknown to me. What's the three-act structure all about? It's all about the idea that you go to an achievement and then you go to a failure

SCREENWRITING BOOKS

There are many books on screenwriting that explore the various aspects of story theory and the business of screenwriting. Here are some of them for you to check out. Never stop learning!

21st Century Screenplay/Linda Aronson (Allen & Unwin, 2010)
Aronson's book has the unique focus of looking at non-linear storytelling, such as the use of flashbacks, flash-forwards, and multi-character (ensemble) story arcs.

Adventures in the Screen Trade/William Goldman (Warner Books, 1983)
An entertaining three-part book from one the best screenwriters of all time. Part One is a collection of essays about working with the colorful characters that make up Hollywood. Part Two looks at eleven of his projects and how they did or did not get made. Part Three looks at how Goldman would go about adapting his short story on DiVinci into a screenplay.

The Anatomy of Story/John Truby (Non Basic Stock Line, 2009)
According to Truby, 90% of all stories fail at the premise and he provides great advice on how to overcome that hurdle. Truby was featured in *The Guerrilla Film Makers Handbook*.

The Coffee Break Screenwriter: Writing Your Script Ten Minutes at a Time 2nd Edition/Pilar Alessandra (Michael Wiese Productions, 2010) The *On the Page* podcast host's "ten minutes at a time" method breaks the daunting task of screenwriting into manageable chunks with the aim of moving a project forward.

The Hero With A Thousand Faces/Joseph Campbell (Pantheon, 1949)
Campbell explores the theory that mythological narratives frequently share the same underlying structure regardless of culture. This "monomyth" is built upon his famous The Hero's Adventure paradigm, which underpins modern story theory.

The Hollywood Standard: The Complete and Authoritative Guide to Script Format and Style, 3rd Ed./Christopher Riley (Michael Wiese Productions, 2021). For those interested in the technical aspects of writing screenplays, check out Riley's tome which takes you through a myriad of different formats one would use depending on what you're creating and for whom.

Into The Woods/John Yorke (Penguin, 2014) Yorke describes why we tell stories in the manner that humans do, exploring the fundamental structure underneath all narratives. He gives good advice for idea generation and maintains that telling stories that matter to you is the pathway to original, non-generic projects.

Making a Good Screenplay Great: A Guide for Writing & Rewriting by Hollywood Script Consultant, Linda Seger:3rd Edition (Silman-James Press, 2010). A pro script consultant takes the reader through the process of generating ideas and developing them into full-fledged screenplays. For those who are more seasoned, it will help give names to things that you know instinctively - like an ear-trained musician who learns the names of the chords afterward.

SCREENWRITING BOOKS (CONTINUED)

The Nutshell Technique: Crack the Secret to Successful Screenwriting/Jill Chamberlain (The University of Texas Press, 2016)
As a veteran script consultant, Chamberlain realized the vast majority of screenwriters approached their stories incorrectly. They were looking at it from the standpoint of situation. She developed a method with eight dynamic and interconnected elements writers can use to tell their stories properly.

On Writing: A Memoir of the Craft/Stephen King (Scribner and Sons, 2000)
While not focused on screenwriting per se, King's post-car accident, five-section book on fiction writing remains a valuable resource and can broaden one's approach to the craft.

Save The Cat/Blake Snyder (Michael Wiese Productions, 2005)
Written in a poppy, energetic voice, Snyder's book has become a favorite of beginners. At its core is his Beat Sheet, which breaks down a screenplay's structure into fifteen manageable sections. He has some good ideas/techniques for generating ideas and pitching projects. Blake Snyder was featured in *The Guerilla Film Maker's Pocketbook*.

Screenplay: The Foundations of Screenwriting 2nd ed./Syd Field (Delta, 2005) A mainstay of the screenwriting world. Field created the first breakdown of screenplay structure with his Syd Field Paradigm. It looks at the entire process of writing a screenplay from the idea to the business side.

Story: Substance, Structure, Style and the Principles of Screenwriting/Robert McKee (Regan Books, 1997) Another mainstay. McKee takes a more academic look at screenwriting than Field, especially when looking at the concepts of Theme and the Forces of Antagonism.

Write Screenplays that Sell/Michael Hauge (Collins Reference, 1991)
Script consultant and story expert Hauge takes you through the process of writing screenplays with an eye toward finding all the authentic moments in your story.

The Writer's Journey 3rd Ed./Christopher Vogler (Michael Wiese Production, 2007) Vogler, when working at Disney, broke down Joseph Campbell's *Hero With A Thousand Faces*, and first applied The Hero's Journey and Campbell's character archetypes to screenwriting in a memo to executives. This book takes the memo and expands upon it in a more academic manner than the other books on this list.

Writing and Selling Drama Screenplays/Lucy V. Hay (Creative Essentials, 2014) Punchy in tone, novelist and screenwriter Hay breaks down what separates drama from genre works and how to create authentic stories that will help get these less commercial pieces financed. This is part of Hay's larger series with other titles looking at characters, thrillers, and diversity, just to name a few.

and then you go to a climax that achieves. That's just another way to say, you've got to have a story. And a story can't just be, "I hope that girl loves me. Oh, she does. Great!" That's not a story. It's got to be, "I hope that she loves me. Oh, boy, she doesn't. She hates me. This is awful. What can I do? What if I jump over this wall? Oh! She loves me now." Then you have a story.

Meg LeFauve - I use a three-act structure because it's how I understand and develop films. I don't have any problem if I'm consulting on a project and they use a five-act structure. They see it differently and that's fine. I may want to know why they think the story needs that, but I don't think there are any rules - there are tools. The tool I use is three acts because, for me, structure is character. It makes sense to me, as the three-act structure helps me keep track of the character. I am seeing where a character is in their transformation and where they see themselves in the world. If you are doing it right, it is also the audience's track because they are having the catharsis with the main character. So I am using it as a discipline to keep track of the main character's transformation, rather than something from which to create the story.

Ron Leshem - When I was a young writer, as I was so eager to jump to the writing, I always avoided any breakdowns. The thing about writing a draft is that it is so hard to find out later on where the mistakes are in the structure. One thing young writers don't realize, is that the word "writing" is a mistake. It's not the right name for our profession. They think it's about choosing words. It's not. It's storytelling. It's exploring what your unique character would do in their unique situation, and exploring where the world might develop in those circumstances. It comes from instincts and for many people, they are there because we've listened to stories our entire lives - like Disney stories. They have the same structure. But many writers jump too quickly to the draft because they are confident and they are in a hurry. They think if you go to the most classic structures, it makes you less of an artist. What they don't understand is that if you take an artist like Tarantino who has the image of a guy who is exploding with chaos and creativity, you see that his stories, like *Django Unchained*, are built on the most classic structure that has been with us since Aristotle. These directors worship this as their Bible. They are trying to make sure the plot points are at the right moment. You are going to have the midpoint exactly at the midpoint. You are going to have the end of Act 1 exactly where the end of Act 1 should be by the book. The most important thing in our profession is this and we should worship our storytelling roots.

I think that the classic structure helps you a lot in identifying what is missing and what type of solutions you should look for. If you don't work with a structure then I don't think it would work and ultimately not be made. And if it is made, there's a 99% chance it will disappear. If you want to write successfully, you have to understand taglines or loglines. You need to understand the motives and goals of the characters and the story. You need to understand what is unique about it. What is the tension? I am trying to build the three acts, even if it is television. I treat the structure of it like a film - both the episode itself and the seasonal arc. I use these tools, I use even something like *Save the Cat* as a checklist to help me, especially when I'm stuck. It helps me look for ideas, but also for my failures. When I start drawing, I want to know what is the story of Act 1. What is the break from Act 1 to Act 2? What is the midpoint? What is 2B? What is Plot Point 2 that breaks from Act 2 to Act 3? What is the climax? I want to know all of these things, both episodically and seasonally. It doesn't make me any less of an artist. I am going to explode with creativity later, but I want to know the roots of it. Sometimes, when we are used to it, this can happen automatically.

Jed Mercurio - I'm certainly not a subscriber to the idea that there's a singular structural model that we should all be following. In fact, I think the very conspicuous plurality of structural models indicates that there is no dominant way of structuring story. If you look at examples in the real world, you will see there are ways of doing things that pretty much everybody adopts. When Dick Fosbury invented the Fosbury Flop, pretty much all the high jumpers in the world took that on. That became the way of setting higher and higher records. If you look at Olympic swimming you have the freestyle event, which means you can swim any stroke you want, but everyone does the front crawl because that's the best way of getting across the pool in the shortest possible time. It's certainly not true of screenwriting that there's only one way to skin a cat.

Josh Greenberg - I use three acts in each episode at twenty-two minutes per episode. Some shows have a little cold open. Some have a little tag at the end of the show. A cold open happens before the credit sequence and there's a little introductory, almost like a prologue, to the show. Not every show has it. You can either use it as a throwaway moment - a funny little mini-play. Or you can use it to introduce what will be the conflict of the episode. In a network show that has a full season order in America, it's twenty-two episodes, which is a lot to do in a year. Other shows have thirteen episodes in a season, and some can be less than that. Generally speaking, you are sort of doing the micro plotting and the macro plotting. You are figuring out what is happening in this episode and discussing story turns and character arcs. But you want to put that in the perspective of the larger season.

Every show that I have worked on, we look at where the show is headed. Sometimes, we are leading up to a giant season ending cliffhanger. Some big turn of events that promises more for the next season. Of course, you want to have the audience come back because of that promise. That is really fun. You are doing everything in service to the larger story. You can't be blind to that. You can't just focus on Episode 3 because it will impact what happens in Episode 10. You want to keep things moving toward that end game, but it's not so clearly delineated as say one third of the way through the season, a specific something will happen.

Dan Mazer - Sacha Baron Cohen and I never really contemplated being film writers. We were asked to write the *Ali G* movie. We came into it as complete neophytes. The longest thing we had ever really written at that point was a five-minute sketch. Very kindly, the people at Working Title said, "Here's how to write films," and directed us towards Robert McKee. I remember just being horrified at the thought that there was this formula and structure that everybody followed. I was like, "No! We are not going to do that. We are going to subvert that and circumvent it and make our own way and forge our own path." Then you realize, no, you can't. It's there for a reason. We all enjoy rhythm and security, especially when we are trying to make a commercial film. You can't really escape all those rules. So in terms of the three act structure and your turning points, Act 2 low points, and your Act 3 storm the castle moment - all, annoyingly, apply. It's kind of irrefutable.

Eli Craig - A horror movie, generally, has a very basic structure. Then you hang the meat on those bones. If you get too carried away from the structure, it just destroys every thought and every great idea you could ever have. So you have to figure out how to put your idea within an existing structure. That's key. Look at good movies and think about how to put your idea within them. If it doesn't fit, then it may not be an idea that works as a movie.

Carolina Rivera - I think in acts. You want to have those little cliffhangers that support the structure. It helps to board them as such. Usually, if it's a half hour, I have four acts. If it's forty-three minutes, like *Daughter*, I have five or six acts. I like to think of the structure in that way because then you have a solid structure.

Tony Jordan - I remember when I first started, I didn't know anything. I went and studied everybody. John Truby, Linda Seger. I went to the Robert McKee *Story* weekend and got mugged for £350. I studied Syd Field. I loved Syd Field. I looked at paradigms; different act structures; trying to find out the right way to do it. The only conclusion you can come to when you study those things is that there is no right way. Once you understand that, it frees you up.

I don't block anything out. I don't do any planning like a scene breakdown. I literally start on page one and when I finish scene one I think, "Where should I go now?" Then I go to wherever, instinctively, I feel I should be. I do that all the way through. This way I become like the audience. When I get to scene seven and I will be like, "Oh, shit! I've left Jenny Jennings in the cab. I better go and sort that out." My logic is that I've had that thought at the exact same time that the audience would have had that thought. So as they think it, it's dealt with. So just when they are thinking where has Jenny gone? She pops up. I think that's pretty cool if it works. I have no idea if it does.

Michael Brandt - For a long time, I resisted "let's lay this out in three acts." I never did outlines because I thought, naturally, I should know how to do it. In fact, I thought not knowing where I was going made me a better writer. But when I got into television for five years doing the *Chicago* shows, I started following a structure almost out of necessity due to the commercial breaks. I had to consider how we built to the opening credits teaser. How do we build to the first commercial break? That's Act 1. Then, we had to do that process again for Act 2, Act 3, and Act 4.

When I got back into features after those five years, that structure muscle in me had developed in such a way that I realized I'd been making it so difficult on myself for so long. Now when I'm presented with a new idea, the first thing I do is put it up on a board and make three columns. I generally will know the ends of Act 1 and Act 2 and write those down. Then, I just have to drive to those points and I'm good. Of course, you start moving little stuff around in the process, but just getting something up helps me see where I'm going, which allows things to happen faster. I save myself a lot of pain and agony by putting a couple of beats up there and knowing that they are now set in stone. It's set in stone because those beats are what I understand; that this point has to happen and this beat has to happen before it. I don't know how I'm going to get there, but I know I have to get there. So it's coming up with what those points are, and those things usually present themselves to you. For a thriller: it's the mystery and who knows what? If you figure all of that out, then, for me, you're eighty percent home. The action is the stuff that fills in the middle and gets you to the next thing. Whether it's a car chase, a foot chase, another murder, or whatever it's going to be, those are the things that get you to that next thing that I have already on my board. So, cool, the car chase happens here, and this gets exposed. Now we're at the end of Act 2. This guy dies, the bad guy gets away, whatever it's going to be, and that action gets me to whatever I've laid in concrete at the end of Act 2.

Ben Philippe - Every room that I have been in has a different language for the exact same thing. On one of the drama shows I did, it was a full three act structure because we were writing for forty pages. In *Only Murders in the Building*, we keep it loose and call them the A, B, Cs. It's this broad beginning, middle, and end. When I teach screenwriting, I say that a lot of screenwriting is coming up with technical language for things that are pretty basic and organic to storytelling. Where are the characters at the beginning of the episode? Where are they at the end? So we talk broadly in A, B, Cs. B doesn't have to be one scene. It can be three scenes coalescing around the same idea. That's the level of the language we use when breaking story. So the B is like the midpoint and every writer looks at it slightly differently. Our showrunner on *Only Murders*, John Hoffman, is really into finding that key central question per episode and my personal style is knowing the central concept. Once I have the key idea, the thing that the episode is about, like it's a flashback episode or a blackout episode, I can then wrap my mind around it.

Danny Strong - For *Dopesick*, a limited series, I structured the totality of the eight episodes with a three-act structure arc. Not per episode, but over the eight episodes. I viewed the first three episodes as Act 1. I viewed the next four episodes as Act 2 with Episode 7 as the darkest of the dark. It ends on the darkest moment of the whole season. The last episode was Act 3, which was this sort of hopeful journey out of the darkness. That was extremely intentional. That did not happen by accident. I very much viewed the whole season as one three-act structure. Within that, each episode had a five-act structure, but I wanted each episode to have storylines that were essentially all self-contained. So that the storylines were, for the most part, resolved in each episode. They had their own arcs to them. Maybe one wouldn't get resolved, but the other three would be. Each one was meticulously designed like that. There was no laziness in that. We didn't just wander from episode to episode.

Emma Ko - On *1899*, we weren't really shaping it episode by episode. It was still more overview. Our showrunner had an outline of what was going to happen in each episode and what the major cliffhanger would be, but that changed. In terms of a traditional structure, beginning, middle, and end, of course, absolutely. In terms of how you plan that out, I mean we still did timelines and what's happening here and what have you, but it always served the purpose for Jantje Friese, the showrunner, to be able to look back at what we've done and then take from it what she needed and discard what she didn't.

Lauren Iungerich - I use two acts or three acts. I've written one-hour shows where there are five acts. Even though my last three shows have been on Netflix where there isn't an act break structure - I don't put the act breaks in the script. I do write acts out, however. I do write as if I am writing to a commercial break. It helps navigate the storytelling as well as structure the plot and emotional turns.

Q: What are the different structures of a sitcom?

Josh Greenberg - I've been lucky to work in both sitcom forms - single-camera and multi-camera. They share some similarities but are also different in terms of formatting and pacing. The overall structure is basically the same. Single-cam is just like little a mini-film. Whereas multi-camera, it's more like staging a mini-play that culminates once a week when you put on a show in front of an audience. You have three or four cameras all filming at the same time live to tape. They are self-contained little stories. They are very satisfying to write. To have those same characters go into a new story next week exercises a muscle that feature film writing did not do for me.

There's not too much difference structure-wise. Different networks will have different act structures, but basically, they all layout as a three-act beginning, middle, and end. There are some pacing differences where single camera is more like a short film. Multi-cam is legit like you are putting on a play, so there's a little bit more of a stagey-ness that happens in multi-cam. They share a lot of qualities, too.

I think single-camera writers used to look down on multi-camera, as, I don't how to put it - less serious, perhaps? I think that's changed. I hope that's changed because when a multi-cam is really well executed, it's just fantastic. With multi-cam, you are basically in the comfort and safety of a studio. You are on the same set that you are always on. Whereas, with single-cam, you do sometimes find yourself in a weird new location sweating from the sun.

Q: Do you have any tips on writing flashbacks?

Ben Philippe - When you are doing a murder mystery, you don't know the life of the character who was murdered. There are no present-day scenes with them. You have to figure out how much of this person's story do we need to see. When do we see the flashbacks? Do you save it for when they are about to die? Or do you show it all at the start? In Seasons 1 and 2 of *Only Murders in the Building*, we did both. In Season 1, we don't know who Tim Kono is at all. He didn't have any friends. He was always in his apartment. He was researching something. He was getting packages and we don't know what any of that is until we get to Episode 7, the silent episode. That's where we find out what he was doing. We delayed it quite a bit until the final episode where we see the moments leading up to his death.

In Season 2, we flip it because we realize that the victim was Bunny Folger, who was the head of the board of the building that nobody liked. One of our rules is that we have to care about the victim. So my favorite episode of that season was written by Ben Smith, and it is the last day of Bunny Folger's life. We follow the last day of this crotchety, older woman who lives alone with a parrot. We see that she's not that lonely. She has other people that she cares about. She's very meticulous and she doesn't want to retire. She takes a lot of pride in her work and she knows this building better than anyone. At the end of the episode, when she goes to open the door and she's murdered, you really feel for her. Ben put a moment in there where our trio could have invited her to their party to celebrate solving their first murder, and they don't because they don't like her. Now, the motivation of the entire season is that we could have saved this person's life by being better neighbors. That propels the story forward even though we spend the entire episode in the past with Bunny's last day. So flashbacks are very powerful, but they have to be judiciously used. That doesn't mean a little flashback, but that it's placed in a way that always faces forward.

Q: In sitcoms, how many locations should you consider in your structure?

Josh Greenberg - Generally, the multi-cam is restricted to how much studio space you have. In so many multi-cam shows there's the living room set, the bedroom set, maybe an office, and a swing set that can be anything. One week it's maybe a bowling alley or something like that. Whereas, with single-cam there are standing sets like an office, but you can go out into the real world and find real locations. In terms of how many per show, that sort of varies. Generally, in a multi-cam, there are three or four basic locations. If it's an office set show, you might have some action take place at the office and then the characters go to, say, a bar to discuss what happened. Perhaps, the conflict spills over into that scene and then, spills over to a home set where someone is telling their spouse or family what is going on. Then, they return to the office the next day. It's all very flexible.

One thing that's very entertaining to me is when we are doing rehearsals on a multi-cam, the whole crew is gathered around watching them put on this little play in the living room set, and then the whole crew does this walk over to the bedroom set. Then, we watch them put on that scene. Then we all walk over to the office set.

Q: In sitcoms, do you carry on jokes from episode to episode?

Josh Greenberg - Character traits or weird little details about a character are really fun to carry over. You can also plant something in one episode and way down the line, pay that off so that the loyal viewer is rewarded. A fun Easter egg.

Q: What are your thoughts about adding themes and messages to your TV shows?

Lauren Iungerich - All my shows grapple with themes and messages. I need to be saying something in order to write something and each episode break of my shows is driven by theme. First, I figure out what is driving the episode - which relates to the episode itself and then as we drive and break the story, I look for the theme that is coming through and we use that to further the break. I have a little motto for my writers - I always say "When in doubt, theme it out!"

Josh Greenberg - I think it depends on the creator's intent. I personally don't love a heavy-handed message. If there's something that can be said with subtlety, that's great. Older shows had some of that where "we learned a good lesson today." But I think most viewers now are sophisticated enough that they sort of reject shows with heavy-handed messages.

Marsha Greene - I think about themes more than morals and messages. I think you need to be true to the character's point of view, so it's difficult to have a message or a moral that

> ## WRITER'S BLOCK
>
> Can't get the creative juices flowing? Try some of these tricks drawn from our group of writer friends to get going again. Also, consider some of the writing exercises listed at the end of this book.
>
> - Exercise - go to the gym, a long walk (Dave Reynolds agrees!), run, bike ride, yoga, etc.
> - Change where you write. A different location can give you a different perspective.
> - Cook or clean something.
> - Take a shower to relax yourself.
> - Take a power nap.
> - Watch movies or TV shows in the genre you are writing for inspiration.
> - Save an idea for the next day so you know where you are going to start.
> - Free think with another writer.
> - Research your idea or concept, but don't get lost on the internet.
> - Write something else - a poem, a short story, a letter.
> - Have more than one project going, so if one hits a wall, you can jump to another.
> - Read your favorite authors.
> - Don't write sober.
> - Keep a notebook of crazy words, characters, phrases, places, and topics. Refer to it to see if it jump-starts your creativity.
> - Some screenwriting programs will ask you questions about your story to help you from being blocked.

you want to tell when that is not what the show or the character inside the show would tell. Maybe you can get those two things to align, but that's why I don't think about it. They are just going to do what they do.

Some people approach an episode or a show from the theme first and then go down. I don't really do that. I think the theme starts to emerge from writing the story. Once I know what that theme is, then I will make sure that the stories are speaking to that theme. That makes the episode better. So if the theme is "the end justifies the means," then you have perhaps, four stories, that are all in some way, grappling with that question even though they are four separate stories. Whereas, if you don't have a theme to hold it all together, it can feel random as you are switching from one person to another. It doesn't feel like they are speaking to each other. Some people can do that at the beginning of the episode and clearly state the theme, but if I feel that it is not coming to me, then I allow the writing process to reveal the theme. "Oh, that's what the story is about!" It could be four people dealing with it on this side and one person dealing with it in the opposite way.

Q: Are there any tips for writing to commercial breaks?

Josh Greenberg - We call that an act break when we are leading up to a commercial. With streaming, they generally don't deal with commercials but I mostly work on network shows that do have those act breaks. They really aren't that different from plays or feature writing where you are leading up to a dramatic turn that will keep the audience hanging on for another three minutes to see how it resolves. The main thing is to have it flow organically. You have all the same rules as in feature writing where you don't want some deus ex machina to come in and suddenly change up the story. It all has to feel like it flows.

Julie Sherman Wolfe - You pretty much need some kind of cliffhanger, or button as we would say back in my sitcom days, that will keep everyone on the hook. But what's funny is, you work so hard to get the act breaks perfect, but ultimately when it comes down to editing, they end up changing the act break anyway! They fade out in the middle of a scene, and then come back right in the middle of the same scene again. It doesn't make sense, but it depends on the editing and runtime. Usually, we're long and they have to cut a few pages. I highly recommend not getting attached to anything you write. Everything's on the chopping block in the editing room, and unless you're producing, directing, or financing the movie... let it go. I can't stress this enough.

DEVELOPMENT DOCUMENTS

Logline: Your whole story summed up in two to three sentences. A good tool to help you with an elevator pitch. Don't be fooled; this is the trickiest of the documents to create.

One-pager: Your story summed up in three to five paragraphs, as if contained on one sheet of paper. This allows you to paint a fuller picture of your story in order to see if it works and to get someone's interest.

Beat sheet: The main moments of your story written out as short phrases. Often done just before an outline.

Outline: The main plot points of your story, sometimes in bullet form, written in sentences or phrases that sketch out the overall structure and character development. This helps you find major holes in the plot or character development. It can also illuminate pacing issues.

Treatment: A prose version of your entire story. It can be as long as it needs to be. Rich and detailed, you can work out all the fine plot, character, and thematic details before you head off into the screenwriting software.

Script-ment: Often used by writer/directors, this is a hybrid of a treatment and screenplay format. This allows the writer to add dialogue between characters, evocative scene headings, action lines, and specific camera movements so as to capture the mind's eye of the writer. Usually, this is an internal document and almost a full script length.

Q: When do you know you're ready to go to draft?

Eli Craig - When I can't outline anymore. When I can't stand it anymore. I don't like outlining. I hate it. I know I have to do it and try to do it as long as I possibly can. I try to do a lot of research. I try not to write as long as humanly possible. Writing the outline, writing about character, I do it until I can't bear it anymore and then I start writing. I feel like a coiled spring and usually, the first act will go very fast. Then, I will spend a lot of time trying to get that first act really working because it's the springboard for the whole story. If the first act is working, even if the rest of the movie isn't written yet, it's going to work. If you have problems in the second and third acts, it usually comes back to problems in the first act. I used to think of the hook as the thing that would grab the audience. But now, I feel it's the reverse. When the story is going one way and it turns on a dime because of some event that happens, like the inciting incident or the kick into the third act that turns the movie in a totally new direction. It was one of those "a-ha" moments after ten years of writing. Oh, that's what the hook is! You want to see things set up in a way when everything turns in a new direction.

Alex Litvak - You just know. Once the road map feels right, it's time to start driving. Have a solid plan, particularly in terms of structure, character journey and big plot moves, but also remember that outline is not a script - it's a blueprint. So don't rush into the draft without knowing what you are doing, but also don't get bogged down in the outline phase.

Q: What is the difference between writing TV and features?

Briana Belser - In the TV world, you have so much answering to whoever is financing it and there are production schedules that go in before you have even typed a page. Before you have even opened that blank Final Draft page, you already know when your work airs. So, I think, in that way, there is a level of completion that TV producers and writers rooms start to feel is the bar - as opposed to excellence and creativity. It's getting from A to B. Is it clear? Did I service that plot point in Episode 3? Did I pick up from 2? Did I set up 4 well? There are some completion-oriented tasks that have to happen in television that don't happen in films because they are contained. The timeline for films is when it gets done - if it gets done. Also, the people who finance film have an understanding of art and there's a less corporate, crunchiness to making films. People are more interested in the process in the way that TV is interested in the result. When does Season 3 drop? In this binge-able world, nobody is tuning in week by week. Content is expected to drop all at one time. Or half at once and half the next week. So there's a financial and entrepreneurial driver that exists in television.

I'm writing features that I would hope to get made and it is just a different experience when I know someone is not breathing down my neck. The other thing is that people watch features in one sitting in a theater. If they go in, they're watching it. Period. No matter what kind of movie it is, they are probably going to finish it. Or they are watching it at home where they can watch it and then pause at their leisure. With television, especially things that air live, if you lose viewers at certain points in the episode, that can impact whether the show lives or dies.

Jed Mercurio - I think the main difference is the writer's status in those different environments. In features, the writer's status is quite low unless they also happen to be directing the feature film. Whereas, in television, traditionally, the writer has much more influence and has a much higher status in the hierarchy. If it's a novel, the writer is absolutely at the top of the hierarchy and similarly with a play. You have to understand how the land lies and you need to align with that. So if you are working in a feature film, you will find yourself in situations where you have to defer to the director. Whereas, if you're in the position I'm in as a TV showrunner, then I work in quite a flat hierarchy where I can have constructive conversations with network executives and quite senior people and it doesn't feel like I am under orders to do it their way.

Ron Leshem - I know that a film is a dictatorship of a director. So when writing for film and not television, I remind myself that my story will become someone else's interpretation and I am very much intrigued by what they would bring to my story. These guys who direct films are used to being dictators in both good and bad ways. When you bring them to TV, they never survive there. In television, they think that if they embrace other people's ideas that they are weak or not an artist or that it's not important to them. They think that the whole idea is to fight and not a single beat or word should not come from inside them. It has to be theirs. But in TV, we are a group and if you choose people who are smart and bring skills that you don't have, then this is a group that will defend the idea. That's the only way to create television. Television brings you two things that I need. I love writing alone. I love being alone for weeks sometimes in bed with my laptop. On the other side, I love being an executive. And being a showrunner is being both. You have 300 people working with you on an idea and sometimes you just lock yourself at home alone.

Josh Greenberg - I started as a feature writer and that's what I wanted to do. But what was frustrating was the logistics of when you would sell something or option something. You would wait literally years to find out if it would happen or not. TV is such instant gratification that the thing you are working on right now will get made. Or you will find out very quickly if it won't get made, and then you are onto the next thing. The other thing is, creatively with a film, you have ninety minutes to spend with a character and then you say goodbye to them. TV is a fun form where if you love a character or a relationship, you can revisit it for hours.

Michael Brandt - Even though I've done years of writing TV, I still find features easier. In network television, everything is open-ended other than your A story. Your A story is about who comes through the hospital doors or what the bad guy did in the teaser. Everything else is you throwing meat to the hungry animal that keeps eating and you keep feeding him. Those are the characters on the show and they're not going anywhere for the foreseeable future if you're successful. So the question is how do I change the diet of what the audience sees this animal eating? And how does that change what the animal is doing? That's not as exciting and it's not easy because you have to constantly find new curve balls to throw at these people. This explains why the main character's estranged mom shows up at the end of Season One. We must continually freshen up the interpersonal stories, which, except for something like *Law and Order,* are 100% of the reason why people watch television.

In terms of the *Chicago* shows, I told Dick Wolf, the executive producer, that I wanted to do more of a *Hill Street Blues* in a firehouse. We would go home with the characters and get into their relationships. He liked that, especially as he wrote on *Hill Street Blues*. But the ramifications of that were that we had to feed those characters. So, on *Chicago Fire*, there was a rule. When the bells go off in the firehouse, and this is true for when a call arrives in a cop show or a patient comes through the doors of a medical show, whatever your main actors are talking about or going through prior to that call, needs to have changed by the time it's over. Something needs to have happened on that call that changes the dynamics of that relationship, otherwise why have that call? Yes, seeing fires being put out is exciting. But something that happens has to affect the characters. Ultimately, in movies, it's a one-time story. Every conversation is really important, every word is more important, as they are not going to have it again.

Q: Any tips on writing spec pilots?

Michael Brandt - The most successful thing about the *Chicago Fire* pilot was the ending. It ended with one of the characters in the hospital after getting injured in the final fire of the pilot. Everybody is there in the waiting room at the end. Dick Wolf, said, "The reason this show works and the reason why this show is going to be successful is that when the camera goes around the room at the end of the pilot, I know every character. I understand them. I want to know more about them, but I know enough to want to know more." It wasn't a conscious design. It was a design of writing well-rounded characters and having them all have their throughlines in the pilot. That's something I've taken away. You can have your mysteries, but make sure the audience knows your characters enough so that they are going to want to come back and see them again. Dole out as much likable or unlikable stuff, so that by the end of the episode someone wants more of that person.

Q: How do you overcome writer's block?

Julie Sherman Wolfe - I don't believe in writer's block. You can't just wait around for the muse to strike and for something to happen. It's your job. You simply have to do it. If you work at the mall, you can't just say, "Eh, I don't feel like selling clothes today." Sometimes, when the writing isn't flowing, I might decide to stop for the day and start fresh in the morning. But if there's a deadline, and an entire production team is waiting for your script so they can do their jobs...you no longer have that luxury. I'll stay up all night and work all weekend to get it done - which was easier to recover from when I was younger! I'm a firm believer in, "The harder you work, the luckier you get." Plenty of people have a great idea for a movie - but very few of them actually sit down and write it. The people who do, aren't waiting for inspiration. They just sit down and write it. Those are the people who make it.

Paul King - Imagine getting writer's block on something as simple as a *Paddington* film! It's embarrassing. But it happens. I got stuck on both of them multiple times. It was never because I didn't have enough ideas. It was always because I couldn't make them fit together properly. The way I go about things is to write a fairly detailed scene list, so by the time I start, I feel I should be able to just go and write it. But then there's a moment where I realize that the blueprint is fundamentally flawed and you have to go back to the drawing board. That, for me, is where the block comes in and that's awful. I'm building a house and the foundation is all wrong and I don't know how to fix it without tearing it all down. For me, the only solution is to go back to the blueprint and question every narrative turn and try to figure out where it all goes wrong.

Michael Brandt - If I think I am writing something shitty, I put on music that I remember listening to when I was writing something good. It rewires my attitude. So if I'm stuck and thinking, "I'm a fraud, what am I doing? They're going to figure me out." I put on something when I didn't feel like a fraud. It immediately gives me self-confidence. It changes my attitude and my state of mind.

In the case of this John Grisham novel I'm adapting, I wrote the first draft a year ago when I was listening to the same music over and over. It was new music that had just come out and it was tonally right. Here we are over a year later, and I'm going to direct this movie, which is interesting because I'm looking at it as the director and at times I'm thinking, okay what was the writer thinking here? I really divorced myself from the person a year ago. I hadn't been in the script for quite a while, so when I revisited it, I was struggling a little bit. So I put that same album on again and all those buttons got pushed. I was immediately back in the state when I wrote the first draft. So music, for me, is a big thing in terms of flipping the right switch.

Dave Reynolds - Take a walk and talk it out. The one thing that I have been doing lately is taking a walk with earbuds so that I can record ideas about my current script. I just start walking, hit record and start pitching out the main beats of what I have to that point. It could be the whole story or just a section you're working on. Do it as if you're telling this to a friend, not a studio exec. That puts a different kind of pressure on the way you'd retell it. Then I come home and I transcribe it. You'd be surprised at what new things you came up with or big story points you dropped.

At Pixar, they structured the campus with walking paths. Mark Dindal (director of *The Emperor's New Groove*) and I would try to walk as much as we could throughout the big animation building. We would go up and down stairs. Sometimes, we would circle a large conference table in the main story room. The important thing was to keep moving. It's the correlation between walking and thinking and actively trying to keep yourself upright. It opens your mind and gives you a new perspective. I'm also a big believer in having some kind of second idea active. If you get stuck on your first idea, you can jump to the second one. And the two ideas should be completely different. Just start putting pages down for that one. I came up with this while working at *Late Night* out of sheer necessity. We had five shows a week, many pieces of comedy per show so you were always trying to generate ideas. I found that having two things going at the same time, unlocks your brain to be thinking creatively on a wider plane. Your brain has a chance to reset and it can give you different approaches. So two things at once for me, works. That and getting up and walking around a bit.

Tony Jordan - There are a lot of myths around writers: You can easily come up with ideas and you can get writer's block. What do storytellers do? We invent things. So I think writer's block is a fictional condition invented by writers to get a bit more extra time before they have to deliver!

CHAPTER REVIEW: BREAKING STORY

- It's usually a good idea to know the ending of your story before you start writing.

- Outlines, beat sheets, synopsis, and treatments are great ways of organizing the story and seeing if there are any holes before you start writing the actual script.

- Feature films tend to be closed story worlds that resolve themselves. Series are open worlds that introduce new characters and issues so it can be told over many series or seasons.

- You'll know when it's time to go to draft when you feel like you can't do anymore to the outline. When you have a good plan, get going.

- If you are working from IP, you will start by figuring out how much of it you want to keep and how much you want to invent yourself.

- Story structure is how the plot and character development arcs are arranged. The three act structure is the most common way screenwriters think about stories. That's generally described as a beginning, the middle, and the end.

- Some people think characters first. They think about what a character wants throughout the story. Some people think plot first. They think about what are the big moments that will hold up the structure. In truth, they go hand in hand.

- Flashbacks and flash-forwards can be helpful storytelling tools by either providing backstory or foreshadowing. Too much of them, however, can confuse or frustrate your audience.

- Themes and messages in your story should always be considered no matter what the format.

- If you're writing a series that has ads, ending each break on a cliffhanger or a question is useful to retain your audience.

- A writer is low on the totem pole when working in features, as the director is the boss. Writers have a lot of power in series because many scripts are needed.

- Writer's block happens. Sometimes, you don't have time for it and must fight through. Other times, you must find a way to relax your mind such as listening to music or going for a walk.

CHAPTER 4

CHARACTER

People watch filmed entertainment to watch characters. They want to love them. They want to hate them. They want to watch them attempt to get past obstacles - win or lose. Our panelists give their insights into how they build their players, human or not, and how their relationships define one another and the story.

Q: How do you come up with your characters?

Tony Jordan - I don't know. It's a bit of a mystery. It's such an organic, weird out-of-body experience. It's really difficult to pin it down. I think, generally, that I have a world, first. I have a world of story. That can be a kitchen if it's a domestic thing. Or a *Game of Thrones/Lord of the Rings* world. It can be a dark, mysterious world of tube trains at night. Killings. Murders. Then the story within that world becomes a thing. Then characters start to inhabit that world. That's why I say the world must come first because how do you know what kind of characters will inhabit it? So that's sort of a three-horse race between story, character, and world. I don't know who's in front or who wins that race. It's the madness of jazz where everything is all going at once and out of the chaos comes some kind of tune. That feels like the reality of it.

Once I have a story, world, and characters, I cast it. I don't wait for real people. I just go online and get images, and I find faces to those characters. They are not just names to me. I print out those images, and I put them on this board behind me. So I have faces looking back at me. Jenny Jennings isn't just a name that rhymes, it's a person. I'm always really shocked and it's a traumatic time for me when we do real casting. I've been staring at Jenny Jennings for six months. I know her, and I know how she thinks. I probably love her. I hate her. She's a person. Then, six months later we come to casting and someone will say that this is Jenny Jennings. No, it's not. Jenny Jennings is the woman from the M&S ad on my wall. It's kind of a weird process.

Ron Leshem - I always try to look for what is fresh with a character. I also tend to choose characters who are my alter ego and who are experiencing something that I've missed or that I will never have the opportunity to explore myself.

Moisés Zamora - When I was first starting out in my early twenties, a lot of the characters I wrote were born from people that I knew. Or my own feelings. Sometimes, several characters, if you put them all together, were me or extensions of my own desires, alter egos, or demons. So a lot of it was inward, trying to pull out characters because I felt that I had unresolved things. I've been doing this for twenty years and you only have so many demons. Once you get a therapist, they are nowhere to be found! It's like therapists ruin your creative process, but they do save your relationships!

Now, most of my characters are crafted almost conceptually. For example, if I think of a

> # MOTIVATION
>
> Characters do things for certain reasons. Those reasons create their motivation to achieve some sort of goal and they come in two varieties: internal and external. Sometimes, this is described as a character's "need" versus their "want."
>
> **Internal motivation** is a character's desire to achieve a better version of themselves; to become self-actualized in a way they think they want. Maybe they want to be braver, less greedy, or more powerful. The journey they go on in the story tests this and, often, what they actually need is something opposite or tangentially aligned to their original desires.
>
> **External motivation** is a tangible and concrete task that a character thinks they must do to get their world/life back into equilibrium. Often what they want to do gets revealed early on in the script, but usually at the midpoint, they begin to realize what they truly need to do. This is the main thrust of the plot such as killing a monster, delivering a package, or sorting out a dead loved one's estate.
>
> A character's flaws will hinder their internal motivations. Obstacles in the plot prevent a character from achieving their external motivations.
>
> Internal and external motivations drive one another throughout the story. If you get a note from a reader that states your characters are doing things for no reason, look at their motivations. Usually, the problem starts right at the beginning, so look at Act 1. Please don't forget this is true for ALL major characters. That means your romantic leads, best friends, villains, and their main helpers.

setting or a world where I want to live and exist because I'm obsessed for whatever reason, then I try to find the character that would be the most miserable in that world. Or it would be for whatever core wound, trauma, or flaw they have, they would have a challenge being in that world. Being in this world communicates where they need to be as a character in the storyline. Then I start filling in the gap. That's when it's an original idea. Of course, we live in a town where they don't really believe in original ideas unless you are one of the greats who have multi-million dollar overall deals. The last two TV shows that I sold were based on IP and life rights/stories. So when I am looking for articles or books that I want to develop, I focus more on the world and what's unique and different. I am Mexican-American. I've lived in different countries and I speak three languages, so a lot of it has to tickle me that way - multi-world, multi-identity. Or just worlds that I haven't seen before. I do gravitate to that type of IP or life rights.

Julie Sherman Wolfe - For Hallmark, you start very generally. What do they do? Where do they live? What's their backstory? Why are we telling their story? I don't even think of specific actors in my head when I'm writing. The characters and their voices, come out of their unique situation. I have to admit that most of my characters have kind of a snarky, sarcastic, edgy bent to them. I try to make the women strong. Yes, they might have been in a situation that damaged their hearts, made them gun-shy, or scared... but it doesn't make them weak. These movies are about people becoming who they truly are. It's not up to the male lead to solve their problems, but be part of her journey to solve them for herself. No damsels in distress allowed! But most importantly, the woman has to help the man, too. It has to be even. The most common note from the network is: How do these two people help each other grow? You have to answer that, or you'll just keep rewriting until you do. As far as voice goes, I personally think that funny women are more attractive, so I try to make them as witty as I can. Then, when they have an emotional breakthrough, it actually means more because they're finally not hiding behind their humor. It's more satisfying.

Q: What are the most important aspects of developing a character?

Bill Nicholson - As a viewer, I must believe what the characters are doing. I've been watching a TV series that my wife and I like very much, Abi Morgan's, *The Split*. She's a very good writer, but there came a point in the first series where the female lead character, married to Stephen Mangan, makes a decision to pursue an affair with a colleague. They have two kids, and he has cheated on her. So she thinks she's entitled to cheat on him. But everything that the writer had created about this character - this woman, her family, and her husband and kids, which was very skillfully done - makes me think that she's invested in this family. So when she's suddenly knocking on the door of the guy that she's going to screw, who is not her husband, I'm saying, no, you have not made me believe she would do that. I'm not saying that a woman in those circumstances wouldn't do that at all, just, you would have to make me believe she would do that. Her husband, Stephen Mangan's character, has gone off and had the affair and he's devastated that he's been caught. He's devastated that he may lose his family. He doing everything to try and undo his shitty behavior. But he's not a shit. He's Stephen Mangan. You think he's an idiot, but you don't think his marriage is over. Firstly, because I know it's going to run for three series! And secondly, I know the lead woman has to maneuver her affair in order to keep the story going. But if you are going to do that, you are going to have to have a couple of scenes before which make us think that we wouldn't want that husband anymore. Instead he has a couple of scenes before that make you kind of love him, which I think was a tactical error. It sort of hurt me. Don't do that! Your kids are going to suffer so much! He shouldn't have done what he did, don't get me wrong. He doesn't want to leave. He's not going to go off with this other woman. So I think you have to make every step of your character's journey believable in terms of the character you have presented. It's no use saying, "Oh, but my friend, Jill, did that." As if that somehow makes it real.

If you are going to have his wife and mother to his two kids decide to go crazy and have a lot of sex, no problem. But you must really make sure you understand that she's feeling trapped and all sorts of things are happening in her that this will release. Then you can sort of go with her on that journey. I've watched it again and again. It would happen a lot in the old days of Hollywood films, what I would describe as an unearned redemption. So you get a character who gets loved after all when they have not been loved. Or wins something after all. It works in strict plot terms because they've had obstacles, they've overcome obstacles and they reach their goal. But it doesn't work at any deeper level.

Meg LeFauve - I would say the most important thing about creating a character is the want. That they want something. If they are adamantly, stubbornly not wanting something, that

> ## FLAT CHARACTERS VS. DYNAMIC CHARACTERS
>
> Tension and release. Conflict and resolution. These dualities create dynamic drama via their peaks and valleys. If you remove the highs and lows, you are left with a flat plane that doesn't contain anything much of interest.
>
> This analogy often gets applied to character and plot problems. If you have a flat character, that means they aren't being challenged internally (see Motivation boxout on page 85) or they are, and they have no response to it. A flat plot means that there aren't enough obstacles or forces of antagonism to move a character to action.
>
> As you can see, these two issues often go hand in hand. A plot with no bumps in it doesn't allow a character to overcome their problems. A character that doesn't move to overcome their problems means an underdeveloped plot.

is still wanting something. As a female creator, it's been such an interesting journey for me because women are inculturated to not want. And yet, want drives story; want illuminates character. It's just a pivotal thing and it seems so easy. It creates agency. So often, we can get caught up in the need, which we do need. What does the character need and what is this emotionally about? That's the first block in the character. I think a lot of female writers struggle with want. That's where my brain has been going lately. And so much of the need is subtext.

The other thing I try to do is understand the poles of a character. They start here and end here. So many actors that I've worked with, that's what they want to know. Where do I start and where do I finish? Then, the theme is in there. The main relationship is going to be in there. So many parts of the engine are going to be in there.

Danny Strong - I try to figure out how to make the character entertaining. By entertaining, I don't necessarily mean they are funny or can sing and dance. What is the entertainment value of the character? What is the character dynamic? Is the character really interesting? How do I root for this character? How do I find as much depth in the character as possible? How can I create a character that feels unique? Something that we haven't seen over and over again? Usually, a lot of details come into play. I try to make my lead characters fun. There's usually some kind of a wit there. Not always.

In *Dopesick*, with Richard Sackler, who is the villain of the show and a villain in real life, I tried to find as many layers of humanity as I could in him because he's famously despised. I made him a little bit funny. The actor who played him, Michael Stuhlberg, understood without me having to explain where every laugh was. So there was a little bit of a warped, dark comedy with that character. Defying expectations.

Then, it is a matter of, what function does the character serve in the story? I perceive that the protagonist's journey is the story and it is thematically, the point of the whole experience; the journey that this character goes on internally. The theme is tied to the character's arc. It's not the plot, but the plot and the character's journey are intertwined, as one. That's the goal. It doesn't always happen. Sometimes, scenes are more plot-driven. They just are. Some scenes are purely character-driven. It's always best when they are happening at the same time, but sometimes that doesn't happen. I will be writing and need certain scenes to happen, then I realize I have several plot-driven scenes in a row. So this next scene, I need to slow it down for a beat. I need to make sure that we are finding another dynamic to it. So that there are different levels to the piece. A lot of character comes out in relationships with other characters.

Character doesn't just exist in a vacuum on its own. Sometimes, it can, such as in *The Conversation*, which is a real masterpiece. There are so many scenes of that character by himself where we learn about him through these scenes where the character is on his own. But then, you'll have these scenes where he is interacting with these other people and they are quite revelatory. He's spent so much time by himself that when he's with other people, your understanding of this person goes to this whole other level. That's a film that has a ton of plot. There's this whole mystery to it. A crime has been committed. There's an underlying dramatic tension to it. Coppola views it as a favorite film of his. It's a real film nerd movie. It's one of my favorites and I feel that its screenplay is a real masterclass in which plot and character intersect for a powerful dramatic experience as you could hope to achieve in a film.

In *Dopesick*, I was very diligent that in each episode my protagonists, and I had a lot of them, all had goals or something they were trying to achieve within the episode. By the end of the episode, they either achieved it or they didn't. The character arcs were over the journey of the whole eight episodes, but, certainly, we were going on that character journey throughout the course of each episode.

Briana Belser - This takes me back to when I visited Spain. I didn't know anything about Spain other than Columbus sailed the ocean blue in 1492. What have you all been up to? There was something so ignorant and unapologetic with the way I showed up and presented myself in that country as an American student. The amount of humility that I acquired just by seeing the Spanish value system and them challenging mine asking me, "Why does this matter to you?" It's a similar thought exercise that I use when rendering characters - why is this that serious to them? I am going to approach a scene by starting at a 10 and then calibrate from there. Maybe I need to tamp certain things down. It's easier to write when I give them real stakes and real beliefs. Doesn't have to be real to the world, but it has to be real to them. I think humor can often come from heightening the tiniest minutiae and keeping it at a 10, never calibrating. It makes them funny and hilarious and breaks our hearts. When they have a vantage point that no one else in the show shares, we get to see them brush up against other characters that don't have the same vantage point.

Lauren Iungerich - You have to really think out who your character is and really get into the nitty-gritty of that person. It's not about what they are wearing or how they associate socially. It's about the underbelly of who they are. For example, in *On My Block*, look at Jamal. In the friend group, he's the one who feels put upon. Nobody sees him and he is ultimately the hero of his friends. He's the one who saves the day. He's unfiltered and he can't keep a secret. So we play with that. He's on the football team, but he hates it. He's doing it for his dad. Then we have this moment where he's actually really good at it, but we don't set him up that way. And he also seems to believe in things that are myth, but he is going to seek the truth of all these myths. He's the guy that nobody believes until they do. It comes at the cost of friendships, sometimes. He feels so hurt by how they have to put him down. You have to get at the emotional underbelly of the character to write their dialogue.

Monse, perfect example. She's tough, but she's got a hard candy shell. She's got a soft, gooey center because she loves César. She's totally ride or die with him. She's also never going to be the girl that somebody takes advantage of. But then you understand why she's so tough and vulnerable. We see that through the prism of her mom who abandoned her. There are a lot of layers to her character, so they are not all one thing or a straight line. You have to find all the different sides of her. Ruby - he's the smallest of the group. He's super-smart and type A. He's the one who will help put the plan in motion. He understands how to solve a problem. They turn to him when they are all in trouble. He becomes his own hero in a way with the girl. He loves the girl, but she doesn't see him. But he keeps chipping away at it. He finally has to relinquish it until she really sees him as a romantic option. You root for him because he's unabashed. He puts up a big front until he doesn't and then he lets his vulnerability out. You think he never will, but he finally does. That's the moment when you say, "I love him, too."

It's really looking at people. These kids may be fifteen, but sometimes the archetype of them are adults that I know or the creators with whom I work. When I realize that, we start to unearth it. So it starts with someone, somewhere very specific, but where it goes as you tell the story and unearth things, you realize that this character is going to go through this and we have to change them. For Ruby, he got shot and almost died and the girl he liked, did die. It changes how he is. He has survivor's guilt. It's the person that you least expect - that he's made fun of and is annoyed by - who, literally, is able to teach him what she's gone through. How she deals with survivor's guilt. How she deals with the bumps in life that she had and how she's come out the other side that sort of becomes the guiding light for him. It starts a love story with them. What's fun is that it is unexpected; seeing two people fall in love that you wouldn't expect. That's life, right?

Josh Greenberg - It definitely helps to have someone as a foil or a love interest for tension reasons. Having goals is really important. A protagonist who really wants something as opposed to being a passenger in the story. Sometimes, you have actors come up to you and ask, "What am I doing in this scene? I don't want to be just standing here in this scene." That's also when you know you've done something wrong. You always want to give characters drive.

Have you heard the story of Patton Oswalt on *King of Queens*? Patton Oswalt was a supporting character on that sitcom. There was a scene where he didn't have any dialogue. A lot of other characters were chatting and Patton Oswald stands perfectly still like a mannequin and now it's like a cult scene. You watch it and it looks like he's been frozen. I think it was some kind of bet but it's really funny and demonstrates that everyone has to have something to do in a scene.

Paul King - If Paddington just sat down and did as he was told, or never made a bad decision, they would be much shorter and more boring films. I suppose that is why most characters - even very nice, well intentioned ones like Paddington - generally need a flaw. They have to have something inside them that compels them to make bad choices. The crucial thing is that the audience understand why your characters are making those bad choices. If the audience think your characters are just doing something for narrative convenience, or because they're idiots, it's kind of frustrating. My great aspiration is for the audience to not even realize the character is flawed, nor that they are making a bad choice at the start of the movie. If your audience think they would make the same choice themselves, then they're personally invested in what follows - rather than thinking all the way through the rest of the movie, "Well, that's what happens if you act like an idiot."

If you can get your audience thinking your character should act one way at the start of the movie, and another way by the end, then I think your movie has done something amazing. Not only have the audience seen your character grow and learn, the audience have also changed. You've changed people's minds about something in an hour and a half. I think that is when things get really good.

Deborah Haywood - There's something satisfying as a viewer when you know somebody has realized something or learned something or grown because of their experience. I do believe we do change from day to day, even if we repeat the same pattern, we've changed in some way, so our characters should reflect that.

Q: Do you do character breakdowns?

Paul King - When I'm writing on my own, I do. But when I co-write with Simon Farnaby, it's more about finding the right voice than a set of traits. Everything follows from that. Hugh Grant's character in *Paddington 2* was weird because the first incarnation of him was very different. He was a sort of gap year hippy guy like, "Yeaaah, I just got back from India. I did a lot of yoga." He was quite posh and almost flirting with Mary. "Yeaaah, you really have to release the chakra." Henry was very jealous because he was quite handsome and had henna tattoos. His voice we found funny, but we couldn't get that character to work in our script, so we went and found another voice.

But even then, once we got together with Hugh who is one of my favorite comic actors, finding that voice again was a real process for him. He had several different Phoenixes and over a week of rehearsals, he found it. "Ah, you want him to be like all the creepy old actors that I used to go on tour with!" He found the character in that moment, and then he could just run with it so brilliantly. He put everything we'd written through his incredible comic amplifier.

Deborah Haywood - If it's not working, I will go back and I'll write where the characters start and where they end; what their needs are; what's their outer problem; what is their inner problem that they need to be solved and how did they solve it. Those kinds of things help me clarify who they are. It's the hardest bit because structure you can kind of learn, whereas with character you have to dig into yourself and figure out what am I battling with? What is still a struggle or an emotional thing for me? Because then it comes across authentically.

I was commissioned to write about the friendship between Freddie Mercury and Kenny Everett. It was all research based and all there. They kept saying there's something not honest about it. So then I went back to my own problems with relationships and stuff and used my own worries and fears, experiences, and things that I am still grappling with and it took off. So I think even if I was writing *Coronation Street* and adapting characters that are already there - if I can put my own problems, things that I am emotional about or grappling with, then it gives it an authenticity. That arc is something that I am still trying to come to grips with myself.

Michael Brandt - Not more than a few sentences. Unless it naturally presents what their history might be before the movie, I don't think I have to know all that. That's not important to me. Now, through the course of writing, that stuff might seep its way into what I think but I don't need to get that on paper ahead of time. For me, the characters are pretty sparse when I start, and this sounds like ridiculous writers speak, but I do let the characters talk. For me, the good writing doesn't start until you actually start writing dialogue and their points of view come out. So all I need to know is who they are and what they want, which is a couple of sentences.

Jed Mercurio - I'll be honest, I'll only do character breakdowns when I am delivering a written pitch document as often it makes the reading experience a little more coherent. Every time a character is mentioned, you give the reader some information about who they are and how they fit into the story. If you lay that out, even if it was just some thumbnail sketch of basic biographical details about the character, it means the reader can always flip to that and remind themselves of who's who. In that sense, I think it's useful. In terms of if it's useful for the writer themselves, then that is up to the individual writer. Personally, I don't do it because I'm moving through the plot and the character at the same time. It's kind of quite a fluid thing. I would never write a whole biography of a character unless it was useful to the plot.

Barbara Stepansky - I used to do character breakdowns, but I don't anymore. Once I figure out what they desperately want: What is the chip on their shoulder? What is holding them back? What do I want them to learn?... then I just go. I used to be so much into character bios, and now the characters just start talking to me while the action is happening. I really like this part of the discovery process. "Oh, this person has daddy issues! Who knew?!"

Q: Do your characters tell you what to do?

Eli Craig - Yes, and sometimes I will find that some of the things that I've outlined are butting up against the reality of the script. Some of the character stuff may not fully make sense. In something I've been writing, there's a girl that's been raised by an outdoorsman, but for reasons of the story, I wanted her to be educated along the way on how to snake hunt. But wait a minute, if she's raised by this guy, she probably already knows how to do it. So maybe she wasn't raised by him. Maybe she's a tourist. So you're midway through and then sometimes you have to back into it.

One of the things I think about when writing is that a movie is four-dimensional. A movie is moving still images, but where those images exist in time is critical. And time is the fourth dimension. People talk about James Cameron doing something in 4D. Isn't 4D just time? Then I was thinking about an art installation with all these images laid out. What you saw before an image affects how you feel about the next image. So when you are writing, the time when things happen is critical. It feels like someone becomes a hero because of what they do into the second act or the third act, not that they start that way. It's the arc of the character that matters. It's fun when you are getting toward the end of a script, say page 90, and you realize that you have to go back and plant a line on page 3. You are trying to connect strings from the plant to the payoff. I think one of the most fun things is when something nonchalant, a seemingly throwaway line of humorous dialogue, pays off in the end. People think you wrote it because it was a funny line, but then, in the end, it connects. There's something very satisfying about that.

Marsha Greene - Characters definitely tell me what to do! I am always asking where my characters are at, when they come into a scene. Sometimes, you want something to happen, which is a plot-related thing, but when you get into the emotional journey of the character, it might not be the right thing anymore.

Josh Olson - I need to know enough about the character going in because story feeds character, character feeds story. I don't believe that they are independent of each other. You kind of find your way. On *Trigger Warning*, my co-screenwriter, John Brancato, and I had a couple of hard and fast rules about our main character that we stuck to, but as your characters evolve, they start to tell you the rules.

Michael Brandt - In the case of the John Grisham novel that I'm writing, there's a character in the book, the Governor of Texas, who was a man that I decided should be a woman. This character is not a great person. What I found interesting is that I had all these ideas of whom this person was when I started writing the script. Then, she started talking. I was typing, but she was talking. She was reacting. She's reacting to the staffers, reacting to the other male state leaders, and reacting to a situation. I found these reactions to be very different than what I thought they were going to be when I started. It was an amazing experience because, well, this is writing! She is telling me what to say and she was saying things that went against what I thought the character was going to be when I conceived her. That doesn't happen very often, but when it does, I just let it go. She did things that changed the story in some ways. Not the bigger beats, but the inner workings of the story and how I got there. That was a really refreshing thing of letting this person say what they wanted to say.

Q: What are your thoughts on creating conflict between characters?

Scott Lobdell - There's an old expression - drama is the story of no. The idea is: if you walked out the door, that is something that you did and it happened. However, if you got up, knocked over the soda and it spilled onto the floor, and then you bent over to pick it up and in doing so, you banged your head on the table - then I would be wondering if you are okay? Should I call your family? If you can put "no" between what a person is doing and what the person's goal is, that's the conflict that drives your story. You could write a story about getting up and walking to the door and you never make it to the door because so many things happen.

Similarly, you can do this with characters. For instance, if you're Riggs and I'm Murtaugh from *Lethal Weapon,* and you say, "I'm crazy and I'm going to go in and shoot everyone and hold a gun to my head," then I say, "Great idea. I'll shoot everyone, too, and I'll hold a gun to my head," there's no conflict. Now, let's say you have two characters, like in *National Lampoon's Vacation.* One is the husband who is all set to go to Wally World and the other is his wife, who doesn't want to go on the trip as she wants to go to France. Because he wants to do one thing and she wants to do another, that drives the movie forward. At one point, she says they should just go home. But he wants to keep going because they are so close. If your main character isn't bouncing off another character, then that other character probably shouldn't be there.

Die Hard is probably the most perfect movie ever. Almost every character who is on screen starts at one place and ends up someplace else. And that almost never happens, especially in an action movie. I think the only one who didn't was the terrorist who reached for the chocolate before the attack by the SWAT team. He gets killed at the end of the film. But the main character needs to have conflict. Not conflict, as in disagreeing as to what to do, but more like a disagreement in point of view.

Bill Nicholson - You have to say what the rules are so that we all understand. For instance, the ticking clock rules. A bomb's going to go off in ten seconds, we have to get the task done. We realize there are many things put in to create tension that didn't exist between the characters. Fake tension. It's all about earning your drama. You earn your drama by setting up a situation where the characters feel the tension because of their own longings and fears. Your drama has to be passed through your characters all the time.

If you have a row of people and they are shot one by one like in a Nazi movie - it's horrible. It's not tense. It's just grizzly. However, if you have a line of people who are being shot one by one, and your hero is number nine - that's tense. Then you have to ask yourself: how does he get out of there? How are we going to set this up so that he doesn't get shot? And you can't say "because he's the star of the film." Either he's got to do something, say something, think something or the person doing the shooting has to have a reason not to kill him. For example, if the whole thing was staged by the person doing the shooting and he knows he's not going to shoot our guy because he needs information from him, that would work. I understand that. The guy on the receiving end doesn't know that's going to happen. He braces for it. We feel for him. It doesn't happen. Then comes the explanation and it works. But if as he comes to him, the lead kicks a stone and runs away you think, "Oh, come on." It's all about character.

Moisés Zamora - If you have two good characters that are not necessarily evil, but if they have conflicting roles, you have immediate tension. You have a couple and one of them wants to get married and the other doesn't; they're good individuals and they have good reasons for their choices. That's why you have reality shows like *The Ultimatum*. That's essentially the basis of that; two good people with very good reasons for not wanting to do what they need to do. When you go deeper into their characters, those things come out. "Well, my Dad left my Mom, I don't believe in marriage." Then you can start texturing that. But then if you put them in a sci-fi space, then other things can represent that essence of commitment. Or in a horror, a monster can represent commitment. But you still have two good people with opposing goals fighting something. Whether they get together at the end or not, it is up to the writer to decide what moral or theme they want to approach. So I think it's a good exercise. It allows you to dig a little bit deeper because sometimes we get lazy as writers. Maybe you shouldn't go for the first five options. Maybe you should go for the fiftieth and push yourself more.

Deborah Haywood - What I've learned is that conflict is more interesting if it's not black and white. Two outcomes that are not good or evil, but somewhere in between. They are both viable. They both have pluses and minuses. Here, we get more involved because there's not a clear answer as to who should have what and why. And I have learned to not give them what they want when they are just about to get it. When they are just about to get it, they are taken onto the next scene. Or something comes in and complicates it and moves them in a different direction. I think that's the biggest thing I have learned about screenwriting. Don't give the "want" until the very, very end. I learned that from watching *Big Brother*. There were these two characters, one had Tourettes, and the girl really fancied him. But he didn't know whether she really fancied him because he was probably going to win, or that she really loved him. You didn't know whether he liked her because she's pretty or because he was intimidated by her and was trying to please her. They were not getting together. Build up, build up, build up. About three nights before the ending, they got together and I completely lost interest in them. They should have gotten together on the last episode and then I would have been satisfied. So you've got to hold people's enjoyment with what is going to happen or you will lose them.

Meg LeFauve - Conflict goes back to want. Every actor is going to want to know: what does my character want in this scene and what's blocking it? Conflict reveals character. Conflict is the teacher of the character. Conflict, to a character is central, even though, as a human I try to avoid it. I have to push myself, as a writer, to conflict. You have to beat up your main characters. That's your job.

Alex Litvak - Conflict is the fundamental ingredient of a movie. It's kind of hard to make one without conflict. For me, there tends to be three levels of conflict. The internal conflict within the protagonist - do I want to turn left or do I want to turn right? Do I want to go forward or do I want to go back? Do I want to rise to the occasion or fold? The best movies are when that tends to be a real struggle within the character. Then the conflict between the hero or heroine and those around them. If it's an ensemble movie like *The Avengers*, it's the conflict between the members of the group. If it's a movie like *Die Hard*, it would be the conflict between John McClane and those who are supposed to be on his side, as well as the building, itself. Everything around him becomes a complication. Then the third conflict is the one between the hero and the villain. And again, the greater those conflicts are, the greater you will engage. At the end of the day, conflict generates friction, generates sparks, generates "I care." It's very hard to get invested in static characters.

Jed Mercurio - I think there are different kinds of conflict. Obviously, physical conflict arises when there is jeopardy. If one person is threatening another physically, then that obviously creates conflict, particularly in the thriller or action genre. But a lot of conflict is about peoples' values. I think there you can look at real world models; that people can have quite divergent values and still believe wholeheartedly that they are right and represent some kind of moral code. I think that's important. I think where things become difficult is where the conflict feels illogical, but it can be easily solved. Or it's exaggerated. There, I think you have to look at situations in which two people can be right. If you were an outside observer and you see them in conflict, you might just shrug and say, "I don't even care. Both of those things sound reasonable. I'm not even going to get involved." That doesn't sound like something that would work in drama, but actually, I think it does. It's credible and I think that the audiences recognize those situations from their own lives.

Josh Olson - Conflict is the essential nature of narrative. Two people have to disagree about something or you've got no movie. It helps to be really emotionally invested. It's essential to remember that your villain does not perceive himself to be a villain. Your villain needs to be human.

Danny Strong - Make them both right. There was a phrase that a great screenwriter, Gary Ross, once said to me. He wrote *Big, Seabiscuit, Pleasantville,* and directed *The Hunger Games.* I was the office runner at his company when I was twenty-two. I would pick up Diet Coke for everybody and do it as well as I could. A lot of responsibility at this office! He knew I was interested in writing and he said a few things that really stuck with me. He said, "Use exposition as a weapon." The exposition is active. The characters are using it as a weapon against each other so that it doesn't feel like exposition. Another thing he said to me, which I loved was, "When you go into the third act, make sure that you are not resolving the plot; that it is ultimately about the characters' journey." All of these things sound simple, but when you are in the middle of writing, it's much harder to execute.

Q: How is conflict used in sitcoms?

Josh Greenberg - Characters butting up against each other in terms of goals. One of my favorite shows is *The Good Place*. The conflict there is so wild because there's a lot of internal conflict where a character is struggling against their inner self. You see that with Ted Danson's character and Kristen Bell's. There's sort of a macro conflict and a micro conflict. TV shows are getting so sophisticated now, that the conflicts can be multi-tiered. It's much more sophisticated than say older shows which were much more simple.

Q: What makes a great protagonist?

Briana Belser - They say that medicine goes down better with a spoonful of sugar. I think heroes have that quality. You can go on a journey with them and root for them. You want them to make it out and there is some plot armor that heroes have where you know they are going to make it out. In *Harry Potter and The Prisoner of Azkaban*, you know Harry's got three more years of school. Protagonists benefit from that in a way that villains don't.

Bill Nicholson - The best protagonist is the one you feel the most powerful connection towards, the strongest engagement. They've got to be really lovable, which does not mean nice, sweet, and syrupy. You can have a torturer who is really lovable, but you've got to find what makes them so. You have to see their sense of vulnerability so you have an eagerness to find out what it is that they want. You want to be able to imagine that the protagonist is you if you were in that situation.

I have a big problem with superhero movies. There has been a whole range of variants in which the superheroes have flaws and problems that they have to solve. However, it's cursory because when they start fighting, they've got this trick that can get them out of trouble. That's when it's lost my interest completely. However, a soldier who is very self-aware of their fear of the battle that they are going into and the fight is not their sole purpose in life is so much more interesting. So you are building a character that you wish to follow into that war. When they get into trouble, your heart is going pitter-pat. My heart doesn't go pitter-pat when most action heroes get into trouble because I know they are not going to get into trouble. I'm totally uninterested in fights where I know the outcome. So I'm no good at action movies. Action movies consist entirely of fights where you know what the outcome is. Much like the fights in *Gladiator*. It's one guy against a lot of people in the arena and he managed to beat them all. I don't know how he did that.

A long time ago, I was asked to write about an extraordinary American aid worker named Fred Cuny. This is a guy who was an engineer and he realized that in crisis spots, often what they need is engineering. They need someone to sort out the water supply or the electricity. So he started up a little group and they would fly into hot spots. He spent a year in Sarajevo during the siege and he did incredible things; he was very courageous. I was asked to write this film with the Mexican director, Alejandro Iñárritu. Harrison Ford was going to be Fred Cuny. What happened to the real Fred Cuny is that he went to war zones, did incredible things, and got an overinflated sense of his own immortality. He then went to Chechnya when everyone told him not to go and there he was pulled out of a car, told to kneel down, and shot in the head. Totally pointless. I remember pitching to all the producers that this movie is going to begin with our hero, Harrison Ford, driving through a forest in Chechnya and the jeep gets stopped and suddenly they are telling him to get out of the jeep. He gets out, kneels down, and we're thinking this is Harrison Ford, he's not going to die. They put a gun to his head and he's shot dead. He falls over and then we go back in time. Everyone around the table said, "Wow! That's amazing. So unexpected!" So I wrote the draft and the studio said, *"*You absolutely cannot start a film like that. Can't be done." I think nowadays, they would go for it.

Josh Olson - If a character holds my interest long enough to write beginning to end, that's a great protagonist. If you find yourself on page 30 of your first rewrite being bored with this person, you've got a problem.

Eli Craig - A lot of people like Iron Man and think he's a fun protagonist. But for me, he starts with everything. He starts on top of the world. To me, a great protagonist is somebody who starts without that much. Someone who starts really down. We want to see a human journey because we all get beat up in life. We all have hard times. We want to go on the journey from not being so sure about ourselves. How are we going to handle this? Is it possible to rise to the occasion and take on the obstacle we are confronting with more resolve? But the obstacle has to be bigger than he can overcome.

> ## ANTI-HEROES
>
> Dark. Complex. Flawed. These are terms associated with anti-heroes. They are fun to watch, but tricky to write because you must balance their dark and light moments to create something believable and rich. If you get it right, they can be great vessels to explore complex themes.
>
> Here are some common tropes for anti-heroes. Consider using them or flipping them on their heads to come up with something new.
>
> - They have done something wrong or illegal in the past.
> - Something bad happened to them and they can't get past it.
> - Guilt and remorse may be driving their turmoil.
> - They want to be better and may do so - for a little while.
> - Often sacrifice themselves in some way to complete their resolution - this often results in their death.

There was a Marvel movie where the superhero just comes down and destroys everything. My son was like, "She's overpowered." If you write a protagonist that's overpowered, then the journey isn't as compelling as when someone feels the obstacles are bigger than them. With the obstacle comes a huge want. So they have to really want something that is, ultimately, identifiable and that people understand. That's why the heart of a movie will often be about love; wanting to get someone to love you. Or it's about wanting to survive. These are big wants in life. I want to live. I want to love. I want to eat. Then, a lot of times with the protagonist, I will try to back them up into a place where they have the ability to overcome great things, but they don't know it, themselves. The audience, though, thinks maybe they can. Empathy is a big thing. You want to love and relate to your protagonist.

In film school, somebody told me, "A good protagonist is one that when presented with two bad options, still makes a choice. Then you follow them down that path." I think the simpler you make that journey, the better. If you look at *Jaws*, we have to get the shark. Then layered within that can be so much of the protagonist's life and who they are. Their inner need versus their outer want and all those other screenwriting terms. To me, it's somebody that you fall in love with when you are writing.

Mohamad El Masri - I've noticed that characters become rich and compelling when they speak for themselves, instead of for the writer. My favorite characters believe in their own argument for why they make the choices they make and can deliver the argument passionately and convincingly.

Alex Litvak - I worked on a project with Stan Lee that he was executive producing during his twilight days. He said, "Remember! The hero is only as good as your villain!" Action films are about going to battle. You are trying to save the people that you love. Trying to save the city. Trying to save the world, all that stuff. So it's courage, ingenuity, fortitude, resilience - all these qualities that, if your villain is weak, become moot. That's why there is this interesting duality, made clear with Batman and the Joker, where one does not exist without the other. This sort of symbiotic relationship.

Al Pacino and Robert DeNiro in *Heat* are both heroes in their own stories. The movie does not have a clear-cut villain. There are tertiary bad guys, but fundamentally you could argue that they are both heroes and villains at the same time. What's interesting is that they are two sides of the same coin. There's the society around them and they both exist both inside and outside the world around them at the same time. They're bound and interconnected and dependent on one another. The same applies to any classic hero/villain dynamic. With Luke Skywalker and Darth Vader, there's even the biological root connection. Batman and the Joker. The two are intrinsically bound together. And conversely, we like flawed heroes. Personally, I've never liked Superman because he's too much of a good guy. He's perfect. I've always been drawn to the guys who carry the scars. They carry heavy burdens. They don't always want to rise to the occasion, but they do because that's what heroes do.

Tony Jordan - I think a great protagonist is different for different people like most things. This is why I have difficulty with people who say that there is only one way to do things. Audiences have to care for protagonists, and people are different. People want to see themselves in the protagonist. Or how they view themselves. This is perhaps over-simplistic, but I like to think there's a little boy somewhere sitting in a bedroom who doesn't have many mates at school, who is a bit shy or socially awkward and he's really rubbish with girls. When someone bullies him, he knows what to say on the way home. But in the moment, he can't think of what to say. I think that when that boy watches *Spider-Man*, he becomes Spider-Man because he needs to become Spider-Man. It's part of his growth as a person to be or inhabit that protagonist. Then, you will have a completely different personality that will need a completely different protagonist. It's true to say there are universal protagonists - the man, woman, or non-specific gender searching for love, who then, overcomes obstacles and finds love. We all need love. But individually, we all need slightly different things, too. We all want to be masters in our own world. We all want to be important in our own world. So, in a way, we all want to be Tommy Shelby in *Peaky Blinders* who seems to know everything and be on top of everything.

To say that there's a kind of element that you must build into every protagonist's personality in order to make them work, I think, is a bit simplistic. You need to be aware of the nuance of the audience. That's why you have genres. That's why you have a *Spider-Man* watching genre. There, the protagonist, perhaps, doesn't work for the 80-year-old in a nursing home who probably wants to watch *Driving Miss Daisy*.

Dan Mazer - I think if you make the protagonist too exaggerated, you immediately lose sympathy. Here's the difference between Borat and Brüno and why Borat is beloved, enduring, and three-dimensional in a way that Brüno isn't. I love Brüno and I think he's a great character, but he is really a vessel for stunts and things to happen. Nobody has ever really met somebody like Brüno. He's always extreme. He was always quite difficult to write for - his world and his opinions. He was really a cipher for other people's extreme reactions, homophobia, and that sort of thing. Borat - there's an innate humanity to him that may not have been there with Brüno. Borat is a product of his environment. His opinions come from his environment rather than from his own extremity. Ultimately, he's a vulnerable and identifiable human who feels real emotions. That's probably why he's more successful and enduring. So if you are writing a comedic protagonist, yes, make them funny, but make that humor based on something real, identifiable, and universal.

Jed Mercurio - It's really important for an audience to be interested in the protagonist and I think that's more important than whether they like the person. Those are the two areas that are most discussed. There is a school of thought that often comes from the executive level that characters have to be likable for the audience to want to follow their story. I think writers tend to have a more nuanced approach. There are plenty of us who think it's just more important that we find a way to a window of the character's psychology so that when they make their decisions, we understand them. It doesn't mean we should agree with them or support those decisions, but we should understand them.

Carolina Rivera - A good protagonist, especially in comedy, is someone who suffers or is tormented in life by their character flaws. Ana in *Daughter From Another Mother* is very controlling and that's what makes her funny. She wants to control everything so she gets into these crazy situations. Marianna's flaw is she has no rules, nothing. She's free. You couldn't put two characters together in a better way. That's where the comedy comes from.

Meg LeFauve - You do ask yourself, in your process as a writer: Why this person? Why is this the person we are following? It's so personal, isn't it, as to what makes a great protagonist? I want to connect the audience to how they see themselves and the world. That they want something that we want. I think any character can make a great protagonist if you connect them to the audience. I love characters that you wouldn't expect to be the protagonist. There's a kind of bravery in choosing to be the protagonist. So many of us choose not to be the protagonist of our own life. There's a certain bravery to, "I'm going to stand in the fire. I'm going to go for it!" I think that our protagonists get to do that for us in good storytelling. Anyone could be that if that's their choice.

Q: What makes a great villain?

Jed Mercurio - I think it's the same as a protagonist. I think it's logic. I think where things start to go awry is when the villain's plans start to be illogical or it just seems it's far too complicated or far too protean to function plausibly within the story. Then actually it's something that is a device to keep creating set pieces for the protagonist, rather than being a genuine psychological arc for the villain.

Danny Strong - I give my antagonists their own antagonists, so they are the protagonist of their own story. It sounds simple, and maybe it is, but that philosophy gives you a completely different understanding of them besides the source of antagonism against the protagonist. They have their own antagonist and their own problems. That's how they become much more multi-dimensional than our two-dimensional, mustache-twirly, bad guy. The more you can make your antagonist right, the more interesting your story is. The more the argument of the sources of antagonism is right or interesting or valid, the greater the depth you have.

> ## SUPPORTING CHARACTERS
>
> You will spend a lot of time thinking about your main characters when building a story. That makes sense as the opposition between the protagonist and the antagonist drives the bulk of the drama. However, you must construct all the people and entities around them with care, too.
>
> - Supporting characters need a reason to be in the story or in a scene. They need to help move the story along and not just be window dressing. Female love interests and best friends often fall into this trap.
>
> - The best way to avoid the above problem is to give supporting characters internal and external motivations. Many times these are similar to the main character's, however as they are their own individuals, their wants and needs will have different tangents.
>
> - The different motivational slants allow you to explore your themes in great detail. Your main character may have one take on the main problem, while their accomplice may have another. The friction caused by these differences exposes the complexity of your subject matter and creates drama as they work out which take is best or correct. It's possible they always will be at odds.
>
> - Supporting characters often say what the audience is thinking. They can provide information or context in complicated situations. They can question choices the lead characters have made. They can speak truth even if the main characters can't hear it yet. This leads to drama, comedy, and character growth for both of them. As such, they can often have some of the best lines.

You are with your protagonist, so they are right, but consider the other side, wow, hmmm... now I am thinking more. I'm in more conflict over what is right. That's the best way to move forward because if I'm in conflict, then my protagonist must be in conflict. All of a sudden, you are having a richer dramatic experience.

Arthur Miller, one of my writing heroes, has a great quote, "In good drama, your protagonist struggles, toils, and then succeeds. A great drama is when your protagonist struggles, toils, and then fails." You don't get to do that often in movies of a certain budget where your protagonist can fail. But I think television has gotten so rich and dramatic starting with *The Sopranos*. Now, your protagonist could fail. They can be duplicitous, an anti-hero, and knowing your protagonist can fail adds a whole other level of dramatic tension to the experience that may be not there in a movie made for over $25 million. There, you know that this is going to kind of work out.

Scott Lobdell - You've heard the saying: Everyone is the hero of their own story. I would love to write a movie about an international thief who comes up with the idea to pose as a terrorist and sneak into a building where there is $600 million in bearer bonds, but suddenly the phone rings and it's a cop in the building. How does he get rid of this New York City cop? In *Die Hard,* you feel it's as much about Alan Rickman's story as it is Bruce Willis' story. *Infinity War's* Thanos is a great villain. You want to feel for the villain. I think the best Marvel villains, so far, have been in the *Shang-Chi* movie. If Shang-Chi was never in that movie and you were telling the story about this guy who had these two kids who left him and he needed them to go back to free his wife from this eternal slavery - how heartbreaking. Look at Magneto. If Magneto was just a bad guy who wanted mutants to take over the world because they were mutants, that would have been boring as hell. But the writer was able to make him Malcolm X to Professor X's Martin Luther King, Jr. He grounded Magneto as someone who had already been through the Holocaust and watched people of his race being exterminated. Suddenly he grows up into a mutant and now there's a whole different set of people who are out to exterminate this new race and he's not going to have any of it. When you look at him, you say, "I see his point. I wish he didn't kill everyone on the San Francisco bridge to make his point, but I see where it is." So if you make a villain someone people don't necessarily have to root for, but, at least, understand, then that makes the best villain.

Moisés Zamora - In horror and science fiction movies, there are very clear villains. Good versus evil. In other genres, in some cases you have anti-heroes. But I think the term anti-hero is a little too reductive because, in a way, we are all flawed. We all have the potential to be the anti-heroes of our own lives. Our flaws get in the way of our best path to success and happiness. We are constantly sabotaging ourselves and our future and our lives because we're just wired that way. Or we're dealing with trauma or living in fear. I feel those kinds of characters are complex, layered and they are really fun. Especially, if they have innate paradoxes in their description. The good thief. The cheating wife. They are exciting because, on one hand, you want to relate to them and root for them, and it makes it real that they make mistakes. On top of it, if the mistakes they make are really exciting for drama, then you are actually rooting for them to sabotage their lives a little more. Like *Succession*. They are such a mess. They are awful. But we love them being awful. We don't want them to be good.

American Crime was very eye-opening because the creator, John Ridley, wanted human trafficking to be the theme of that season. And with human trafficking, it's very nebulous when it comes to evil vs. good. Obviously, human trafficking is bad. But we learned from our research that every human being, no matter who they are, has the potential to torture another human being if they have full control over their lives. Learning that was shocking. At first, you're seeing characters on *American Crime* that are in that gray space. They are actually good people who end up doing really horrible things. How does that person get there? I think that's what John Ridley wanted to get at and leave it open-ended. There's no, "We caught you, killer! Boom! You go to jail." That's not necessarily what happens in this sort of situation.

With *Star*, it was a little soapier, so you have those villainous kinds of characters. And also, anti-hero characters sabotaging their own lives in order to create drama. Now, I do feel that, even though I love genre, I'm gravitating to some of the classics like Chekov. Good versus evil, everyone is down for that, but when it's good versus good, then that elevates the story. Take two inherently good people and put them at odds with each other. Chekov's family dramas were all about that. That's interesting when two good characters come into conflict. What's that drama? Because we are going to root for both of them and it's going to be juicy. Or some people will root for one and some for the other. So that's sort of what my ambitions are now where even the villain is good. If you want to say it's anti-hero versus anti-hero, that's the thing about writing, if you see something that attracts you or has a little light that sparkles to you, keep on going to see where it takes you. That's how art is created.

Deborah Haywood - To make a great villain, make them as scary as possible, but not in a pantomime way - in a realistic kind of way. Like the bully in *Pin Cushion*. She is vile, but I gave her a glimmer of reality. Let's see her side of the story. It's not her story, but let's have a little glimpse so that she becomes more three-dimensional and real. So, yes, they are vile, but there's always a reason for some kind of behavior. Let's have a little glimpse of that in some way. I actually find in drama, villains can be scarier than in an action or horror story. Like Begbie in *Trainspotting* - the scariest villain for me. I was absolutely terrified of him. Someone else like Freddy Krueger or whatever, it's not real.

Bill Nicholson - I think a great villain is the same as a great protagonist. Both need to have energy. They need to be vital characters. Even if the vitality is cloaked under, say, depression or shyness. You need to feel an energy.

You have to, as a writer, create characters that embody psychological tension. So if you have a villain, he needs to be someone you want to see threaten your protagonist - that threat has to be credible. It's obviously not enough simply for the villain to be more powerful. When a villain points a gun, they have no power. The gun has the power. When you realize that the villain has got qualities that have made him able to be in a position of power, then it starts to get more interesting. So villains and protagonists are the same, but you are giving them a different journey. With protagonists, you love them and want to go with them to some conclusion, some sort of redemption. The villain has to evolve and change too and, for me, I want to understand why they are villainous. If you think about the Coen brother's film, *No Country for Old Men,* Javier Bardem went around with the cattle prod killer thing. I really, really found that tedious. Who is this guy? Why is he killing people? I understand that was sort of the point. It was supposed to be this blank, affectless killer. As a result, I felt blankness and affectless, myself. I didn't believe it.

If you have ever read anything about people who do really evil things, to themselves, they are not evil. This is not somebody who says, "How can I be really wicked?" It is someone who says, "I am prepared to take the really hard decisions to achieve a really desirable and worthwhile goal. It may be protecting my family." Usually, villains have enemies of their own. They know if they don't kill you, someone will kill them. They have worked it out and they are okay to do it. That's much more interesting. I have a lot of frustration with James Bond villains. In *No Time to Die*, I simply couldn't understand what his plan was. He had some plan to do something dastardly to the world or to people; something to do with poisoning specific people via their DNA. I simply didn't know what was going on and I couldn't get behind it. Whereas, with some Bond villains, you kind of get the idea of someone who has almost become insane because of things that have happened to them. Damage that may have been done to them. It might be crudely laid out, but you get it. It works.

The best Joker is the one whom you realize, to your horror, has no motive. It's just nihilism. Now, why would someone be that nihilistic? That's psychological damage and you can kind of understand that. What do you do with someone who isn't after anything at all, except let me just cause pain and destruction because in me is so much pain and destruction? That's interesting and I can believe that. I think to create a great villain you have to, as much as you do with a protagonist, think about what does this person want? Why are they like this? When you know what they want, you will know what they will do to get it. Then you can make your confrontations credible.

Briana Belser - Oh, man. I love villains. It's probably my favorite part of storytelling. The thing about a villain and their pure storytelling function, which you learn in 7th grade literature class, is that ideally, the antagonist is driving the protagonist to make choices. As much as we are aiming in television for the hero to push the plot, I feel villains do the same thing. They, for me, as a screenwriter, can be the hero when I'm like, "What now? What happens? Let me see what my bad guy is up to." In terms of philosophies about villains, I love the ones who have pure conviction in what it is they are doing. Heroes have their nice, little flaws. They have to be likable and redeemable. I like the villain who is like, "I know what I am doing and I am going to go for it by hook or by crook." I often think that ruthlessness is the thin line that separates heroes and villains. Heroes take into account context, nuance, and feelings, while villains get stuff done.

There were two villains on a pop culture front that really surprised me in recent years. One was Thanos in the Marvel films. He was like, "Look, I understand all those details. Big picture? Done." I liked how it really forced the main characters to reckon with someone who won't play ball. He's not here to negotiate. He's here to execute on task. It really poses a question to the heroes of how bad do they want to achieve their goals because they are up against someone who will do anything to achieve his. The other was Eric Killmonger in Ryan Coogler's version of *Black Panther*. So much pain and legacy and so much bedrock of storytelling before the events that by the time he went head to head with T'Chala, there were legitimate questions about whether he was just evil or was it more about who made him evil. To what extent was T'Chala responsible? So I love when villains are entwined with heroes in that sort of way. I do love a villain who has pure conviction.

Another villain that I think is fun is Frank Gallagher in *Shameless*. He's fun to watch, horrific, makes your stomach hurt, and makes you laugh. He's grounded and he's real. His goal is: I'm drinking. I'm going to get over and I'm drinking. If you are going to get in my way, if you are going to stop me drinking, we are going to go toe to toe. There's a simplicity and clarity to that. If everything that you know is Frank is looking for a drink, then the fun becomes: How does he get it? Who's in the way? Villains that have that mantra make them so fun to write for and I think it can also challenge a hero. How do they keep themselves from becoming single-minded? How do they stay open-minded and complex? How do they grow? Villains often don't grow, I don't think. But they can help push your protagonist.

Josh Olson - One of the things that's fun with villains is a long storied tradition where the villain gets to speak the writer's truth to the audience. Hans Gruber says a lot of stuff in *Die Hard* that somebody actually believes, which I think is really fun. I have a lot of Black leftist friends. They were excited for *Black Panther*, but they were upset that the villain was a Black nationalist like they are. He's one of us and everything he says is stuff we believe, but he's the villain! I was like, guys! That's literally how you get that into a movie. There's a reason why there's a load of people with this character tattooed on their arms. They are saying stuff that if you put in the mouth of your hero, no studio is going to get behind. Make him your bad guy and you get to say whatever you want. It's not necessarily a judgment on that because he's the villain. He's the delivery system.

Dan Mazer - I've never really done anything with the sort of conventional villain, to be honest. I've done rewrites on stuff where there have been villains and baddies - big studio movies. The stuff I write is more grounded in the everyday, rather than broader and villain based. But I would say, it remains true for all characters, if there's something in that villainy that is based in reality and identifiable, whether that is a fragility based on family or lost love or envy - everything needs to be rooted in something we identify with in our daily lives. The boss at work who is taking it out on you because he was bullied at school and is now given a position of responsibility and is getting payback. That you can extrapolate to a villain in a more heightened environment. So to base everything on something that resonates on a daily level is probably a sensible course of action.

Tony Jordan - I think stories are our way of working shit out, as a species. It's a way to get better to cope with situations. I think it's fundamental, really. Thousands of years ago, there was no Netflix, though it's hard to think of a time before it. People sat around campfires and strangers would come and say, "Can I share your beans, mate?" They were all Cockneys in those days! "Yeah, absolutely, how have you been doing?" "Well, you will never guess what happened to me." They would tell a story and the other people around the campfire would be on the edge of their seats for a number of reasons. One, they wanted to know what happens. What happens next? That's important because the next time I am in that situation, in a pass with a saber-toothed tiger, how can I get a good outcome? You are trying to learn. You are trying to grow. That's within our species. That's what we do. That's what experience is. That is what I think storytelling is at the most fundamental level. That's why you have to care about protagonists. If we don't, it's not a story worth telling because it doesn't apply to you in some way. It's the same with villains. Why are they threatening? You can have a villain that threatens that order in one way or another. That's basically what villains do. So in a love story, the villain is the person who will stop the love from happening, or who will make the person be with the wrong person for the wrong reason and it makes

---

CHARACTER IDENTITY

How we see ourselves in the world is sometimes very different from how others see us. We may think we're cool and smooth in any given situation, but those around us may see us as arrogant and aloof. Or we can see ourselves as clumsy and awkward, while others deem us lively and quirky.

Screenwriters can use this disconnect to their advantage when building characters and their relationships. A clueless blowhard is a classic place for a character to start in many comedies. When going up against forces of antagonism, these traits can both help and hinder them as they try to reach their goals. They can force their way out of confrontation via their wit, but use it against someone not charmed and a physical fight may break out.

Challenges to identity can lead to character growth as the story progresses - unless you've created someone completely obstinate. They can also help explore your story's themes, as characters in their path can represent opposing views on an issue. The friction created can expose the complexities of your subject matter.

our teeth itch. They can change the natural order of things. Boy meets girl, falls in love, has babies, and lives happily ever after. Happy days! It attacks that order. It can also be an evil Bond villain who is stroking his white cat and wants to change the sun to make it burn something. That changes the order. I don't want to live in a bunker and serve a global despot. I like what we do. That was a really long-winded way of saying I think a protagonist needs to be in search of and deliver order and an antagonist needs to trip all of that up.

Eli Craig - A good villain is somebody that you can understand where they come from. If you can draw out a villain and show why they think the way they think, that's great.

Alex Litvak - It's back to that symbiotic relationship with the hero. Your villain needs to be as strong as your hero. If you pivot the movie and it's the same story from the villain's perspective, then you kind of understand where they are coming from. Thanos, from the Marvel movies, truly believes, "I am saving the universe. You fucking idiots don't understand that everything I am doing is not because I am sadistic or brutal. It's because I am the savior of worlds and you are just standing in my way."

There's also got to be some compelling or redeeming or emotionally relevant quality in the villain that you can latch onto as an audience member. We feel sympathy for the Joker because of what happened to him.

Obviously, there are exceptions to this. Hans Gruber just wants a bunch of money. What's wrong with that? We all want money. But a lot of really compelling villains have to have a justified reason. Darth Vader didn't just want to restore order to the galaxy. He wants to make the Empire great again. It's all justified.

Briana Belser - As much as we're ingrained to know that a protagonist will succeed, we're also ingrained to know that the villain will not prevail. That assumption can be so useful as a writer. When you assume that the audience knows the bad guy is going down, you can tell the hard truths of life. For example, Thanos is environmentally friendly. He's like, "There needs to be less of us. I'm not going to be picky about who goes." There's something so legitimate about that. We understand overpopulation and overcapacity in our world where we have climate change. I'm not trying to extrapolate a large political crisis from a Marvel film, but as an audience member, there is a brass tax to Thanos' villainy - there are more people than there is water to provide for them. Somebody is going to be thirsty!

With villains, if you seek their motivations from these hard truths, the hard truth can be the springboard to make them act. I love that phrase. It could almost be a tool to generate a villain. Identify a hard truth and a person who is going to do something to address it. And how, in that process and that journey, do they become "villains"? What are the worlds in which the hard truths have prevailed? Our world is full of death and disease and sin, and whatever other ways you want to contextualize it. It's fun for a writer if you take those plot assumptions and subvert them. What if the hero doesn't win? Or what if the hero wins, but the victory isn't as sweet? Especially in television where you want the story to evolve, stemming from a place of hard truth and pure conviction, it can be a great way to make a villain continue to shift and change and create problems for the lead.

Ron Leshem - The only character that I have written that I wasn't attracted to was the assassin in *Incitement*, a film about the assassination of Prime Minister Rabin. I was disgusted by him. The assassin was a religious guy, a law student, who decided to kill the peace process by killing the Prime Minister. He was working as a messenger from God or a kind of messiah. He had a God complex and an inferiority complex at the same time. The idea of writing a story about a guy that I was disgusted by, was awful for me. But I thought it was important because I wanted to show what makes this personality do what he does. It was important to show who influenced him. The world was and is becoming so violent via social media. *Incitement* is part of politics now. Everything is fueled by hate. However, I wanted to feel empathy towards this guy unlike when I was writing the antagonist in *Euphoria*. I needed this character not to be lovable, but to be relatable.

Meg LeFauve - A lot of people would say this, and I agree, that the villain thinks they are the hero of the movie. They don't see themselves as a villain and they have a legitimate point of view. That's why it's so scary. They are not just a baddie. They could sit down and have an argument with you about why they are right. And you could be like, "Oh, my God! I kind of understand." But how they are going about it is totally wrong. Also, a great villain is part of you, too. And they are part of the main character. They are the dark side of the main character. They don't have this transformation.

Chris Cullari - Sometimes, the most frightening thing for me is a horror villain whose motives aren't quite clear. Those are very hard villains to write because you get into questions of rules. But villains like in *The Strangers* or *Blair Witch* or, even though it's not a movie, the horror in *The House of Leaves,* is a very dread-based, existential kind of horror. It's not an evil or a villain you can negotiate with or explain something to. It's just coming. I think that can be really effective.

Villains are tricky to nail. The more explanation we get of why Michael Myers does what he does, the less effective it gets. I think a lot of times the villains that are most effective aren't necessarily the ones the creators thought were going to be eternal. There's just something about them that worked for scaring so many people. It's a hard line to walk where the villain needs to clearly want something, but you don't want to explain everything about why.

Jennifer Raite - If your movie has a formulaic beat where you completely understand what the villain is doing and why they are doing it, I think it takes away from the horror. For instance, "Now I know how this is working, I can stop it." But this is so unlike the things in life of which we are so often afraid. You need the anxiety.

CHAPTER REVIEW: CHARACTER

- Your world can dictate what kind of characters are in it. This comes from doing lots of research in your subject area.

- Your characters must be believable or else the audience won't empathize with them. If they are too exaggerated, then they may become one-note.

- The more specific you can make a character the more authentic and unique they become.

- All characters have internal and external motivations. Internal deals with their character development. External centers on a task they have to do via the plot. Sometimes, this is referred to as the need versus the want.

- Characters, like real humans, should have assets to their personalities that help them succeed and flaws that hold them back.

- No person is truly all good or bad. Balanced characters help make them believable and relatable.

- Make your characters entertaining and give them a function in the story. A dull character with no purpose is hard to get behind.

- As your characters go through the story, they should learn or realize something about the world and/or themselves that helps them grow as a person. Unless you are on a sitcom where the characters remain more static.

- Character breakdowns can be helpful when figuring out their point of view of the world, as well as their internal and external motivations.

- Having characters with different points of view on the main theme allows you to explore those concepts in greater detail.

- Your characters will tell you what they want to do. Be open to that.

- Conflict between characters drives drama. It can be especially interesting when two good characters have an issue with each other.

- Anti-heroes are complicated characters to write because they are lovable, but very flawed. If you get them right, it can be satisfying.

- One way to round out an antagonist is to give them their own antagonist. This helps drive their internal and external motivations.

- Villains allow the author to tell the hard truths of life.

CHAPTER 5

DIALOGUE

Putting words in other people's mouths can be tricky. How do you make sure it sounds authentic? How do you make your characters feel distinct? What do you leave out for greater effect? How does an actor's performance enhance what you've written? All of that and more get reviewed in this chapter.

Q: How do you approach dialogue?

Briana Belser - I'm a Southern woman and I am also Black. Mainstream America is White and either West Coast or Mid-Atlantic in how people talk. That's normal American speech. I think coming from an African American perspective, we have a subculture and a means of dialects that don't always resonate with the mainstream. There are things that I can say to my homies that I can't turn into a paper in my English class. I am always very clear about my audience; when and why shapes how I say a thing. And that is strictly on cultural lines.

In terms of generating dialogue, I almost always act it out. I go one character at a time and think, what are they getting at? To whom are they talking? What is their status relative to this person? What mood are they in? Are they tired? Are they irritable? Is this a person with whom they are in love? Are they telling the truth? Can we trust them? Using those contexts, I write whatever comes to mind. The longest version of what it is. Then I move to the next character in the scene and try to shift perspective. And then from there, try to cut it within an inch of its life. Trim and trim. Say less. I love when my script has as much white space as possible. Minimal description and action with mostly dialogue on the page. But I don't want over-talking. I'm not writing monologues.

Then, is it fun to read? Is it something I want to see? Sometimes, I read sample scripts and I'm like, "Oh boy! I can't wait. Put this in this actor's mouth and that in that actress' mouth." There's something really exciting about that. There are also times when I have gotten bored with my own writing and I'm like, it doesn't feel real. It's too mechanical.

Good dialogue should fly off the page. It should be clear on the first read. If you are having to go back and check and check and check, it's probably not written to the best it could be. You should do another pass. I think the last thing is specificity. If there's a character who has a stutter or an impediment or who uses metaphors frequently to speak, then those things should show up on the page.

Deborah Haywood - I don't think I write the dialogue until the last minute. I've got the story in beats and treatments and outlines and all the rest of it. Then I do a step outline, which still doesn't have dialogue. When I have the story, I know the characters so well, the dialogue writes itself. I do think, what does this character want? Because if you know what they want, then you know what they are going to say. I remember reading David Mamet, who said, "Every time we speak, as people, it's to illicit something from somebody else." So if I feel that my dialogue isn't working, I always go and look at that. What are they trying to get in the scene? And if they are not trying to get anything in the scene and if they aren't trying to get anything, I scribble it out.

Meg LeFauve - I envy my playwright friends. They've had so many years of learning dialogue through the plays they've written. I have no insight into dialogue. I try to write how I hear people talk. I so admire Aaron Sorkin who, to me, is just a magician. He can make dialogue sound like music, yet still remain authentic and human.

Bill Nicholson - I've written a lot of historical things, but I do not use a historical form of speech. If someone says, "I don't know whereof you come," they do so because they think that is how people spoke in the past. It's not. It's how people who wrote books in the past, spoke. They spoke similar to us now in a squished together sort of way. People think that the minute it's Jane Austen's time, people might say, "Who is this I see before me?" No, it's "Who's this?" You don't use stuff that's out of date. You keep it plain and simple, but colloquial vernacular.

If you know your character, your world and its rules - which you will do because you've researched it - it's really easy writing dialogue. As you're writing it, you're acting it. Being it. You feel it. When I am reaching a crisis point, I know what he's going to say and I'm longing for him to get the chance to say it. Then you write it. And then rewrite it before anyone sees it. And probably again. With each pass, it's kind of tidying up the initial outburst. If I do this before anyone sees it, it means I can be free to take any risks that I want. Sometimes, some of the riskiest things are the best. What would happen if they just did that? Well, let's try it. Then on the rewrite, I think, "Ah, that's silly." So before it gets to anybody, it's been through three layers. I find that liberating.

This is the trick; you have to be a fountain of originality all the time. Then you have to be a fountain again. And again. The minute you start to anticipate criticisms, it goes wrong. The minute you start thinking that you better write it to fit some external requirement, it goes wrong. It's got to be all the time coming purely from you. Then it's out there and okay, then you can start kicking it around. When you're writing, you really must love it and be passionate. I think that is the hardest trick to pull off - to be passionate through the process, which is very wearing on the whole. I think you need a particular character for that. You can't be so insecure that you are terrified that you will get it wrong. You have to think, "What the hell? Let's go for it." It helps to read other peoples' scripts because mostly they are so bad and you can think that you are not going to be that bad even at your worst! And it helps to know that the people working around you don't have a clue, either. You have to be a bit fearless. Then you get wounded. Then you have to be fearless all over again.

Moisés Zamora - When it comes to crafting dialogue in a scene, I think it's important, no matter where it comes from or whom it's inspired by, that the scene has to work. It has to be clear what character A wants and what character B wants. Hopefully, it is in conflict. Or if it needs to be contextualized for character A, where maybe, character A has cancer, but without saying that. I feel that the way I process dialogue is: what do I need to tell the audience in the context after I have the very basic, on-the-nose dialogue? Then I take another look and put subtext into it. Maybe you talk about the mold in your house to tell the other character that you do have cancer; that you are suffering from something that actually will bring you down. Whatever it is, it has to feel right to the piece, the genre, and the tone. Subtext is great, but sometimes I feel on-the-nose dialogue gets a bad rap. I think there are a lot of examples of movies that have on-the-nose dialogue that have won Oscars and been nominated for Best Screenplay. You don't notice it because of the context and the way the scene is crafted. The way the characters interact with each other is so compelling that you forget that their dialogue is very on-the-nose. In fact, because it is on-the-nose, it makes it funnier or more compelling.

Here's an example. *The Wrestler* has lots of on-the-nose dialogue. When he tries to make a connection with his daughter, it's very on-the-nose. This is what I want. This is what I am trying to do. There's no subtext. But because it's Mickey Rourke as the wrestler and the situation is that his daughter hates him and she tells him so, you don't notice it because of the way the scene was crafted. I'm not saying write all your screenplays this way. It depends on the style you want to do and sometimes that calls for on-the-nose dialogue. Obviously, your executives are going to go, "This is on-the-nose. Can we have some more subtext?" You will get those notes, but it may not be your style.

Michael Brandt - I used to be an assistant editor for Robert Rodriquez. That was the best film school in terms of helping a writer know when to get in and out of a scene or in and out of a piece of dialogue. It helped me realize what I needed and what I didn't. One of the best compliments I ever got was when an executive said that he was standing at his kitchen counter when he opened the first script Derek Haas and I wrote together, and when he finished, he realized that he was still standing at his kitchen counter. Now, I know that script wasn't great, but it was a page-turner because the pace was right.

We wrote that script when I was cutting scenes with Robert. I was very much in the frame of mind of what is necessary and what isn't. Robert is a great filmmaker and the best thing about his filmmaking is his editing. He cuts all his movies. His sense of pace is really great, so I think that helped me with my own filmmaking. I think the executive's compliment came less from that it was a really amazing screenplay, but rather that we got in and out of scenes and dialogue quickly. To me, white space is a giant deal. I go to great lengths to make sure my scripts don't look dense. There is nothing worse than opening a screenplay and you can tell they've changed the kerning - widened it or squeezed it. If I see that, I know it's going to take me four minutes to read just the first page. I want it to be airy. The words have to be the right words, but perception is also an important thing. This is a marketing document for a movie, not a script. In my mind, I've never really written a script. I've only written movies. And I want movies to move. That doesn't mean fast cuts, that means the pace at which characters get to the point and move on.

Q: Does your dialogue come naturally once you're immersed in the story?

Josh Olson - Yes. You get to a point where you sort of hear it in your head.

Deborah Haywood - I do think I get that thing where if you are in the zone; you get a gift from somewhere. You don't know where it really comes from. I don't know if that's from the characters, your subconscious, or from the Gods. When I am in that zone, it's beautiful and

I think that's why I do it. It's like a drug when that happens. It's so euphoric. More of that. Oh, my God! Let me get out of the shower and write it, quick!

Tony Jordan - I create the world, characters, and story. I, then, put those characters in my head in a scene, in a situation with a dynamic and I fold my arms and wait for them to start talking. Then I become a reporter. I'm not thinking of anything. I am not thinking about what they would say. I have no fucking idea what they would say. I wait - this is weird. I don't think I've ever said this out loud. I wait until they speak and then write down what they say. I'm actually struggling to keep up, sometimes. I can't type fast enough because they are talking faster than my fingers can go. Like a court typist. That's how it works for me. I don't know if that is the same for anyone else.

Q: Some shows now use a mix of languages due to their characters' origins. How is this written in the screenplay?

Moisés Zamora - America doesn't like subtitles, at least not the older generation, so we wrote the dialogue of *Star* first in English. The newer generations who have Netflix have read so many subtitles so they don't care. We knew we would have subtitles and we started in English because we wanted our executives to understand what was going on. Also, to me, the blueprint of the screenplay has to flow. You don't want to look things up. You don't want two dialogues competing with each other. On the page, it looks like something you don't want to read. The way you experience a screenplay, it has to flow. We start in English first and then it gets approved. For *Star* specifically, we made sure the slang was right because Benjamin Bratt's character is from Peru. There are a couple of things in there that would make sense in Spanish. Or a Peruvian-American would say even if it's a little off because the Spanish is not perfect. That's okay and I think it gives it authenticity.

For me, I do like to venture into those language things, especially if the story calls for it. *Selena* calls for it. It was part of that identity, experience, and journey. We had to create that and it was wonderful. But if it doesn't, don't contrive it just because you know another language there and expect the reader to look it up. They are not going to look it up. Everyone is too super busy to go into Google Translate to figure out what that sentence is. That is just not what people do unless they are a super, mega-diligent reader, but most people in the business don't have that time. So create an experience that gets the point across. Maybe put something in there like italicized dialogue will be translated to Spanish and that's it.

Emma Ko - Everything on *1899* was done in English. Then the actors came in and converted it to other languages. My characters speak Cantonese, which is slightly different from a European translation because there is a lot lost in translation to English from East Asian languages. I was really adamant that our showrunner and the team understood that. Luckily, one of the actors who was cast is a friend of mine, so we could liaise. Then, it turned out that they hired two extraordinarily competent Chinese women to do the translations in the edit, and they also helped the director in takes. I was so heartened to hear that they had used pros. There are ways you can translate something and it loses something. It's a lot like what happened with *Squid Game*. Korean speakers were saying a lot was getting lost in translation. I don't think that is going to happen with this.

Q: Do you have any tips for writing sitcom dialogue?

Josh Greenberg - The main thing is realism. I think people tend to think that a sitcom is a heightened reality, so characters are going to speak like broad caricatures and it's not true. They can speak that way and it can work, but when something is truthful, it's funny. That has served me well on single-camera and multi-camera shows. The more grounded, the more truthful you are to the character, the funnier it will be.

Q: How do you approach dialogue so that each character sounds unique?

Eli Craig - Yeah, that's really key. Screenwriting is pretty sparse. You don't get a lot of time to say what's going on in somebody's head. That's a big difference between screenwriting and novel writing. You don't get inside anyone's head, ever. Sometimes, the only way an actor is going to understand a character is through their language. How do they speak? Do they speak with confidence? Are they demure? Do they downplay themselves? How do others speak to them? All of that will give a sense of character. Sometimes, you will read books and it doesn't matter that the dialogue is stilted. You can get inside the story and it reads just fine.

In a screenplay, the characters really come through the dialogue. It's essential that you find the voice, however you do that. With *Tucker and Dale*, I was watching *Dumb and Dumber* and *My Name is Earl*. He was Dale. Not the brightest, but a kind, loving guy. I also draw from friends that have a certain voice. Or through combined friends. This is kind of like my friend Scoot mixed with my friend Tom.

Jed Mercurio - I don't really try. That's quite hard to do. I'm sure there are some writers that are great at it, but I'm not. I tend to write characters that work in the same institutions, so they often talk the same. The individuality comes from their choices and their values rather than the way that they talk. Obviously, if you are creating a character that has some regional specificity or cognitive specificity that's reflected in the way that they talk, then, of course, that can be distinctive. But it's also a double-edged sword. You do run the risk of stereotyping by doing that. Sometimes, a really good screenplay can be undone by the feeling that the dialogue is stereotyping people from a certain demographic.

Emma Ko - Personally, I have a problem with sounding too much like me in my characters. I have to consciously write not like me. I read something by John Wells, who said that on *ER* they used to do all the drafts and when they got to the point when they thought it was ready to go into production, they would go through the script and take out all dialogue past the fourth line in a speech. Then, they would read it, and if it still made sense, they would leave it.

The other thing I've learned as a writer is to understand how much a really good actor will bring to your role that doesn't need to be expressed in words. I remember the first time I had a table read of my script. It was excruciating because of self-consciousness, but it was a CBBC show and the kids were already so good. They brought to life my dialogue and made it even funnier. I was gobsmacked! In everything, but especially in comedy, just one eyebrow lift can remove half a page. That is completely and utterly down to the performance. That's the collaborative effort of something. The perfect script in the right hands. If I have a philosophy of dialogue, it would be to keep it short. And if you are going to monologue, make that monologue amazing. Most people are not amazing monologuers.

Danny Strong - First and foremost, I try to give them unique voices. How does this character sound? How does this person talk? What is their rhythm? I don't try to show off in the dialogue. I want the dialogue to feel very real. But I have a voice as a writer and mostly that voice comes out in the dialogue. That voice comes out in the scene structure and things happening. It's a totality of storytelling. The goal with dialogue is that people shouldn't be noticing it. Don't belabor it. Sometimes, I will write a scene very quickly because I know what it's about. Then, I'm playing the scene as the actors and I'm writing it and I move on. I will come back to it and edit it, but it's not like each sentence is a masterpiece. There should be something bigger going on in the scene than the dialogue. The dialogue is in service of the conflict of the scene, not the scene is in service of the dialogue. Some people disagree with me and their work is about stylized dialogue or innate dialogue, where the dialogue is the star. I usually find that work very boring. I'm bored out of my mind. I don't know what's going on. I don't know what they are talking about.

Then, you have some shows that I've worked on as an actor where it's both. The dialogue is stylized and entertaining, but there's great conflict. I've been on *Gilmore Girls* and *Billions* and with those shows, that's why they've become massive successes. *Gilmore Girls* is legendary because it has incredible characters, conflict, and the dialogue is extremely entertaining. It's all humming together. My own dialogue is not as stylized as some of those pieces I've worked on.

Sometimes, it's not dialogue. It's just what they are doing - how they are behaving. What their actions are. Sometimes, how they speak defines the character and sometimes it's the type of person they are by what they are doing. It's multi-factored. Sometimes, it's what they are wearing that can define a character. I also try to not overthink smaller characters. If someone has a few lines, I usually won't give them a whole world of backstory. It gets in the way of the story. But if someone has a decent amount of screen time, I like to find a way to give them some significance that ties into the themes of the piece.

Josh Greenberg - I've always felt that when lines can be interchangeable between different characters on a sitcom, that's bad. That's a sign that you've done something wrong. I have seen sitcoms where characters just riff jokes, sometimes pop culture jokes, which are fine - they are really funny. But going back to a classic show like *Friends*, each of those characters was so specific in their worldview that everyone found something to relate to about them.

Julie Sherman Wolfe - On *Everybody Loves Raymond*, I think what made the show exceptional was that all the jokes came out of the character, more than the situation. If you can't look at a line of dialogue and tell whose it is without seeing their name, then, in my mind, you're not doing it right. You haven't drawn a complex enough character with a voice. When the show started hitting its stride in Year 2, you could see the audience laughing on show night before the actors even said their lines. The audience knew the characters so well, they almost knew what was coming. It can still be set up, set up, punch line, but when the punch line comes from character, it's a home run.

Marsha Greene - I don't think so much about distinguishing them in terms of the dialogue, I think about making sure that what I am writing feels very specific to the character. In *The Porter*, what Marlene would say and what Lucy would say should be wildly different. They are very different people. If it seems like something that someone else would say, that's when you have a problem.

When I worked on *Mary Kills People*, I started making a character report in Final Draft, so I could see all the lines of dialogue of that one character. It can help to see if you need to give them better lines. You can read it and see if it seems like them. Does what they are saying have personality and character? Because that is how you will get something to feel different, but still in the world of the show.

Q: Do the actors bring more to your screenplay?

Danny Strong - They bring everything. Whatever anti-actor sentiment there is in the arts or the industry is completely foolish. Actors make it all come to life. There's a stereotype that actors aren't really all that intelligent and that is the opposite of my experience. I find, for the most part, they are some of the smartest people in the process. I trust that. When we are shooting, it is all about them now. It is not about my script or my words. It's about their performance and making them comfortable. If they tweak things or they say things, I don't care. I just want them to be loose, in the moment, and really listening. Sometimes, it's a problem. Sometimes, they will have great ideas for changes. Sometimes, they will come up to me and say a line is sticky for them and my response will be, "Say whatever you want." It's almost always pretty great. It's from them and for the character in a way. In film, you can have big action sequences - things that are less performance-driven. But, in television, 85-90% of the show is actors talking. I want great actors - they can elevate it. They can find nuances to it. They can really take it to another level.

Josh Olson - Yes. Viggo Mortensen in *A History of Violence* is amazing, and I got to be there for a lot of that. The scene outside the house where you see him change back and forth between Joey and Tom. How are you doing this? The one who blew my mind was William Hurt because that character was so hard to do, and he's pivotal; he's essentially the villain. But it was impossible to do anything with him on the page that would make him jump out. I fretted more than David Cronenberg did because he knew what was coming. I was there the first day that Bill worked. It was the only day I felt any kind of despair because he seemed like he was in a different movie. I can't say anything. David seems happy. What the fuck am I going to say to David Cronenberg and William Hurt? The first time I saw the cut - meh. Then, I saw it with an audience and you feel it. Oh! He got that Viggo is entering a different movie when he gets to Philadelphia. To this day if I am ever doing a Q&A on *A History of Violence*, I always show William Hurt's scene because it's my favorite part of the movie.

DIALOGUE TIPS

- People rarely say exactly what is on their minds, so avoid on-the-nose dialogue by using subtext, metaphor, and euphemism.

- Exposition slows down a read. It can kill dramatic momentum. Use it if you have to get certain information out, but make it interesting and dynamic.

- People usually speak in short sentences using simple words. Keep it spare.

- Don't overuse exclamation marks. People rarely yell.

- Actions are worth a thousand words, so consider more showing and less telling. Or no dialogue at all.

- People often say the opposite of what they want or are doing.

- People are different. They should sound different, too.

- Eavesdrop on conversations in a cafe. Notice how real people speak.

- Dialogue tells you where your character is from (New York, London), their education level and social status (highly educated, working class), and their habits (pedantic, magnanimous).

Jed Mercurio - It varies. Generally, you are talking about quite small things if that happens and it's completely unpredictable. If it's a larger departure, then it has to be discussed. It may well seem right for the scene, but it may not be right for the episode or the series, as a whole. That's where the showrunner comes in because you can talk about the arc of the series and how something functions within that. What it usually boils down to in that discussion is what the intention is of the scene. So it may be that the execution needs to change or there's a better execution of it. You absolutely need to stick to the goal of the scene in terms of what the overall arc of the story is.

Marsha Greene - I have worked with some actors who stick exactly to what is written. They don't want to improvise. Other actors improvise more than maybe I want them to. On *Mary Kills People*, the actors told us that the dialogue was very natural, so it was easy for them to memorize and say it. They didn't have a lot of notes. Whereas, on *The Porter*, because you are dealing with period language, we would change it more to help it feel comfortable for people to speak. The actor should feel good. Sometimes, you can explain to them what you are going for and that will be enough and you don't change a word. Other times, you are tweaking it if they are struggling with it. I worked with Alfre Woodard on *The Porter*, and I think because she is such a wonderful and seasoned actor, she can put her own spin on it. But it's essentially what you wrote. She knows what you're going for. Great and seasoned actors know how to keep the essence of what's there and yet make the character feel real to them. That's what you want.

Michael Brandt - I love it when an actor has an idea about something. I have no problem being challenged by an actor about, "Why do I say this now?" Or "What if I say this instead?" I really want the best idea to win. The difficulty comes when an actor really digs their heels in on something, which you know as the writer, director, or creator, is the wrong move because of the reveal it's going to give or the tone it's going to set for something later. I want to understand where they're coming from and then find a way so they can make it their own. But I need to get what I need for the show. It's not what I want. It's what the show or movie needs.

Conversely, it can happen the other way where the actor can call you out on a bad story decision. In *Chicago PD,* for whatever reason, we had a flat episode. It may have been a combination of the script, the director, or sometimes, in the course of a twenty-two-episode season, you get one that's a bridge to a more action-packed episode. However, this one was going to be on air in a week and needed help. An idea was thrown out that a character should rough up this guy who is in a holding tank in order to instill some ass-kicking into the middle of this episode. I flew to Chicago to direct this reshoot and get this scene done. We rewrite it, prep it, and go to shoot it. The actor involved asked, "I'm not really sure why I'm roughing this guy up?" Now, I can't say, "Because the episode is lame and we just need you to do this." I had some bullshit answer and he seemed to believe it.

So we block the scene, it's all good, and we call the crew in. Now, there are a hundred people there. Everything seems fine until we get to the point where he's supposed to rough this guy up. The actor turns to me and yells, "This is bullshit!" He loses his temper, "Why am I doing this?!" The whole time he's yelling at me, all I'm thinking is, please keep yelling at me because the longer you yell at me, the more time I have to think of how to respond because I don't have an answer. The truthful answer is, "You're right. The episode is lame and I just need you to beat the shit out of this guy." But I can't say that. Finally, he stops yelling, and luckily I had thought up an answer that he half-bought, so he stalked off, and came back saying, "I'm an asshole." I said, "Yes, you are!" But he was right.

Ben Philippe - While writing *Interview with the Vampire*, we didn't as yet have a Louis or a LeStat, so their characters were very much in our heads. At some point, halfway through the room, we got our announcement of who was going to be our Louis. We knew he was going to be Black because it was an updated adaptation set in New Orleans. Once we got an actual person in the role, it felt like we were writing for that person. And Selena Gomez on *Only Murders*, was very good at dry, witty, and acerbic dialogue. Once we knew that, we could write to that. Oliver, Martin Short's character, I love, because we have a specific sound that he makes and in the script, it's written, "Znnt," and we just write that in because we know what it means. Once you are writing to those actors, it becomes a whole different experience.

Paul King - I remember for the first *Paddington* film trying to write this banter-y dialogue between Harry and Mary, played by Hugh Bonneville and Sally Hawkins, who are extraordinarily brilliant actors with enormous range. I said I felt it was important for there be conflict between them, and they really ran with that idea. But suddenly, the movie felt like a horrible divorce drama, that we were watching two characters who hate each other and should split up. I'd never done this before, but in the end I asked them to watch *Manhattan Murder Mystery,* the Woody Allen movie which has him and Diane Keaton playing this lovely couple who are always bickering but deep down clearly love each other to pieces.

And because Hugh and Sally are so fab, they latched onto this tone and by the time we got to filming, they were perfect. It was just about toning it all down, which isn't always the instinct in comedy.

Actors that good can make the same scene play in so many different ways. The same dialogue can seem like they love each other or hate each other, or for one reason or another they are getting under each other's skin. Pitching that right is their job and the director's job, of course, but it makes you realize that scripts are not bulletproof. They can go wrong in a million ways. It's like you are walking through a minefield and there are a million choices and you can probably only get two or three big ones wrong before the whole thing is irredeemably broken. It's sort of a miracle to me that any film is any good at all.

Q: Does having acting experience, help you write dialogue?

Danny Strong - I think my acting background is crucial in my journey as a writer. I've spent so many years as an actor playing scenes, being inside plays and TV shows, film scripts - reading and working on them. So when I am writing, particularly the scenes themselves, I'm very much writing them as an actor playing a scene. Less so, when I am structuring the script as a whole. The outline and the structure and the story - my background as an actor doesn't collide with that. But when I am actually writing scenes and doing character work, it couldn't be more helpful. It's sort of my secret weapon.

Dave Reynolds - For me, it did. I studied improvisation through the Second City training company in Chicago. Through those classes I ended up meeting some very creative people, one being Robert Smigel, and creating a stage show of sketches that ran successfully for almost two years. Once, we needed an understudy for one of our cast members and when she came in, she asked to study the scripts for her scenes. We all exchanges looks. That's when we realized that we all had the two-hour show in our heads because we originally wrote it through improv and honed over time.

For me, improv opened my mind to the most important thing for every writer, how to approach rewriting. You need to learn to LOVE rewriting. That's when your scriptwriting really begins. Steve Martin once said, "You don't write a screenplay. You rewrite a screenplay." Everyone knows you don't take your first draft and start shooting. You need to realize that your polished draft that everyone loves, the one you've been working on for years, for dozen of drafts is, in the studio's mind, the "first draft". The quicker a writer can accept this, the better. You have to be able to cut or change things you love. Defend these precious babies but be ready to lose them. Remember, if you want to make movies, TV shows, plays, even podcasts - you need to be open to changes. A lot of them.

Q: Does being a director affect your writing?

Barbara Stepansky - Not really. Directing means analyzing and that's a part of my brain I shut off when writing. I just want to put the best possible story on the page.

Paul King - As a writer/director, there is a danger that when you encounter a problem, you try to solve it by rewriting the script. It's hard to keep faith with the screenplay when the scene isn't working so you think I'll just change the words. Whereas, if you're directing somebody else's script, you'd probably be a bit more respectful and initially try to change the performance or the direction. Really, the director is the custodian of the tone and can influence things enormously, so it's important to remember that before rewriting every line at the first sign of trouble.

Eli Craig - It helps to know how an actor might view these things. I think writing good dialogue is part of the screenwriting process. Writing realistic dialogue as to how people really talk. I do put "um" and "uh" and all those little things in that sound like how people really talk. Sometimes, I've had a line of dialogue where someone says, "Uhhhhhhhhhh." That's the way people talk. They talk over each other. I think that helps actors. Of course, when you are shooting it, there's some improv and you are letting them get to the dialogue the way that they naturally do. What I've found is that improv gets them back to the dialogue that's back on the page. If they aren't sure about the dialogue, I will absolutely let them do their own line. Then, they usually go, "That was all right. Let's try it your way." And sometimes their way is better, but sometimes they say that my way was right. So I like to write as people speak to some degree. You don't want too much stuttering in there, however.

Q: How should writers indicate something like a stutter?

Briana Belser - Trust an actor to do their job. If I say the character stutters in the character breakdown, maybe I will remind the reader one time when the character first appears in the script, and then the actor should do their job. If it's interruptions, I'm going to write interruptions in. I might write one or two stutters in if it's not an impediment, like the manner of the character's being, but, rather the moment has created a loss or struggle for words. It's the same way I don't write a lot of camera direction - that's the director's job. I think for me as a writer, I need to put words on a page that creates a blueprint with the clearest vision. I need to make it as specific as I can so that people come in and add their talents. I know they are going to morph and change it continuously. I really don't have the right or the interest in doing someone else's job for them. I want to see what they bring.

Q: Can exposition be a common fault?

Danny Strong - If there isn't a way to get around it, then you're fine and the audience doesn't even think about it. It may even be interesting. They want the exposition. I don't think you can do it that much. I've seen huge movies where so much of the scene is the characters explaining the story to each other, as opposed to following the story. I think it can harm the piece, but sometimes you need it and you get away with it. In procedural dramas, cop shows, or law shows, there's usually a scene or two that kind of explains the case, and the audience is right there with them. They want to know what the case is. It's not as if exposition is a sin. I would just prefer the exposition to be hidden.

In the first forty-five minutes of *Marathon Man,* you don't know what's happening with your protagonist, which is a great dramatic technique. You are as confused as your protagonist. It's a great way to create suspense, tension, and mystery. Then there is one scene where Dustin Hoffman's character is in a car and he explains what's been going on for the last forty-five minutes. And you are like, whoa! So that's what's been going on! It's just pure exposition in this scene, but it lands like a thunderbolt to the audience in the best possible sense. When I was rewatching the movie, I couldn't believe how much of it rests on this scene working. What if it didn't work? What if it felt expository or corny? What would you do?

Q: What are your thoughts on first-person narration/voice-over?

Lauren Iungerich - I think VO is commonly used as a lazy narrative device. I used it in *Awkward* but I used it with intention - it was the inner voice of a character who was afraid to be her true self. The idea was the inner voice and outer voice would ultimate catch up to one another and the use of VO would be eradicated - but I left my show before I was able to do that.

Barbara Stepansky - I personally don't mind voice over as a device but I don't like it when it repeats what we see on-screen. As long as the voice-over adds something new to what we're already learning via visuals and dialogue and doesn't feel redundant, it can be very poetic and impactful.

CHAPTER REVIEW: DIALOGUE

- Acting out dialogue is a good way to gauge if it sounds authentic to the character in that situation.

- People very rarely say exactly what is on their minds. They usually speak around a topic using euphemism and metaphors.

- Sometimes what is not said speaks louder than shouting. A facial expression can say everything.

- In a scene, characters want something. The dialogue should express that either textually or subtextually.

- The old adage of coming into a scene as late and leaving as early as possible is a good way to think about dialogue.

- People usually speak in short sentences and use relatively small words. You can write monologues and use large words, but only when necessary.

- Dialogue should be in service of the scene, not the other way around.

- If lines of dialogue could be interchangeable between characters, then you haven't made it (or the character) specific enough.

- Actors can take your dialogue to places you didn't expect. They can also be a good barometer as to whether the dialogue is authentic.

- Acting, doing stand up comedy, or sketch comedy can give you some strong insights into what actors want from dialogue. Give it a go!

- Exposition is fine when you need to get some important information across to help orient the audience. Too much, and you will bore them.

CHAPTER 6

RULES?

Screenwriting is an art and there should be no rules, man! Is that true? Does that work the best? Or are there some rules, either imposed or self-imposed, which can help guide you through the process? Let's hear what our panel has to say.

Q: Are there any rules for the length of scenes?

Jed Mercurio - No, I think you have to make a virtue of those things. If you are pushing for a scene to be very long, then you need to justify its length. If you are writing in a way that feels very fast-paced and cut-y and you are going from one short scene to another, again, it's got to be justified. Sometimes, that can lead to incoherence. In a long scene, the danger is stagnation. The scene isn't developing, it's just staying at the same level. So I think you just need to apply those analytical tools to your writing and not necessarily worry about the length of any particular scene.

Scott Lobdell - Some years ago, I had a deal at Dimension Films and as I was working on my first draft, I sat down with Bob Weinstein. He told me that no scene should ever go longer than two pages. When people are talking, there should never be more than three lines of dialogue. Dimension certainly had its brand and they were really good at it. And if a character needed to talk more, I wouldn't think twice about putting as many words in their mouth to convey whatever they need to convey. But I do believe his two-page rule is very good. It's a little different with TV because you don't want to keep setting up new shots. With a movie, if I read someone's script and two people are talking about their relationship and it goes on for four pages - no one is interested in this. So if one of the characters gets annoyed and goes back into the living room, add a new slug line for the living room. Or perhaps there's a knock at the door and he has to step into the hallway - breaking that up into separate scenes helps. There's a really strong case for that two-page rule. If you go to YouTube and watch movie scenes like the scene in *Die Hard* where John McClane says "Yippee Ki Yay" or "Wrong answer, Hans," you see that scene is only two minutes long. Maybe two minutes, twenty seconds.

You know that famous scene in *Erin Brockovich,* where they are in the boardroom with the polluting power executives and they say they only have so much water? Then, Erin says that they brought in water, especially for them. Again, two minutes. When people will comment on my scripts, they often say that the pages really moved. And that's why it moved - because you don't spend ten minutes on things. Unless you're Tarantino, who can do anything he wants because he is a master.

Tony Jordan - I hate slide rule writing. I even hate it when people say how many pages it should be. I have to have that discipline because I have to fit into a sixty-minute slot. I understand it, but I still hate it. So don't tell me that a scene has to be a certain length. I don't care. I'm not interested. It can be twenty seconds or thirty minutes as far as I'm concerned. Sometimes, it's wrong to think of them as scenes. You have to think of the story as a whole. What does the story need? That's probably why I don't break it down into chunks before I write. So what does a script need at that moment? What does the story need? If it needs that big, powerful two-hander that goes on for seven minutes, so be it.

In the 1980s, there were three record producers, Stock, Aitken, and Waterman. They worked out the perfect formula on two levels. One, to get airplay time. So if a song is, I'm guessing here, two minutes and three seconds, it was the perfect length to fit in between the ads and the news; it's the perfect air time; you automatically get on the playlists. Two, the song itself had to have a certain number of breaks at certain times and if the name of the song was repeated so many times, it was a hit. It makes no difference who is singing it. They were called The Hit Factory. They had all these songs coming out exactly the same, no matter if they gave it to Rick Astley or Jason Donovan or Kylie Minogue. It didn't matter. It was the same, and song after song was a hit. You can teach that. And you can have a Robert McKee *Story* weekend. You can teach that style of writing.

But after The Hit Factory, a little guy came along from Zanzibar called Freddie Mercury and he wrote *Bohemian Rhapsody*. It was seven and a half minutes long. They were told no one would ever play it. It's got opera in it. It's got hard rock in it. It's a ballad. It's fucked up mental-ness. His record company threatened to drop him and he said he didn't care. It was the story that he wanted to tell. So I always ask people who say, how many scenes should it be? Who do you want to be as a writer? Do you want to be Kylie Minogue or do you want to be Freddie Mercury?

I know baby writers really love to hear that if you make scenes thirty-two seconds and if there are twenty-five of them and your script is fifty-four pages, you've hit it. But you are doing them a disservice. What you are suggesting is that as a creative person, as a writer, there's a secret and you know what it is. If you show it to them, then they can become Russell T. Davis (*Queer as Folk, Torchwood, Doctor Who*). That's not true. Russell T. Davis is a genius because Russell T. Davis writes whatever the fuck Russell T. Davis wants to write. I can tell you that he doesn't worry about how long his scenes are or how many pages it is. It's not even in his thinking. So you have to figure out what kind of writer you are. I do know that the ones that succeed are all trying to be Freddie Mercury. The ones that write a few episodes of something and then disappear are the ones who are trying to be Stock, Aitken, and Waterman.

Q: Are there any rules for the length of scenes in sitcoms?

Josh Greenberg - Generally, there's no hard limit to the length of a scene, but since each scene itself is a mini-play, that goes for film, too, where every scene has a beginning, a middle, and an end, then you can feel when you have started to overstay your welcome. There are very short scenes and there are scenes that will go on for a few pages. You rarely have a scene in a sitcom that is super long. That would get tiring. But all in all, it's flexible.

Q: Are there any rules when writing action lines?

Alex Litvak - Leaner or spaced out is always better. I believe that as a writer you only control the words on the page. What happens after you turn in the draft is completely not up to you. You need to both write your heart out in order to tell any given story and then immediately shut it off the moment it's off your plate, which are two polar opposites. You need to care so much to force the reader to care. If you don't and you're phoning it in, it comes across. So this needs to be your blood, sweat, and tears; your brainchild on that page. I always say, as a man I don't know what it's like to give birth, but I do know what it is like to give birth to 120 pages of paper filled with ideas and images. So you have to care and you have to force the reader to care and that is how you overcome the problem of people who just don't want to read. I know people who just read dialogue. They don't read the scripts.

There are some tricks like bolding some words or putting them into caps if it's important. But fundamentally, you need to care, and you have to make people care and then forget about it and move on. It's going to be damn torturous when you don't hear anything about it for weeks, or they call you and say they love it and now they want to hire another writer. Or we love it and now we want to totally change everything.

Briana Belser - I don't know of any real rules, but as to the actual mechanics on the page, I have found many writers do not read their scripts aloud and that can really underscore when some things are not working. When can't you say your own shit dialogue? When can't you say your own scene? Sometimes, you read it and you're like, "Uh uh. Nope." Reading aloud is one way to check work.

Eli Craig - I frown on writing comedy that doesn't play on the screen. Not in the action, but in the screen description. Sometimes, you will read a line of comedy that makes you laugh, but you aren't going to see it. I will say, occasionally, if it helps lend to your voice, and it's not frustrating, then you can use it.

Josh Greenberg - I like keeping action lines clean and simple. Sometimes, I can be a little more stylized with them. But that is more employed in a single-camera format. There's really not much room in a multi-cam for stylized action. It's more utilitarian, like 'Steve walks up to the bar and sits down.' But in a single cam, where there are so many weird, cool things happening, the action lines can almost be like an action film. You can have a lot of fun with it.

Scott Lobdell - When I was in college, we were being handed out papers we'd written in Russian Literature class. The professor came to my desk and put the paper down and he said, "Not a word wasted." What a nice thing to say. That has been my guiding principle for years. So when I come across something that is so brilliantly concise, like *Die Hard* or *Inherit the Wind* and *Singing in the Rain* - almost every line has meaning and is there for a reason.

Q: Are there any rules on writing action?

Josh Olson - You break it up into shots and beats. You don't say "shot," but every paragraph break is essentially a cut. It's such a frustrating thing to do, especially in an action movie because you have to make it really exciting because it's going to help you sell the thing. But you know for an absolute fact it's going to get changed. It always makes me crazy because we have to go through this dance. We're going to set you up with all the characters. We are going to give you all the beats. What matters in an action scene is that you care about the characters and you care about the context - you understand what is happening. You know what the consequences are. The fact that I have to sit there and figure out a stunt that is going to change the instant a stunt coordinator comes on, drives me crazy. Their entire job is to come up with a stunt that's way better than anything I can. I got to speak to Martin Campbell on our podcast and he said, "Yeah, I hate that. It's frustrating."

Do you know how they described that amazing parkour chase in *Casino Royale* in the script? *'What follows is the greatest parkour chase you've ever seen.'* I loved that! They say it's a collaborative art form and then you have to spend all this time coming up with something that's never going to be shot. What happens now? Well, probably a car chase and James Bond has to live. Two henchmen have to die, but the villain escapes. Go! That's all that matters. That's what I need to tell you as a writer. And stunt people don't give a shit! They're not going to read that. They will do their own thing. It's just to satisfy some antiquated notion of what a script ought to be.

It reminds me of a stint I had in the 90s of writing some Showtime/Cinemax soft-core porn/erotica. It would be: "Ding dong! I'm here with your pizza." Then you write *"sex goes here"* and then you go onto the next scene!

Jed Mercurio - If you go into an action sequence and the reader sees blocks of stage directions, they understand it's an action sequence. I do think you need to convey the physical reality happening so that the reader can picture it. You don't need to do any detail beyond that, unless by adding detail you create more jeopardy, tension, or suspense. Those are the qualities you are aiming for as a writer, not to do the job of other departments. You don't need to describe every single weapon or every single piece of clothing, whatever it is. There are departments that will do that and they will offer them up to the director and the director will choose what looks best and which is the most logical fit for the scene. But you do need to solve the basic problems of how a character gets from one place to another; how they negotiate physical challenges and so on.

Alex Litvak - You could give it all to the second unit guys - to the stunt coordinators, and they will have tons of their own ideas. Having worked with Chad Stahelski who did *John Wick*, he has a ton of them. But unless you are writing for a particular director, you kind of need to be your own stunt coordinator. Because if it's just, *"The hero and the villain converge and they have a furious fight. The hero wins."* Great. That's the scene. But do I care? No, because you haven't told me anything. Maybe because I'm such an action junkie, I do block it out in my head. I don't go move for move. I give you the cool moves. I don't need to tell you every punch, but if there's a punch where there's a fistfight and the villain holds up a table and the hero punches through the table, that's cool because it

SCREENWRITING PODCASTS, WEBSITES & BLOGS

If you want more discussion on the rules/philosophies of screenwriting, here are some recommended places you can check out.

Podcasts

Script Notes (John August, Craig Mazin)
The Screenwriting Life with Meg LeFauve and Lorien McKenna
The Q&A with Jeff Goldsmith
Bulletproof Screenwriting Podcast with Alex Ferrari
On the Page with Pilar Alessandra
The Movies That Made Me/Trailers From Hell (Josh Olson, Joe Dante)
Selling Your Screenplay Podcast by Ashley Scott Meyers

Blogs/Websites

Most of these entities have both blogs and websites, so we've put them together so as not to double up.

Bang2Write: bang2write.com
The Bitter Script Reader: thebitterscriptreader.blogspot.com
The Black List: blcklst.com
Deadline Hollywood: deadline.com
Final Draft: finaldraft.com
Go Into the Story: gointothestory.blcklst.com
Good in a Room: goodinaroom.com
Industrial Scripts: industrialscripts.com
Inktip: inktip.com
Internet Movie Script Database: imsdb.com
International Screenwriters' Association (ISA): networkisa.org
JohnAugust.net
Roadmap Writers: roadmapwriters.com
Reddit Screenwriting: reddit.com/r/Screenwriting
Save the Cat: savethecat.com
Screenwriting from Iowa: screenwritingfromiowa.wordpress.com
Script Angel: scriptangel.com
Script Magazine: scriptmag.com
Script Reader Pro: scriptreaderpro.com
Simply Scripts: simplyscripts.com
So Create: socreate.it/en
Stage 32: www.stage32.com
The Story Department: thestorydepartment.com
Studio Binder: studiobinder.com
Variety: variety.com

instantly gives you an image. The fist going through the table and the splinters flying. I want to put that in the movie.

Stunt coordinators always break it down in terms of moves. If there's a cool move you have in mind, give me that. Another word for it is 'gag'. They talk in terms of gags. A term that goes back to the olden days when they did pratfalls and things. But what's the action gag of the scene? Sell me that gag, rather than giving it to the stunt coordinator to come up with it. I don't need every single move for move, but I do need to know this is why this action set piece is going to be cool. So, personally, my answer is that I try not to overload the reader with details particularly knowing that execs hate reading, but at the same time I try to make it sparse and spread out, but give enough to a reader who does enjoy action to reward their attention.

Danny Strong - I'll write a pass of it in the script and when the director is staging it, putting it on its feet, it will become a whole new process. With a big film with big set pieces, it's not like they are reading the script and doing exactly what is written there. It becomes a huge process of visual effects and stunt people. Hopefully, the director is in charge of the whole thing and hopefully, the script is a template to help you through the sequences. At the end of the day, there's a lot of big decisions involved. A lot of expensive decisions.

Michael Brandt - I put it all down. I think you have to. I don't know why you wouldn't or how you couldn't. Your characters are doing the action, so it has to be written in there and it has to be specific. Now, if your action is two meteors colliding at the beginning of the movie and a piece of one meteor gets sent toward Earth, all I care about at the end of the action is the one piece heading toward Earth. How that visually comes together, I won't necessarily have figured out completely.

A good example of not having everything figured out but knowing what needs to be done for the characters, is the opening of *Wanted*. In the beginning, a woman meets a man. They are doing a business deal and she gets a bullet in the brain. Then we cut to a guy on a far rooftop who's pulled the trigger. The important thing is we get a little feeling of who these people, the woman and the assassin are and why they are important. The director, Timur Bekmambetov, brought to the scene that when a bullet flies through the air, it breaks off into three stages like a rocket. That wasn't in the script, and it wasn't important that the bullet had three stages - that was Timur's crazy, amazing, childlike, cool brain coming up with that. And that's what you want directors to bring; that's when it works best. The characters got serviced, the director brought in cool visuals, and when those are put together, it works as one.

Q: Are there any rules about writing camera directions into your script?

Eli Craig - I try not to, but as a writer/director, I do. It depends on where I am in the process. If it's the first draft of a script that I am not sure I'm directing, then I will try to keep it clean. As I move toward directing more and more, it's sometimes easier to say "CU on Hans grabbing the gun." Visually, you know it's a close-up shot of a guy's hand grabbing a gun.

If you are writing for someone else to direct, sometimes people don't want you to be that descriptive. At the same time, I really like minimalist scriptwriting. Not a ton of dialogue. Not a ton of scene description. It's not a novel. It's a script and scripts are sparse. Sometimes, the shortcuts of camera moves do help convey the visual of what we see.

Jennifer Raite - Personally, I don't mind it. I would rather someone be overly prescriptive in their directing on the page than not. I don't think a lot of people think that way, especially since we work in television so much. The writers are really the voices of the show. I remember we were meeting with a director on a pilot we were doing and she seemed to vibe and compliment us for that like, "I know exactly what you are looking for with how you wrote this opening sequence." Then she could jump into a lot of the specifics. I think it's great to bring your audience and your filmmaking team into what you want to do instead of having it be like, "I'm the director and I'm keeping all of this private and away from you." Why would you want to do that? You're just making it hard for everyone.

Michael Brandt - I don't put camera moves in. I let the director figure out how that's going to happen. I feel that's cumbersome reading and prevents you from moving on and going forward. I'm writing a movie, so I don't want the reader to be distracted. I want them to come away from a scene saying, "I can feel the way that would feel in a movie."

Dan Mazer - If I am writing a film that I am going to direct, I make sure there are far fewer night shoots! They are the worst. So I will turn INT. STUDIO - NIGHT into INT. STUDIO - DAY a lot, so that's the key thing... Ha!

No, when directing, it doesn't really change anything in terms of how you write stuff. Whether it's you or someone else directing, you want it to be the best and funniest that it can be. You are putting yourself out on the page. I never really write for somebody else. I think you have to write what you think is funny and assume that they have bought into your take, taste, and personality, as well.

Paul King - I pretty much want the script to work as a reading document. If there's something really important for the flow of the read, or to understand how the scene works, then yes, I put that in. But otherwise, I just want it to make sense and read well. I do try to imagine the scenes while I'm writing, but not get too bogged down in the details. I find it so hard to write that I simply don't have the brain space to figure out the direction at the same time.

Bryan Woods - When Scott Beck and I first started out, we would really lean on camera direction in our prose. It would very often be "Tracking with this person," or "Close up on this person," and that's just because writing and directing went hand in hand when we were kids. We grew up with the camera in our hands. The more and longer that we've done it, we've come to appreciate and respect the written document as a form of storytelling unto itself. Now, we almost never write camera directions into the script. We want the reader to get immersed in the story. There's nothing wrong with putting camera directions in a script. I have no problem with it. I wouldn't want to discourage people from doing it, but for us, any barrier to having a reader be immersed and be into the story is something we like to eliminate.

CHAPTER REVIEW: RULES?

- There are no rules on how long a scene should be, but develop a sense for when nothing is happening and it's time to move on.

- Keeping your action lines lean and sparse is a good practice, but that doesn't mean that you have to do it always.

- Reading your work out loud is a good rule or practice to do. Your writing sounds very different than it does on paper.

- If you find that your writing is doing the jobs of the other production departments, then you are probably overwriting. You don't need to describe every bit of weaponry, set dressing, wardrobe, make up, or visual effect unless it's pertinent to the story later.

- When writing action scenes, write in a few cool moves to give the reader a sense of the pace and tension, even if it all changes once the stunt department get their hands on it.

- Directing on the page is something you should be doing to help bring your script to life, but try to do this without camera movements.

CHAPTER 7

FINDING YOUR VOICE

Producers, agents, and managers often talk about finding a writer with a unique "voice." But what does that mean and is it really important? If so, how did our panelists go about developing theirs? Can you have more than one voice?

Q: Is it important to have a voice as a screenwriter?

Tony Jordan - It's the only thing you have, and what new writers should do is protect their own voice. It's the only thing that makes us unique. No one else has my voice as a writer. There are better writers, different writers, and a whole world full of writers, but I've got my own voice. When we think about writers like Russell T. Davies, he has a very distinctive voice. Same with Jimmy McGovern. Sarah Phelps. Andrew Davis. Amazing writers. Jed Mercurio. If you've seen something on the telly where there's a hook in three seconds, and something that blows up, it's Jed's voice. It's what he does. It's the way he tells stories. We all have our own unique voices.

When I left *EastEnders*, I didn't really watch it in the way that I was writing it. It was always on when I was cooking the evening meal. I'd hear the scene between two people, and I would know it was Sarah Phelps who wrote it. She's mad as a bag of frogs and brilliant. No one else can write that. Then I would hear a clap of thunder and it would be dark and members of the same family were sleeping with each other. I would know it was Simon Ashdown. Then you would have something really random and weird and that would be Jeff Povey. Then you get something really warm and, oh, James Payne has written that.

You have these voices, and it's the only thing you have that makes you unique. It's the only thing that commissioners want. That's the other reason why this quantification, if that's a word, is a bad thing. It has to be five acts or seven acts. Scenes can't be longer than this. If you take on that, everyone's voice gets taken and we all sound the same. In a world where everyone sounds the same, nobody excels. No genius can grow. You have to hold onto your unique voice and not let the industry or the machine take it away from you.

Deborah Haywood - Yes, it's important. I don't really know what that voice is, but I think it's when you are being as really honest as possible. We tell so many lies and cover ourselves as much as possible. I think if you can let yourself out, then people spot that and that's what makes it compelling to read or watch. Whatever that nugget is. It's like writing when nobody's watching. Or writing as if nobody is ever going to read it. Like a diary, or something. Try to get your thoughts on the screen because that is gold dust. We're all our own gold mines, and if we can get ourselves out, then people can smell that reality. All of our subconsciouses know that we are all full of bullshit, so it's trying to cut through our ego to get to the real stuff.

Bill Nicholson - I think you have your own voice whether you want it or not. You just do, so I don't think you should worry about that. It's kind of odd because the stuff that isn't dialogue is normally written in a very terse way. Nobody is going to thank you for writing it like Virginia Woolf. As for the dialogue, you are trying to ventriloquize your characters. So I think your take on life, or, your voice, comes with every decision you take within your script. Do what your instincts tell you is good and right, and it will be you.

Carolina Rivera - I feel like I am a bunch of people. Throughout life, you go through so many stages, so I've had a bunch of different voices. I like comedy and I think I have a filter in life to see humor. I can't help it. I guess that's just a shade of the voice, not the voice. The voice changes. Sometimes, you want to write about different stuff, maybe at a slower pace. Sometimes, you are in a phase that's really fast and that's how you write. There's not one voice for me. I've been able to write other people's shows and that's not my voice. Of course, in a writers room you express yourself when you give ideas, which come from your experience. I'm not the same person that I was thirty years ago. I'm experiencing being a grandmother for the first time, and that gives me a bunch of information about myself. I'm learning all the time.

Jed Mercurio - I think that having a voice is a concept that relates maybe to the kinds of subjects that you're interested in; maybe to your own personal values or personal politics. I think there are plenty of writers who write within that kind of context; where they are telling stories that are fundamentally about the same values - either those values being promoted or challenged. I think that can be incredibly useful. It's important that those values are widely shared. If they're niche, then it means that your writing may not connect with many people and may be alienating people.

Eli Craig - I think that's why I'm hired. It's for that voice. The most well-known screenwriters absolutely have a voice. There are the structuralists that can screenwrite, and there is an army of writers that are doing that. I haven't done that. But there are a lot of people who can write in other people's voices. Great! Fantastic! For me, having my own voice is essential.

Marsha Greene - It's very important to have a voice as a screenwriter, particularly when you are trying to sell a show or even when you are trying to be staffed. When I read a script, I look for "the personality." I look for "I would never have thought of that." I am drawn to things that are outside of what I would consider to be my own skillset. I don't want someone who can do what I can do.

My only caution is that when you are staffed on a show, your job is to write in someone else's voice, so you need to have that skill, too. It's what's good about writing specs; a spec script in television is writing a script for an existing show. It used to be very popular and people would read them because that's how you know that someone can do the job. I wrote a *Modern Family* spec many years ago and people can read it and see that I understand the show. It's partially the voices, and it's partially what the show is. You need to understand the mentality of that show; what kind of stories do they do.

Specs like that used to be popular and I think, at least in Canada, people don't really write them anymore. Now, they focus more on originals. Originals are important in terms of

SCREENWRITING COURSES

If you're someone who likes to learn via instruction, there are many programs and labs that you can apply to outside of a traditional university or college format. Some are easier to get into than others and some service certain demographics. It could be a great way to get a different perspective on your writing and meet some like-minded people.

Accelerate Fellowship (disabled screenwriters)
BBC Writer's Access Group (UK, Ireland, disabled, deaf, neurodivergent)
BBC Writers Room (UK, Ireland)
BFI Flate x BAFTA Mentoring
CBS Writers Mentoring Program
The Black List Programs (various categories)
Cartoon Network Mexico Children's Animation Writing Program
Channel 4 Screenwriting Course (UK, Ireland)
CineStory Feature Retreat and Fellowship
Circle of Confusion Writers Discovery Fellowship
Digital Storytellers Lab
Disney | ABC Mentoring Program
Feature Film Screenwriting Lab (India)
Film Independent Amplifer Fellowship
Film Independent Screenwriting Lab
Hedgebrook Screenwriting Residency
MasterClass
Michener Center for Writers MFA Program
The Minority Report
NBC TV Writers Program
Native American TV Writers Lab
Netflix/Sky Screenwriting Fellowship
Nickelodeon Writing Program
Norman Jewison Film Program Writer's Lab (Canada)
On The Page Writing Classes/Pilar Alessandra
Outfest Screenwriting Lab
Roadmap Writers Diversity Initiative
Sesame Street Writers' Room (childrens TV, underrepresented racial groups)
Stowe Story Labs Fellowship
Sundance Screenwriters Lab & Intensive Lab
Television Academy Foundation Summer Internships
The Thousand Miles Project (Asian & Pacific Islander stories)
QALAMBAAZ (Pakistan)
SFFILM Rainin Grant
UCLA Writers Extension
Universal Writers Lab
WeScreenplay Diverse Voices Lab
Warner Bros. Discovery Access Writers Program
Women Write Now
The Writers Lab (Europe oriented)
Young Films Foundation

getting representation or being staffed. When you are doing your own work, you write in your own voice. It's tone. It's taste. It's style. It's formatting. When you go on a show, it's more like you are bringing your POV rather than your voice. I'm not writing it in my voice, I am writing it in their voice. But I am bringing what I like about stories to it and putting it in the house of what that show is.

Ron Leshem - You know what the executives are going to tell you. They are looking for a voice that is A, B, and C. If you have A, B, and C in that voice, you know you are going to get a green light for development. But your biggest fear is that you are going to disappear among 500 shows. On the other hand, if you have a very unique idea or voice, you are going to struggle hard to prove that it will work. In your head, you say that it does have the truth. It's relatable. I know everyone is telling me my formula doesn't work, but I can prove that it does work. It happens to every successful show. It happened to *Breaking Bad*. *Stranger Things* got a pass from all twenty buyers that they went to and they all said the same thing - you can't do a show from the point of view of the kids. You have to make this about the FBI. So everyone said "no" to it. Eventually, Netflix did say "yes," and it turned out to be the most-watched show ever because it was different.

Meg LeFauve - I think it's essential to have a voice. You can have craft. I'm not going to say there aren't people who have made a career from just the craft because it's a hard craft. Trust me. That alone could take so many years to learn. But to be elevated out of the pack of people learning the craft, the voice is your personal, emotional, vulnerable, insightful view. If you are asking your protagonist to be brave, the first person who has to be brave is the writer. They are willing to go and talk about, through metaphor, this complex idea. It could be just a question they have. Why do people do whatever? The voice can also come from how you write it on the page, which can develop as you write more and more and more. That's just something organically coming up. I think it's also about the questions you're asking in your story. I love my characters so much that my voice comes through them.

Lauren lungerich - I think there are writers that can adapt to voices and then there are writers who have voices that are so strong that they come through all their work. Those are the voices that usually cannot adapt to someone else's voice. I have a career because I have a definitive voice. You can see it in everything I've done. You can hear me and you can read it in everything I've ever written. I don't know if that is the only thing that equates to a career, but for me, it's given me a career. I have a lot of friends who are successful and they don't have a definitive voice. So I don't think it defines success to have a voice but I think it sets a writer apart from others in a great way.

Paul King - In the *Paddington* movies, I was aware I was treading in Michael Bond's footsteps, so it was more about finding yourself within his world. Sort of like a marriage. I was aware that if I made it too me, it would break. There's a Venn diagram where you find that middle bit where it's a bit of me and a bit of you and you need to be in that sweet spot. If there's no crossover, you are probably the wrong person for the job.

Danny Strong - I think if you don't have a voice, maybe you have the wrong job.

CHAPTER REVIEW: FINDING YOUR VOICE

- Your voice is unique to you. It's your main selling point.

- Being honest and letting yourself out is a good way to find your voice.

- Don't force a voice that doesn't fit you authentically.

- Write as if no one is watching.

- Sometimes, your voice can change as you grow older and have different perspectives on life.

- If you are hired to write on a TV series, you will be writing in the voice of the creator or showrunner in order for it to be consistent. What you say and the words you choose, though, allows some of your voice through.

- Sometimes, your voice might stand out from the crowd and people will take notice. However, be prepared to perservere if it takes a while for your voice to find the right collaborators.

CHAPTER 8

SCREENWRITING COMPETITIONS

———

How do you break into the screenwriting trade when you don't know anyone and live far away from Los Angeles, New York, London, Mexico City, Toronto, or some other media center? One possible route involves entering screenwriting competitions. Doing well in one could get you some exposure. Or will it? In this chapter, hear about the pros and cons of them from two people who found success in two of the larger ones in the USA, as well as a prominent UK competition for emerging writers. There's also some discussion on screenwriting classes which may help your entries.

Q: Are screenplay competitions worth it?

Barbara Stepansky - Yes, the Nicholl Fellowship really changed my life. The Academy Nicholl Fellowships in Screenwriting is an international competition that's well known by aspiring screenwriters. They consistently get thousands of submissions a year. If you win, you get paid to write a screenplay for a year. It's a wonderful competition and they cultivate that feeling of family. I've been applying to the Nicholl for at least a decade. January comes along and you start to prep your application and screenplay because the final deadline is in May. You have to get into the top 25% to get into the quarterfinals. And then you have to land in the top 10% to be in the semifinals. And then they really whittle it down from 100 people to ten for the finals, which is a big jump.

I had sent in *Sugar In My Veins*, the script that would eventually win the Nicholl, at an earlier point. It did get into the quarterfinals but in a very different iteration. After that, I took a break from writing for a few years as I went to the AFI to study Directing. After that, I took a UCLA class that was run by Billy Mernit, who wrote the book, *Writing the Romantic Comedy*. He's a really great instructor. It was a year-long course where you were accountable for pages every two weeks. I pitched *Sugar in My Veins*, and I wrote a version which was very different from the one I had submitted before. By the end of the course, I kept the names of the characters and pretty much had chucked out everything else.

I worked my ass off for that screenplay and I finally got to a place where I felt that I had channeled something rather than written it. People read it and liked it so I sent that version of *Sugar* around for people to consider me for work, as I didn't have representation back then. Nobody read it. When the Nicholl said I made it to the quarterfinals, I sent out another slew of emails. And still, nobody was interested. I made it to the semifinals, but by then I had given up emailing anyone. Then, I got the call from Nicholl saying I was to be a finalist. I was speechless because my script was a coming-of-age drama, which are both really bad words in Hollywood! I then got everything I wanted from being a finalist. I got my manager. I already had a lawyer who was dealing with my contracts for a year before, so I was happy to keep him. Then I got my agents about a month after winning.

Ben Philippe - Having won the BlueCat Screenplay Contest, I guess I am a little biased, but I do think that it's very much worth it. It gives you validation, which is the first obstacle to making a career out of screenwriting. There are many, many doors that get shut in your face. I know so many talented writers who went to the same MFA program that I did, or were as good as I was or even better, and they eventually got tired and gave up. They

SCREENWRITING COMPETITIONS

Some people hail them as a great way to break into the industry, especially when you don't know anyone. Others decry them as rip-off schemes that prey on the hopes and dreams of screenwriters. As usual, the truth is somewhere in the middle. The larger ones have sizable cash prizes, which is always helpful. More importantly, they offer exposure to producers and representation as part of the prize package, which is how a career is built. Smaller or more specialized contests mean a better chance of winning and/or being read by those that really care about your topic or genre.

On the other hand, competitions of all levels cost money to enter, which can add up quickly if you go for a wide range of them. And there is a lot of competition. Some of the smaller ones may promise things they can't deliver or may be too niche to get you any notice. There's also one undeniable fact - **there must be a winner.** That doesn't necessarily mean the winning script is amazing. It means that it's the best of what was entered.

Here's a short list of some of the larger ones from around the world. A Google search will yield dozens more. Or you can use **Coverfly (www.coverfly.com)**, a service that allows you to submit to multiple competitions all at once via their platform. Make sure to read all their terms and conditions to find out if you're eligible, what information they require, and what format they want your submission in. Keep your eyes open for early submission deadlines to save money.

Academy Nicholl Fellowship
Atlanta Film Festival Screenplay Competition
Austin Film Festival Screenplay Competition
Big Break Screenwriting Contest
BlueCat Screenplay Competition
Final Draft Big Break
Nickelodeon Writing Program
Page International Screenwriting Awards
Page Turner Awards
Raindance Script Competition
Roadmap Writers Shorts Competition
Screencraft Competitions
Script Pipeline
Scriptapalooza Screenplay Competition
Shore Scripts Short Film Fund/TV Pilots
Slamdance Screenplay Competition
Titan Awards

picked something that was not lucrative, but more immediately rewarding. I think those competitions are very useful in setting clear guidelines in the world. They are goalposts that you can hit. And they keep you writing. You are never going to get your first few scripts made. Contests are a great way of finding a life for them. They are really important in fostering new talent.

I had written four pilot screenplays that I thought were complete when I hit "The End." The one that I sent to BlueCat became my ongoing sample when I was trying to get staffed or representation. That was the one I was most proud of. Every writer thinks they are good enough to keep writing, but the more you write, you realize which ones are special. This one had something that I wanted other people to read. That was one of the appeals of BlueCat because they gave you feedback. So even if I didn't win, I was going to have an objective person, who is not my friend, read the screenplay and give me 250 words of objective feedback which is incredibly useful.

I used to read submitted screenplays for the Austin Film Festival when I was doing my MFA in Texas and I would have to give them a grade. They liked to have two people read every screenplay and they got thousands and thousands of entries. I would read people's pilots and one of the metrics for judging them was: Does this stand on its own? I also taught screenwriting at the beginning part of my career and that was something that I tried to impart to students. You only have those sixty pages, at most. In most cases, you have ten pages, so state your goal early. Many times when we watch TV you say, "It doesn't really get good until Episode 7." You can't really do that as a writer and I think it's one of the hardest things to learn.

When I found out I was in the final five of BlueCat, it was very thrilling. It was sort of a countdown that never went away. I did not get representation right away. BlueCat is sort of good about sending your information out to people and they get emails from people wanting to know who the winners of each cycle are. Representation didn't come through BlueCat but the BlueCat win is a medal that never goes away. When I am emailing CAA agents or others to get representation I would say, "This is my sample. It won the BlueCat." That definitely caught a few eyes. It made people take me more seriously as a writer and it gave me a level of confidence about the script.

I got representation because I had written some YA novels and an executive wanted to see if the rights were available, which they weren't because I was very young and broke and had signed away all the rights. But it just so happens that his partner came to join us for the meeting and he was an agent at CAA. I asked him if he was looking for clients. He said sure and I sent him my BlueCat sample. He read it on the plane back to Los Angeles and emailed me and signed me. It was a very serendipitous encounter.

There's no contract signed when you sign with a legitimate agency. From the outside, I always thought I would get an envelope via FedEx and you will sign a bunch of papers. No. It's just someone saying, "I'm, your agent now." That's it. Then you get emails from their assistant setting up general meetings for you for staffing opportunities. That all came from the script I had with BlueCat.

I live in New York City and it was pre-COVID. My agent told me to come to Los Angeles, as people wanted to meet me. Zoom was not a word yet. I went out and the first general meeting I had was with Jess Rosenthal, a producer on *This Is Us* on NBC. General meetings are very strange as they are somewhere between interviews and first dates. You can get very excited. I had a general meeting at Bad Robot (JJ Abrams' company). I had a general at Disney. You meet them. You talk. It's lovely. You leave and that's it. In my meeting with Jess, he said that they had just staffed a room for season three of *This Is Us*, so they didn't have anything, but he would keep me in mind. I wasn't disappointed; that's how things go. I didn't think I would hear from him again.

One year later, right before I went into a movie at AMC, I got an email that said Steve Martin was developing a pilot and they were looking for New York-based writers and Jess Rosenthal had recommended me. I met with John Hoffman, our showrunner. Then I met with Steve Martin. By that point, things were happening on Zoom. So I'm on my computer and all of a sudden, Steve Martin appears! That was my first staff writer gig.

Tony Jordan - The Red Planet Prize has never really been about a winner. For us, it's about finding new voices and giving new writers an opportunity. So we try to take the top ten to fifteen writers, and when I say top, I mean those that got to the very final round. And rather than just pick one of those - they're all brilliant otherwise they wouldn't have come through 3,000 scripts - we try to mentor those writers. We bring them in; we try to help them. Do whatever we can. Robert Thorogood didn't win the competition, but during the mentoring process he came up with the concept of a Caribbean cop. Then we helped him develop it over that mentoring scheme and it became *Death in Paradise*. That's the apex of the competition. That's what it was set up to achieve. That was huge. We've had smaller successes where writers have gone on to earn money through Red Planet episodically, or they've gone on to other companies and they are doing their thing. It's tough to do every year, so we do it every eighteen months or so.

THE BLACK LIST

This website platform asks a multitude of film executives and high-level assistants to state their "most liked" non-produced spec scripts they read that year. The results are tabulated and those with the most mentions end up at the top of The Black List. The list is circulated throughout the industry and frequently great scripts that were overlooked get a second chance for exposure.

Scripts that made The Black List include *Whiplash, Juno, Don't Worry Darling, Argo, The Unbearable Weight of Massive Talent, The King's Speech,* and *Free Guy* just to name a few.

Over the years, The Black List has grown to offer other services for screenwriters. For a fee, writers can post their work on the platform and get professional feedback plus a score. If it rates high enough or the logline sounds interesting, producers and representatives can contact the writer directly and solicit the work. It's a possible avenue to get exposure, especially if you live far away from a media center.

In addition, there are several feature film and television writing lab and residency programs you can apply to for both feature film and television writing to help improve your craft. There are many other educational resources as well.

https://blcklst.com/

Q: Are screenwriting classes helpful?

Moisés Zamora - They were essential for me because I was terrified of the format. I was terrified of the network of Hollywood, and I just didn't want to leave it to chance. I had tried to get some books that help teach you how to write, but I wanted some professionals to tell me, "This is right and this is not right." I came across a teacher that was so picky about format. He wanted the script to really look professional. The kind of caps that you use. Don't novelize, which is where you put in the action, the thoughts that you would never see on screen. He was very purist that way, but it was compelling because it put me in a different mindset. I was a novelist! So everything is all flowery. But nobody can see that. So what is this? It's flavor and tone - no, no, no! Quickly, the first thing I did was figure out how to master the format. There's a wonderful book called *The Hollywood Standard*, which is about formatting for screenwriters. I carried it with me everywhere. Final Draft has a lot of stuff to teach you on how to format, too.

The classes were also important because the class environment, more or less, mimics the writers room for television. Something people forget is that these people taking classes with you, essentially, are going to be your peers at some point, maybe, in a writers room. I remember one classmate of mine, we hit it off and she's done really well as an indie film producer. Now, she's hustled a TV show, slated to be a co-showrunner. You never know who you are going to meet again down the road, so you better behave and act professionally because people remember the crazy things you say or if you were not a very kind person in the class. UCLA was essential for that. It allowed me to gain confidence. I know how to do the format. I know how to develop characters for the screen.

Also, they have guest speakers. Lee Jessup was very vital in helping me decipher Hollywood. She is someone who helps junior scriptwriters, and she was instrumental in helping me break into television. She recommended a different set of workshops that I swear by, called Script Anatomy. They focus very much on the TV structure of the half hour and the hour. They are just wonderful. They are a foundational course that a screenwriter should take if they don't want to go to a film school or something like that. It's very valuable and a hell of a lot cheaper. Film schools, I feel, give you the entire experience - the theory, all that other stuff. But these ones get to the nitty-gritty of how to structure a pilot or a spec if you are applying to the writing fellowship programs. So out of these second round of workshops, the pilot I had started developing at UCLA and finished and revised at Script Anatomy was the pilot that changed my life. It got me my manager and it got me my first job. And my second job. And my third job. One pilot.

CHAPTER REVIEW: SCREENWRITING COMPETITIONS

- Screenwriting competitions are one way to get exposure to industry professionals. But that only happens if you are a finalist. And usually a finalist in one of the larger competitions.

- Screenwriting competitions aren't too expensive to enter individually, but it can add up if you want to enter many.

- Look for competitions that offer quality prizes. Exposure and meetings with industry insiders are often more important than money or a new laptop.

- Screenwriting competitions are always looking for people to read submisions. It's a great way to learn what stands out from the crowd.

- Screenwriting classes are helpful because they make you write, which is really the only way to get better.

- Screenwriting classes provide a room full of people who can read your work, and you, theirs.

- Screenwriting classes will give instruction or refresh your memory about screenwriting basics like formatting and structure.

- You'll never know who you'll meet in a screenwriting course. The person sitting next to you could become your writing partner or the showrunner who hires you down the road.

CHAPTER 9

WRITING TEAMS

Some say that two brains are better than one, and having an extra set of eyes when writing can be helpful. However, that means two personalities who can be at odds with one another creatively. How do our writing team panelists navigate their relationships? How does the work get split? And how does the industry view them?

For clarification, the writing teams that follow are:

Scott Beck & Bryan Woods
Chris Cullari & Jennifer Raite
Hilary Galanoy & Elizabeth Hackett

Q: How do you work as a writing team?

Elizabeth Hackett - We come up with a premise first that we both like and then just sit in a room, sometimes with a glass of wine, and just start talking about it. Who else would be in the story? What do we think happens?

Hilary Galanoy - We break story together, back and forth, and, then one of us goes home and writes a page of notes. Then we usually have a second session where we talk about that page of notes. It starts to form into a couple of paragraphs - a beginning, a middle, and an end - and who these characters are. Liz and I usually don't work in the same room and that was true pre-pandemic. We almost always work over email and chat. Then we go back and forth adding more to the story until we get a two to three page narrative. If we're doing this for someone else, at this point we would show our producer and get some notes. If we're going to do a formal pitch at the studio, we could just pitch those three pages to Netflix, but otherwise, we would build it out to four or five pages and that would be a 20 minute pitch. That would be the beginning, middle, end, the characters, and some funny bits that happen. If they buy it, we go into a deep, full outline.

If we were to write on spec, we would do that whole same process but start outlining from the three-pager. We write out every single scene of the movie in order as bullet points and sometimes put in dialogue. Normally, we don't do index cards, but recently we did use them because we were having a really hard time moving around a bunch of different scenes and the cards really helped. I had such fun with them that now I'm thinking maybe we should use the cards more often. Our outlines are usually very detailed - around fifteen pages or so. Sometimes, we break out the outline and each write a portion, but more likely we will do it round-robin style. One of us starts and writes the first twenty pages and sends it to the other who rewrites those twenty pages and writes fifteen pages more. And so on.

Elizabeth Hackett - It's a really detailed road map, so you don't get off track. And even if things change, you still have that map or compass.

Chris Cullari - The bulk of Jen's and my work together is cracking the story. We will sit and create a detailed outline of every scene. Once we have that, we will split off and take chunks of the script, sometimes based on "I like this character more," or "I want to write the action scenes." It depends on what's most appealing to us in the script. We then write those pieces and put them all back together. Then, we read the script and give ourselves notes. Sometimes, we address those notes together and sometimes we go off and address them separately depending on how big they are.

Jennifer Raite - We do that until the last rounds of fine-tuning when we'll end up in the same space together. When we first started, we tried to do it together at the same time and that's crazy. Some people write that way, but that wasn't for us.

Chris Cullari - When we are together, it feels fun like we're playing ping pong. It's going back and forth. But when you sit and write together, there are just long pauses where you're both just staring off or thinking, and it interrupts the flow of that. We never discuss it. It's just when the fun ping pong stops and the really hard thinking starts, it's better to be separate so that we're not just staring at each other.

Bryan Woods - Scott and I learned early on we should never write in the same room together. We would just be laughing and making jokes; not getting any work done. A lot of our writing process over the years has become conversation and discussion and really talking to each other and rolling ideas over in our minds. We have Google Documents that we share with each other where we place ideas.

When we get into writing the actual script, it's different on every project. On *A Quiet Place*, one would write ten to fifteen pages and then we would hand it off to the other person. They would react to the work that had been done; rewrite and revise it; pitch some ideas as to where it could go and then take a stab at the writing process. Very often with us, it's the process of handing over work, reacting to it, and being each other's audience. Fresh eyes. We like to go from page 1 to 120 in order, but we skip over scenes sometimes that are difficult to write or are less fun. More than anything, our process has become a series of whatever is the most fun, that is the best place to go. If something is interesting or exciting we follow that. Follow the fun.

Q: When you read each other's drafts, do you do a pass of notes on each other and then in person battle it out?

Jennifer Raite - It's kind of a mix. We use this software called Writer Duet that's great for teams because there's a real-time function like Google Docs where you can see people changing things as you're going. So sometimes, we will just tweak stuff and we'll have a record. So if I change a line and Chris hates it, he can click this little "back" button and we can fight about who is going to say what there. Sometimes, we'll change things. Sometimes, we'll make notes and talk about it. It will also depend if we are on a deadline or not. But usually, when it's that first big bulk, we go from no pages, to we've written half the movie.

Chris Cullari - It's project to project. If we are getting a lot of notes from executives, we're less likely to give each other a lot of notes on scenes and pages because we're already wrestling with all the notes from the execs. It's sort of ongoing, as we're reading each other's stuff, commenting on ideas. I think part of the reason we like to do that big detailed outline is so we get a lot of, "Is it this or is it that? Does this character arc work or does that character arc work?" We get that done before we go off so when we come back there's not so much, "Oh, I thought the scene was going to be this way."

Jennifer Raite - We love the detailed outline because it puts so much of the brunt of the work into the outline, but I think we both find it very liberating for the script because then we are just executing the outline. Sure, you are adding things and bringing it to life, but there isn't the pressure to figure out the movie on the page. Let's get this first draft done, and then we'll say what's working and what's not. Writing the first draft almost feels like a reward for having broken a very detailed outline.

Scott Beck - We will be on the phone or on Skype and then use Google Docs. It's massively helpful because we can be on the phone and edit the document in real-time. We live in different places, now. Bryan is primarily in L.A. and I am primarily in Iowa. I used to live in L.A., but it was funny, we lived eighteen miles apart, but with L.A. traffic we were doing this digitally anyway. So we're pretty flexible with the process.

Q: Do you have your own strengths writing-wise?

Jennifer Raite - We do and sometimes that will vary on different projects. I think sometimes one of us will really home into a voice in a character, and we realize that person will write that character really well. Generally, as much as it pains me to say it, I think Chris is funnier than I am. Sometimes, that's very helpful, and it always makes me enjoy reading his pages. I think I'm a little more sensitive to character. I think Chris' brain is always going "What's the structure of this?" So we're always trying to find a balance there.

Chris Cullari - I am more plot-oriented. I get bored really easily, so a lot of times I will be very cognizant, saying "It's been two pages, now what? Something better happen." Dialogue is a strength. Jen has a character strength. Plot and tone are kind of a back-and-forth between us where I think we have our strengths in that world. I have strength at pushing the plot forward and Jen is very good at being able to edit plot. She can say, "This is too much. We're losing what we're trying to say or losing the character's journey. He's going from here to here to here and we only need one of these things. You don't need three." It's definitely a plot strength, even if it's not…here are a million ideas. Being able to see through the million ideas to see the one is also a plot strength.

Jennifer Raite - This happens on the page, too. Chris tends to overwrite and I tend to underwrite, so there will be a balance of that. So if Chris sends me ten pages, if I were to edit it, it would go back to eight.

Chris Cullari - That's true and if she sends me ten, it will turn into thirteen.

SCREENWRITING SOFTWARE

If we can borrow from Michael Crichton and David Koepp...you *can* write your screenplay in Microsoft Word, Apple Pages, or via some plain text program. That doesn't mean you *should*. Yes, your ideas are what rule the day and a good story is a good story. But properly formatting it with screenplay software makes it easier to read and more professional looking. The odds are already stacked against you, so don't give a reader an easy out of having a poorly formatted screenplay as the reason they reject you.

Below are some of the more common programs. They are all fine to use for writing screenplays and most have useful functions such as making production drafts, reading your screenplay out loud, searching for scenes with the same character in it, collaborating with others, adding pictures, writing alts, and so much more. Try them all and see which one you like best. They often have discounts for students or organizations.

Final Draft
Celtx
Writers Duet
Highland
Movie Magic Screenwriter
Arc Studio Pro

Hilary Galanoy - Liz and I can both do everything, which is nice, but the way we put it is this: I like to build the house and Liz loves to decorate it. I love the challenge of the structure and Liz loves all the little details. The last step of our writing process is that we always do the last draft together to make sure we have all the really fun jokes and the best dialogue. We were doing that yesterday using Final Draft's Collaborate function for six hours. I would have given up, but Liz is so good at the little things that push us over the top. We didn't give up, and we probably got ten more jokes into the script.

Elizabeth Hackett - We each have our own things. She's definitely better with structure. Dialogue is my thing. And we've learned from each other.

Hilary Galanoy - Yes, there are times when Liz is like, "This structure isn't working." And I'm like, "Oh, my gosh, you're so right." And once in a while, I write a really funny joke. When we talk to people about why you should be in a writing team, we will say that if you have people with complementary skill sets, it can make a script really strong.

Elizabeth Hackett - Filmmaking is such a collaborative process anyway. After we're done, the director comes in and gives their thoughts. Then the actors have their say. Sometimes, they read it out loud and you realize something crucial, be it a dramatic moment, a romantic confession, or an important argument, isn't working the way it did in your head and on the page. It's nobody's fault; it's just not working. So you need to come up with some "alts" (alternative lines) to make that moment more convincing. Or they say it out loud and you realize this particular actor is adding something fantastic and better to it, so you listen and try to find more moments where that can happen.

Bryan Woods - We say that we're both equally mediocre at everything. Our process is to challenge each other and call each other out if it wasn't our best work. We try to one-up each other. We have a very friendly, but competitive spirit. We like to dig in and be detail oriented and we like to focus on every little piece whether it's writing or filmmaking and poke holes and challenge each other.

Q: How do you resolve disagreements?

Scott Beck - Any creative endeavor is going to have differing points of view. You can call them disagreements, I suppose, but they are never heated. At most, they are passionate because we believe in what the answer is. The nice thing, because Bryan and I have been working so long together, is that we can have it out and have these passionate disagreements. But we'll say that we will take the day and think on it and see where we come out tomorrow. More often than not, we have swayed each other to the opposite way the next day. We flip-flop. We are very respectful of each other's ideas. When we started working together when we were teenagers, there was more ego built into the process. You quickly realize that you have to shed that. Not only do you have to shed that between the two of us, but you have to shed it because you are going to start getting notes from producers and executives at a studio and actors. You are hearing notes from a hundred different voices. You have to remember what's best for the story. You still need to believe in what you want the story to say, but you have to be open enough that everyone else in the room should be treated as being smarter than you. Then you are really using the best ideas and keeping your antennas out to make sure you are picking them up.

Elizabeth Hackett - We've worked together for twenty years, so you figure it out as you go. We both have sisters, so we're used to "sister negotiation" during a tough moment. Ultimately, we both agree on the final product we want, which helps. We have a common goal. Like any group project, you figure out how to best get to that common goal.

Chris Cullari - We definitely argue. That's one of the great things about having a writing partner. It's having someone who is not only talented but whose taste or outlook is a little bit different; just like when you have a songwriting team. A lot of the best stuff comes from two hardheaded people trying to find the best version of something and really trying to stay true to the principle that "the best idea wins." That can definitely be hard. We don't have a lot of really big fights. We both get very quiet when we get angry. When we fight, it's more sulking than yelling. We just sort of talk it out. I did work with other writers in college on and off and I grew up making movies in my backyard with my friends. It was always very collaborative, so there's always been a collaborative element in me to the creative process. So it's a matter of talking it out. Sometimes, it takes a week until one of us has an idea that makes the other one go, "Oh, my God! Why didn't we think about doing it that way a week ago?" We just force each other to come up with a better idea.

Jennifer Raite - Sometimes, it slows us down and other times it makes us go faster. There's an interesting rhythm to writing with someone else. Even when we are stuck on something and we just see it differently, it forces us to be very analytical and really look into why we think a version is better. Is it really better? It keeps you from getting carried away in your vision and not realizing that there may have been something wrong with a scene all along if you had been chasing it on your own. So even though there is conflict all the time, we are not hot-headed people, so we'll be grumpy. When we are on the same page and something has been refined enough, that's sort of its own indicator in the process. By the time we're on the exact same page, it feels awesome and we can fly through things. You know that it's working. It's coalesced. We are both saying the same thing. That's really fun.

Q: What are the advantages and disadvantages writing as a team?

Hilary Galanoy - The advantages outweigh the disadvantages. You have a built-in sounding board. And there's always another half of the brain that can step in when you're out of steam or ideas. If you're stuck on page 55, your writing partner is there to pick up where you left off. A good team combines strengths and combat weaknesses. The one disadvantage is you split the pay. On the flip side, you also split the work and therefore can work twice as fast and get more accomplished.

Bryan Woods - It's a challenging business because you are putting your heart out there when you write something - you open yourself up to criticism. There's both creative and professional disappointment. So the best thing about having a partner is another shoulder to cry on. Suffering the rare highs and the many lows.

Scott Beck - The disadvantages allude me. From what I've observed from outside our partnership, sometimes the partnership doesn't come to an agreement on what they want to write. Meaning, someone is really passionate on one idea and someone else doesn't feel it. I don't think Bryan and I have done that. Usually, our process is a rolling stone that gains momentum. The more we think on it, the more we get excited and lured into it. Our sensibilities are very similar.

The other thing I see, is sometimes the work ethic is different between writing partners. With Bryan and I, that's not so much the case. We are always juggling different things because we are not in the same room, but we know that if Bryan is writing pages, I am working on another script or a pitch.

Bryan Woods - That's a good point. You have to find somebody who has the same work ethic. Otherwise, it's going to be frustrating.

Chris Cullari - Everything is more polished when writing as a team. Your first draft is really more like your second or third. Or fourth. Or the hundredth draft. You've already done so much of the work. I don't know if you consider ego death a positive or a negative, but you very much don't always get your way. One practical disadvantage is you make, at least here in the States, the same as one writer, split in two. So financially, it is tougher. The old saying that we heard when we came into the industry is that writing teams work twice as much in TV because you are two people for the price of one. You're a deal! So people are always going to hire you. I don't think that's really true anymore. I'm not sure it ever was. Rooms are smaller and a lot of the ideas of what a writers room was has kind of gone out the window. So you make less money, you won't always win, so face the fact that you are not always right.

Jennifer Raite - The accountability is great. There's a lot of compromise in what projects you do. My passion projects aren't always the same as Chris'. The more practiced we become, the more we're trying to find ways to say, "You love this more? You lead and I will follow and vice versa." Which is a newer thing that we are trying to learn how to do. We were once a couple so there's an added level of closeness, trust, and intimacy from our former relationship that allows for honesty. This really helps in production or situations where we have to be in two places at once, where we trust each other to make decisions.

Chris Cullari - In most ways, it does make it easier. At one point, we were so afraid of people finding out that we were no longer a couple. We thought people would think that our projects would be ruined, but it was the opposite. People found out that we were still working together, and they thought we must be really good at this if we can make this work! We came into each other's lives one way and it turned out to fit differently than we thought. We were lucky to have the wisdom to notice that.

Jennifer Raite - We probably have extra practice in conflict resolution because of that!

CHAPTER REVIEW: WRITING TEAMS

- Having someone to bounce ideas off, is very helpful.

- You can, theoretically, be in two places at once or work on two things at once.

- Try to find someone who has complementary skills, such as one of you is good at plot and the other good with character. One may be a better idea person and the other a better editor.

- Writing in a team means that you are accountable to each other to get work done on time and to a certain level of quality.

- Too many disagreements can lead to immobility.

- The industry considers you to be one writer, so you will have to share/split any fees or commissions from your writing.

- Because you are deemed as one writer, series showrunners like the idea of getting two brains for one price.

- If you decide to go off on your own, it is sometimes seen as starting over in the eyes of producers and financiers. They don't know what you've done in the partnership.

- How you work in a team situation is up to the two of you to figure out. It seems that most like to do the original brainstorming together and then do the actual writing apart.

CHAPTER 10

THE WRITERS ROOM & WRITING ON SET

Once an exclusively American entity, the writers room concept has seeped into other markets as a way to create series. While each room has its own culture and politics, there are some universal things to know before entering one. What does a showrunner do? What makes a good one? How do you get heard in a room full of loud voices? Our panelists give first-hand accounts of their times in writers room across genres, platforms, and countries.

Production is a crucible where the theoretical meets the challenges of reality. In other words, your script may not work entirely when the cameras start rolling. How do make those adjustments when the clock is ticking? And what happens when you are called in to fix someone else's story? We talk to writers who have found themselves writing on set.

Q: What is a showrunner?

Barbara Stepansky - The showrunner sets the tone and he or she is our guiding light. They set the direction of what they see as the arc of the season. Season and character arcs is something that we discuss for a while. Though if you are new to the room, you spend a lot of time just sitting back and listening. I feel you have to figure out what's what before you open your mouth.

Lauren Iungerich - Showrunners are different on different shows. For my shows, it's an all-encompassing job. I'm the head writer. I'm the head visionary. I'm the boss. The buck stops with me. I report to the network. I have a whole team of amazing people who work underneath me. I have to be the team leader. I always say when you are making a TV show, there can be only one general. You can have a lot of sergeants and captains, but you can only have one general. I've co-showrun a show before with someone I love and it's not as fluid. So to me, the showrunner is the general - you make all the calls. You definitely consult with everybody - all the experts in all the different jobs. You want to make sure to take into account what they think; that's why you hire them. For me, being a showrunner is being a boss who hires and consults great people to make all the decisions.

Marsha Greene - A showrunner, as the title suggests, runs the show, which is to say that the showrunner oversees all of the different departments of the series and usually does that in partnership with the producers of the production company. Every department answers to you insofar as they are executing your vision. You oversee wardrobe insofar as they are picking clothes that you feel are the right clothes. So you might not be in there every day, and I don't think, as a showrunner, you should be micromanaging everybody, but it's your job to be very clear about your vision for the series and give clear direction. You also need to be available and accountable to people who are working hard for you. For instance, if you get an email on the weekend from a department. I'm not saying don't take the weekend off, but they aren't getting the weekend off. Yes, of course, you have to find time for yourself, but these people are working for you for your show. If you say that you are not answering any emails on a Sunday, that's fine, but on Monday you need to respond because people are waiting for your answers in order to do their jobs. That is a responsibility, I think, that we have to take very seriously.

Q: What makes a good showrunner?

Lauren Iungerich - I'm an artist, but as a showrunner, I have to manage. I'm managing other artists that I've hired because I love their artistry. But now I have to lead them to see the art through my lens. It's the hardest part of the job. So to be a good showrunner means being able to get others to see your vision by being able to articulate it well. You have to be incredibly decisive. I have a point of view on everything. Sometimes, if it's a this or that situation, I will go to the experts and ask which one is best. I get the answer and say to go with it. Done. Being a showrunner means making decisions very quickly. Nine times out of ten it will be the right decision if you go with your instincts and the one time that it's not, the train doesn't come off the tracks to take the time to go back and tweak it. So be decisive and have a vision. You need to know exactly what you want.

Carolina Rivera - A showrunner is a person who can make the hard decisions - the ones no one wants to make. You are a leader and people look up to you. If there are decisions and you're shaky or you are not sure of them, you still have to make them. Someone has to make those decisions and it had better be you. A good showrunner is one that makes decisions quickly for people to do their jobs. In all the shows I've worked on as a staff writer or whatever, the worst thing that can happen is a showrunner who doesn't make decisions. What do we do? Where do we go? Here? There? We need to know. Also, someone who can lead a bunch of people in a happy way. There's a thing in Hollywood where it's accepted that a showrunner yells at people in a bad way or treats people badly. Bullshit. You are not entitled to treat people badly even if you are a showrunner. You're not saving lives. You're just doing TV. You have to treat people well.

Briana Belser - I think so much of showrunning is, first, hire well. Know what you can do. Know what you can't. And hire the best person for all the tasks you cannot achieve. I think that can be painful, probably. But there is a lot of humility that comes from "I don't know. I'm the boss and I don't know."

Second, I think showrunning is a management job. People talk about it like it's this intense creative writing job. And there is a lot of creativity there. A lot of them can write really well. But good God, you better know how to manage people and a lot of different ones. I'm talking about actors and their managers and agents, lawyers and PAs, editors and audience members, and publicity and press and executives. I hope you have that skill set. You know to whom you are talking and when and why. You know how to control your face and your tone. That has made me really excited to continue staffing because I want to get as great at writing as possible because should I get the blessing to be a showrunner, writing will take a back seat to managing and all the operational stuff.

Then the third thing is trusting the people that you have brought on to do their jobs. There is just too much work. There's not enough time in the day. Have the confidence to say, "You take the first pass and I'll come back tomorrow and look at it." Delegate, delegate, delegate. Trust that people are going to bring something to the table that you can't think of, which means what you thought of might be different from the final, but it can still be amazing. That's an excellent showrunner.

One person whom I've heard so many stories about and would love to meet and work with is John Wells (*ER, Shameless*). I've only heard fabulous, point-blank, unrelenting, creative, amazing stories about this man and his expectations for people. "You are going to come to set off-book actor as we just don't have the time." "Hey writer, every time a new draft of something comes out, I would like notes within this amount of time. You don't have to come into the office five days a week, but here are the expectations." That probably feels rigorous, but I've heard these narratives from these people who say it's the most fulfilling work that they've done. They did their jobs! And they watched that show knowing that they impacted the final product. That emotional investment, to me, is so important.

Moisés Zamora - I like showrunners who are accessible, fast decision-makers, and can sell you on their vision really well. We are going to get shot down by studio executives - something happens and the story that you fell in love with got shot down. Not because they didn't like it. Sometimes, it's that they can't do it. It could be a production issue or something like that. It can be very disheartening to start all over again, and you need a great leader to bring back that spark. To get that fire; to get writers to show up with their best ideas. There are tricks to do that. I use emotional manipulation, to a degree, in the room. It's Selena! It's emotional! People already had an emotional relationship and connection to Selena's legacy. So when we were beaten down after breaking an episode, I said, "Let's listen to some Selena! What would she do? What would she say?" I mean, she was living in a bus. We would go back to her interviews to hear her laughter and her songs. And then *Bidi, Bidi, Bom, Bom*, we're back in there. That's what I used. Sometimes, I would give them little treats to appreciate the work that they have done. Tell them I know it's devastating that we have to change that storyline. Here are some treats. Take a moment and then come back and start all over. Also, the best showrunner, reminds you of why you love writing.

Emma Ko - The best showrunner I had was not actually a writer, she was a script editor. She wasn't a producer, but she was hired by a production company to facilitate a room. The best showrunners, first of all, set the culture of the room. She had three rules: no phones, let someone finish talking, and be kind. Done. This industry is full of people with egos. The more insecure, the bigger the ego. When you come across someone like that running a room, you're contending with a psychology of obstacle versus an ability to get the job done. Multiply that by whoever is in the room with the same conditions and it becomes very challenging.

A really good showrunner is confident. They know their show, but are completely open because they know that collaboration makes a show better. If you are one person creating a 10 x 60 minute Netflix show, it is almost impossible, especially if you only have a couple of years' experience, to have every idea in the world. So if you populate your room with clever, smart people who come from their own places of lived experience - who have their own little story scenes to share, you will elevate what you see on the screen because it's fed in by so many different influences, styles, and thoughts. At the same time, there is a point where you have to say that you don't think an idea is working. You will always have time constraints. So it's understanding that you have to let an idea run and run through a room until it comes to a time where you have to say no or yes, let's put this idea on the board.

Danny Strong - There are many factors to what makes a good showrunner. First and foremost, being a good writer. I think you need a good temperament with people to be a good leader. Those are the two most important things. Then being good in post. Post-production is huge. It's just as big as everything else. I'd love it if my showrunner can deliver these cuts.

Marsha Greene - A good showrunner is someone who takes into account what everyone is doing and is trying to be clear and firm in their choices, decision, and vision, and doing so with timely and clear feedback. Also, I think you have to be flexible and open to other people's ideas. I think it can make it much more special. Other people have ideas that you would never have and that's a good thing. You get the script and it's exactly as you want it, but now you are handing it over to a lot of people. Now, it's going to change in some ways that you don't like, but maybe it's going to change in ways that you really love - ways that you never would have thought. You need to be open to that feedback and open to that feeling about it. To be resistant to the feeling that it's all being ruined.

You have to be more than just a visionary because you have to be a manager. You need to be cognizant of that part of the job. That it's not about just being a creative genius. It's about managing people. And being a good manager is helping people do their best work. I had an interview with a showrunner recently, and he was so amazing, I wanted to work for him so badly. He said all the things I think. He said that the job should be fun. You should want to go to work. You can be working long hours and still be having fun. It's an all-encompassing job, and you really need to find the joy in it. I think you need to be grateful and humble that you get the opportunity to do it. And I think you need to be kind.

Q: What is your experience of being in a writers room?

Mohamad El Masri - They've all resulted in a tremendous amount of learning, growth, and relationships that will last a life time. The valuable part of a writer's room, for me, is seeing the layers of collaboration and the number of stakeholders involved in bringing a series to life. It's a tremendous amount of work, time and resources put forward by many people across multiple crafts. In general, I've learned that everyone has a super power, no matter what they do. I've worked with amazingly talented people and leaders who know how to empower and platform others, and inspire the best in people around them.

Barbara Stepansky - Being in a writers room has been the highlight of my life. I don't feel alone anymore. If there's a problem, we can all solve it together and I like getting to the best idea. Sometimes, I have an inkling of an idea and then someone else makes it better. And then person three makes it even better. That takes us hours and hours, which is why it takes us months to go through a whole season, but it's so much fun. I had been working in a writers room for the past few years but recently I've been working on a new spec feature script. So I'm sitting here by myself and I have no one to ask and I have to figure it out myself. I was used to it before the room but now, I realize I do well in a creative exchange.

Briana Belser - My first job was as a writer's PA on the FX series, *Snowfall*. It was created by the legendary John Singleton. It was about a Black kingpin in 1980s L.A. during the crack epidemic. My job was to keep the fridge stocked. To print the paper. To wipe the table. To wipe the board. Administratively assist the writers in writing. That's a lot of staples and paper cuts. I enjoyed it, but going into the room knowing nothing, bright-eyed and bushy-tailed was eye-opening. The concept of the show was drugs and gangsters. Crime, law, CIA, cartel, and all this stuff. The writers who are hired for such content, often, can speak directly from personal experience. So a writer would be like, "Yeah, my parents are in the CIA, and here's this story and this story." Oh, my God! Guest speakers would come in and be like, "Yeah, when I was gang-banging in the streets of L.A..." There was a moment for me when I realized that this was not just an invention; that so much of this stems from real experience and personal anecdotes. The words that you see actors perform as their characters often stem from the human writers that no one ever sees in that room around that conference table. That was something that blew my mind. The second thing I learned was that hierarchy exists in the writers room. You knew who the boss was because they were talking. They were the ones writing on the board. As the fridge stocker, I quickly learned to speak when spoken to and when to get out of the way. The beauty of that is I got to be in any room as long as I wasn't detracting.

Going on to being a staff writer in other writers rooms, I've been able to see how the showrunner is the one who sets the tone of how the room will run and operate, and also that the show content will establish the tone of what makes the table and who is in that room. I've seen the difference between the hire of "old school" versus "new school" writers - new school being writers who are hired for a storytelling standpoint. They share experiences that are being experienced by the characters of the show. However, the best experience I've had from being in writers rooms is that every single writer that I have come into contact with has offered to help me on my journey. They have listened, checked in, and given me advice and criticism, whether they were constructive or not. Each writers room, I walked away a better and stronger writer - and more business minded.

Moisés Zamora - Every writers room can be a little different, but it boils down to a bunch of writers coming together to pitch story for the episode at hand or even the season at hand. In a way, it was similar to the advertising work that I had done. You get a bunch of creatives together for an advertising campaign. It's about being creative in the room when it comes to your pitches. Being clear. Being able to sell your ideas because you don't want to ramble on. To be succinct is really important. For *American Crime*, John Ridley's was a particular room because we only had four hour days. He knew what he wanted for the season and he trusted that we were going to deliver those pitches. He was very good about the decision-making of the stories.

There was a lot of material and articles we had to read. Often, things that he was inspired by. We had consultants come in because it was human trafficking. Also, he hired us due to our particular backgrounds. He read my script and usually when you get an interview to meet the executives or the showrunner for a show, your writing has to be great already. There are lots of writers with great writing samples. But after that, your interview is, are you right for the job? I prepared tremendously for that interview. Both for the John Ridley interview and the *American Crime* interview. First, I met the executives, and then I met John Ridley. I came from an agricultural area in California and I had a lot of stories that dealt with the exploitation of field workers. I shared those stories with the executives and, actually, some of them, from the interview, ended up on the screen. By the time the room gathered, we were already working on those pitches. We also knew ahead of time that the room was only going to be three or four hours a day because John was going to come in at 11 a.m. and he needed to pick up his kids from school at 3 p.m. Family is important to him.

MINI & ALTERNATIVE ROOMS

With networks and streamers opting for direct to series projects with the hope of attracting top tier acting and directing talent, they had to find a way to minimize this financial risk. So they decided to set up proving grounds with project incubators called mini rooms.

As the name states, **mini rooms** have a showrunner/creator with a smaller number of writers than a traditional writers room who work out the first few, or even all, of the episodes of the first season. This is especially useful when complex world building is needed. This gives executives a chance to see the project up on its legs and they can decide to proceed or kill it before spending lots of money. While once a strictly American phenomenon, other countries' industries are starting to adopt this model.

As usual, there are pros and cons to mini rooms. They create opportunities for newer or less experienced writers to work in a professional setting with a showrunner. The work time frame is shorter, which may be an advantage or disadvantage depending on your personal situation. However, the pay is usually lower, so writers unions like the WGA in the USA recommend negotiating above union scale rates. The showrunner may lose a bit of their power later as many story points have been worked out already. And there are no guarantees that the show will go forward unlike when a traditional writers room is set up.

Another kind of room that a writer may find themselves in is a **breakout room**. These function within the traditional writers room model. Here, a group of writers work on a specific task such as creating a episode outline or punch up scares or comedy.

Though rarer, feature films can have writers rooms. This usually happens when sequels or parts of a "cinematic universe" require lots of brainstorming during the world building phase. Results from this have been mixed over the years.

It really gave me the confidence to deliver. It's a group of smart people. Great writers. Why can't you get this done in a very efficient manner? He knew what he wanted and when he got it, he put it on the board. And it stayed on the board, and then stayed in the outline and stayed in the episode.

Star was a little different because we had tons of characters. It wasn't a nuanced, thematic sort of thing. John Ridley's season for that year was eight episodes. *Star* was eighteen. It was a different process because the number of storylines and pitches made it more of a factory. Boom! Boom! Boom! There are advantages and disadvantages to both, I think. When it was my own time to lead a room on *Selena*, in a way, it was a combination of both. We needed to go pretty fast with some of our storylines and some of the episodes. There were no four hour days. You have multiple boards. We are following a family, so there are more storylines. There was historical stuff we needed to add, and we were, at times, replicating events or videos that you could actually access. So we were trying to see if all of that would fit into the puzzle of the journey or the theme. So it was a different process with *Selena* being about a real person, whereas these two other projects were fictional.

Emma Ko - My philosophy in writers rooms is that no idea is shit. Rule number one is no phones, two, let someone finish talking, and, three, be kind. Rule number four is throw anything on the table because no matter how bad it is, you are saying it for a reason. I would say that I don't know where this is going or what this means, but I am having an idea, for instance, of an image of a chicken and it's running. Then somebody might come in and finish it off. You never know where something magical comes from. The saddest thing, particularly for writers who are under-confident, self-conscious, or young and don't want to say the wrong thing and get fired, is censorship. There's a difference between saying anything in your head, and self-censoring because you're worried about looking stupid. For me, the best way to work with other writers is to be encouraging, particularly if I know it's quite a big deal for them to throw something into the room. The first few days in a writers room, you have no idea who somebody is. If somebody is really quiet, shy, and shuffly or whatever, it's quite easy to discount them, but they might be the person with the Pandora's Box of the most extraordinary stuff. You need to be able to encourage that to come out. I have been in the room with absolute assholes. You have to work out why they are being an asshole. But for me, you have to take everything that is being said in the spirit of collaboration and serve the showrunner's purpose of getting the best show out there.

Julie Sherman Wolfe - Sometimes, you have a wonderful experience with people you love hanging out with, and spend the entire day laughing. You never want the show to end. Sometimes, you get into a room that's very negative, toxic, and soul-crushing and you can't wait for the show to get canceled. I've had both, and I think it ultimately gives a writer the thick skin they need to survive for more than just a handful of years. Network sitcom notes can be rough, and come every day, so I got used to the fast pace and sheer volume of writing that has to be done by morning. It can definitely throw people when they get sixteen pages of notes on a thirty-two page script. An effective showrunner has a plan to address the notes, doesn't procrastinate, or wait until 10 p.m. to start writing, and makes fast decisions when the joke pitches are flying. This high-pressure pace prepared me well for my time at Hallmark, especially when they need the script ASAP. I'm considered a fast writer, and that's absolutely due to my time in the sitcom trenches.

Karen Walton - You're in the writers room by about 8.30 a.m. or 9.00 a.m., Monday through Friday, with four to five other staff writers, and the showrunner. The walls are literally covered in whiteboards. You may be there for six, eight, or ten to twelve hours a day - depends on how the room is run. If it's a serialized show, you don't write one episode at a time and wrap it. In Canada, we're not writing the entire season of scripts in advance. We're shooting while we are breaking episodes, coming up with a single main question to answer or layered mystery to solve gradually, at the end of each season. Each episode contributes to a big picture story. We're revising stuff all the time because we are fine-breaking say, Episode 6 in the room, and we realize that what would be good in Episode 6 is a clue we'd need to seed in Episode 4, which we are shooting right now! Let's tweak tomorrow's big scene, so it all works later.

So you are always thinking about what's in production at the moment, writing for what's coming next, and making changes on the fly, because every single beat has to lead up to something five hours later. A very different experience than writing a movie, or an episodic procedural. Personally, I love writing serial drama. But it is an all-consuming endeavor, at least for me, as a writer.

With that kind of room, you spend all day breaking stories with a team of writers, unless you are on set supervising your latest script, at camera. You attend prep and production meetings for your upcoming episodes. Somewhere in there, often at night and over the weekends, you are writing your next script, and you are reading the other staff writers' episodes, giving notes and feedback; working together to crack a challenge on any given script or season-arc issue as they arise. When Production breaks for lunch, you attend table reads with the cast for the next episode, gather the final pre-production notes and get those revisions out.

You get home and you're sleeping. You still have to deliver scripts on Monday, and be ready for the next episode's production meetings on Monday. Sundays - you are writing, reading, and doing the laundry. I used to do it and fold it on my dining room table near to the back door. I'd get up early on Monday, dress at the table while I had my coffee, and then walk out to my car and go.

When I started out as a junior staff writer on the original US *Queer as Folk*, I would go to the writers room every day. You'd sit with incredible talents who made shows you watched in abject awe. "Oh, my God! I'm here!" You get to watch writer-hyphenates who have done series for twenty years and figure out how it all works, every single hour, every single day. You see how series characters are developed, everything. So for eight hours a day, you are sitting in a room with writers. Then production starts. *Queer as Folk* was only different because for the first season, which I was not on, they were in L.A., but they shot in Toronto. For the second season, they hired me and Michael MacLennan, who is now a Canadian showrunner, as junior writers. They brought the writers room up to Toronto during production, so the L.A. writers would actually be in touch with the set, instead of one co-showrunner being up here and everyone else being down there. Twenty years later, the writer's experience is the same.

Tony Jordan - I love being in a writers room. I don't know if I have the personal discipline to come up with a show and then lock myself away for eighteen months to come up with all eight hours of it. Writing is the loneliest profession in the world. I like people. I stayed at *EastEnders* ten years longer than I should have done. I was creating all of my own shows, but then going back and working at *EastEnders*. Not because I had a burning desire, but because I loved the story meetings. I loved being in the room with twelve other writers making up stories. I love that. I like being with other writers. I'm doing one now for six episodes. I'm writing two and we've brought in three other writers. They will read my pilot and talk about it. We will talk about character arcs and serial arcs. We come up with guest stories. Lots of stuff. I love to work that way.

Ben Philippe - My experience on *Only Murders in the Building* was great because John Hoffman is a really good showrunner. I was in a room with writers who had decades of experience on shows like *Modern Family* and *Family Guy*. It was really inclusive and, I don't want to use the word mentor, but he was a really great boss. John had worked on *Looking* on HBO and *Grace and Frankie* on Netflix and he was just the nicest, kindest man. We were all on Zoom and I didn't really talk for my first three weeks there. Someone made the joke that I always look frozen in fear like I'm going to get fired. And with a brick wall behind me on Zoom, I looked like I was at the bottom of a well, which prompted me to put up a mirror to break the illusion.

The first lesson you realize is that the writer of the show is the showrunner so you are serving their vision, so you pitch stories and learn about their sensibilities. There were eight to ten different voices converging into one voice - the showrunner's. Because the show is a wonderful, magical show that has elements of character building, comedy, mystery - a bit of everything - we all found our footing. John was very empowering in letting me and Stephen Markley, another novelist, who was also a first time TV writer, pitch high-concept ideas like when we had an idea for the silent episode. The episode would be from the perspective of Theo Dimas, a deaf character in the building. John just ran with it.

The first draft we co-wrote. Co-writing, alone, is a challenge because when you are a writer, you're used to having everything in your head. If you decide the vase is purple, it's purple. Now, you have to have a conversation with someone who sees the vase as blue. So there were some creative growing pains in combining our voices, but we came up with what I thought was a really special and amazing episode. In re-reading the episode, we were definitely first-time TV writers because I think the budget for the episode would have been at least $15 million. John was very kind and never shut us down. He always massaged iteration after iteration until it became the studio draft that went to production. It was a great experience. I am in the middle of another season now and I make it a point that if I get offers to join other rooms, if it conflicts with *Only Murders*, I don't take them. I want to see this show all the way through because I think it's special. It's been the best experience.

Josh Greenberg - As a group together, you are finding out what a character would or wouldn't say, or what a character would or wouldn't do, while serving the vision of the showrunner. That's all you are there to do, which is great. If the showrunner wants something very broad and wacky, then that is what you have to deliver. If the showrunner wants something grounded and more subtle, then you are there to do that. It's a great writing muscle to exercise. I never knew that being a writer could be about sitting in a room with a bunch of people who soon become your friends and laughing a lot as you construct characters. It's really joyful. I feel really lucky to be doing it.

Q: How long does a staff job run for?

Karen Walton - It really varies by show, in Canada. And we saw plenty of adaptations to room scheduling and booking over the past few years due to COVID: running rooms on Zoom and so on - your days "in the room virtually" tend to be shorter, which I felt was a good thing for the writers. Television seasons have gotten shorter as well. When I started in TV, you'd be booked for twelve or twenty-two episodes; you get paid weekly as a staff writer, and then you get paid on top of that for the scripts you are the credited writer on. On that classic model, it's quite lucrative; you can raise a family in the biggest city in Canada quite comfortably. Now, you have eight or ten episodes a season, and fewer staff writers. Fewer writers write more of the scripts on shorter seasons. Plus, Canadian networks are making fewer new shows, domestically. So now your staffing jobs are fewer here, and shorter in duration.

Barbara Stepansky - It depends on where the project is set up and its stage of development. Mini-rooms can run for around ten weeks, regular rooms for up to twenty weeks.

Q: What is the lifestyle of a senior writer?

Karen Walton - As a senior writer on *Orphan Black*, I would start in April/May with the showrunners and I think most of the writing staff and I would wrap in December/January. But we don't have "Pilot Season" up here in Canada. A green light is a green light for a show, and your room can start and your show can go at any point in the year. Generally, the more experienced writers see the season through, but as I say, it varies by show and resources. Where I work, we often wrap writers before the end of the season is out of production, as the showrunner is taking the finale scripts, and the staff writers aren't needed after we've sorted the stories for those, in principle.

Once you are wrapped as a room writer, most writers are already committed to, or hunting for, the next thing. That's when you are going to write your own development deal work, or take something of your own out to pitch. In Canada, it's very popular to have one-week or short-term, no obligation Development Rooms. This is where you get all your favorite and available people together and just work on a project you've landed formal development partners for; the network or production company is paying you, and it's a week to flesh out the new stuff in development. You may also be consulting on less-experienced creators' series in development. So you are keeping your fingers in all those pies.

Q: How do you break story in a writers room?

Lauren Iungerich - I have an idea of where I am driving to - the general idea. I might have ideas for the character arcs already. I may have the beginning, middle, and end for all the character arcs and that is what we talk about. The big broad strokes. Then we just start pitching and for any great idea, we write it down. We create a vomit board and write each idea under each character. Every show, from the jump of a pilot, you can already see what the arcs are, where the story is going, and what the big thematics are. You really start to map that out. So I get into a room with the basic ideas and then we vomit ideas until we start to see the big picture stuff. From there, we start to lay it out in more specific detail from a global perspective, so we go macro to micro. However, through the course of a season, as we break episodes, we may go back to things and switch them around and move them asking where do we need to pull or push story out?

Emma Ko - On *1899*, there was a huge amount of underlying work that had been done by Jantje Friese, the showrunner: the premise of the show; who the characters were. Genre was front and center. It is a mystery to the extent that Jantje did not want to know what was going to happen in Episode 2. It was a very interesting room to be in. Basically, the shape of the show was, this is what we think is going to happen. But at any point, and she's a very visceral writer, to serve the mystery better, she might change things and therefore I never got too attached to any one idea because it might be thrown out. I got to the point where it was less about the story and more about what can we introduce that is so fantastical and crazy and spooky and weird and mysterious, that it leads to more story. She did have an endpoint structured over three series, but she also said it could go out the window. That was very unique and when you see it you will know why.

If you've seen *Dark*, then you'll understand as it gives an explanation as to why what she's saying isn't as ridiculous as it sounds. In *Dark*, the older character with the beard who comes back, appears in Episode 1. When they were writing it, they didn't know who he was yet. They just called him "The Stranger." They just knew a stranger had to come. But it wasn't until later that they realized - SPOILER ALERT - that he was the older Jonas. Do you see how that serves the story of the timeline thing? It was a difficult way of crafting the story. There were many people in that room who couldn't cope. Most of the tentpole stuff in the first five episodes is laid down, but what's happening in episodes 6 to 10? She only wanted something like 80% of the idea there in case something better came along.

Barbara Stepansky - Once we know what the season has to feel like and what we approximately want in each episode, then we go in and start breaking the episodes themselves. We do the index cards. We do the beats. We put them up on the board and discuss them at length. Some cards are vaguer than others, so before you can go to outline, you can always double check in the room, "What is this card, really? What happens?" The great thing about the *Outlander* room is that they value opinions and new ideas. I had some really strong opinions about some material in my first season and there was a moment where I thought I may have opened my mouth when I shouldn't have. But everyone was really supportive.

Ben Philippe - It goes from the top down. First, we do the blue skying: What is this season about? The longer you take on that, the better. We had moments in Season 2 on *Only Murders in the Building* where we went by the blue sky very fast and we went into breaking. We know roughly what the season is about, let's start breaking Episodes 1, 2, 3. Then we would hit a bump because we realize we hadn't answered some of the bigger questions. Who is this character? What are they about? So we threw out those scripts and went back into the room to talk it out and go back into the specifics. We had to talk about who these characters are, generally, if we are going to make them believable people to entertain. Then you go into where they all are this season. What are their arcs?

So for Season 2, it was set up that it comes on the heels of Season 1 where our trio is arrested for the death of Bunny Folger. So there is no flash-forward to six months later. It happens straight away and it's clear they are being framed because they were so proud and loud about being podcasters who solved a mystery. The murderer planted evidence in all their apartments and now everyone thinks they killed someone else for the attention. Once we figured that out for the season, we could see what that would look like in Episodes 1, 2, and 3. Then, 4, 5, and 6. Then, in the final turn, 7 through 10. That's the seasonal version of the A, B, and C - beginning, middle, and end. What do they each hold? Then we do the micro of it. Episode 1, what do we have to cover? Then we go into the A, B, and Cs of that particular episode. Then, we go into the A. What must that cover? It's always funneling down into the micro-scenes. I think there is a way where if you do this poorly it becomes like tying strings together, but there isn't really a basket holding it all together. It's just yarn and red strings on a board.

You need to give everything an identity. Episode 8 is the twist of the season, so we have to start looking toward the person who actually did it. Our gang is coming together after being fractured. But it needs a thing…oh, it's the blackout episode! Everyone is stuck in the building and the elevators aren't working, and you have to talk a lot. Once I have that, now I see what the episode is about. It was written by Madeline George - an amazing episode.

John, early on in the first episode of the show added a touch of fantastical visuals so that occasionally we break with reality. In the pilot, which he co-wrote, every character is living their life and something bounces. Steve Martin makes an omelet. He throws it out and it bounces back onto his plate. Mabel is playing with a ring that she got from Tim Kono. It bounces off and goes back around her finger. Martin Short gets a loan from his son and the other two have agreed to do the podcast with him, he falls on the ground and he, himself, bounces. It was the visual idea that these people are finding their second wind. That is not something you would see on *Grey's Anatomy.* He likes to go back into the season and add surreal touches. In Season 2, Episode 5, they are throwing a party, and we see it all from the perspective of a period Martin Short. He's got a ponytail and everyone is in gorgeous period costumes. That is a sense of surrealism that really works for us. Everything comes into focus as the season goes on.

Q: How are episodes divvied up by the showrunner?

Emma Ko - What happens on a show like *1899* is the lead writer writes Episodes 1 and 2 and also the end. The other writers write the difference. We all kind of had our own characters. We were writing the main narrative story for that character per episode. So it was divvied up by that, really. It didn't end up quite being that because a lot changed and some writers got fired. Basically, I knew that I was writing Episode 3 going in.

On other shows, there is no episode guarantee. The likelihood is that you will get episodes if you have been part of the process to develop the show to where it is. Mainly, because it's a waste not to. You know it. But when I was working at CBBC, you would pitch an idea per episode. I would be in a room to talk about the shape of the show and then I would send in six or seven episode ideas. From that, one would get chosen and might be commissioned. Then, I would send in other ideas and in a thirteen-episode series, I might get two or three episodes.

Marsha Greene - In Canada, I'm not sure this is as true in the U.S., but the writer, typically, knows going in, how many scripts they will be writing - it's negotiated as part of their contract. On *The Porter*, I was writing two episodes and Annmarie Morais was writing two, excluding the pilot. We knew we had eight episodes, so we had four left. So how many people could we get? Most writers want a script to take a job. So, in that case, we are not going to have seven people because we only have eight episodes. The more episodes you have, the bigger the room.

In terms of who gets what script, the standard thing is for the showrunner to take the first and the last. Then, it depends on the show. Sometimes, in Canada, there is a hierarchy where the co-EP will do Episode 2. The Supervising Producer would do Episode 3. But that is not always the case. Sometimes, it's based on the subject matter. If we are all coming up with ideas and someone pitches an episode about horses and that becomes Episode 3, they are going to write it, especially if they have a lot of experience with it. So you may assign episodes based on what people pitched or what they feel connected to. Or if there is a story that has a specific culture that you are part of, you can speak to it and you might do that episode. If it's more open where anyone could write it, then they would use the hierarchy. But if it's an episodic show, then it's what a person has pitched. The very worst case would be based on the schedule. As you go along, you lose people from the room. So if you give your co-EP Episode 2, then you are losing them really early. But if you give them Episode 5, you get to keep them in the room while other people leave. So you can think of it in the strategy of whom do you want to stay in the room to help move it along.

Lauren Iungerich - I used to assign things ahead of time. Now, I don't do that. If you are a writer on staff, it's not a guarantee that you are going to write an episode. If you are new to me, I've got to hear that you understand the show before I'm going to assign you an episode to write. Outlines are written in my room, so much of the writing is done when the episodes are broken. It's so detailed. More and more as I run a show, I've become a stronger hand in the writing. It's wonderful collaborating, but I've discovered my shows are better and more cohesive the more I write.

Q: How many writers are in a writers room?

Josh Greenberg - It really varies. The largest writers room I've been in was *Raising Hope*, which was a huge room with nineteen writers. That was wild. Then I have been on shows where it's five or six writers. Every room that I've been in, finds its equilibrium. You are dealing with different personalities. You often have one person who is an alpha character, who insists on being heard. You often have people who are a little shyer. It's sort of a weird microcosm of life or any office where you have to deal with different personalities.

Marsha Greene - The biggest room I was ever in was twelve people sitting around the table, but one of them was the writers assistant. Not to say that he didn't participate, but he wasn't a writer. That's a big room. When we did *The Porter*, there were six of us. Myself, Annmarie Morais and four other people. Then, at one point, it went down to three other people. There are some good things about a big room, but one important thing is that when you are doing a show and breaking the episodes, at some point people have to go off and write them. At that point, you are losing people from the room. When you have twelve people, it's great, the room can still function. You still have a lot of voices. When you have a smaller room, it's harder for it to keep going. Typically, in a small room, you will do all the work together and then you will break. You stop the room and everybody will go off and write and then everyone will come back. If you want to have the room going on as the show goes on, then it's important to have more people. The first show I ever did, there were eight or nine of us. Even so, when we got to the end it was like, "Where is everybody?" Some people's contracts had ended. Some people were on set. Some people were home writing.

When you have a big room, this is when, as a showrunner, having a vision and knowing what you want becomes even more important because it's more people giving you ideas. And you need to steer the ship because it can be going all over the place. You have to say what you like and then tell people to go with it. When there is a small room, there are five or six of you sitting around and you can be much looser. You can throw ideas around, but it doesn't get as unruly as a large room.

Ben Philippe - *Only Murders in the Building* is on the bigger side. We have around eight writers and that includes producers and John, the showrunner, and a writing team, who serve as one writer. I've been in other rooms on other shows like *Interview with the Vampire* for AMC. The showrunner there, Rolin Jones, wanted a really small, mini-room, of only five people. It was a book adaptation and it can be helpful not to have too many voices in the room. I like the mini-room format, it can be helpful. But if you are writing a comedy with eight writers, you can get eight different jokes. It gives the showrunner more options to streamline everything.

Q: As a staff writer, do you have to take on the voice of the project you're on?

Karen Walton - Yes. You are working in service. You apply all your craft and imagination seven days a week, plus writing at night, weekends, in service of the writer/showrunners who invited you. You are working as a member of a team of writers and your job is to collaborate and support a singular vision that is not your own. That's television. Or at least, that's staff writing jobs in dramatic television. And especially in the culture of "rooms."

Emma Ko - My belief is: If I am invited into a writers room on someone else's show, regardless of whether I think it is a good idea or a bad idea, my purpose there is to help that person get the best show they can to the broadcaster. I'm pretty adaptable. It took me a couple of days to get Jantje Friese's style on *1899*, but once I understood that conventional rules are out the window and because I watch so much stuff, I thought about what is going to help her the most. It's a multi-national ensemble cast, so we all had our own characters to look after. I was there to shepherd my characters and their story arcs. In terms of story, my characters were the least developed when we went into the room, so I had to come up with that. I think I did fifteen different options in the three-week writers room. But in terms of the greater storyline, what is it I can do when I go back in to serve Jantje the best? She doesn't need me laying down what is in Episode 8. What I realized is that I could feed her ideas or motifs or themes that would guide her gut to say what feels right and it might feature in Episode 8.

Ben Philippe - I think you can still have your own voice. I think it's the responsibility of the showrunner to find people who have their own voices, but whose voices match the show. As a showrunner, it's their job to read twenty-five to fifty pilots of writers that the network has sent them. They're trying to find the person with the right sensibilities. That's someone with little bit of an original voice, but a bit of a humor that they find funny and a bit of dramatic heft that they respond to.

Barbara Stepansky - Whether it's the first season of a show or the fifth, you always want to adapt your voice to the genre, tone, and style that pre-exists you, so to say. But there's also a reason you were hired, that's the original spark that is your own voice and it's always good to add that to the mix. Call it an additional spice.

Q: Are there any rules you must follow for a show?

Ben Philippe - With *Interview* we have more scares. They are vampires so there has to be one moment in every episode where you see them being vampires. If you are going to see *The Fast and the Furious*, you want to see cars. If you watch *Sex and the City*, you want to see dresses. With vampires, you want to see fangs. So that was a mandate that we had in the room.

With *Only Murders*, we learned some things along the way and they became unwritten rules. We like to see Steve Martin, Martin Short and Selena Gomez's characters together. The most fun we have is when the three of them are at the mystery board trying to solve things. Sometimes, because they are different characters, we tend to go off with each one. Charlie is doing this. Oliver is doing this. Mabel is doing this. How do we tie it all back together? While there aren't scares, as it's not a scary show, pretty early on we realized that no one is ever going to think that they committed the murder. That's a twist that you expect in murder mysteries, that one of the detectives is the murderer. We cashed that in pretty early with Mabel being this young, mysterious woman in Season 1 who knew the victim. So there's something there and we paid that off. So our three leads may have secrets; they have personal lives; but they are not the killers. That's a rule…until we break it, haha!

Those rules aren't universal for every show. Our showrunner is very adamant that every episode should end on a turn that sends us in a new direction. So if they are investigating the neighbor from the second floor in one episode, we can't go into the next episode following that storyline. So maybe at the end of the second episode, we learn that he was talking with the janitor and now we are on to the janitor. And a new "rule" that we are trying to do is that we don't want anything to be a filler. If you are watching twenty-two episodes of *The Simpsons* or *Will & Grace*, you are not really following the plot. You can miss one here and there. But if you are following a murder mystery and you think that you can skip that one, you have failed, especially if it's only ten episodes. Everything has to build into the mystery even if it's in ways that people don't see yet.

Barbara Stepansky - On *Outlander*, we follow the books as it's an adaptation and we write Scottish characters in their Scottish dialects. Other than that, every episode is carefully crafted by the whole writers room so when we move into outline and then script, we have a very clear road map.

Q: Do writers change each season?

Barbara Stepansky - Yes. Season 6 of *Outlander* thinned out a bit because we lost two writers to other projects. We replaced one. Season 7, where I wasn't part of the writers room, had a bunch of new writers again. I only did a freelance episode.

Marsha Greene - My experience has been mostly mixing it up. I have worked on shows that have had pretty much the same people and I am the new person who is coming in.

The shows that I did, we did have new people each time. Sometimes, it's just availability. Time has passed and that writer isn't available anymore. On *The Porter*, it was so hard because we had this small room and we read so many writers. The first year of *The Porter*, we consciously decided to have an all-Black writers room because we were making history in all these ways. It was the first all-Black creative team in Canada. For that first season, we wanted to make sure that everybody felt perfectly comfortable and safe sharing their personal stories. We felt that would be easier to accomplish in an all-Black room. But we read many writers that we liked in Season 1 and we were excited to be able to hire different writers on Season 2 and give other people the opportunity that we were excited about being on the show. On *The Porter*, we knew we were going to bring different people in for various reasons. On *Mary Kills People*, it was different. It was just more circumstance that Sherry White was in the first season. She was running her own show the second season. People were doing different things so we had that turnover. Ideally, you don't have a lot of turnover.

On *Mary Kills People*, it was myself, Tara Armstrong, and Tassie Cameron; we were always on the show. The other people were changing. You want that because, not only do people get to advance every year, but they know the show really well. They know the actors. They know the crew, so they can be on set more. It's valuable to have the same people come back for multiple seasons.

Q: Are freelance episodes common?

Barbara Stepansky - No, they don't usually do it, but it's something that can be done. The only freelance episodes that have been given out consistently have been for Diana Gaboldon, the author of the *Outlander* books. She gets an outline or a beat sheet that we've broken and she writes her own episode. That functioned a little bit like that with me this year. I got the beat sheet and we discussed it for a couple of days over Zoom. Then I was up to speed and I could go ahead and write that episode. It was kind of fun. After you've been with a show for so long, you know all of these characters, it's really easy to fall back into their shows.

Q: Can you work two shows at the same time? Or if you're a staff writer on one show, can you write an episode on other shows?

Ben Philippe - You typically wait until the first one is done. One of the things that happens is, different projects have different priorities for you. My manager says, "writing for a show is your job and developing your own independent projects is your side job." If you sell one of your own projects, the show that you are writing on has priority. When the show that you're on ends, you can staff on a different show if your agent can get that into your contract. At one point, I had four projects with a ranking of priority that if I sell my pilot or it gets green-lit by someone, that would break the contract that I have with *Only Murders in the Building*. If I am on a different show for five weeks and *Only Murders* starts up again, then I leave that show and go to *Only Murders*. You can't do projects concurrently.

Karen Walton - The model of working for television in Canada has changed. You used to be able to pop in for an episode on a variety of shows, and that money would support, say, your film writing habit or allow you to develop your own spec work, or work with many different styles, forms, writers and directors. That's how I started in TV writing; people read my film scripts and invited me in as a junior writer. That model vanished here when we imported the US writers room model in my country. Now, you are either in for as long as they can afford to contract you, or you're out. A certain number of TV writers room jobs exist, and then they are no more. It becomes more like a crew position, in the sense that if you land a staff position, odds are you want to say yes and keep doing it for multiple seasons if possible. Otherwise, you will lose your spot in the shrinking hiring hierarchy. And as you advance on a show, you make more money, write more of the scripts, in that hierarchy.

Barbara Stepansky - It depends on your contract. If it is an exclusive contract as a staff writer on a show, then no. If you have a non-exclusive contract, then yes, it's possible but it is extremely time-consuming and showrunners want you to focus on their project.

Q: Does working in a writers room help with your own writing ability?

Barbara Stepansky - When I'm writing features, I'm at a computer by myself, listening to notes and typing out the notes. There's some talking involved with producers, but it's not extensive. When you're in a writers room, you sometimes do nothing for weeks but just talk about the story. So for pitching open writing assignments or TV shows, I look at the story and what works best for the project. It's also allowed me to read between the lines as to how this job is going to be and if I want to do it.

Ben Philippe - If a script comes in at forty pages, it's too long and you have to find a way to cut four pages out of that. That's a place where having other people in the room is extremely useful because when I write something I think, "No, you people don't understand. This is forty pages of brilliance. I spent weeks on it. I can't remove a single word." You give that to a Kirker Butler and two hours later it's thirty-two pages. I didn't need those eight pages; I just couldn't see it.

Q: How do you balance being a showrunner and a director?

Danny Strong - Sometimes, I'm both and that's easy to balance; I just do whatever I want. As the showrunner, to other directors, I want them to feel empowered. I want them to have a good artistic experience. I want them to give me their best. I always tell them to make it cinematic. Go for it. Don't feel constrained. Don't make the whole experience about trying to make your day. You have to make your fucking day, but really see if you can get some cool, interesting shots in. Do it in your blocking. Don't just have them standing around talking in every single scene. Sometimes, directors do that because it's faster and easier to shoot. Then, all of a sudden, you have an hour of scenes that sit there like lead because everyone is standing there talking.

Most showrunners want the director to have everything in their first cut. I am not like that. I say go for it. If you think there are scenes that don't work, cut them. I don't need to watch it in the cut. Although, I will usually review the stuff that is cut. I view all the directors that I hire as really talented people. I want them to try and put their best artistic foot forward and then, I will step in as the showrunner. Sometimes, I will be an executive producer where I am not the showrunner, where I will be the last stop of a cut. I'm not there to service the director's vision as it's the showrunner who has the ultimate vision of the piece. However, I want the director to feel free to come up with ideas because what if they have some great idea that I would never have thought of, and they would never have tried had they felt constrained. A great example of that is in *Dopesick*, there's this scene early on in one of the first episodes where it was two separate scenes and then Barry Levinson intercut them. It made it so that one scene was in the head of the character in another scene and we were going back and forth. It was a fantastic idea. Loved it! Check! Great job! Oh, that's why you're a living legend! I want the directors to feel that they can go do that. I feel it's a great spirit to have.

Jennifer Raite - We directed one episode of *12 Deadly Days* for Blumhouse. I think they wanted us to direct more, but when you are showrunning, it's so hard to make time for just being focused on directing. I think it makes sense a showrunner directs the first episode or the first two episodes, or the last or last two episodes. Then everything can coalesce and they can just focus on that one thing. After we had written the majority of that show, so much of the process was being able to be in two places at once. We were in pre-production on episodes while we were shooting other episodes, so one of us could be in a meeting, and one of us could be on set. Nights and mornings, we watched cuts. The only time we were physically together for any real stretch of time was the three days when we were directing our episode. It was super fun, but challenging and it ended up being in the middle of the run. We had to bolster what was going on in the episodes that were shooting before and after us. There was a lot of catch-up.

Lauren Iungerich - I was a director before I was a showrunner and before then, I was a working writer. It makes it easier for everyone on my team to only have to listen to one voice all the time. Directing in the TV space is a very strange thing. Directors inherently want to be in charge and in television they're not. I'm still in charge as both showrunner/director. I have a very strong point of view. The directors I work with come in and I'm collaborative, but at the end of the day, if they want to do something and I don't want them to do it, they are going to have to do what I am asking them to do. As I've gotten more and more seasoned, I've directed more and more, and I get asked to direct more and more. There are a lot of TV directors who are journeymen. They come in to direct and they don't watch the show or know the show. They are not interested in engaging and getting under the hood to know the show. I always love it when directors come in and want to get to know the show and love it as much as we do. I personally think it best to be a showrunner/director and do it all. At least for me and my work - it allows the work to be more cohesive.

Q : What is the difference between Staff Writer, Story Editor, Executive Story Producer and Supervising Story Producer?

Ben Philippe - It's a ranking for the Writers Guild of America for your pay scale. Staff Writer is the lowest position. You are in the room, so there's a minimum they have to pay you. I think there's a cap as well. You can go from the Writers Assistant, which is not a Guild writer position to Staff Writer, which is a Guild writer position, to Story Editor which is the next level, to Executive Story Producer, which is what I am currently. Again, it's a matter of pay. All those pay grades are set by the Writers Guild and that's why there have been so many contentions, fights and strikes. It's all a little bit arbitrary and establishes everything as a pyramid, which allows people to get paid their worth. For example, sometimes it can be a matter of who has the best agent; the one who can haggle the best deal for you. It's not really a meritocracy of: is this person participating more in the room? Is this person a better writer than the other?

Barbara Stepansky - It's the ladder you have to climb once you start your career as a TV writer. You start out as a staff writer and work your way up the credits. Being a Supervising Story Producer on set is an important task as you're representing the showrunner. You want to make sure that story strands don't get lost. That, for example, on *Outlander*, we don't slip into modernisms. That the point of the scene that we discussed in tone meetings, is hit. Probably the most important part of the day for on-set writers is rehearsal. Once a scene is on its legs, the actors are comfortable and the director knows how to break up the scene, then you can kind of lean back a bit. But it's important to be there in rehearsals so if there's a question, you can answer it. When the actor says a line isn't working because circumstances have changed, you can jump in and help adjust it so the scene still flows and makes sense. I'm trying to make the show the best it can be and sometimes when we run out of time or daylight, it becomes a logistical issue. Can we live without this coverage because we couldn't get to it? Since I am a trained director, I can see if we are missing something or if something isn't quite right. Does that necessarily mean that's bad? No. It's part of the process.

Q: How do showrunners balance the creative with the business of making a TV show?

Danny Strong - As a producer, that's the job - the business side - and that's what they are there for, to help the director and the showrunner on the business side of things. Not that they aren't there creatively, too; they are. But you want your producer to step in certain places where it wouldn't be a good use of your time. The showrunner has to be very cognizant of the business side of production and staying on budget. In film, directors go over budget sometimes and sometimes they go way over budget. That director needs to be very successful or they won't get to do another film because you need to be responsible. There are some directors that just don't care because they are so successful. You can't do that on a TV show. You can go over budget a little bit, but if it's episode after episode, you aren't doing the job right. That's part of the job; keeping the trains running on time. I take the budget very seriously. I brought in *Dopesick's* eight episodes, hundreds of thousands of dollars under budget. I was so far under budget that I was mad at myself! I should have

> ## TV & STREAMING PRODUCER CREDITS (USA)
>
> This is the hierarchy for the USA market, but it is gradually being adopted by European ones. Please use as a general guide.
>
> **Executive Producer** - often the showrunner or head writer of a show. Also EP credit is given to seasoned show creators with other writing credits, long time writers on a show, or the head of the production company that produces the show, and may not write on it.
>
> **Co-Executive Producer** - just below Executive Producer. They manage the other writers and the production/post-production crew. They contribute significantly in the writers room and may write scripts, too.
>
> **Supervising Producer** - these producers oversee script rewrites, help new writers in fictional shows. They are active in the writers room and often write their own scripts.
>
> **Producer** - producers will have written the episode and will be the main point of contact on set. They are active in the writers room.
>
> **Co-Producer** - a co-producer may not have written the episode, but contributed significantly through table reads, discussions, and/or revisions.
>
> **Story Editor** - this position manages junior writers with their drafts by giving feedback. They will pitch in the writers room. Story Editors may be the keeper of the show bible so that the storytelling is consistent.
>
> **Staff Writer** - the entry-level position on a series. They will pitch ideas in the writers room and help develop ideas into scripts. They may work alone or collaboratively with another writer.
>
> **Writers Assistant** - provides clerical and administrative support to the writing staff. Assistants won't write scripts, but may be in the writers room on some shows and give ideas/opinions when asked.

used that money on stuff. It's not like they reward you for it. But it's part of the job. I think from the network or studio's point of view, that's one of the big sins. If you can't bring these shows in on budget, you're fucking out. When you are going up for your next job, they will call the studio and ask what they thought of you. Constantly over budget. Bad.

Lauren Iungerich - It's the worst part of my job, as it's not creative. I also find that the rules are different for women. Where I would be passionate and tough, people have a problem with me not being sunny or cheerful all the time. I've definitely fallen prey to the, "Oh, I don't like her tone." All I am doing is being direct and professional. I am usually very warm and kind but sometimes I'm all business and I'm just the boss. People still don't like female authority so I find that being a woman makes my job tougher than it should be.

Marsha Greene - Lots of writers want to be a showrunner. It's kind of the ambition because you want to have your own show. My first job in television, before I was ever a writer, was being the assistant to a showrunner, so I was very aware of how demanding the job was. But I think I still had stars in my eyes about him being in charge of everything and executing his vision. The truth is, when you are a showrunner, a lot of the job is creative adjacent. It's not quite the same as the joy of being in the writers room and just dreaming up stories. Now, you are making creative decisions based on business decisions like budget and time. That's an adjustment in your thinking because it isn't just the rosy making of my show where anything goes. There are realities of production that you become aware of when you are a showrunner. You have to think about every decision creatively. If someone says we have to cut something or that we can't have something, you have to take that business decision and try to filter it back through your creative brain and what you want for the show. So instead of just saying "yes" and it makes it bad, or just saying "no" and making everyone else's life hard or whatever, you have to try to find a way to make the situation work.

There's an expression for when you get a note from the network: Pretend it's your own note. If you gave yourself this note, how would you change it? I remember clearly a director on *Mary Kills People*, Norma Bailey, had two people sitting in a car. One sitting up front and one in the back. She said, "This is a really tough day and it would be easier if they were sitting next to each other. That way I don't have to move the camera to get all the coverage." So we went home and we thought about it. We tried to rewrite the scene, but it just wouldn't work. The dynamic of them sitting next to each other changed everything. I went back to Norma and said, "I'm really sorry. I can't make it work." And she said, "I really appreciate you trying. I'll figure it out." I had every intention of trying to make it work for her. She is a great director and it was a difficult scene on a huge day. I knew it was going to be a problem, but I just couldn't do it. Sometimes I have changed things and thought it was better.

Q: What advice would you give new writers in writers rooms?

Josh Greenberg - There are two kinds of big sins for writers in the writers room. Sometimes, when you are brainstorming an idea, either a scene or dialogue or a story point, a new writer might say, "I've got it, everyone! I've got the answer." That's going to doom you. It's a curse. All you are trying to do with this group of people is throw ideas out. Brainstorm. Someone puts out an idea and then you build on that idea. It's got to be a lot more free-flowing, rather than someone declaring they have the definitive answer.

The other thing that's maybe a bigger sin than that, is when an idea is on the table sometimes a new writer will say, "No, that doesn't work." That's fine to say that something doesn't work, but you have to have a suggestion to replace it. To just tear something down isn't constructive. I also recommend that every comedy writer try stand-up. It's a really great exercise for being a writer. In a writers room, you're not in front of a studio audience, but you are in front of your peers. You have to be sharp and funny. On set, if a joke doesn't work, you have to quickly provide an alt. I've done a lot of stand-up and I find it really satisfying. It is a really fun thing to do and it teaches you how to work live.

Marsha Greene - One of the best pieces of advice I ever got was from my writing instructor at Humber College. He said, *"Be a joy to be around."* I always think about that. I go to work every day with a smile on my face and a good attitude, ready to work. I think it's important. If people are coming in with that energy, that's the energy of that room. You don't want to be the energy sucker. I would suggest that people are vocal about their ideas even when they are nervous. You learn from being wrong, too. Putting yourself out there is what is going to make you better at the job. Also, in terms of being vocal, try and find something in the material that you connect with or have personal experience with. The first show I worked on was a medical show. I got hired with this other writer and we were both new in the room. Her father was a doctor, her mother was a nurse, her grandfather was a doctor - everybody was in it. I didn't even have a family doctor - that's where my life was at. But there were sisters in the show and I have a sister. I was living with my sister and we were incredibly close. That's where I am going to focus my energy. Rather than pitching medical ideas that I don't know anything about so they won't be any good, I will focus my ideas on what I do know. That can make it a little easier. Maybe there are times when you are not saying anything for a long time and that's okay. You can't always be quiet; you have to find something where you have some ideas. Go home at night and come up with ideas and get ready to share them. Or find a moment with your showrunner and tell them you had some pitches, but you couldn't get a word in. Find a way to be seen and heard in the room. It's really important and it will make you a better writer.

Barbara Stepansky - Know the expectations of your showrunner because every room is slightly different. Some showrunners want new writers to speak up, some want them to listen more. Feel it out and then contribute the best you can.

Q: Are there any challenges or advantages to writing on set?

Jed Mercurio - We all like to get our scripts into the best possible shape, but when filming, sometimes things come up that weren't predicted and they need to be discussed. It's a great advantage for a writer to be part of that conversation so to help find solutions.

Hilary Galanoy - For *Falling Inn Love,* the director, Roger Kumble was very supportive of writers. He was one before he became a director. He feels the writers should be part of the process and he wanted us there at the table read in New Zealand. It was awesome. We found out a bunch of things that didn't work. We left the table read and wrote for five hours even though we had just landed in New Zealand.

Elizabeth Hackett - Roger Kumble had been hired quite soon before *Falling Inn Love* started shooting. There were tweaks to be done. There is something to be said about being there in person with the actors and hearing it out loud. Also, we are Americans writing for New Zealanders. Most of the cast were from New Zealand and they were like, "Actually, we would say it more like this." Great! Tell us! How would you say this?

Hilary Galanoy - Also, what's useful with being on set is that sometimes things come up with a location. This happens a lot. With our Australia movie, we got called by the producers who say a scene isn't happening because something is up with the location. Or maybe we lose an actor. If we are trying to write stuff here in the U.S., it's already tomorrow, mid-day in Australia. Our producer would call frantic because things change and they need help. It helps to be on set to write for that circumstance.

Elizabeth Hackett - I'm a night owl and Hilary is an early bird, so there's always one of us up at some hour so they can get us here. But it's much easier being there.

Marsha Greene - What I admire so much about directors and actors is that they have to do their jobs with an audience. I typically don't have to do my job with an audience. We do our jobs in the privacy of our own homes or the privacy of the writers room. So for someone to say, "This isn't working. Can you fix it?" Then, on the spot, I have to come up with something better; that's my nightmare. I don't like it at all because I feel the pressure of having to come up with something good in the moment in front of this audience. But it's not a problem that I have been asked; that's my job. It's just my own insecurity. But if I'm on set while the actors are blocking and going through lines, and I realize a line isn't working, then let me write something else. That's fine.

Other showunners that I've worked with are much more strict with the script and there are good reasons to do that. It saves time. But I like to watch the scene and see if it's working. Sometimes, what you wrote on the page isn't how it's translating because other people are making choices. The director is making choices. The actor is making choices. The way you wanted it to go maybe just doesn't work. In that situation, I have no problem rewriting it. I feel no pressure. I've cut out whole chunks, half a scene. The actor asked if we were cutting it because we were running out of time. No, I was watching it unfold and wondering why all of this was happening. It had all been said and just wasn't needed. So I don't like doing it when other people ask because I feel self-conscious about doing my job. But I do think, generally, it's important to have a writer on set for the reason of rewriting lines, but also because the writer knows the whole story and the characters. They are able to be the keeper of that knowledge for the people on set.

Carolina Rivera - I wish we were writing on set here in Mexico. Instead, they tell you what the problem is and you fix it. You're not on set, which is bad. I have so many things to say about my story. And I've been in the room. I know what's coming and what was. I can help.

Julie Sherman Wolfe - When it comes to my Hallmark movies, going to set is mostly for fun rather than work. By the time they start shooting, most of my writing is done. I've already worked with the director, done production rewrites, and made tweaks to the script when they change locations or need to make cuts. Still, I prefer to be involved all the way through production, even on the smallest line changes, because you can tell the difference when someone else, like a producer or director, writes it. It doesn't have the same tone.

Being on set or not, that's up to me. But I love going. It's always incredibly rewarding to see how every single person on the cast and crew bring the script to life and make it even better than you envisioned. Most of the time, I'm thrilled. Sometimes, a line gets read and I think, "Oh, man, that's not how it's supposed to go." But again, on a Hallmark movie, I'm not a producer or director. I can't give a line reading note. But saying that, if it's glaringly wrong, and if I have a good relationship with them, I may whisper my note to the producer, who may or may not whisper it to the director, who may or may not say it to the actor. But you didn't hear that from me.

Michael Brandt - The movies I've written that have turned out the best, happen to be the movies where I was on set a lot. It's not because of me. It's because the writer was there. I think if the director is strong enough in terms of what his job is and what he's bringing to it, allowing the writer to handle the writing, takes so much off his plate. Assuming the relationship is good, of course. On *Wanted*, the director wanted Derek Haas and me on the set. He thought it was important because the actors felt better and he did as well. Eventually, we were off the film and it was rewritten by other writers who were servicing other masters. Because of that, the script didn't make sense anymore. What was put in didn't take the whole movie into account. To the point that sets were built that no one had any idea what they were for. We were brought back in last minute to try and make it work.

The number one way movies go off the rails is when there isn't someone guarding the story. Yes, it should be the director's job on a feature, but I've directed and it's really hard. New ideas enter the fold from a stunt coordinator, an actor, a studio exec, or a producer that may sound really good, but fuck up Act 3. An actor may want to change a line now, but there are ramifications of it that nobody is thinking about. So you have to tell the actor why they can't do what they want to do for story reasons. Usually, they will thank you for guarding that.

Ben Philippe - When the writers are on set, the Story Editor might be at the Video Village giving notes while the scene is filming. There might be times when an actor wants to try something different. Sets are very much the showrunner and the director's domain and the writers are looped in if they are needed. When I went on set for the shooting of our episode on *Only Murders*, it was more like, "The writers are visiting," rather than, the writers have all the power.

I've heard nightmare stories of writers on set being upset that the lines weren't being delivered correctly. The fact is, you are low on the totem pole. I'm always nervous on sets because everyone is an expert at what they are doing. When you are a writer, it's just me and my laptop. On set, it's tactile. The grip, the person doing the electrical work, the person moving the camera - they all know what they are doing. I am in the corner because I don't want to be in the shot and someone has to yell at me to move. Sets stress me out.

Barbara Stepansky - Fixing lines on set happens sometimes when circumstances call for it, but we want to avoid cutting out or replacing anything because it's a trickle-down-effect to the other episodes. That's why it's good to have a writer on set because they can tell why we need a line or an action, as it can set up a story point down the line.

CHAPTER REVIEW: THE WRITERS ROOM & WRITING ON SET

- The showrunner is responsible for the overall vision of a series. Often, they are the creator of the show.

- Showrunners must be good and fast decision makers.

- Showrunners are managers as well as creatives. They deal with all elements of business, including talking to financiers and representation.

- Showrunners set the culture (supportive, competitive, etc.) for the writers room. A good showrunner hires writers that can thrive in these conditions.

- Writers rooms work well when composed of a diverse set of writers with different life experiences and viewpoints.

- Writers rooms are collaborative spaces and many writers love them as they sit in a room with a bunch of like-minded people and make up stories. They feed off each other's energy to get the best ideas into the show.

- Senior writing positions on a series can be very time consuming.

- Writers rooms generally operate in the same way. Bigger questions about where the show is headed and what the series/season will discuss are dealt with first. Afterwards, the individual episodes are shaped so they work with one another. Finally, a showrunner will divvy up the episodes amongst the team unless they do all the writing themselves.

- Staff writers have to remember to write in the voice of the show.

- Staff writers may change with each new series/season as they go on to other jobs, but the showrunners and senior writers tend to stay the same.

- There's no set number of writers in any writers room.

- When you are working on one show, you are on that show until your contract ends. You can't really write on two shows at once.

- Showrunners must keep shows on budget and deliver episodes on time.

- As a new writer in a writers room, you should be listening a lot to figure out what's going on. You can offer suggestions, but be careful how you present them. Tearing people down with no way to fix ideas or saying you have the best solutions is a good way to not be invited back.

- Writing on set allows you to solve problems as they arise. This could be anything from a dialogue issue to a location problem.

CHAPTER 11

REWRITING

It's a given in screenwriting; you're going to get notes. Sometimes, they are direct. Sometimes, they are cryptic. In either case, you need to figure out if the suggestions work or not. In this chapter, our writers give their perspectives on getting and responding to feedback before they embark on the other given of screenwriting: rewriting.

Q: What is your experience with notes and rewriting?

Briana Belser - Oh, my God, the rewriting. They say that writing is rewriting and Lord, it is. Even on set. The actors are waiting and I'm typing up revisions. It's just not over until it's over. And then it's shot and you're ADR-ing and you're still writing dialogue! Then it's the day before the episode is going to air and the executives are reaching out to you for the logline summary that you put on the story area eight weeks ago. I wake up every single day and I am sitting at my desk between 9 a.m. and 10 a.m. and I am writing until the evening. I clock in every single day on my samples, my pitches, and my ideas. Writing is rewriting. The point at which I was hired was not the moment when I began to write. I had been doing it for years. The scripts that I am only now just starting to pitch to develop, have been written going on ten years ago. It doesn't mean that they will ever come to fruition. Writing is rewriting. It is so solitary. It is so emotional.

Also, nothing is a wasted draft. I have all these aphorisms. It's funny, I met somebody who has done quite a lot of stuff and he said, "Yeah, I don't get notes from anybody. The only people who give me notes are the people who pay me." Well, I don't feel that way. I have a couple of people that I go to and ask - I just want a read. What do you see? I don't necessarily want you to fix it. What isn't in there that I think is in there that needs to be in there? Especially with stuff that I want my reps to send out. I will do that before I send it to my rep with the idea that I am not really looking for notes from my rep. If they want to give me notes that's great and if I agree, fine. But when I give it to them, I feel like I've got it to a place where it could go out. That is different from the way I would've done it ten years ago. You have to manage the self-doubt.

Josh Olson - On *A History of Violence,* there was one brief pass with the studio. So brief. And I got some good advice from someone. If it's a small amount of notes, don't charge them for the rewrite even though it is in the contract because you want to be the guy they have to call when they get a director. They would not have booted me off at that point anyway, but it was good advice. It took a day to do the first round of notes from the studio. Then when David Cronenberg came on, he and I sat there for literally a week and walked through the entire script. Talked about everything. And that was pretty much it. I did a few tweaks here and there, but basically, my second draft is what got shot.

Scott Lobdell - My friend John McLaughlin (*Black Swan*), told me years ago that when you get notes from a network or studio, they will say, "It doesn't work that Sam takes out a gun at the restaurant and shoots Andrew. So take it out." But as the writer, you're thinking that's the most important scene. How can they take that out? John told me when someone gives you a note that's against something you really like, chances are it's not Sam shooting Andrew in the restaurant. It's a previous scene with Sam on the gun range that needs reworking. Often you need to rewrite something earlier so when Andrew is shot in the restaurant, the audience says, "Oh, of course, Sam shot him. Good, he should have shot him."

So the trick is, sometimes you have a moment in your script, which works as a set piece that you love, but you have to ask: did the characters earn the set piece? And if not, you have to go back and set it up so when the studio exec reads it, they understand now why that scene is there. You do want to build things up and to me, that's the fun part of writing. The opposite of the fun part is when you are shooting for 102 pages and you're at 95 and have to go back and build things in. Or if you're at 120 and you realize that nobody in the world is going to read a 120 page horror script. No one's attention is that long, so then you have to go back and start shaving down stuff you have set up. That part is tedious. Sometimes, if you are on your eighth time re-reading the script, you can feel like you can't take it anymore. Then, you see something and get through it. But the way I stay engaged is through the mechanics of making sure the story works.

After I've written a script, I send it out to my producer to get notes. My friend, Frank Hannah, who wrote *The Cooler,* says, "You can't just send in first drafts. That's not how this works. You have to talk to people and make edits." But to this day, once I write Fade Out and take care of any typos, I send it out straight to my producer. However, what I've also learned is that you need to have the right producer as otherwise, you get notes back like, "I love the action. I love the characters. I love the humor. I love the resolution. I love this movie, but it's the Senator's wife who is dying, so he's the one with something at stake. So *Bypass* has to be about him, not the two EMTs." To me, that is like you turning in *Jaws* and somebody goes, "I love this. I love the setting, this small Rhode Island beach. I love the sheriff that doesn't swim. That's a great idea. He's a sheriff in a beach town. And you have the ornery fisherman who comes in. But here's the thing, people don't like sharks. Make it about a dolphin because people love dolphins. That's your movie." That's not my movie. So make sure you find a producer who wants to do your story. Not one who wants to do another script.

Moisés Zamora - Everyone dreads notes and, of course, there is a part of me that dreads that, but I think it's fear-based because it triggers your self-esteem - I'm a bad writer. If you put yourself in a growth mindset, notes are actually the best thing in the world. Some of them are really wack. When they are really wack, you have to realize that the people giving them to you are obviously smart individuals. They have been doing well in Hollywood. Why are they wack? That means that you're not, as a writer, doing a great job in being clear on the page with your execution and intentions. If it's just one wacky person and the others are somewhat okay, then I think you need to take a look and contextualize where this is coming from. When you do that analysis, it actually helps you discover something in your writing that you are not seeing. And I think it's important to go through that process.

I used to get upset when getting notes, but now I just kind of love them. It's like when you go and work out. I get myself prepared, it's stressful, you've got to get up. When you are in the middle of it, it's kind of exciting. Your adrenaline is pumping and all these things are firing in your cells everywhere. I treat notes like that - like it's going to be a Boot Camp

> ## KILLING YOUR DARLINGS
>
> The rewriting process is difficult. Sometimes cruel. You've been slaving away, carefully crafting characters, plot, scenes, and dialogue for weeks or months and it seems perfect. You love it! Every word. Then you or other people read your creation, and invariably, something isn't working. You need to rewrite something, or worse, cut it for good. This can feel awful.
>
> So you go through the five stages of grief, but eventually, come to the acceptance stage and realize that you must make the changes. Usually, time is the best friend you have. With distance, you can apply story theory to your work objectively to figure out what's gone wrong. More often than not, the changes do make things better, so don't be afraid of this process.
>
> If it makes you feel better, directors, editors, composers - any art form, really - experience these feelings, so you are not alone. And despite the title of this section, what you've written doesn't have to die. Perhaps it can be saved for another story down the road. So save it!

workout. When I go back, I do let them sit for a second. I do simmer a bit because they do trigger something. Usually, when they trigger something, they are speaking to your creative process and I pay attention to what they are triggering. And I'm getting better at deciphering what's the note behind the note - everyone says that expression and it's so annoying. No, the note is the note. You're the one who gives it meaning and it's important to know how your process works. If you are pushing back and are going to burn the house down because they told you to do this or that, well, you're not going to get that $50 million. And you want to get there. Obviously, if you have an Oscar...John Ridley didn't implement any notes on *American Crime*. He was like, "Thank you for your notes," but didn't implement any. Not a single one. But they are not going to be wagging their fingers and saying, "John Ridley, why are you not putting in that note that I gave you?" He'd probably just put the Oscar on the table and say, "Come again?"

But it's a collaborative process and people giving you notes allows you to sell them again on your vision. You have to do that throughout. You have to sell the PA on your vision. You have to sell the actors on your vision. Grandma, you have to sell her on your vision. There are different ways to practice that. There's a different type of language that you have to use and the best writers and creators know how to sell the same vision to a five-year-old all the way to the actors and all the way to the owner, the head of the studio. The note process allows you to express and use the vocabulary necessary to keep selling your vision.

Danny Strong - With notes, I am very collaborative. I am not insecure with notes. When someone gives me a note, I don't consider it an attack on my intelligence or talent as a human being. I take it as there may be something wrong that we need to fix. It doesn't mean they are always right. I like to have a few people read things, so I can get a sense of where I'm at. Sometimes, people's tastes or opinions are theirs and other people disagree with them. Unfortunately, the people that pay you? You do have to listen to them. You don't have to take every note, but if you are combative about everything then it can be a problem.

CHAPTER 11: REWRITING 187

Notes usually mean there is something wrong or there is something confusing. It could be better. The goal isn't to satisfy the notes so the studio or network is happy. The goal for me is to take the note and figure out how to improve the piece with this note. I'm trying to make it better from my point of view and, hopefully, other people's points of view. I think maybe there's a problem here and how do I make it better, rather than, I'll just satisfy them. Sometimes, I will think they are wrong and I will talk them out of it. Usually, I'm listening to 75% of the notes and figuring out how to improve the script. Sometimes, more.

Emma Ko - Sometimes, the notes have nothing to do with your talent or the writing. They have to do with what's happening in the politics of the broadcasting industry. We are, in some ways, completely and utterly at the whim of what is going on out there. I had many friends developing projects with the BBC when the head of production left. Years and years of work may have been shelved. And there's nothing they can do about it. My sitcom went on ice because the head of comedy at Channel 4 left to go to Apple.

It can work in your favor, sometimes. My sitcom is set within the entertainment world. It's about an actress working in the UK industry. When the commissioning editor came on board, he said that both he and the head of comedy were unsure about it because there is, or was, a belief in commissioning that people aren't interested in watching shows set in the TV/Film industry. However, after some time *Starstruck* had come out on BBC Three, the Rose Matafeo show about falling in love with an A-list actor. Minnie Driver is the power-hungry Hollywood agent and it's done incredibly well. So between the first meeting that was originally meant to happen and the subsequent one a few months later, things had changed. He was more open to my idea because *Starstruck* did so well. It goes both ways and one just has to take a Zen-like approach to it all. Everything takes time and within that time you can get bad news and good news. The other thing to add is that any meeting with a broadcaster will get postponed at least three times.

Dan Mazer - I love getting notes. I may be perverse and unique in that, but because writing is so solitary, you sit there and you torture yourself. And even if notes are bad, they are good because they force you to think and react to something. And you'll always make something better. If someone says they don't like something, then you have to justify it. And in that process of justifying it, you might make it better or come to another realization. The truth is I sit on my own stewing over stuff for months on end, so any external impetus to that, like the read through, is oxygen. You don't have to agree with them. Sometimes, you can and that's even better. Even if you don't agree with them, they will make you think and they will start a dialogue and one thing you don't have as a writer on your own is a dialogue, so I'm all for it. The more notes the better.

Eli Craig - I've gotten to a point now where I have to get the script to a place where I can stand up to the notes. You can get really pressured on time. When you have weeks to write a script, either it can be a glorious ten weeks of wow, it all came together, fantastic! Or none of it is working: you're eight weeks in and I hate this thing. What do I do? You feel the deadline is really important and it is to them, but it's inevitably worse to turn in a draft that you don't like on time. Then, you get all these notes that you already knew about; you know what's not working. Often, you will get notes on a draft that you don't like, but then there are elements that they fall in love with and don't want to change, but you don't like them. Then, everything becomes a mess because you are trying to make their script work.

DEVELOPMENT TERMS

When providing feedback on your work, development executives may use some jargon that seems vague or broad. Here are some of the more common things they may bring up and how they should be translated.

Beat: A moment in a screenplay.

Character doesn't track/Story doesn't track: the development of the character's growth or the plot isn't fluid or smooth.

Contrived: When a story beat or character action that hasn't been set up comes out of nowhere. Usually happens to get around a hole in the plot or other story problem.

Dense/Overwritten: Too much writing on the page in either action lines or dialogue. Slows down the read. Hard to read. AKA: too much black on the page.

Derivative: A story that seems taken from or based on an already made project usually to inferior standards.

Elevated: When a genre script has a new or sophisticated approach to the storytelling.

Familiar: A story that seems like it's been done before. Doesn't offer anything new.

Get into it faster: Extraneous scenes or dialogue must be cut to move things along.

Like the arena: The world you have created is interesting and engaging.

Lost the character/Not with the character (POV shift): Leaving the main character's vantage point for so long that their character development gets hampered.

Needs more tension: Not enough drama occurs.

Not likable: A character isn't sympathetic to the audience. Means they will not root or care for them.

On the nose: Too close to what something should be - a lack of subtext or subtlety.

Pay off: The result of a set up. A promise to resolve.

Predictable: The plot or the characters' actions didn't surprise the reader.

> **DEVELOPMENT TERMS (CONTINUED)**
>
> **Raise the stakes:** Where you add more risky obstacles for your protagonist.
>
> **Set piece:** A sequence of scenes generally revolving around one location that has important ramifications to story and character. Often moments of these will appear in the trailer or marketing.
>
> **Set up:** Planting an important seed of either a character's persona, an action, a prop, the style of the writing, which will come into play later.
>
> **Structure problem:** A main story beat or act is either missing or in the wrong place.
>
> **The bad example is...:** What a note giver states when they are about to give you a suggestion of a fix, but it's not meant to be exactly what you're supposed to do. It's to get you thinking in the right direction.
>
> **Tone shift:** Something has happened in story that doesn't fit with the set up genre/style.
>
> **Too fat/Too thin:** Too much or too little of something (act length, dialogue, character development, etc.)

Whereas, I really think good notes are just trying to hone in on your vision for something. If you are 90% percent there, then good notes are seeing the script as an organism, and what would make this organism tick better? Rather than trying to make a bunch of different people's egos and ideas kind of fit within a project.

Meg LeFauve - I wish I knew whom to credit for this, but I met the writer of *Spotlight*, who told me he had a friend with a great take on notes, "Getting notes is a three-step process: fuck you, fuck me, what's next?" Yeah, that pretty much is it. When you get notes at first, you can get very defensive because I think at some point your brain thinks you are being killed. You are your story. You go into survival instinct. That's why I always record notes when I am first getting them because you aren't going to remember half of them and you have no objectivity. You are just down in survival mode. Then you can turn that against yourself. "I suck. I don't know why I am a writer. I should quit." That's the "fuck me" moment.

Eventually, if you give it enough time, it will turn into "what's next?" What am I going to do next? How am I going to fix this? As a pro writer, you may have to go through all those stages in the room with the director and the head of the studio. They don't care about the fuck you/fuck me stuff. They want to hear about what's next and have that conversation. Sometimes, you can't. You have to take time to think about it and have another meeting. You know that you are just getting too riled up about it. You know you have to get out of that part of your brain, or better, you use it for the material.

THE FIRST 10 PAGES

In a world where distraction is ever present, it's imperative that you capture a reader's attention from the start of your screenplay. In addition, most experienced readers know if they like your writing straight away. So while you obviously want your entire screenplay to be engaging, you should pay particular attention to the first ten pages. Here are some things to keep in mind to help you out.

- Make sure you've set up the world clearly. Where are we? What time period?

- Clarify the genre and the tone. Is it a comedy? A thriller? A dark or slapstick comedy? A psychological or action thriller?

- Introduce your main character or characters. Show their assets and flaws preferably via their actions.

- Start your film with something engaging. This could be an action set piece, a murder, a large dance routine, a comedic sequence, a misdirection that plays on the reader's expectations, or a prologue that creates mystery.

- Some writers like to have questions posed in either the dialogue or the action lines at the bottom of a page so a reader is compelled to turn the page.

- If are able, end this section with the inciting incident so that your characters realize the stakes of the problem they will have to overcome.

- Be descriptive of location and character, but keep it as brief as possible so as to not bog down the read. We don't need a lot of details unless they are important to the plot.

- Make your dialogue as crisp and real as possible.

- Read it out loud. It's the best way to see if your dialogue and action lines are moving along well.

I think that a lot of people who are not great note-givers are sometimes just shadow artists; they really want to be the writer and creator and they are using you as a tool. Those notes generally don't work well. But there can also be wonderful, amazing note-givers anywhere. It can be a studio executive. There's this idea that they don't give good notes. But they do, they've made a lot of good movies. I just try to stay open and I always ask questions back to the note-giver. I have to understand what is really going on here.

Note-givers are giving you the symptoms of the disease. So your job is not to just do those notes because you will just get different symptoms. You have to go down deeper into the engine - the creation of this thing, and figure out why these symptoms are coming up. That's the deep work that the writer needs to know how to do.

Ron Leshem - Writers, when they are criticized, believe that the reader doesn't understand the story or understand them. That they are trying to make it more commercial or cheaper in all ways. When they listen to the executive and they give solutions to the issues, they hate the solutions, either because they are really bad or it's not to your taste. The executive is not the writer. What they are doing is giving you the warning sign that something didn't work. Don't listen to his solution; it is just an example. Don't get stuck on the solutions. When you get where the problems are, the warning signs, you will most likely have to go put this draft in the drawer and go back to the blank page and start drawing the structure of the three acts. Then you can see what doesn't work in the plot points.

When I wrote the first draft for *Beaufort*, I was lucky to work with a brilliant director who was eager to listen to my story and embrace it. I wrote the first draft in two weeks. When I brought it in he was amazed that I wrote it so quickly. He said, "You realize that not even a single page will get to the screen." I was confused. He told me that we do twenty drafts. Some of these drafts are rewrites. Some are you throwing it all into the drawer and starting over from scratch. But what survives at the end of the day is worth it after twenty drafts. I couldn't understand this because I was a journalist. We have deadlines at night for the next day's news. Why not write now what would be the twentieth draft? Why do we need to go through erasing everything? It doesn't make sense. Only when I became more mature in my writing did I realize that when I looked for shortcuts and didn't do the whole process, it would never be made, and if it was, it wouldn't be good. So I want the long process.

The other side of this is that you get to a point when you are so tired of rewriting. You want this to be made, so when a producer, director, executive, or network comes and gives you ideas, you just embrace all the ideas because you are so tired and just want to move on to your next project. You want it to be this? No problem. You want to cut this scene? No problem. Then you lose your story.

Alex Litvak - One of the challenges of writing, whenever you are dealing with notes given to you by friends or your employers, is that you cannot say no to everything or you will never work again. And you cannot say yes to everything because you will run it into the ground.

One of my early experiences when I first sold a TV show was that it also included a blind deal for my next thing, which meant I had to pitch ideas. I pitched ideas until I was blue in the face and we settled on an idea, which I don't think was the best idea I had. Then, I was pitching ideas for the pilot. I pitched ten ideas and number ten was the one they said yes to. Not the best idea for the pilot. As I wrote it, they would have all these notes. And every note was the greatest note ever. You want it in red? Here you go. You want stripes? Brilliant, stripes it is. Even though the script is well written, it has no identity because I lost sight of what the story was about.

I lost sight of the question - why do you care? If you think the executives know, they don't. They are working on a hundred different things. They woke up this morning thinking, why don't we try this? And sometimes they are correct in identifying the problem, but it's on you to solve it. They may say something feels off. Let's amputate the leg. Or add more ketchup. And, it's your job as the physician or the chef to say, "Right. Let's not amputate the leg. Let's try an antibiotic. And, yes, something is off taste-wise. But ketchup is not the answer. Let's try a pinch of salt." That's the tango that you are always doing. You cannot say no and you cannot say yes, so how do you find the maybes? That's incredibly challenging.

Julie Sherman Wolfe - After twenty-five years writing professionally, I like to think I know what I'm doing. But sometimes, I get so wrapped up in a script, I can't look at it objectively anymore. My producer and/or the network exec can read it and say, "Hey. You missed this. And this. And this. And this." And then I have to go back in and fix it. Sometimes, you'll have multiple sets of notes, and go back in multiple times. It can be pretty brutal, and sometimes it stings when they don't like what you thought was "brilliant" work. But it happens to everyone.

That being said, if you have good relationships with the executives and producers, and have already proven yourself as a writer they can count on, you can have a conversation about the notes. You can explain why a certain note gives you pause. You can even explain, respectfully, if a certain note pulls a string that upends the entire movie. But if you want a long career, it's very important to remember that you ultimately have to make the network happy. You can discuss a note all you want, but if they say, "Do it anyway," DO IT! Because they're paying you. You work for them. Nothing you wrote is that precious. Kill your babies, as they say. That's part of the job. I can't tell you how many people have done one Hallmark movie and never get asked back, because they argue with the notes and couldn't just let something go. That's the kiss of death.

Dave Reynolds - The first thing you need to embrace is that any note you get is NOT personal. Even if it feels like it is. This is natural because we're presenting ideas that we thought up and someone is telling us they don't like it or more likely that "it's wrong". Many times they won't tell you what the "right idea" is because that's what they're paying you for. On the surface, getting notes seems pretty personal and reacting to it makes sense. Here's the difference. It's Hollywood. Someone is paying you to tell a story. They will have thoughts, sometimes insane thoughts, on how they want you to tell it. As long as they are paying you, you need to make the changes they want as best you can. It's not personal - it's just business.

When I was new at Disney years ago, I learned about the "note within the note." I remember an executive coming in and saying he didn't like a ballroom scene. After he left, my co-writer and I looked at each other like, "What just happened? We've been working on this thing forever and that person never had an issue with it before today." That's when you look for the note behind the note. You realize that they didn't like the dynamic between these two characters. They didn't believe them. Or why is this or that happening here? You pull apart the thing that was seemingly working ten minutes earlier. You now look at it from different angles and see if it still works. That exec couldn't pinpoint the problem, only that there was a problem. And if they were bumping on it, it most likely means that future audiences would also.

When you get a strong note and you think you have to rewrite the whole thing, it is a good idea to see what you can save first. Sometimes, you need to be more like a detective to find the problem. If you can, ask that producer or executive what they specifically liked or didn't like. This way, they pick it apart and you can pull out what bumped. "Oh, it was this? So if I made this change, would that work? No. Okay, how about this?" Then you start to figure out exactly what they didn't like.

Q: Have you ever been rewritten? How do you deal with that?

Barbara Stepansky - I went into the *Flint* script knowing that at some point someone is going to have to come in and adjust the tone. My tone tends to be sarcastic and dry. I didn't have an ego in that sense, at all. It was a difficult phone call for them to make; telling me that they need to have someone new to come in. But I knew because we had talked about it upfront. They were pleased with the reaction because writers are usually a lot more sensitive. I had a step left in my contract so they could come back to me. And that's what you want, for them to feel they can come back to you, so why would you put up a fight? I did three director drafts for Bob Beresford for *Flint*. I remember the second one was a big step backward. And I did the third one and he was happy with that. Then they hired another writer to rewrite me to get the Lifetime tone a little more out. Then that writer's contract ran out and they hired me back because I had one more rewrite on my contract and because I had done all the research, I could go into the script and figure out what still needed to be done for production. I has happy that a lot of what I had written was left standing. I'm actually a lot more of a brutal re-writer so if you hired me to rewrite, you will probably get a page one rewrite.

Alex Litvak - Writing is rewriting. So I have rewritten people - and I have been rewritten. I also rewrote myself, revisiting scripts from years ago, so you are coming in with a completely different perspective. Your first task is do no harm. There's always something in the material that's working, the diamond in the rough, even if there's a lot of rough. Hold on to that and improve the rest.

As far as dealing with being rewritten, the script stops being your baby the moment it's out of your hands. So wish the next writer the best of luck and move on to another project. A shark keeps swimming to stay alive. A writer keeps writing to stay sane.

Q: How important is it to be open to producers' changes?

Jed Mercurio - Everybody gets notes at every level of the industry. That's usually because we are working for people who are paying for the production and productions cost a lot of money. Obviously, people can make their own short films on a shoestring and then there are no notes because there's no significant money involved. I think it's part of your development as a writer to be able to communicate with executives and to find a way to collaborate with them. I think it's always best to work with the notes, rather than against them. It's down to your own interpersonal skills to be able to do that. Clearly, there are examples, and people end up talking about this, which is how you deal with the terrible note. And then it's really about the person who gives the terrible note, not about you. If they give a terrible note, but they're a reasonable person, if you politely and professionally talk through how the note doesn't help, then a reasonable person will accept that. It's when you get that combination of an unreasonable person and a terrible note - then you're stuffed. There's no way past that, really. In an ideal world you get out of that relationship, but that may not be something that is possible for you. I'm afraid I don't know what the solution is there.

Eli Craig - Writing is rewriting, so notes are always useful if they come from a thoughtful place, even if you decide to ignore them, they might give you some insight into something the script is missing. You should always be open to feedback and changing things, but it really depends on the situation and the producer. Is it an assignment? Are you adapting a book, rewriting a script, writing your own material, writing for a director, or are you directing? Is the producer Steven Spielberg or a first time producer that has high hopes and no clue? Since I am usually only writing stuff I plan to direct, I have a little more say than if you're writing on assignment for a producer. In general, a producer is probably pushing you in whatever direction they think the studio is going to want, or will help them sell the script and market the movie. Ideally, your producers are giving you notes to help draft a cleaner, more marketable script for the budget you have, but that's not alway the case. Basically, it all depends on how much you value the producer's insights and your relationship with them.

CHAPTER REVIEW: REWRITING

- Often times, a problem with a scene is not in the scene itself. It's something that preceded the scene.

- The goal of notes is to make the project better. Notes mean that something in the script is confusing the reader or it isn't as clear as you think.

- Some people love notes because writing is such a solitary process. It's nice to be collaborative for a change.

- It's natural to be defensive when you first receive feedback on your script. Just don't let it ruin your relationship with the note givers - especially if they are paying you.

- Be openminded, listen, and ask questions when you receive notes if you think they aren't being clear.

- Figure out the note behind the note. Often note givers aren't sure what the problem is. They just have a feeling that something is wrong.

- Only work on the notes that make sense. If you do notes just to please the studio or a financier and they don't work for the project, you will only make the script a mess.

- Writing is rewriting. Sometimes, you do the rewriting. Sometimes, someone rewrites you.

CHAPTER 12

ACTION & THRILLER

———

Some of the highest earning films and TV shows are the ones that get your heart racing, but they also tend to be very intricate genres to write. And they can be expensive! So how does one handle fights and other action scenes? How do you sustain tension for long periods of time? Should you write with the budget in mind? Are the stunt people ever consulted in the writing process? This next chapter promises to be a page-turner (we hope!)

Q: What makes for a good action thriller idea?

Alex Litvak - The answer to that question is the same as the answer to the question: What makes a good story and why do I care? Every story regardless of the genre should have that special sauce that you add to make the scenes more exciting. To make the villain more compelling, clever, formidable, whatever. To make the hero or heroine more courageous. But all of that is wallpaper. At the end of the day, the question of whether you want to live in this space comes down to: Why do I care? Why do I get invested in this world, in these people, in this situation? And there it really goes to two places. It goes to the head and it goes to the heart.

To start with the head: Does this idea, the big "what if?" make you go, "Ah ha! That's cool." Do I see the trailer for that movie in my head? The moment I say, "This is a story about a bus that if it goes less than fifty miles per hour, a bomb will explode," you get a trailer in your head that says, "Oh, that's cool. I want to see that." Or do I have your attention and curiosity with this intellectual piece?

In action movies, you're kind of there for the action. It helps when you like the characters and you get invested in them. I would argue that the classics of the genre are the movies where you really enjoy being with the hero. Obviously, there are exceptions. Look at the *John Wick* movies. I don't know if there's anything compelling about the guy. He's just a really great killer, but you really enjoy him doing his thing. He's a master chef in the kitchen of murder. Ultimately, it's always good to have some level of emotional investment. It's not like it has to have that chase or it needs to have this gunfight. As you build it, it absolutely does. Structurally, there are certain expectations in an action movie. You have to have a certain number of set pieces because that's what the audience wants to see. But when you start with a premise, it's the same for any genre: why do I care?

Michael Brandt - Recently, my wife and I heard a horrific story about a kid who was murdered by someone he'd gone to school with years earlier. Within a day, the police found the deceased boy's phone, saw the messages, figured out who did it, and arrested the murderer.

After we heard it, my wife said, "Wow! You've got to write that movie." But it's not a movie. It might be a good television episode, but it's not a movie because within twenty-four hours, we know who did it. And while there are certainly stakes for the kids and their parents, as a removed writer, I can see there are no stakes for the police doing the investigation. There are no twists and turns and straight-ahead stories don't make movies. People hear something emotional and think that's good enough. You need emotion, of course, but then you need to have the four or five other things that the audience, or the police, don't see coming, in order for a thriller plot to work. Now, if we had found out that the deceased set up this fucker because he was harassing him in high school years ago and he wanted to commit suicide and take this kid down with him... well, then you might have something.

Then we have to know what's the point of view. Are we omnipotent? That's one way to do it, but then we definitely need the twists and turns. Is there a cop character who's going to drag us through the story? Is it the mom who's seeking justice and is going to find out who did this and why? Ultimately, we have to figure out who's going to take us through the story. Lacking that, you don't have a movie. You have a story, but not a movie.

Finally, for me, I have to have an inherent gut feeling that a story's three acts will lay out clearly in front of me right off the bat. In the case of this story, there are only two acts: what happened and the fallout. One of the oldest adages in Hollywood is: What's the second act? If you have to dig really hard to find a second act or find yourself manufacturing one over and over that doesn't seem to fit, that's probably a bad sign. If the second act doesn't present itself to you right away, I think you're ultimately wasting your time.

Q: It's been said that you need seven set pieces for an action film. Is that true?

Josh Olson - Sounds reasonable, I guess. It's always been intuitive for me. I watched a lot of movies, I know the beats. If you're a rock and roll songwriter, you don't need someone to tell you about bridge/verse/chorus. I can read a script that I wrote and know that there is way too much time going on between action scenes. I really need a car chase right now. This is an action movie and we need to put more action in it. You write for yourself and the audience.

Jed Mercurio - I think that's more about genre expectations. If you're setting out to deliver a thriller and you've persuaded the audience that that's what they are going to be watching, then there are expectations that you must absolutely deliver on. I don't think it's as prescriptive as the old Hollywood model of needing seven set pieces in a feature film or anything like that. You may have an incredibly thrilling movie that only has one set piece and everything orbits that. It's about delivering on the basics of thrillers, which are jeopardy and mystery. There is infinite variety in how you can present those two qualities.

Alex Litvak - A lot of writing is intuitive. It's like interior design; what looks good? Seven episodes? It sounds reasonable, but I can tell you, depending on the movie, it may be too much or it may not be enough. Let me talk you through the classic, tried and true model. This doesn't mean every action movie should look like this because there are values in subverting the model, but with a classic action movie - BOOM! Opening set piece. That would be number one because, as with any story, I need to get your attention and I need to get your attention quickly. If you don't own them in the first twenty pages, you've lost them. And as it would be in real life, if I was telling you a story of how I just had this crazy day, I better hook you in soon, or else you are going to start thinking about your own crazy day.

That's where, especially as a writer, you are dealing with people with very short attention spans who are inundated by material.

Stepping into an action movie, the expectation is you are going to wow them with some cool, edge-of-your-seat stuff. So set piece one. Usually, once that is over, you set up the world and the characters, so by the end of Act 1, you present the problem the hero or heroes are going to go on. That is usually set piece number two. Now we are done with Act 1, we are going into Act 2. In Act 2, you are going to have at least three and possibly four action set pieces, and this is where I think the number is flexible. You are going to have a big action set piece at the midpoint, which is the hinge of the movie. The midpoint is invariably where the audience is like, "Okay, I'm getting a little bored." So you have to hit them with something that gives them another jolt of energy and sets them up for the second half.

The end of Act 2 is usually the "all is lost" moment, so you are going to have something there action-wise to set up the further complications of the problem we are trying to solve. But now we are trying to tell the audience there is no way we are going to solve it. We're doomed. And then, somewhere along the way, you are probably going to have one or two more. Then, obviously, there is going to be the final battle at the end where we manage to save the day. So if you go by that model, you have two in Act 1, four in Act 2, which gets us to six, and then seven in Act 3. The four in Act 2, depending on the movie and depending on the size and scope of the set piece is either plenty and just right or too much and not enough. And also, what level of set pieces are we talking about? It needs to be instinctual.

Always look at other media to compare movies. I talk about interior design in terms of what looks right in the space that you're operating. I also go to cooking: What's the meal look like? If it's seven courses of action, you can get overstuffed. Sometimes, I watch great action movies where taking it apart scene by scene, they're tremendous, but piled on top of one another, I'm kind of done. I'm exhausted. So you have to not look at set pieces by themselves, but at the totality of them. Like at the end of a great meal, you want to walk away saying, "That was great! I feel very satisfied." Not, "Oh my, gosh, I wish I had more. I'm hungry for more." Or, "I'm totally bloated now and I don't want to eat anything else."

Paul King - Somebody said movies have a currency, a sort of contract with the audience. So if I am going to a *Mission Impossible* film, I want there to be seven action sequences or one every ten to fifteen minutes. But the currency of a *Paddington* movie is comedy, so I felt we probably needed a certain number of comic set pieces amongst the story and emotion.

We also wanted an exciting third act and action doesn't come naturally to me at all. I slaved over those sequences to make them even halfway decent. The museum chase was really hard, as was the train chase. We had miniature train sets and then you get to the end and it's only alright. Not exactly *The Lone Ranger*. I don't think Gore Verbinski would watch them and learn anything from them. I read enviously about those writers who get to put, "They fight," and then Doug Liman takes it away and the rest is history. I've got nothing to offer on that front whatsoever.

Michael Brandt - Seven set pieces for an action film seems like a ridiculous notion if the story isn't dictating those set pieces.

Q: Do you think about budget when writing action?

Alex Litvak - In *The Three Musketeers*, the best action set piece we had, we never filmed. Afterward, one of the producers said, "Dammit, we should have found the money. We should have filmed it." It was a great idea and it would have been an awesome set piece. I was very proud of what I did on the page. It was fun. It was clever. It was really well choreographed because it involved a multi-tier sword fight.

The idea was the Three Musketeers are on this mission impossible. They are going to go to London to steal the Queen's diamonds, which are in the Tower of London. That set piece is in the movie and I'm sort of proud of the moves within that set piece and how it unfolds because there are a lot of clever reversals, which made it into the movie. In the book, there's a series of chases and escapes which we didn't have the budget or the time to do. So I said I want to have a great set piece of them getting out of France. So they get to the port at Calais and the harbors are closed and the Cardinal's men are everywhere. So if we can't go through legal channels, we will go through illegal channels. They go into my version of Mos Eisley cantina, which is like the smuggler's den. I wanted to give the *Star Wars* feel where there's all these characters there, so there's the Barbary Coast pirate, and here's a guy in a straw cap in the corner. The whole place is being run by a Russian cossack and all that stuff. They walk in and Porthos has a friend there who is the cossack and they start negotiating the price. But what they don't know, and what they discover over the course of the sequence, is that the Cardinal anticipated that move and he put a bounty on their heads. So all these killers are there and they are all waiting. What ensues is this awesome fight against all these awesome characters. There's a belly dancer on the stage and she's an Arabic assassin. She's using different chains on them. The guy in the straw hat is a ronin and a samurai, so you have a Musketeer fighting a samurai. Then there's a guy in the corner with a basket and he's a snake charmer and the snakes come out. And because it's a multi-tier thing you have one person fighting on one level which impacts someone fighting on another level. So somebody cuts a chandelier and it falls and kills someone on the bottom level. I was so proud of it. But ultimately, it was going to be too expensive and we didn't do it.

Michael Brandt - I definitely don't think about the budget early on. I wrote a *Fast and the Furious* movie and didn't think about the budget. There were no budget conversations until the second draft was turned in. Then, the conversations changed to, "Okay, we're shooting in six months. Let's start to think about what this would be." So don't think about the budget at all early on. You will handcuff yourself. As you get closer to the movie actually getting made, or you understand who might be financing the movie, then you will think about those parameters.

Early on, as much as your script is a screenplay, it's a marketing document to let the financiers know what it could be. Everyone knows that every little beat of action in the script might not be in the final cut. It may not even be shot. But the flavor of what goes into the script, aka the marketing of it, to the people who are going to greenlight it, is really important. An example of that is in the second *Fast and Furious* movie. The first movie was about straight-ahead drag racing. So in the opening race of the second movie, we wrote it so the reader thinks it's a drag race, and then reveal that the cars turn and that it's actually a race around Miami. You aren't given any other information, and, suddenly, the cars make a turn. Wow! You want the readers to experience it like the audience will experience it.

What we added was, when the cars make the turn, the side of the car clips a curb and the hub cap goes rolling down the street. It's just flavor for the script. There was no story reason for that hubcap. It just seemed cool for the read. Nine months later, I'm in Miami and the stunt coordinator comes up and says, "Man, we're having a hell of a time with the hubcap gag." It turns out that in Miami there aren't really curbs, and all the cars we picked, they all have these different wheels. They had spent a week trying to find the right curb and the right wheels. I was like, cut it! We don't have to have that! That's when you realize that the power of the pen is very important in getting the universal gods, the literal gods at Universal Studios, to think, "This is cool. Let's make the movie." At that point, you start taking budget and real-life considerations into it. However, I think it's really important to put that flair into the early drafts so people understand the kind of movie, the tone of the movie, and my marketing of the movie to you, the reader.

Q: How long can a set piece be?

Alex Litvak - The one in *The Three Musketeers* was six or seven pages. You don't want these things to go too long. So six or seven from the entry point. What was cool was everybody was fighting their own fight, and the fights were linked. *Predators* was the same sort of thing. The ending of the original script was when the hero, Adrian Brody's character, puts on the Predator armor and leads the original Predators against the upgrades. It was a Predator versus Predator battle. Fucking *Braveheart* with Predators! Ha! That was insane.

Q: Is there a structure to an action set piece?

Alex Litvak - Action is a little bit like choreographing a dance number. As with every dance number, there's a beginning, middle, and end. So first, engagement - the two partners are engaged in a series of movements with one another. Okay, I'm following the dancers. Inherently, as with the structure of an action movie, there's a moment where all is lost, where our guy or girl is going to get the shit kicked out of them. They are going to lose. Then, there is the pivot where they find a way to turn the tables.

It can't be too short. One, two, it's done. There are exceptions of expectations being subverted. In *Raiders of the Lost Ark*, the famous scene where the guy wants to engage in the sword fight and Indy just shoots him. Boom! One move. That's cleverly subverting the expectations. But for the most part, the classic action set piece cannot be too short, nor can it just go on and on and on because it becomes exhausting. It's finding that Goldilocks, just right model.

Q: How do you make a set piece stand out?

Michael Brandt - First, it has to feel organic to the story and the characters in it. Then, it has to feel different, which is the hardest part. The way out of that involves thinking about what can be added to the set piece that changes the stakes from something that might feel familiar to something that feels fresh. How can you bring another element into the set piece that changes the stakes some way through? In *Indiana Jones,* he's fighting a German and at some point, the plane starts to turn and now there's a propeller involved. Then, more Germans show up and start shooting at them. Later in the scene, the gasoline catches on fire and the whole thing is gonna blow. So what goes from a fistfight between a big guy and a little guy, which is a set piece we've seen a million times, it is now elevated multiple times to something incredible. The easiest way to elevate your set piece is to add an element to it part way through that is different, giving your protagonist a ticking clock or an additional danger.

Q: What are the most difficult aspects of writing an action thriller film?

Alex Litvak - One, making it fresh because it's such a well-traveled genre, but that is true of many well-explored genres. You need to make it comfortably familiar, but refreshingly new. You need to not reinvent the wheel, but put a fresh tire on it. You have certain expectations when you walk into a genre movie. You've consumed a lot of stories in that genre and you expect that a lot of this new story will adhere to the standards of that genre. In the same way, if you are going into a steak restaurant, there had better be a steak there. If they have lots of pasta, that's great, I love pasta, too, but I didn't come to a steak restaurant for pasta. At the same time, you need to be comfortably surprised. If you walk into the steak restaurant and it's the same steak I could have had at twenty different restaurants, I'm never coming back here. As opposed to, ah, I like the sauce and how you seared it and the cut. I can't wait to come back. Again, it's about finding a way to deliver on expectations and subtly, artfully subvert them. This is true of the action genre and true of other genres. As a great man once said, "There is nothing new under the sun, it's how do you make it new-ish."

Two, how do you make those set pieces cool and fresh without just saying let's just throw a lot of money at it? Three, how do you find a good ending to the story and a character you can get behind? Why do I care? Also, one of the challenges is the story has to be simple enough, yet complex enough. When the story becomes way too simple, it starts to become like a B movie if there are no layers to it. Unless of course, it's executed like *John Wick.* That's a very simple story, but it's transcending the genre because the artistry of the scenes themselves is undeniable. It's ballet. For the most part, you want to have layers to your story so it feels like there is more going on than meets the eye. I'm engaged in figuring out the puzzle. At the same time, it can't be so complex that you lose me.

Jed Mercurio - I think the most difficult aspects of writing thrillers are the ones that relate to the expectations. If you're writing thrillers, then you have to deliver thrills. You have to deliver twists and turns, and you have to deliver jeopardy and mystery. You have to keep on delivering those all the way through the piece. You can't be too far away from any of those qualities within the story. Obviously, you can dig into people's personal lives and that can be incredibly enriching for the story and the audience's grasp of the character. However, you still keep needing to go back to what you are asking them to expect the story to be like.

Michael Brandt - It's the thriller part. The action is its own thing. The action serves a purpose; puts people in seats; cuts a good trailer; it is what makes the movie an action genre movie. But the thriller part, the twists and turns, and the choices that you make as the storyteller of who has what information at what point, are the most difficult. What you withhold from your main characters to create a mystery in a thriller is important. Who did it? Why did they do it? Where are they now? Where's the body? How you decide to withhold that information, and to whom you give it, is critical as those are the beams that hold up the 2 x 4s of your story. Those are your signposts along the way that are your act breaks.

Q: What are the cultural differences in writing action movies?

Alex Litvak - With the Chinese market there are certain things you are supposed to stay away from; certain rules to follow. Some of which are very easy and some of which you can't work through. One of the things I'm working on that's funded by Chinese money is a heist movie. The note from the China side was: Thieves need to be caught at the end because in China every crime gets punished. First, I don't know if that's true. Secondly, in *Ocean's Eleven*, you aren't rooting for the thieves to get caught. You're rooting for the thieves to get away. So we have a fundamental problem. You can't work with that one, so you have to ignore it. You are writing for a particular culture, a value system, and as much as possible you try to be respectful and understanding.

Q: How do you reduce predictability in a thriller to keep your audience on the edge of their seat?

Jed Mercurio - I think expectations have to function off predictability. If the audience comes with expectations in relation to the tone and style of the piece, then you have to deliver on those. That's where the predictability lies. They also need to be able to formulate a prediction of what might happen in order for you to subvert it. So to create a twist, you obviously need to have a coherent story, which is pointing in a particular direction, so that the audience can then be confounded by the story lurching in a different direction. If they aren't following the story; if the story is incoherent, then twists just don't work.

Barbara Stepansky - Easy! You figure out what the predictable or expected next step would be and then you don't do it. Or subvert it. Find a different way to get from A to Z.

Q: Do you have any tips for writing fight scenes in an action sequence?

Bill Nicholson - Yes, there should be rules. The first of which would be: How would my protagonist lose? What would happen? For example, if his sword is knocked out of his hand, he's dead. That's it! You don't let go of your sword. You understand that rule. If his sword is knocked out of his hand, he does a somersault, flips over a tree and picks it up, and starts again, then, honestly, it's like those Chinese martial arts movies where they do spectacular dances through trees. It's wonderful and I love to see it, but there is absolutely zero tension in the whole thing.

I remember seeing a Russian film called, *The Red and the White.* It was about the Russian Civil War, right after the Revolution - the Red Army and the White Army. It started out with a group of soldiers who were in a White cavalry troop who were riding through a forest. They come to a river and they unpack, make a little camp, and chat with each other. You spend a good fifteen minutes with them. Then, suddenly, the enemy Red group comes into the scene and they have a terrific fight and all the White people are killed. And then you follow the Red Army. You think - what? Wow! That's war. Then, the Red Army soldiers get captured and they all get killed! Then you follow the next lot. It was a very striking breach of expectation.

Michael Brandt - Besides trying to create a fight scene that no one has seen before, I always think about what I can set up thirty pages earlier that pays off in the fight scene. Having a reveal or throwback makes the fight scene more than just two guys fighting. Hopefully, the audience has forgotten about it, which makes it fun for them. They may go, "Oh, I forgot that guy had a pocket knife," or "Oh, I forgot that guy is allergic to poison ivy!" And the more personal you make it, the better, and it's going to change the dynamics of the scene. If it's not personal, such as a prisoner and a prison guard, with no relationship, fighting, well that's one thing. But if you've seen the prison guard treat the prisoner like shit in Act 1, then that changes the dynamic of the fight scene. So think about what you can do to make the fight personal, which will bring emotion to the scene.

Q: What makes a good action thriller protagonist?

Michael Brandt - To me, a good action protagonist has to endure a lot of pain, which humanizes them. It's why in *Terminator 2,* you needed the new Terminator to be bigger and better than the old Terminator. We knew the limitations of Schwarzenegger's Terminator, and for him to now be a protagonist, we have to have Robert Patrick's Terminator, which is scarier and better. Ultimately, your protagonist can't be the biggest and baddest in every scene. If Jean Claude Van Damme walks into a room, he's going to beat the shit out of everybody. People love that scene in *Oldboy*, where he just kills everybody. But there are no stakes to it because you know he's going to beat up everybody; it's just a matter of volume at that point which became cool because it was so ridiculous.

I used to work for Quentin Tarantino and we've seen what he does with his protagonists. We see what a badass Uma Thurman is in *Kill Bill*. Then, Quentin puts her in a coffin and she had to punch through all that wood in order to get out. To see her go through that pain and imagine what it would be like if we were in that spot, softens her character and makes her relatable. It changes the way we think about her, versus just watching her beat the shit out of everybody in a room.

Barbara Stepansky - Both protagonist and villain are two sides of the same coin. Both have to have a strong want and drive. Both have to have equally strong obstacles. No human ever thinks of themselves as a villain so what makes these characters interesting is that they're willing to do the wrong thing for what's right for them. That applies to everyone in your script. Ideally, you give your characters diametrically opposed agendas and see what magic happens as they struggle through it all.

Q: What makes a good action thriller antagonist?

Michael Brandt - I think being smart would be my number one thing. Also, you want your antagonists to be likable. Part of me is rooting for the antagonist because he's just so funny, cool, smart, or fill-in-the-blank, that I enjoy being with him. He's not just a knuckle dragger who wants money or power. I want to spend time with him and I want the audience to want that, as well. Yes, we want to see him die in the end because, ultimately, he's in the way of our good guy. But it's so refreshing to have an antagonist who is also as worthy, not just physically, but mentally, as our protagonist. It really puts them on an even playing field in terms of all those categories that make a good protagonist. The more you can even those two out and change what the villain wants, the better chance you have at creating an interesting dynamic between the two.

Q: Is it easier or harder to write action thriller for TV than for features?

Michael Brandt - Even though I've done a bunch of years writing TV, I still find features easier. With network television, which I did for five years, everything is open-ended other than your A story. Your A story is about who comes through the hospital doors, or what the bad guy did in the teaser, and let's go get him; and we get him at the end. Everything else is you throwing a meal to the hungry animal. He keeps feeding, and you keep throwing meat at him. Those are the characters on the show and they're not going anywhere for the foreseeable future if you're successful. You need to keep that going. So the question is: How do I change the diet every now and then of what the animal is fed? And how does that change what the animal is doing? That's not as exciting, so, in some ways, it's not as easy. Because you're constantly finding new curve balls to throw at these people, that is why, suddenly, the estranged mum shows up at the end of season one. Or you're thinking, what are the things we can continually try and do to freshen up the interpersonal stories, which, let's be honest, except for *Law and Order* are 100% the reason why people watch television. We weren't making *Law and Order*. Our show is driven by the characters. Whatever reason those bells go off in the firehouse, when the characters return from the call, something needs to have happened on that call that changes the dynamic of a character relationship. The change somehow makes it better, makes it worse, or adds a new element, all of which is helpful, but also it does get a little repetitive for me. Ultimately, in the movies, it's a one-time thing so this conversation is really important. They're not going to have this conversation again so every word is more important.

CHAPTER REVIEW: ACTION & THRILLER

- Don't write with a budget in mind on the first few drafts. Once you get closer to production, then you can start making those changes.

- Action set pieces (or any set piece or scene) should have a beginning, middle, and an end.

- The stakes need to keep rising throughout an action set piece. Start off with something mundane and keep adding elements to it that are different and make it fun and original.

- If you are writing a thriller, you need to thrill them. You can't get too far away from that by going deep into character.

- Writing the twists and turns of a thriller is the hardest part to plot. Consider what your characters know and what you want to withhold and then reveal them.

- Setting up how your characters can lose via the rules of your world goes a long way to adding tension to fight scenes and the rest of the plot.

- Planting elements early in your plot can be brought out later to create tension and jeopardy. It can also be used as a way to state how a character might get out of a horrible situation.

- A good thriller or action protagonist has to go through a lot of pain to achieve their goals. This makes them more relatable.

- A good thriller or action antagonist is as likable and smart as the protagonist.

CHAPTER 13

HORROR & SCI-FI

It seems that no matter the year, no matter what is going on in the world, horror films are always in demand. People love to be scared! With missions to Mars on the horizon and AI entering our lives, sci-fi offers seemingly endless opportunities to explore and test the human condition. What are some things to consider when writing in these two popular genres? How many scares do you need? Are there any taboos that you can't cross? How much world-building is really necessary? Our horror and sci-fi writers give their opinions on this and more.

Q: What makes a good horror or sci-fi idea?

Scott Beck - It's definitely the characters. When we wrote *A Quiet Place*, we ended up making a genre film that was a silent film mixed with the touchstones of Ridley Scott's *Alien*. That was very much the first thing that came to mind, but that's the gimmick of the movie. You can't sustain ninety minutes of someone's attention by only having the gimmick. So who are the characters? It was very much diving into it and making it a drama about a family that cannot communicate. If you stripped all the genre stuff away, it would still be a valid drama; a story that would stand on its own. The same for horror. It can be the scariest situation imaginable, but without those characters, you don't have anything that you're really rooting for or caring about.

Jennifer Raite - It's usually a character in a world that we find interesting, a thematic piece that we want to explore, or something that seems a little scary or evocative that we can't stop thinking about.

Chris Cullari - Jen and I gravitate toward a character whose problem is rooted in something that is equally emotional and supernatural. Then, we build the world out from there.

Q: What do you find special about horror characters?

Chris Cullari - Sometimes, it's as simple as in *Halloween*, where you find the hero is a hero simply because they are going through this horrific life-changing experience. Sometimes, it can be that you find a hero who has a much more specific conversation about where they are in their life and what that supernatural threat is going to represent. One of the reasons I always go back to *Halloween* is because it involves the essential nightmare of a teenager coming to face the fact that she's going to die someday and there's nothing she can do to stop it. That's not necessarily in the movie, but what's so great about horror is that you find those metaphors and say, "Oh, I can tell a really simple, scary story about this very human thing and it comes with all these rich undertones that are baked into the concept."

Jennifer Raite - Both of us grew up in very rural areas with "the woods," "the dark," and "what's out there?" Taking any character through what's frightening to them or to us, just feels very natural to us.

Bryan Woods - The thing Scott and I keep coming back to with our characters, is: What is relatable? Who are the people that you really love? How personal can you make it to yourself? Inject the things about you that are very specific, unique and true. Then, somehow transplant that into the characters. That's the most important thing. It's hard to scare an audience if they don't connect or relate to the heroes in the movie. I think there was this weird run in Hollywood, particularly in slasher movies, but in horror movies, in general, where some executive said, "We need to have really unlikable characters because it will be fun to watch them die." That doesn't really work for people. If they don't identify and connect, then it's almost impossible to scare them.

Scott Beck - And this is not just from the hero's perspective, but also from the villain's. What are you saying about the villains? As an example from our own work, there was a movie called *Haunt* that we did in 2019. On the surface, it's masked villains that are coming after these people in a haunted house. Everything bad that is going on is real. But how do you latch a theme onto that? How do you dive deeper? That helps facilitate the writing process. Whether or not the themes or the layers land with the audience, it is up to the eye of the beholder.

Haunt takes place on Halloween, and it's all about characters wearing masks, so our hero is someone who puts on a front; they are hiding something deep within their soul from emotional abuse. How do you activate that from both the hero standpoint and the villain standpoint? It's something you can always lean back on when you are writing a scene. It's not just about someone being chased. It's about someone putting on a facade and having layers beneath it. That helps activate a little more imagination and substance than you wouldn't otherwise get. In some good horror movies, you do have the ability to peel beneath the surface and reveal some layers that gives you something if you are looking for it.

Q: Horror is such a saturated genre. Do you feel you can still find an original story?

Chris Cullari - It's tough. And sometimes I think you take a swing and see how people respond to it. Our film, *The Aviary,* is from a whole horror sub-genre of people on the run from a cult. Sometimes, they have been on the run for a long time. Sometimes, they have been on the run for a little while, but, the cult always shows up. Sometimes, they are wearing Satanic robes, surround the cabin or the house and then there are supernatural twists. There is always this big, faceless entity that is coming after them. We like that genre, but we've seen that a lot. With *The Aviary*, we looked at how do we tell a story in that genre that is, one, more focused on the heroes, the women fleeing this cult, and looking at them as survivors; and, two, how do you tell that story without doing robes and Satanic sacrifices? By keeping the focus on the women and keeping it grounded in reality, we think it's a new way of telling that story. Whether that is enough to stand out and people will gravitate to that, only time will tell. I would say *Martha Marcy May Marlene* is the closest thing to what we were trying to do, but we were trying to do a more visceral, horrific thrilling piece. *Martha Marcy Mae Marlene* is all of that on an emotional level. We were trying to make something in a sub-genre that we love, in a different way.

For us, the swings have been getting bigger because so much has been done in horror already. We have a slasher idea that's very big and very weird. We have a haunted house idea that's almost too esoteric that we're not sure it will work as a movie, but if it did work, it would be brand new. No one would have seen that before.

Jennifer Raite - It turns into a puzzle and a challenge. We love horror, but we love all movies. When you are watching so much stuff, I think this is when the conversation of "that's not horror" or "this is horror" happens. Part of why this has become an argument is that there is this fluidity of people bringing horror elements into other genres or vice versa. Are you using the filmmaking techniques of horror in a drama? Horror-comedy is very much its own genre at this point.

Sometimes, it's creating an existential drama like *The Humans*. You are pulling in horror film techniques to create this extra sense of dread and discomfort in a scene where they are eating dinner. You're understanding these familial conflicts. Then, I feel that there are these horror movies that are doing the opposite. They are bringing in conventions from other genres. I think that is where a lot of the fresh stuff comes from. That's why we, and when I say we, I mean the horror audience, that's why we love genre horror movies so much. I feel like Robert Eggers is absolutely telling original stories in horror night now. We haven't seen this kind of movie in this kind of setting with these kinds of characters.

Chris Cullari - I think the horror genre is going to drift more into period films. I'm not going to say that horror films were better before the world was more connected because there are great horror stories to be told in a hyper-connected world. But just in conversations with other writers and filmmakers, we're all sick of having a scene where the cell phones don't work. That conversation is already fifteen years old. Either movies are period pieces, or movies like *It Follows* are in a vague period-ish space where it feels modern, but nobody has a cell phone. That one girl has a clamshell thing. The movie is telling you we are not doing cell phones. We are not doing texting. We are not doing video chats. We are not doing any of that. A lot of horror, in one way or another, whether literal or emotional, is about isolation and it's about distance. It's about people not understanding. In a connected world, that's so much harder to do. It may be better for the sake of our world because we are more connected; we are more understanding; we do help each other more often; but in horror, you don't want to deal with those things.

Bryan Woods - The cool thing about the horror genre is that it's always been this great entry-level genre for writers and filmmakers going all the way back to the 1970s. Francis Ford Coppola, Peter Bogdonovich, and Johnathan Demme - a lot of them started with these small horror films. I think the reason why it's such a good entry-level genre is that, more often than not, the budgets can be smaller. The genre is the star of the movie; you don't need Tom Cruise. A horror movie will show up because it's horrifying. The horror genre is a great playground for experimentation and concept. It's a great opportunity to bring bold ideas to the table. That's why you get *Get Out, It Follows, Nope,* or even *Barbarian*. It's a wonderful place to just think big. We always try to take that opportunity.

Q: Is there a particular structure for a horror movie or a horror series?

Chris Cullari - With *The Aviary*, even though we knew it was going to be a movie in the desert with two women when we were writing it, we were very cognizant that something has to happen every ten pages, which changes the nature of this story. In a slasher movie, you would probably have a kill every ten pages, but we only had two characters, so that's not going to work! And there are other movies, like *Honeymoon* and *Bug*, two touchpoint movies for us. Structurally, you do want to make sure you are delivering on the promise of the movie. I guess if the promise of the movie is that you are building toward something horrific, then you are structuring it in a way where the build is very important, which is what we were doing. If the promise is, there's going to be a giant body count, then you have to structure it so that you deliver that for the audience. Sometimes, you can come out of left field and have something like *Mandy*. I can't speak for how the director thought that movie would be marketed or received. It was marketed as a Nic Cage, bodies hit the floor, this is going to be a wacky, zany time, but the movie is a long, turgid, bad acid trip, fever-dream that finally delivers those things in a surprising way. But structurally, that movie is not at all what I thought it would be.

Jennifer Raite - That's another place where horror can try to be new. Something we like to do is make a list of movies that feel similar and different. Watch all of them, break all of them down. This works really well. This doesn't work. Then put that up against what we are trying to do. And at the same time, thinking about the surprise element. How can this be in the conversation with movies that have done similar things and how can we also write something dramatically different that is exciting and satisfying for us and the audience?

Bryan Woods - A structure in a horror movie is sometimes a risky prospect. One of the things that scares us the most is the fear of the unknown; the fear of not knowing what's coming next. At times, it can be a trap to lean too heavily into a traditional structure for a horror film. Something like *A Quiet Place* is traditional at times. It's *Jaws* in many ways. You introduce how dangerous the monster is upfront. Then, you spend the rest of the movie fighting back against the monster. Sometimes, you can turn a structure on its head and use it in an unexpected way but it's all about chasing that unexpected unknown because that is where fear is.

Q: Does the studio or network tell you that they need a certain amount of scares?

Chris Cullari - They can do that. I think the desire to have those scares sometimes comes from a creative standpoint and sometimes from a commercial standpoint. How, as a horror screenwriter, you react to those notes and what you create to fill those scare beats, I think, is the very practical meat and potatoes of horror screenwriting. Trying to figure out how to make those beats work without resorting to fake-out scares or cat scares. A lot of those times, we've found that the stronger projects that we've had are the ones where the character conflict is such that there is a fresh, unique scare in there somewhere that we can figure out. So that when somebody says, "Oh, we need some more scares here. There's not quite enough." We can go back and look at it and realize, "Oh, well this character wants this thing, but in order for him to get that he'd have to go into the basement." As opposed to a scene where they are eating dinner and maybe a tree branch hits the window. There are ways of pulling those scares out. Certainly, that's one of the lines between a commercial horror film and an art-horror film. I don't think anyone is going to Ari Aster and saying, "Hey, can we fit another scare in here? Maybe a guy in a mask?" His movies are more specific than that.

Jennifer Raite - Sometimes, there's just a loss in translation, too. I think a lot of people, if they were to read an Ari Aster script, it's not an Ari Aster movie in their heads. I think often that when someone says we need another scare here, it's a mismatch of the pace. The pace the writer is putting the script on isn't necessarily the pace the reader is looking for. Sometimes, you can get lucky and there are other things you can change that will make that work for them. It's always that note behind the note. They might be asking for one thing, but what they need is something else. And sometimes, you have to work as that translator because you're the writer and you know the story best. Even a bad note often has a real symptom of something behind it.

Bryan Woods - The studio always want more.

Scott Beck - Once you are bringing it to life, they'll want to oversaturate it. For us, and now having worked with Sam Raimi who is a great master of this, it's more about suspense than it is about scares. Nobody did this better than Hitchcock; he really did understand what the audience wants and what they react to the most. The term "jump scare" is so thrown around these days that it is just another indicator of how tired tropes can become. It's a challenge, as a writer and director, to understand the psychology of what you are trying to put on screen. You can't just go one step beyond the audience's expectations. You have to go three steps beyond and unravel what you think an audience thinks is going to happen. But, then the audience is thinking about what might happen, so it's this weird Rubik's Cube of trying to put it all together and hope that you deliver. Part of the process of that is hopefully getting a movie made and then you need to play it for an audience and see how it feels. You don't need to have them say whether it's working or not; you can feel it in the room. If there's a tension that overcomes them or pure boredom. It's fascinating.

Q: When you build tension on the page, is it important to reflect that in the actual words that you choose?

Jennifer Raite - I think it's very helpful, especially for the readers who need their hand held through it a little more. Working towards having good pacing and clear images on the page; breaking up lines and slowing things down as you build towards a scare is really helpful. Sometimes, I think readers will just breeze past something that is meant to stretch out if you don't do that. Chris likes to do more capital letters, underlining, and italicizing and I think there's a constant back and forth of me undoing those and him putting them back in. We are in a very similar place with how we like to break up the language and have shorter sentences over more lines versus compact action writing.

Chris Cullari - It depends if you're writing for yourself or if you're writing for an executive. If we're writing for ourselves, I think the language is more important as a reminder of what we want to do on screen. Not every exec is the same, but a lot of times, execs gloss over stuff when they read. This is where the underlining and capitalization come into play - especially with scary scenes. It helps especially when they are on their fifth script of the night. This way they get the feel, like Jen said, with the fewest number of words. Maybe they won't necessarily get that it's scary by reading it, but you can shape the page visually in a way that makes them understand that the story is slowing down. Then, they see a big underlined word and see "knife" nearby. I think it can help. It's a blueprint and you want to make sure people are following the rhythms.

Jennifer Raite - Sometimes, they will see the accent and if they have been rushing through, they will go back and that is where I think Chris' technique works. The capitalized, underlined section, they are not going to miss that piece. And if they wonder how they got there, they will go back and get the more measured read that I want.

Chris Cullari - When you are writing something that is going to go up the commercial ladder, you're both telling a story and writing an instruction manual at the same time. So you might do a pass where you tell the story to a reader, and after a long sequence, you find a way to summarize what just happened in an action line at the bottom of the page. So in case someone is lost or reading quickly, you're giving them a summary as they go. That, we've found is important. I used to be - here are five paragraphs of description and it's going to tell you about the floorboards creaking, the wind, and the shadows. Doing that is like drawing a blueprint with a multi-colored marker. Nobody really wants it. They want the instructions and they want to feel them, but they need them delivered to them.

Jennifer Raite - And when we do use the colored markers, we use it on the first page to really set the tone, but still trying to do it as little as we can. Or we use it if and when there's a huge tonal shift. So being more limited, but more with the stylistic hand-holding as you can be.

Scott Beck - You have to find the sparseness of the words or how you present them, but you are trying to prolong time. That's hard to do because everyone reads at different speeds. Whereas, on screen, you are giving them the actual length that you want. It's a challenge. In the past, when we are combing over one of our scripts in the rewrite stage, we notice that we may be going right to the scare. It doesn't allow what you're trying to suggest once it comes to the screen. It's a really difficult thing to translate.

On *A Quiet Place*, one thing we did with the sale draft script was play with font sizes and play with the positioning of words on the page. There is a four or five-page run where there is just a single word on each page. It was the idea that our lead character was running and he's getting closer. Then you flip the page and he's getting closer. And then you flip it again, and he's getting even closer. That was a deliberate choice about how else can we communicate how suspenseful this should be without letting some design and wordplay happen on the physical page.

Bryan Woods - We would also use onomatopoeia for certain sounds. We would shrink the font sizes when a sound was getting very quiet. Sometimes, we would blow up a font size for a loud noise. We were doing it for impact on the story, not to screw around. Those choices can get out of hand really quickly, but if it was a dramatic turning point in the story for a sound, we would do it.

Q: How does the format, either streaming, TV, short, or feature, affect the writing of the horror genre?

Chris Cullari - When we sold our first pilot in 2014, the really big horror hits on TV were, *The X-Files* (from the 90s), *The Walking Dead,* and *American Horror Story.* Those first two or three years, people were only looking for maximalist horror where it was everything and the kitchen sink. Then, *Hannibal* and *Channel Zero* and certainly, *Haunting of Hill House* really changed that and opened up a lot more doors for what horror on TV can be.

Structurally, we don't really think about things that way. Genre doesn't influence the structure for us as much as the medium does. The structure of a TV show, even an eight-episode limited thing is going to be much more different from a feature film. There are certain stories that work better in a TV space than in an hour-and-a-half/two-hour feature space, so that's something where we will look at an idea and think about how big is the world. How multi-faceted is this character's journey? Does it work for a movie or a TV show? Sometimes, it's both; it can be either/or.

Broadly, we found that villains who are one note, like a slasher, which is not necessarily a bad thing, generally work better in movies because you are going to resolve the story. In a TV show, the appearance of that character, and this is why you haven't seen a *Halloween* TV series or *Friday the 13th* TV show, is because Jason can only kick the door in so many times. But that's what the audience wants to see, so now if you have to do ten hours of Jason chasing teenagers, there's not as much to explore there. Freddie Kruger might be better, in that regard.

Jennifer Raite - It's the same reason you don't have a *Jaws* TV show.

Chris Cullari - Exactly! They got one great movie out of it and then the rest of the movies are diminishing returns. Whereas, Freddie Kruger or Hannibal as villains are much better suited to a television show because they are interesting characters on an emotional level. They can drive story. You can spend time with them. Also, they talk, which Michael, Jason, and some of those other characters, don't. The *Chucky* show did so well on SyFy because Chucky is a layered, interesting villain.

Jennifer Raite - And there are interesting things to explore. Is this a character that we find out more about their backstory or people that are important to them? Is that additive and interesting to the character? Or does that make them less interesting? Do you want to know that stuff about Michael Myers? Is that successful or not?

Chris Cullari - We went through the process on a *Texas Chainsaw Massacre* TV show for a minute. That was an interesting one where Leatherface is obviously not going to be your lead, but *Texas Chainsaw* comes with a town and a family. You start going down those roads and that opens up possibilities. Certainly, there could be more *Texas Chainsaw* movies, but if you dive into this other part of the world, there's a lot of materials, characters, and storylines that can fill multiple hours worth of TV. That's where the genre blend comes back around, too. One of the ways we approached that process was you're really talking about a Southern cannibal murder mystery and there are elements that, once you boil it down, could cross over to *Justified*, a little bit. Or you could see something structured like the *Fargo* TV show - an exploration of these insular TV worlds and communities. You are still talking about something frightening, visceral, and scary, but you are bringing in these other elements of a detective show or a small-town soap. It doesn't dilute the scariness. It just gives you another lens to view some of that stuff through.

Scott Beck - There have been a lot of changes. I would say you get less of the wild sci-fi movies. One that comes to mind which I don't think would get made today, is *Event Horizon* or Danny Boyle's *Sunshine.* Those are movies that I can't think of a direct comparison of size and what they are saying these days. But I feel that the format offers fun flexibility. Certainly, with platforms like Shudder that cater directly to a horror crowd. They do really incredible programming. Whether it's acquiring movies that might not otherwise find a distributor that would put them out to the right audience, or playing with the format. Bryan and I for the longest time wondered why there isn't the flexibility of some sort of show, whether it's an anthology, that's twenty-two minute episodes. This was years ago when it was mostly network television and such. Now, I feel as though the floodgates have opened up for filmmakers and artists to have the flexibility to pitch these wild ideas and sometimes find the right homes for them. It's exciting from that standpoint, but the caveat is maybe you don't get those wild, bold swings on a more massive scale, which would be theatrical.

Q: There used to be a taboo about killing children in horror films. Does that hold up today?

Chris Cullari - We screened our short film, *The Sleepover*, and at the end, this woman at the back stood up, screaming, "You killed a child! How can you show this in such a violent world?!" I don't know how we answered it, other than it's sort of tongue in cheek and kids face real horror and villains all the time. I think it's a bit of a generational thing. We grew up reading *Goosebumps* books and kids die in those books all the time. It's not graphic on the page, but a lot of those books ended with, "and a wolf backed her into a corner, snarling and drooling from its mouth."

Jennifer Raite - When there are these unspoken rules like it's a kid so a kid can't die, you then have bumpers on the movie. Yet you want that sense of potential chaos. *Trick 'r Treat* is an example of a movie where a lot of kids die. You love it because you are surprised. In the *Scary Tales to Tell in the Dark* adaptation, which is a big studio commercial movie - a lot of those kids don't make it out and it's fun to see.

Chris Cullari - None of them die in a particularly graphic way, though. In *The Sleepover* and all these other movies where kids get killed, it's not a sinister thing. A lot of us came to the genre when we were young. It's a piece of horror that taps into a younger part of us. When you were reading the *Goosebumps* series of books, you weren't imagining everything was okay. Part of the scare was that these kids were dying. It only feels natural to have kids die. We wrote a feature based on the *Black Eyed Kids* legend on the internet. They are monstrous children. There is a lot of kid death and that never got off the ground, partially because of that.

Bryan Woods - It's always a concern. Anytime we wrote scripts in college we would open with a child being murdered and it was met with an immediate and hard "no." It is taboo, and it's not something that can really be done. But we did it in *A Quiet Place* and I would credit 100% of that to John Krasinski who was a co-writer, but also the director and star, and his wife and co-star, Emily Blunt. They were really able to insulate that movie and push certain buttons that are hard-nos to everybody else. They were able to protect the movie in a way that we are super grateful for. Any time there was studio interference, the deck was stacked in our favor on that one. We got away with some things. Taboo. That is what horror is. Looking at the things you're not supposed to say or talk about.

Scott Beck - As the father of a young child, there are things that I've seen recently that provoke me in a way because they deal with the loss of a child. It makes you feel powerless as a parent. It tests even my willpower to go with that, but I acknowledge that is the journey that you do want to be invited on, so to speak. To a certain degree, the worst sin in a horror film is to just do the same thing that you've seen ten times over. If you are not evoking a memory or a moment in the movie or TV show that can invoke a nightmare as an adult, then it's probably not as powerful as it could be. That's the real challenge in a great way. How can you test someone's endurance in a horror film?

Q: Blumhouse has become *the* horror production studio. How is it working with them?

Jennifer Raite - Often, when you are working in a horror space, there will be a lot of people in the creative process who aren't that familiar with the genre. That's not Blumhouse. I think Jason Blum surrounded himself with people who understand the genre. We've worked with them more on the TV side, but on the feature side, it is still very director oriented. We wrote a movie for them for a director and it was all about collaborating with him, taking his ideas, pushing them in interesting ways and making all the pieces come together. It's a lot more like problem-solving.

Chris Cullari - A lot of the execs' notes on the feature side were check notes that I really liked. I think that is to keep it director-focused. The notes would often be like "I don't believe this moment. Audience will roll their eyes." That kind of stuff. In a way, those are very helpful notes because it's not an exact getting in there to try and shape what the movie is. It's that they've made 600 movies. And 99% of the time, those were moments where we went, "He's right. This wasn't really the best version of why a person would do this. Would they really go upstairs? No. But that's where the scare has to be. Well, now we have to find a better way to do that scare."

Jennifer Raite - They trust the director to bring a specific style and flavor. Therefore, they will interrogate moments, instead of big structural issues. If it really needs it, they are more than capable of those kinds of notes. The development focus is: This movie is going to get made. They're getting on board this moving train and trying to make it the best version of what it is moving towards. Broadly, as a creative, it is a great way to work.

Chris Cullari - We were mostly working on TV pitches, but then once in a while, features would come to us. They would have a script that needed to get fixed or a director that they wanted us to sit down with, so we were kind of ping-ponging back and forth. We had a little office there and were kind of a multi-purpose tool.

Q: Can you go wrong in any way when writing sci-fi?

Scott Beck - Yes and no because I would never want to exclude anything. I would suggest that one would want to find a relatability inside of it. It's not so removed. That being said, I've never read the script, but I bet the script for *WALL-E* was bizarre because you are following a robot. But there is such an element to how that robot reacts that on the page you are finding a relatability. If you read something like *Star Wars* back when George Lucas wrote it, you might be like, "I don't understand this at all, whatsoever." But when you watch the movie, it's about a kid on a farm who feels like his life is going nowhere and how does he get somewhere? To me, it's always relating to character. Sci-fi elements and the technology could be as weird as possible, but as long as you have some sort of human element to it, you are forgiven on the page until you can get that on screen.

Q: Is it important to set up the rules of the world in sci-fi or horror?

Bryan Woods - Setting up the rules is always super helpful in order to help get the audience invested in taking the ride. In sci-fi, though, there is always a risk of over-explaining. George Lucas or Steven Spielberg, one of those guys who are smarter than us, said that in sci-fi, the worst thing you can do is explain how a teleportation unit works. As a writer, it's very easy to go,"there's this futuristic technology with teleportation and I am going to explain how this thing works through the characters' dialogue so the audience believes it's credible." That's absolutely the worst thing you can do. The best thing you can do, is show it working. Just show one person warp from here over to there. Enough said. We buy into it. So with sci-fi, we are cautious of over-explaining.

Scott Beck - You want to set up the parameters of where you can go so you're not throwing everything into it or spiraling into things that become inconsistencies later. As a writer, you need to understand your rules because that will give you the box that you can paint inside. You have to put all of the rules and world-building in there. For the sake of *A Quiet Place*, we knew how the family got their electricity. We knew why they were staying in one place. We knew how they were surviving and where their food source came from. But to put all of that in the script and on-screen would not be the most interesting version of that film. What you really want to know is that these characters are surviving and what is their journey ahead. If you have those answers, you can lay them in as subtle as possible. Sometimes, you don't lay them in at all. It just becomes an answer you can give when you're in production or to your producers or to people on Reddit who are tearing apart the logic. I think being prepared is the biggest rule of thumb.

Bryan Woods - Those world-building conversations translates to the audience. The audience doesn't need to know all those various details, but they need to know that you know the answers to those questions. It filters into a kind of confidence in the storytelling where the audience can feel comfortable.

Q: How much detail do you go into describing monsters or aliens?

Scott Beck - You want to go into it enough that it paints some sort of visceral picture for the audience, meaning the reader. So with *A Quiet Place*, it wasn't like defining it so that it eats up a whole page of description. They are on four legs. They are completely blind. Get into some texturing that gives you an aching or scared feeling; something that evokes as much of an emotional response as possible. But you don't want to go so deep because you are going to lose the reader at a certain point. You will be spending time on details that don't really matter. Ultimately, you know there are going to be geniuses, whether in physical effects or visual effects, who will have their own creative slant on things that will be so much better and much more realistic.

Q: Any tips on writing horror films that may be void of dialogue?

Bryan Woods - Our biggest fear with *A Quiet Place* was that it was going to be a very boring script to read. More often than not, the scripts that are very easy to read are the ones filled with dialogue. The pages turn faster. We could have had 100 pages of dense description with no breath of air for the reader. So we devised this odd style that was quite gimmicky and new to us; not something that we had ever done before. We incorporated wordplay such as describing the font sizes. We used images in the script if there was an important moment. An example of that is a Monopoly board. We used a Monopoly board in the script as a visual signifier of when they are playing Monopoly, this is going to be a big dramatic scene in the movie. But it also was an opportunity about how they had taken the Monopoly board and turned it into a makeshift map of their farm, which painted a picture in the reader's mind of the geography of the farm, how it all worked, and how the various set pieces corresponded to each other. This way we didn't have to weigh the script down with long descriptions showing how everything is connected.

With that script, in particular, we really tried to stretch ourselves and make it readable, entertaining, and exciting, and to sell this idea to the studio that just because there is no dialogue in the movie, doesn't mean it's not the most fascinating thing you've ever seen. It can be a real asset. With other genres, the story moves forward from a motivation within characters, but often with sci-fi, it comes from an unexpected impact from the outside,

Scott Beck - I think it depends on what type of sci-fi film you are going for. Using *A Quiet Place* as an example, it's about the mystery of what are these creatures? Where did they come from? And letting that mythology, even if you are not directly answering that on the page, be a point of provoking the audience and creating the mystery of their presence. And then, letting these creatures be omnipresent whether they are on the screen or not. How do you create suspense when they are not there? You can do that through a multitude of ways whether it's a visual presence that they had been there, or via sound. In creating that suspense, you give a driving force to the story. That translates to the horror genre, too.

Q: What are some of the best horror scripts that you think writers should read?

Chris Cullari - I would say *Alien,* especially if you are a horror writer who overwrites like I used to. I read *Alien* and was like, oh, there's a different way to do this. That's an inimitable style, so you can't copy it. It won't be as good. But there's definitely a way that it feels creepy and the pages are just impossible to not turn. As far as horror comedies go, I would say Brian Duffield's, *The Babysitter* is a knock-out horror-comedy script. It's really funny. It's violent. The scary parts are frightening. I would study the structure of *Shaun of the Dead*. That's definitely a movie that is on a list with *Back to the Future* of pretty perfect scripts. And even if you are writing a straight horror movie, you won't have all the funny callbacks and stuff. You still can understand the placements of setups and payoffs that are so well designed in that movie. I would also put *The Strangers* on that list. I go back to that script a lot because it does a lot of things really that aren't my strengths. There's not a lot of dialogue. It has a lot of sequences that could feel repetitive on the page, obviously not in the movie. Every sequence in that movie is soul rattling on the page. It's a lot of people walking around the house being quiet; faces appearing behind them, but it is still so fucking effective even on the page.

Jennifer Raite - The *Hannibal* pilot is a great pilot script. That's definitely one where I felt that Bryan Fuller is really good at directing on the page without it being intrusive to a read. He's very skilled at that.

Chris Cullari - I think some of the dialogue hasn't aged very well, but structurally *The X-Files* pilot is great. That network mystery-style of TV has gone out of style a little bit, but in terms of every line and moment telling you more about a character and setting up a character, that pilot is great. Even if you are looking to write an eight-episode Netflix-style show, you can learn so much from that pilot.

Jennifer Raite - There's an efficiency to the writing from the very best writers who came from a network style and now work in more serialized stuff. It's still in their DNA in a way that I think is very beneficial. Like the Vince Gilligans (*Breaking Bad*) of the world.

Scott Beck - The best horror script that comes to my mind immediately is *Alien,* the Walter Hill, David Giler draft. The sparseness on the page painted such an incredible atmosphere. That's one that both of us have gone back to many times over. It's also a fun read.

Bryan Woods - A script I would recommend is *Gone Girl*. I read it before the movie came out and it was an adaptation of the novel by the author. The expectation is that it is going to be very flowery, heavy on prose, and really enamored with its own sense of style and tone. It's the exact opposite. It's so matter-of-fact and simple and clean and economical. It's a script I return to for its writing style. It's a great example of a page-turner. It's scary when it needs to be scary and it's dramatic when it needs to be dramatic. It checks all those boxes. It's a great piece of screenwriting.

CHAPTER REVIEW: HORROR & SCI-FI

- The best horror and sci-fi stories focus on an interesting character in an unusual or engaging world.

- Take a character through the things that scare you. That will make it feel authentic and natural.

- Isolation is a key element of horror films. One way around that is to set a film before mobile/cell phones existed.

- Sometimes, a studio's desire to make more scares is really a mismatch of the story pace that the writer has in their head versus what a reader has in their head.

- If you want a scene to be scary, then write it scary. Fewer words on the page and shorter sentences can convey tension. Underlining, bolding, or capitalizing important words can focus weary or distracted readers. Likewise so can playing with font sizes or other techniques to enhance the storytelling. Just don't overdo it.

- Characters that are one-note, such as in a slasher story, work best for movies as the story gets resolved. Series require complex characters and worlds that can be explored over many episodes.

- Many of the taboos of yesteryear in storytelling have disappeared. It's really down to the taste of those financing a project as to how far or extreme you can go. Horror should be about things that invoke nightmares in adults.

- You can be as weird and imaginative as you want when building a sci-fi world, as long as the characters have something relatable about them.

- Don't try to explain how your sci-fi world technology works unless it's important to the story later on. Just show it working and the audience will get it. If you have to explain, keep it tight and short.

- Likewise, you don't need to spend a lot of page time describing your world or the monster or aliens in it. Just do enough to paint a picture in the reader's mind and then let their imagination take over.

CHAPTER 14

HORROR COMEDY

These two genres are supposedly at odds with one another. How can you be laughing when you're meant to be scared? How can a funny situation be frightening? Do financiers really hate this hybrid? Our horror comedy panelists discuss how they balance the hilarious with the horror.

Q: What kind of idea gets your attention?

Scott Lobdell - An idea that can surprise me and one that can surprise the readers or, if it's a film, the studio. If I was going to write a story about my youth when I was a sickly kid and I read comic books and became a comic book writer, you would doze off. You see movies like that all time - a story of someone's life and they have ups and downs. Whereas to me, with *Happy Death Day,* you could say it's the story of a sorority girl who keeps getting brutally murdered. And people go, "Keeps? What do you mean?" But every time she wakes up, she gets clues as to who's trying to kill her and how to stop them. Then all of a sudden they are intrigued. So if you can surprise them every ten to fifteen pages or so, whether it's in the concept or in the writing, then that's a great idea.

Q: What have you found makes for the best scares, and in contrast, best laughs in a horror-comedy?

Scott Lobdell - The mechanics of setting someone up for a scare is basically presenting something they know and then startling them with something they didn't know was coming. We've seen it a hundred times when someone is shaving in the mirror. They open the mirror in a closed room, they close the mirror and there is someone behind them! It's that normal-ness, set up of what we think we know and then something we didn't know. And really, it's the exact same setup with comedy. If I say, "This guy walks into a bar," you know to expect he's going to order a drink. You've walked into a bar. But if you say, "This dyslexic walks into a bra," now the audience has to go in their minds and picture the upended expectation, "Oh, it's the reverse because he's dyslexic. So is it a bar or a bra?" The set-up of comedy and horror are the same idea of introducing something familiar and then surprise the audience by going somewhere else.

Eli Craig - To me, real horror can only happen after you've fallen in love with the characters. Only when you're invested in them and care about them does the tension really escalate. Of course, there's all kinds of scares in horror movies: jump scares, the slow walk of the knife wielding killer, the tension of knowing something might happen and then it doesn't. Even the tension that a character you love will die and then you'll hate the movie and everyone who made it. There really is no best or right way, that's what's fun about the job. For comedy as well, it just depends on the project. I don't know if I'll ever write a better comedic scene than when Tucker and Dale are trying to figure out why these college kids are attacking them and come to the conclusion that these kids are killing themselves all over their property in a suicide pact. While I was writing it, I just kept thinking of Steve Martin in *The Jerk* when he's getting shot at and the shooter keeps missing him and hitting the cans and he comes to the conclusion that "It's the cans! He hates these cans!" Lovably dumb people make great comedy.

Q: Do you find comedy or horror harder to write?

Scott Lobdell - I'm writing a thriller right now and there's a lot of humor in it already, but in the first twenty minutes there's a scene that makes people tear up. My inclination, though, is to be funny. Not ha-ha jokes, but more like, this is how this character is reacting to different things. I know when I get to the end of this script, I will go back and pull out the comedy to make the thrills a little more nerve-wracking. Sometimes, I have to be cognizant of not making things funny unless it is a comedy and not too funny if it's a horror or thriller story.

Eli Craig - I'm more inclined, frankly, to the comedy. I do enjoy writing some of the horror. When I look at horror, it's surprising how freaking scary it is. When I am watching *Us* or something, I'm watching it through my fingers with one eye open. It's horrifying! How can a comedy guy write such great horror?! I admire Jordan Peele. He's amazing. People say *Get Out* was a horror-comedy. I don't think so. It was a horror.

Ben Philippe - The more I try my hands at different things, the more I develop a taste for them. For example, there is some action in *Interview with the Vampire*. They are super-beings who sometimes get into fights. When I was first writing, "Louis punches LeStat." I didn't know if it was good. But after a while, I could imagine the choreography, how the characters would move, and how to write it in an impactful way. It's fun, but it is an underdeveloped muscle for me as opposed to people who have been on *Cobra Kai* and other action shows.

I enjoy writing a scene of horror here and there. I might enjoy writing a slasher horror like *Halloween* or *Scream* because even though there is a lot of horror, there's a lot of suspense building. Someone walks into the house and the door is open. Is the killer in the house with them? All of those elements work toward building a crescendo to the horror. I love writing those elements. *Interview with the Vampire* is really a romance and that was the pitch for the show. In the book, they were a homosexual couple, which is only alluded to. They spent sixty-five years in domestic harmony until Claudia came along. That's two men living together and then they suddenly have a daughter who never ages. That's an entire show. It became a *War of the Roses* domestic thriller, so extracting the horror from those elements was really fun. But they are vampires and if they throw a party, they are going to kill everyone at the party. I don't know if horror is my natural go-to, but, with the magic of a writers room, other people add to your ideas and you add on to theirs.

Q: How do you balance between the two opposing tones?

Scott Lobdell - There's a scene in *Happy Death Day* that didn't make it into the final cut. In the movie, the main character, Tree, references that each time she dies, it's taking more out of her. In the original script, there was a scene where she was in the bathroom and her roommate was on the other side. You hear these moans and you don't know if she's drunk or hurt or whatever. Then you go inside the bathroom and she's literally using duct tape to hold in her ribs. Her body is falling apart. That didn't make it in. That could have been a scary scene. Look what's happened to her! She has to wrap up to hold her collarbone in or wear a tight shirt to keep it all together. Or it could have been very funny. It depends on how it's shot.

There's also an alternate ending for *Happy Death Day* on YouTube. In the original script, she survives where she's in the hospital and asks the doctor for something for the pain. The doctor says "no" because he needs to know what's going on and asks her if she can hang on for a night. She says, "Trust me, I can hang on for a night." He pulls the curtain and then, a nurse comes in who takes out a syringe. Tree tells her that the doctor told her not to have anything for the pain. The nurse says, "Not for your pain. My pain." And you see that this is the wife of the doctor with whom she was having the affair. She says, "Did you really think you would ruin my marriage and get away with it?" Then there's a look on Tree's face where she's like, "You gotta be shitting me." I wrote it very specifically to be a funny sting. But instead it was shot in a way where it was "Really, you're going to kill me now?" It was like a cake deflated. Test audiences hated the ending. The director did not like the ending and so he shot the ending in a way that there is none of the fun and vibrancy that is in the rest of the movie. But the fact, that I can give you one version that's funny and then that exact dialogue makes you go ugh, is kind of interesting. So when you say, how do you find the balance, you find your own balance, but when the director comes, it is what it is.

I did a pilot for Warner Brothers. It was a modern-day telling of *Alice in Wonderland* set in New York City but as a cop show. I wrote in a *Royal Tenenbaums* tone; I loved that there was 323rd Street Y. Where's that? Yonkers? And anytime they needed a taxi cab, a beat-up gypsy cab would come up. Obviously, that doesn't actually happen in real New York City. In our pilot, I loved that we created a New York that we recognize, but it's different. So the pilot I wrote felt very much like that - whimsical. When the director came on, he turned the script into a *Jacob's Ladder*. If someone had said, "Write a scary version of *The Royal Tenenbaums*," maybe I could have done that. But imagine giving *The Royal Tenenbaums* to John Carpenter. On one of the last days of shooting, there was a big party that had to be shot. I was in Canada and got a call from L.A. saying that the scene had to be really whimsical because that is what I sold them. I had zero control over what was being done. At that point, I knew there was no way this pilot was getting on the air. So, to your point, sometimes all the balancing in the world can mean nothing once it's out of your hands.

Eli Craig - I definitely have a gut feeling that there has to be more horror in certain parts and more comedy in others. And the transitions between the two is really important. There's a term I really like: contrast and affinity. That's maybe why I like horror writing because you get used to a certain thing when you are watching it, an affinity. You have an affinity for both visual styles whether you are shooting in a flat space or shooting a comedic scene. Then you have a contrast where you are shooting in a deep space shot with tons of smoke and now you are in a horror space. It feels like, "Oh, no! This is a horror film." It feels scarier because of the affinity of the comedy that has been set up. There's a lot of time when I will be reading along and I will get carried away with my jokes. I'll be entertaining myself with the comedy, but then I look at the script and I realize I need to throw in the horror scene right here. That's why I think this is four-dimensional because the timing of where that goes is as important as the scene itself.

Q: Is the horror comedy genre too predictable?

Eli Craig - But that's the fun of horror comedy. It's taking those tropes and inverting them. Showing them in a new light. I think there is some joy in seeing the thing we've seen before in a new way.

Q: Are studio executives wanting originality in horror comedies?

Eli Craig - They say they do, but they really don't. They really do want a really well thought out pitch that fits into the mold of a lot of things. I would say more recently that has changed, and Netflix, God bless them, was a big part of that. They created some stuff that really defined convention. I think you are always trying to push that boundary, but not that far. You want to make something that reminded people of what they've seen, but in a new way. We don't need to reinvent the wheel, which, in a way, is reassuring. There are so many geniuses that came before us that have done this really well. *Little Evil* was based on Richard Donner's *The Omen*. I was like, okay, I'm just going to take that structure and I am going to invert the tropes and add different characters that don't really belong there. One of the things about horror comedy is that the characters don't really belong there. They shouldn't be in this movie. They should be in another movie. That juxtaposition is funny to me.

Q: How is horror comedy viewed in the marketplace?

Eli Craig - It's negative. People generally don't want to make them and there's this perception that they don't do well in the marketplace, but I think that's totally inaccurate. *Ghostbusters*, *The Goonies*, *Zombieland*, *Scream*, those are all horror comedies and they all did amazing at the box office. They're all downright classics until the end of time. So yeah, horror comedy is a genre that can work like almost nothing else sometimes and last the test of time. With that said, many times I will be asked, "Can you take out the comedy?" That's just not fun. I don't really want to do a straight slasher movie without a touch of satire. It's not my personality. But there's a feeling that comedy is local and not global. Horror plays more world wide. There's definitely a push to go darker. Leave the comedy for sketch and silly hi-jinx. Grounded comedy gets rarer and rarer to see.

CHAPTER REVIEW: HORROR COMEDY

- The set up to get a good scare and a good laugh are similar. Start with something familiar and then give the reader the unexpected. Inverting the expectations always keeps an audience engaged.

- Balancing horror and comedy is challenging, especially during the transitions from one to the other. It's primarily a feel and timing issue.

- Horror comedy can be problematic for financiers' marketing departments. They aren't sure how to sell it.

- Horror comedy allows you to manipulate the tropes and expectations of the genres, thereby producing the possibility of satire or social commentary.

CHAPTER 15

TELENOVELAS

———

With high drama and fun characters, telenovelas are the highest-rated shows in most Latin American countries. They are so popular that their characteristics are finding their way into non-Spanish speaking markets. What makes them so irresistible? And how can those elements translate to other formats? Top telenovela writer/producer, Carolina Rivera, discusses her time making these programs and how it informed her writing on others.

Q: What are the similarities and differences between telenovelas to American and British soap operas?

Carolina Rivera - Telenovelas are the pornography of emotion. You have to take emotion to the extreme. It's very intense. Mexican telenovelas are very melodramatic. We didn't have a studio system, so in Mexico, the three main telenovela networks, Televisa, Azteca, and Imagen are like studios. When writing the telenovela, you are only behind production by two weeks. As I was writing, the networks/studios were monitoring minute by minute the ratings of the show. They were able to measure: Here comes Juanita, and the ratings go up because they love the character. Then, here comes the bad guy. He's not a good antagonist and so the ratings go down. They were monitoring minute by minute the show and they would tell us that people don't like this character, so we should kill him. So as a writers room, we would have to be able to react immediately, so we could kill off that character and come up with a different storyline. What happens, though, is that our only link to the production is the ratings and we are supposed to move the story and react. It's very complicated. You practically don't have a life. You live there. You're basically waiting for the results of the monitoring.

There's also a focus group every Thursday. It's basically women commenting on different aspects of the show - even the wardrobe. They would say, "We don't like that wardrobe. It's too sexy. It's too much. We're all very Catholic or conservative." The telenovela is like a live animal; needing something different every week or every day and you have to feed the animal different things from different points of view from the production. The producer has to modify the look - the wardrobe or the hair - based on the focus groups. And we might have to veer the story somewhere else.

Q: Are you able to do any long-term storytelling when things are subject to change so quickly?

Carolina Rivera - Yes, once the network greenlights a telenovela, the room produces a bible that contemplates long story arcs. But, as a room, we need to be prepared to react fast and make changes, as needed. Even the long story arcs. What we do is put the storyline on hold. The character might suffer an accident or might end up sick in a hospital, and that gives us a little time to react, but not much, because production still needs to come up with forty minutes of air time every day. So not much time to react!

Q: How many episodes are there in a telenovela?

Carolina Rivera - They are closed stories from 120 to 360 episodes, depending on how well the telenovela is doing. If the ratings are up, then we would have to come up with more stories. It all depends on programming and ratings. Basically, it's a love story with a bunch of obstacles. Most of the obstacles are the same. All telenovelas are kind of the same story but in different locations. There are all the telenovela tropes that we all know and we use them like that. These two meet and they fall in love, of course. If they are from different social or economic backgrounds, it's best. If she's poor and he's rich. They are very traditional and conservative. She is good, good, good. And he's good, good, good. And all the rest of the characters are in service of the love story. Some are for the love story. Others are against the love story. The villains are very bad - very villain-y. There's no room for inclusive love stories. It's always a man and a woman. There's no room for gay love. Maybe a little bit now, but still very conservative. It's a love story full of obstacles, but in the end, they succeed and get married. Everyone is expecting a big wedding at the end. Or the big, we are going to be together forever. The end. They are very popular. Even with all the streamers coming to Mexico - Netflix, Amazon, and HBOMax, everyone - telenovelas are still top-rated.

Q: How many writers are in the writers room?

Carolina Rivera - It depends. I always liked fewer writers than more writers, mainly for communication. The pressure and the way you have to move fast, sometimes many voices are not best for a project. Say, for example, I would have six writers at the most who were writing 120 hours of story. It's a lot, but we have all the usual tropes, like the twin brother that nobody knew about and deaths. We all thought that he was dead, but no, he survived the accident and he's back! We know what to do with those.

Q: Since the shows run so long, do they ever pull in current events to give more story opportunities?

Carolina Rivera - Yes. We put current events in all the time because it's very immediate. The writers are starting two weeks before production and production is just two weeks before air. It's very fast-paced. We shoot forty minutes of air time every day. So you are shooting in studios and you don't go to locations too much. You build sets, but it's very static and has a bunch of dialogue. Telenovelas are meant to be heard. They come historically from radio soaps. We were always told by the studio or the networks that women in Mexico do their laundry or some housework as they are kind of listening to the telenovela. And then something catches their attention and they turn to the TV. Then they are back to whatever they are doing. There's a lot of repetition because they air Monday to Friday always at the same hour. So you create a habit. People do what they are doing and then they sit down and get ready to watch their telenovela. Usually, there's only one TV per household because we are talking about Mexican telenovelas airing in countries that are not very rich. So you have to keep it light for a family viewership. Family orientated. Although, in Mexico, telenovelas run from 4 p.m. to 9:30 p.m. If you are writing the telenovela for the afternoon schedule, you have to be very familiar. Kids are around and watching. Night telenovelas are very sexy.

The way we work is the same as any other show. We have boards and you kind of put your week on the board. The weekly arc. The big event is on a Thursday, not on a Friday, because people go out and have dinner. So the big event has to happen on a Thursday. The big event means the couple gets closer or the kiss.

Q: How often do you have a cliffhanger?

Carolina Rivera - You need to have a good cliffhanger every Friday. It depends on where you are in the story, but you have to set up the main obstacle for the next week. It is usually something the villain sets up. It's always the villain that moves the story forward setting up the new obstacles. But viewership goes down a lot on a Friday. People go out with their families. The thing is you have to keep the tension going up and a cliffhanger to bring people back on Monday. It just won't be as good as the one on Thursday. It's complicated and there's a lot of repetition. Remember, if you can't watch on a Wednesday, you have to be able to understand what's going on the next day. Online viewership is not as good as live viewership in telenovelas. It's been changing a little bit, but since we are a poorer country not everyone has the internet. So people watch live because it's free TV.

Q: Are telenovelas good for learning to write dramedy? Or is blending comedy and drama difficult?

Carolina Rivera - It's interesting because telenovelas, at least the ones that I was writing, were melodramas. Big dramas. But I was also writing comedy films at the same time. I love comedy, but I always tell my students or the writers I work with that you don't have comedy without tragedy or drama at the same time. It's kind of boring when it's just punch line after punch line. Drama goes deeper and good comedy comes from tragedy. So I feel, at least in *Jane the Virgin*, you have all sorts of tones going on at the same time. We had these storylines with Petra and characters that were absurd - the mysteries and killings. It's a kind of comedy that's way up there. Then we have the other comedy, which was very funny coming from grounded characters.

Then we had melodrama; all the crying and being very melodramatic in a good way. Sometimes, I think that melodrama is looked at as a minor genre, which I don't think it is. It's easier to make people cry than make people laugh, true. But you still have to tell good stories and entertain people. It's hard. So we had all sorts of tones within an episode of forty-three to forty-five minutes. Jennie Urman, the show's creator, was very good at boarding the scenes. We would try to avoid putting a very absurd scene next to comedy, then next to a very emotional scene. It was asking the audience to go from one emotional state to another very quickly. You would go up and down on *Jane*, but always in a smooth and organic way. At least, that's what we tried to do. That's not what I was doing in telenovela. When Jennie Urman hired me on *Jane the Virgin*, it was because she wanted an expert in telenovelas in the room. It was very interesting because when we killed the main character, Michael, the room was divided. "No, we can't kill Michael. What are we going to do? It's the second season. People are going to know that people are going to end up with Rafael and that's it." I was the one on the other side saying no, we can bring him back. Then they would be like, "He's dead! How are we going to bring him back?" I'd have to remind them, "It's a telenovela! We can bring him back. We are doing all sorts of absurd things, why can we not bring him back?" And we did. He had amnesia.

Everyone watching a telenovela knows the couple is going to end up together and get married. We know it and we don't care. We just want to see the obstacles that the writers are going to create for these two to overcome before they get together. We know the ending and it doesn't matter. Who cares? The audience is not there for the ending, they are there for the ride.

Q: Is there a difference between Mexican telenovelas and American soaps?

Carolina Rivera - It's a different mindset. When I was writing telenovelas, there were not that many shows that were not telenovelas in Mexico. We didn't have access to American shows unless you paid a bunch of money to be able to watch. And, even so, there was not a lot of TV series coming into Mexico. So people just watched telenovelas. But now, there are a lot of shows on the air and people are getting more internet so they can get Netflix. Now, people choose what they want to watch. If you choose a telenovela to watch, you know what you're getting. The suspension of disbelief of things. Of course, I prefer the other kind of TV where you don't know what the ending is going to be and you are surprised all the time.

I remember that the first Netflix show we watched in Mexico was *24* with Kiefer Sutherland. I remember what I liked about the show was you didn't know what was going to happen! Especially, when they killed the wife. Wow! Anything can happen in this show! I really liked that because, to be honest, I was tired of writing the same thing over and over again. I feel like telenovelas are very much like author Judy Bloom said, "Little kids want you to tell them the same story the same way, every time."

Q: Must telenovelas always have a happy ending?

Carolina Rivera - Yes. I once wrote a telenovela that ended not on a marriage, but on a divorce and it did so badly. The studio was like, "We have to change this because it's an awful ending. People are not going to want it." So we didn't go all the way to divorce. We went to, "Let's get a divorce so we can get married again!" I was trying to write a different story and the audience was saying we want our telenovela. We want to watch what we know. We want the dream of the perfect love story and love conquers all. We want them to get married. To be madly in love.

Q: What do you think about when shaping female protagonists and antagonists in your shows?

Carolina Rivera - Something I think people should know is that there is no good and bad. Only in telenovelas. The shows I am writing now, there is no good or bad. It's just complicated. Women are complicated just like men are complicated. I concentrate on what they want. I have a show called, *The War Next Door* on Netflix, and these two women are crazy. They always fight with each other. In a way, I think they both want the same thing: what they think is best for their families. It's just they are different and they are not willing to listen or learn from each other until they do; until they watch the other one. What happens is that it depends on the moment you are in your life as to what you write about and how you tell them. You learn. That's the best scenario - you learn from life. Age is something that is good, not bad in writing. What I try to write in my characters is that they all have a vision of what is best for them and their loved ones. In the case of *The War Next Door*, these two women are not willing to accept that the other has something they can learn from, but still, they are just watching. They learn little tiny things, but mostly they learn to appreciate the other one.

Most of the things that I have learned, like a piece of knowledge that is very, very useful in life, has come from a woman. And you appreciate it like a treasure. I am a woman and I live life as a woman and whatever I learn from other women, I cherish. There's one piece of advice, I remember from a long time ago when my kids were young. My best friend's mom who has an amazing, beautiful relationship with her two daughters and her grandchildren, came to me while I was trying to cope with little kids, work, and family. She told me, "You can't compartmentalize life. You can't be a mom all the time. You can't be a working person all the time. You can't be a wife all the time. You can't be a daughter all the time. You have to be all of those things at the same time, all the time." As a mother, especially as a Latino mom, you feel guilty because you are educated to be like the Virgin of Guadalupe. The perfect woman, mother - the mother of God. Ugh! So as a woman, you feel very guilty not wanting to be a full-time mom and do other stuff. Or even enjoying sex, while being a mother! As a Latina woman, with Catholicism around you, you are expected to be pure and a great mother. So I was feeling very guilty back then. This woman was saying you are the mother you can be to your kids, not the mother you are expected to be in Mexican society. I can't forget that piece of advice and all my characters are like that. They are expected to be different and that gives them a lot of conflict. They are expected to be a different woman, but in the end, they realize they can only be the woman they can be.

Q: Can one's society and culture be a source of antagonism?

Carolina Rivera - Yes. That plays very much into the arc of all the women in my shows. In this other show I have, *Daughter From Another Mother*, the two female leads are expected to be a certain kind of mom, but they are very different women. In fact, in *Daughter From Another Mother*, there's a businesswoman who is on her way to the hospital and doesn't want her husband to know she's giving birth because she promised him that she would stop working if he agreed to have this third baby. He wants her to be a full-time mom and not what she was like with the other two kids because he feels that's not okay. In Mexico, there is still that thing in most of society where they still expect you to be a full-time mom.

Even our President has closed up a bunch of guarderías, nurseries, where they take care of little babies. They were free to use if you applied, and they were for working moms. All the feminists, a lot of people went out to the streets asking why he did this. He said, "Let the grandmas take care of the grandchildren." What if we're not around? I'm a working grandma! I have dreams and things I want to do. So it's a very conservative country and as a woman, we're expected to be a certain way. Men, too, are expected to be a certain way. So I feel all my women characters start out as that - what they are expected to be in my society, then gain consciousness. I feel the inciting event always questions that. The switch of babies and now having to give them back because the government says so and cut all communication because that's how it's supposed to be. And they decide not to do that and keep seeing each other and we'll figure things out.

We're starting to shoot the new season of *Daughter From Another Mother*, and where I want them to end up is creating their own family structure. Not the typical one with a mother and a father and kids, but something different. A community of people raising these two babies. Families are the people who nurture you through life and that might not be a blood relation. That's where I want them to end up. Completely different from where they started. In the second season of *The War Next Door*, there are also changes in family structure, too.

My female characters start with being what society wants them to be and the inciting incident destroys that and they have to figure out who they want to be. I am starting a new show on Lucha Libre called *Against the Ropes*. This is about a bunch of women who wrestle in Mexico. Dads do not want their daughters to become wrestlers. That's the most anti-feminine thing you can do. I'm very excited about it.

CHAPTER REVIEW: TELENOVELAS

- Telenovelas follow many of the same tropes and storylines, but just in different locations or situations.

- Telenovela writers rooms have to be very nimble. The networks are monitoring the ratings minute by minute and use a lot of focus groups, so you have to be able to change the storyline quickly.

- There is a lot of repetition in telenovela stories so that if you've missed a day or two, you can catch up.

- The biggest events in telenovelas happen on a Thursday. The previous days of the week have been building up to it. Friday has a big cliffhanger usually instigated by the villain as a way to get the audience back on Monday.

- Telenovelas' absurdity gives you lots of freedom. Just because a character died doesn't mean you can't bring them back!

- Telenovelas have happy endings because the audience demands it. And that happy ending usually is a big wedding.

- Society can be an antagonist in drama, especially if a character is going against what a specific culture deems as normal or expected.

CHAPTER 16

COMEDY

───────

This genre often gets dismissed as being silly or not serious, but the truth is, writing something that makes people laugh remains one of the hardest things a screenwriter can do. And the most satisfying. In this chapter, we talk to comedic feature film and sitcom writers who give insights on creating comedic characters, writing jokes, ad-libbing, and other things to tickle your funny bone.

Q: When working with a comedian, do you allow for ad-libbing?

Ben Philippe - Yes, although less than I think some people expect. I always get asked about the bloopers reel for *Only Murders in the Building*. We have them, but they aren't as funny as they could be because the comedians are very involved in the writing process. Steve Martin is an executive producer; he co-wrote the pilot. He sees all the scripts and we have virtual table reads. So when they have notes and thoughts on jokes, they just give it right to the writers, so those things are already massaged into the actual script.

Dan Mazer - It's always my default and preference that everybody in a comedy should be funny and have the ability to ad-lib or extrapolate, ameliorate, what's on the page. That's the beauty. To me, the script should always be a starting point. I sit in a room or at a cafe writing a script and sort of imagine who will be in it, but by the time you are shooting it a few years later, you've got different actors. It's now a completely different beast to what you imagined. I think it's a massive mistake to stick to what is on the page through pride or ego or vanity. Let funny people be funny. As the writer, you are going to get the benefit of that because people will imagine it's your words. You've provided the kernel of that anyway. I'm a huge fan of improvisation. The caveat to that is I think it should be structured. I always think you should get the version of what is on the page because what you think is a great idea on the day may not be when you get to the edit where you think it was a terrible idea. The truth is, a lot of people forget that by the time you write the script and get to production, you will have done thirty drafts of that scene. There's no logical reason why on the day some actors improvising will make it better. They might do and you should absolutely give them the chance, but equally get the scripted version down.

Josh Greenberg - Yes, though it depends on the performer. In the case of Tim Allen, whom I worked with for a few years, it was crucial. When he was in front of an audience, the audience just loved him. They just loved him. He would take that energy and give it back. So he would riff and there was no way you were going to tell him, "Please don't do that." It was great because he would do the lines as written, but since it's tape, he would try different ways of doing it. We have this term called "alts," alternative lines. Someone runs in with an alt and says, "Why don't you try saying this line?" What's so great is that it's in front of the studio audience who have seen the scene play out already, but they are seeing it a second time, but it has a new ending and they go wild. So you have even more energy.

With both single-cam and multi-cam sitcoms, you sometimes can get frustrated because you have to repeat a scene over and over again. But in front of a studio audience, you have the added pressure of losing the crowd. The audience is getting really bored watching the same scene shot over and over again. Once you do it three or four times, you really have to try to move on.

Carolina Rivera - I try to get actors to stick to what's on the page. We worked really hard as writers to come up with those words and they've been approved by Netflix or the studio. Of course, there's always room for ad-lib, but I try to keep it to a minimum. My shows are very fast-paced and ad-lib trumps that. So often I will let the actors say what they want, but then give me what's on the page.

Q: Is there a danger of staying with a joke too long?

Josh Greenberg - Yes, absolutely. It's funny, I grew up a big fan of Stanley Kubrick. There were all these legendary stories of doing a hundred takes of Jack Nicholson walking into a room just to get the right moment. Film students tend to idealize that. That you keep doing it over and over until you get it right. But, with comedy, you start to lose something. There's a certain sort of magic that you capture and then you can crush that by continuing to beat that dead horse. So and so is looking for a punch-up, that is the joy. You can sit there with a blank page and spend months and months toiling over a script for the same amount of money that you would get for two weeks of punching up somebody else's script.

Q: Is being hired for on-set punch-up writing fun?

Dan Mazer - Unbelievable! It's my favorite thing. Not only is it insanely lucrative, but all the hard work on the script has also been done. All the structure and character work, the logic work that drags you down has generally been done at that point and you're just there to pep it up. Frankly, you are sort of the hero. Everyone is tired of the script at that point. You come in and pep it up with a few jokes and everyone thinks you're great. People will reject the stuff that is not good and take the stuff that is good that makes it through. Everything that you do is additive and a bonus at that point. People are so desperate for the oxygen of new material, that even if they are clunkers, people don't realize they are. I've known people who have been employed for eight weeks at six figures a week and who ended up with two lines in the movie. That's just joy. It's like the reward for doing all that hard work over your career. When you get that call from your agent saying that so and so is looking for a punch up, that is the joy. You can sit there with a blank page and spend months and months toiling over a script for the same amount of money that you would get for two weeks of punching up somebody else's script.

Q: How do you plot out a comedy film?

Paul King - I think plotting is incredibly hard and no one ever really appreciates that. Even the way you're paid reflects it. You're given a few weeks to write a treatment and then far longer to write the dialogue as if that's the by far the hardest bit. To me, once you know what you are doing, writing the scenes is comparatively simple, whereas charting out stories is so very, very difficult, which is why everyone is looking for the Holy Grail formula that tells you what to do.

What I did learn doing *Paddington* was how useful other films could be; how they work. More for emotional through-line than comic through-line. With *Paddington 2*, I was obsessed with Frank Capra and doing a community movie. I watched *Mr. Smith Goes to Washington* about a dozen times; really trying to break it down. Not to copy it. It's nothing like *Mr. Smith Goes to Washington*, but just to see how those characters play out - the road map of their development. There's that scene where he sits on the steps of the Lincoln Memorial and you have this great, hopeful patriotic character who has lost all faith in the system. That's his nadir. That scene I found very emotional. So I tried to figure out how they got there, how they made me feel what I did? How it worked? And also how it didn't? Even in a film as great as that, one of my favorite films, there were moments where I thought I could maybe do a little better.

Simon Farnaby, who I work with a lot, always talks about the comic motor, which is great advice. What is the game that we are going to be playing here? I guess the first film is just, let's put a bear in a family home and see what happens. The second film was, let's put a bear in prison, which seemed a funny place to put Paddington. The first one, we were sort of obliged to do by the source material and the second one, there was more room for exploration because there was more of a blank canvas narratively. That sounded like a funny place and he can meet funny people. There will be fun conflict. But then, building a story around that would be difficult.

Q: Is it important to keep the tone of a comedy even?

Dan Mazer - I think the most important thing in comedy is the tone. There's no right answers to what the tone should be, but it's important that when you are writing your script you are aware of what it is and you stick to it. This way you have a voice and an identity. So if you want to write a gentle comedy, then that's great, but then you will be focusing on keeping things real and rye and witty with nice lines. You can't really alter that. You can't, all of sudden, throw in a crazy scene where there's a naked fight or a cage fight because that's not the tone you've set. That's because when studio executives and producers are reading it, they want to know and understand what they are reading. If you alter that, then people are confused, especially without a director saying how they want to change the genre with all these crazy things. I think it's very unlikely that people are going to sign up to a script that veers tonally as it goes through. It's important in your mind to know the tone of the script you are writing and, within reason, stick to that tone and not veer from a scene that is incredibly grounded to a scene that's extreme. That's hard because you will often get seduced by a joke or comic idea that is independently really funny. But the damage that does to your credibility or the universe that you've created will be irreparable if it's not consistent with the tone of the rest of the script.

Josh Greenberg - It's very important to choose a tone. *30 Rock* has a very specific, fast-moving, wacky tone and that wouldn't work on *Everybody Loves Raymond* or something like that. Some shows are more grounded. Some shows are more silly and broad. What's funny is that I love all those different tones, but it is crucial to know the tone of the show that you are working on.

Q: Can you go too over the top with comedy?

Dan Mazer - Absolutely. If you are writing an extreme comedy, then go for it and write it as extreme as you can. That's great, but know that's what you're doing. Don't dress it up as something else. It's about creating rules and sticking to them. This one is going to be extreme and anything can happen. This one is grounded and set in reality, so it has to adhere to the rules and have logic and a basis in reality.

Josh Greenberg - It depends on the project. I don't know if you've seen *What We Do in the Shadows*, which a USC classmate, Yana Gorskaya, produces. That show goes crazy places and it's hysterical. It's amazing, but that's totally in keeping with the tone of that show. Gonzo bananas. I admire that they can do that. It's always fun in a writers room when someone pitches, "What if this crazy thing happens?" Everyone cracks up. I've even been on shows where they do it. It may not be really in keeping with this show's tone, but screw it! Let's do it!

Ben Philippe - Yes, you can. I've been very lucky that all the shows I've been on have a bit of comedy to them. I've been on five seasons over three shows and the trickiest one for me was the drama. I couldn't be as comedic and I was used to the mish-mash style of *Only Murders in the Building*. I am used to things being funny, but they have to be grounded. Sometimes, there may be a funnier joke here, but would the characters really talk that way to each other when they are researching a murder? For example, in the pilot of *Only Murders in the Building*, they are all neighbors and they go into the apartment of the person who just died via a gunshot wound to the head. At the conceptual level, there could be a wacky bit where they are slipping around on the blood on the floor. That was carded up on the board for a while and then we realized that they wouldn't do that. That would be too glib and dark for the show. So we have a little dramatic moment where Mabel is put off by actual blood in her neighbor's apartment. It's just modulating how much comedy you want. I've never been on a full *Modern Family* or *Family Guy* type comedy where it's just joke, joke, joke. I think I would struggle a little bit. I enjoy character-based stuff.

Q: What makes jokes kill?

Dan Mazer - Wow! If any of us knew that, then there would be a formula, we would write it in a computer and I would be a gazillionaire! There are a million factors. It's where a joke comes in a script; what's preceded it; what tone you've set. Have you gone two minutes without a joke and you have this thing that's insanely brilliant? Are the characters lovable enough to carry the joke off? There are a million mitigating factors in what does and doesn't make a joke work. And I will often be absolutely blindsided in that first preview of a movie as to what hits and what doesn't. The biggest laughs in things that I have made, I didn't even consider jokes. People would just love it because you set up a character with whom people have fallen in love. And then there are things that I would stake anything on in absolutely killing and being the greatest and it falls down to absolute silence.

A great tip I would give writers when writing a comedy is that as soon as you feel you have the script in shape, try to get a read-through. They don't have to be brilliant actors or twenty of them. Just five actors playing different parts. Sit in a room and just listen. Even if there are four people watching, you will get a sense of how those people will react. The brilliant thing about comedy, about laughter, is that it's empirical. Either something works or it doesn't. You hear a laugh at a point where there's a joke or you don't. If you hear a laugh, it works. If you don't hear a laugh, it doesn't. I've been lucky to go through the preview process and, generally what you do is if a joke doesn't get a laugh, you cut it out. As long as it's not integral to the plot or the script, it goes. I've been foolish and arrogant enough to go, "No. They're wrong. They will laugh next time." They never do. If it falls silent, it falls silent and you're wrong. You've just got it wrong.

I've been writing jokes for nearly thirty years in one form or another. Scripts for twenty. I'm pretty good at knowing what will hit and what won't, but by no means do I have a 100% record. Nor do any of the directors or brilliant producers or brilliant actors that I've worked with who are some of the biggest names in comedy - know what is a cast iron joke. I've had nice discussions with Sacha Baron Cohen over a joke having to stay in because it's great. And then either him or me saying the opposite. Then you play it out and people either laugh or they don't. Sometimes, I'm right. Sometimes, he's right. Sometimes, neither of us is right. It's not a science.

In the last *Borat*, the sequel, I never saw the Mike Pence bits at the Republican Party conference as being funny. I didn't understand it. I was in favor of losing it. But some people come out of the theater saying that was their favorite bit. Then events came along and made it funnier. I liked it when there was a father and a daughter doing a dance when she's on her period. People find different things funny. Stuff that my Mum finds funny, I could watch for eight hours and not find a laugh in it. That's the beauty of the genre and it's also the frustration.

Josh Greenberg - Wow! That question is so tough. Now we are getting into the theory of humor. The easy answer would be "the unexpected"; something that you could not have predicted. That's sort of the most basic comedy rule from Buster Keaton on. Then, there is a lot of comedy that is clever wordplay and subtlety. I always come back to character stuff, that when someone says something or has a specific attitude, you know they are going to feel that way because that's who the character is. It's delightful.

Dave Reynolds - If you stay true to your character and your character doesn't go out of their way to tell a joke, the joke will resonate longer and you will want to see it again because it's true to the character. There are a lot of funny movies out there, especially animated movies. The jokes are coming from every direction bang, bang, bang. They are hilarious. Then you ask someone if they want to see the movie again and they say no. Why? Because they've seen the jokes and they have nothing to do with the story. When you rewatch a movie, even a comedy, you're watching it for the story and the characters. Yes, the jokes are there and they're still funny because they're based on the characters you're rooting for. Jokes do better if they have meaning to our main characters.

Q: What do you find hard about writing comedy?

Josh Greenberg - Trying to do something that is new - that's fresh. Our generation and generations younger than us grew up with so much television - just this massive cerebral influx of TV - that really influenced us. Sometimes you use those things as a model, like this is how a show is done. You do A, B, C, and D. Some shows like *What We Do in the Shadows* just completely shatter the mold of what's been done before. Unfortunately, you also bump up against executives who love what's been done before. They don't like taking risks. They don't really want to shatter that mold. They think, "Well, this worked, why don't we just copy that?" So creatively, the biggest challenge is trying to do something really new, fresh, and funny.

Ben Philippe - It's the balance. It's like a sandwich, which needs to have lettuce, bread, and meat. So writing has to have a bunch of elements like characters, comedy, and drama that work together. It has to be funny, but you can't shoot for the funniest thing possible. You have to be realistic and live within the characters and live next to the mystery. For example, my episode, *Putting the Pieces Together,* for Season 2 in *Only Murders*, was about Mabel stabbing someone on the subway and then having a fugue state because she doesn't remember whether or not she did it. There is a stalker around New York City and she's having memories of her father who died when she was young and she blocked that memory out. It's very cerebral. It's very character focused. There's a lot of grief for her character. When you are writing an episode like that, the comedy can't be the first thing you go to as opposed to an episode like *The Tell*, where Martin Short is hosting a murder-mystery party where it's joke, joke, joke. It's calibrating where you want there to be comedic verses, where you want the comedy to still exist but take a step back.

Dan Mazer - The solitude of writing, generally, is hard. One of the reasons I direct is because it's the opposite of that. It's incredibly social and you have to answer a thousand questions a day. You have to deal with 500 people a day. Writing, you sit for ten hours on your own and try not to spend all your time looking at the internet and trying to find inspiration.

I find that at this point in my life, I know I can write a funny script. I can sort of coast through it. I can rely on a scene that's like a scene that I did ten or fifteen years ago. I have a massive bank of material that has been made, nearly made or not made. When you've been doing something for twenty years now, it's hard to come up with new stuff that feels fresh. You constantly have to challenge yourself to do that. Tastes move on. Sensibilities change. You have to keep abreast of that.

For example, when I started writing movies, I was doing *Ali G Indahouse.* Everything then was gross-out comedy - *American Pie, There's Something About Mary*, the Farrelly brothers. I loved all that, as it was my sensibility. Now, nobody is interested in that. Frankly, fewer and fewer people are interested in comedy which in America, they call R-rated comedy. Adult comedies. Very few of those are being made. So you have to diversify and keep fresh and try to think of new ways to be funny. That's the challenge.

Q: What is the first thing you think of when writing a sitcom?

Josh Greenberg - Character. If you look at so many examples of successful sitcoms like *Frasier* or *Friends* or *Everybody Loves Raymond* - they're filled with jokes, but the reason people keep coming back is because of the characters. They love these characters and they want to spend time with them every week. You can have a really wacky or unique or cool premise, but it's always about finding a character that people would want to spend time with, possibly for years.

Q: Do current events ever come into play when writing sitcom characters?

Josh Greenberg - We are in such a divisive time right now that it's challenging now to have something that is a direct commentary on current events without upsetting someone. However, political commentary can sometimes bleed into what you are writing.

Q: Do you think comedy is very specific to culture?

Dan Mazer - I think often with comedy, specificity is what makes it funny. I would probably say that for all films. When you take someone into a new world or idea that we haven't seen before and it's fresh, then that is often what is exciting. I think that is what will get producers and audiences engaged. But, at the same time, within that specificity, there has to be some sort of universality, as well. I think as a writer, it's about being as non-generic as you can be. I think if something is good and fresh, then it will find an audience. It's wrong-headed to think people in Azerbaijan will think this is funny. For example, we never thought *Borat* would translate the way it did. We thought it would be a little niche indie movie that a few people would see. But it had something about it that appealed to people from Australia to Austria and beyond. It was pretty across the board. It was very specific and very focused. I think the worst thing anyone can do is go into a script trying to make it appeal to everyone because then it will probably appeal to nobody.

Josh Greenberg - I love that you are seeing all these different types of comedy and different perspectives on comedy that I don't think you would have seen even five years ago. It's great because you have new voices who are showing you something that wouldn't have been on TV or streaming a while ago. It's awesome. Everyone has their own comedic perspective. They all have something universal about them. I can watch something that has nothing to do with my life and still completely relate to a character or conflict. I think the audience is getting used to seeing different types of cultures on TV. There was a time when half-hour comedies were homogenous and that is changing.

Q: What do writers get wrong when writing comedy?

Dan Mazer - The belief that comedy needs to be extreme is wrong. Sometimes, the more subtle and nuanced it is, the better. Look, I wouldn't say that my work always pays heed to that, but a lot of the stuff that I like watching, certainly, does. Again, I am not a great exponent of this, but having faith in letting something breathe and relying on character is really important. Ultimately, all stories rely on us loving the characters and investing in them. The joke should never supersede that. The joke should really come out of character and feel organic. And don't sort of try to force stuff in. Sometimes, I've had to get rid of that set piece that I thought was the very fulcrum of the movie because it didn't serve the plot or the characters well enough. While, in isolation, it would have been a really funny scene, it did more harm than good by either jolting people out of the story or making people less invested in the character. Even in a comedy, you need to get people invested and that comes from identifying with characters.

Q: What are the differences between writing sketches and features or TV?

Dan Mazer - A problem that I have is that I get seduced by a funny idea or a funny scene. Laughs are so precious and hard to come by and if you've written something that you think is funny, you just want to cling to it even when it doesn't service the entire film. There's that old adage of where sometimes you have to kill your babies and I think that is particularly true in comedy. You have to think about the holistic situation of the movie, and sometimes a misplaced scene or laugh can jolt you out of the movie and undo all the good work that you've done. Again, I am preaching advice that I don't necessarily follow, but there is a benefit to thinking of your movie without jokes. Strip out every joke and see that if this was a drama, would this work? And then layering in the jokes on top of that, which, obviously, lift it. The plots of the *Borat* films are super simple. The plots of most successful comedies are super simple, but they work. Yes, by all means, embellish that and make the laughter the thing that makes it distinct and elevates it. But if you stripped out all the laughs, a question you would have to ask yourself is: Would the film work on that basis?

Josh Greenberg - I love sketch stuff. That world seems really hard to me; the world of *Saturday Night Live*. That seems really challenging. In terms of the feature versus sitcom world, writing on the feature side was such a solitary exercise. I did start doing comedy features and it was just me and my computer in a cafe or in my apartment staring at a blank monitor. They didn't tell us that writing for TV is more of a social thing. You are having to work with these other people, which I think is awesome. You will throw out an idea that's not quite fully baked and then someone else will go, "Oh, that's great. Why don't we do this?" Then, someone else will say, "Oh, then you can do this!" That's really hard to do in isolation. It's just you and your brain trying to figure out the story. That's a huge difference. In terms of storytelling, they are similar. You are doing the same stuff. But the experience for a writer is different.

CHAPTER REVIEW: COMEDY

- Allowing comedic actors to ad-lib lines can generate lots of jokes that are better than what you originally wrote. However, always shoot what you've written because you know that will work with the logic of the rest of the story.

- Alts or alternative lines can be written into a screenplay if you have different ideas for jokes or gags. Most screenwriting softwares have a function for alts.

- Too many takes or alts can loose the magic of the comedic moment.

- Comedy works best in short bursts.

- Figuring out a story's "comedic motor" can help with building the plot.

- Choose a tone early on in your screenplay and then stick to it throughout the story. Veering from it will confuse a reader.

- Read-throughs are very helpful with comedy. If the jokes make people laugh, it works. If they don't, it doesn't.

- Do not force comedy or push for over the top comedy. Often, subtle comedy can get the biggest laugh.

- Comedy that is based on the characters you're rooting for will give jokes longer lasting power. And they are the films and shows that keep people returning to them.

CHAPTER 17

ROMANTIC COMEDY
&
CHRISTMAS MOVIES

What's more entertaining than watching humans deal with the most human of all issues: romantic relationships? It's one of the prime drivers of our existence! Now take that and add in one of the most popular times of the year and you may have a real winner.

In this chapter, two rom-com writers talk about how they get us to literally fall in love with their characters and plots. Later on, a Christmas TV movie writer discusses how to keep the ideas fresh when there are hundreds of this genre made - each year! Oh, and how much Christmas do you have to write into the script? Read carefully as you don't want to make it onto the naughty list!

Q: How important is it to know your market when writing rom-coms?

Hilary Galanoy - It's more important to be a fan of romantic comedies because I think your market is always there. For a long time, I think Hollywood ignored romantic comedies. They were out of fashion, which is silly because the audience never went away. There is a built-in audience for them all the time. People are always going to want a feel-good love story. I am the audience. I've always been the audience. So I think that's all it takes - being a huge fan of romantic comedies. Then, you will automatically know what people want to see in romantic comedies.

Elizabeth Hackett - You've heard "write what you know?" It's also "write what you love." Everyone loves love stories. Even when I watch *Die Hard*, I'm like, "Well, their marriage is going to be saved, right?" Romance lines are the things that keep publishing houses alive. The biggest mistake studios made was shifting away from rom-coms because once the streamers came along, there was a huge appetite for them. And they want more! It's getting harder to come up with ideas because, "Oh no! That's already been done!" It's something that we love watching and are happy we get to write them.

Q: Is there a fixed formula for writing rom-coms?

Hilary Galanoy - Yes, absolutely. You can deviate from the formula a lot, but there certainly are a lot of tropes in romantic comedy. Like, "Oh, no! I need a date for the wedding," or "I'm on a mistaken date!" One of my favorite romantic comedies of all time is based on a trope, which is *Working Girl*. She was pretending to be someone else. But that one was done so well that it got nominated for an Oscar. And then, there are the romantic comedies that are more character based like the Nancy Meyers kind like *Something's Gotta Give*. But they definitely follow a formula. It doesn't have to be competing love interests, but there's definitely a "meet cute" and there's an arc where your characters are butting heads. And of course, they end up together in the end. It's not a romantic comedy if they don't end up together in the end. Some could argue that *My Best Friend's Wedding* is not a romantic comedy, it's just a comedy because they don't end up together at the end.

Elizabeth Hackett - There's a formula for a reason. It's like a cookie recipe. Some people make better cookies than other people. Some people add stuff. Some people stick to the playbook. You want to figure out a way to make it so it's not the same old chocolate chip cookie.

Hilary Galanoy - And you definitely want to avoid the cookie where somebody put raisins in it because that ruins the cookie.

Elizabeth Hackett - One of my favorite movies is *Palm Springs*, which is a romantic comedy, but it plays around with the genre.

Hilary Galanoy - And that certainly was a trope. They did *Groundhog Day,* but it was so well done. As Liz said, they made it a cookie of their own.

Q: Do Hallmark and Netflix have particular formulas or sets of rules that they want in their movies?

Hilary Galanoy - At Hallmark, there really isn't a set of rules. The producer just says what they are looking for.

Elizabeth Hackett - Any time you're pitching anywhere - studio, streamer or network - you do your research about what they're interested in buying. What's the word on the street? What are they looking for? What do they already have in their pipeline? They want this; they don't want that; they already have two scripts like that. You find out from your producer or exec what is officially off the table or what they feel the development slate is missing.

Hilary Galanoy - They told us that a mom and a teenage or pre-teen daughter should be able to watch it and not be like, "Shut your eyes! Don't watch this part!" There's probably no eight-year-old daughter that wants to watch a romantic comedy.

Q: How do you make a rom-com idea stand out?

Elizabeth Hackett - There's a formula in terms of structure, but you have to look at what the movie is about. What is it trying to say about relationships? What are the themes they are playing with? In *Something's Gotta Give*, it's an older guy who's always dating younger women and finds himself falling for the mother of his girlfriend. Or *When Harry Met Sally*, men and women can't be friends. The better romantic comedies have some sort of thesis underneath them and are trying to say something or prove something or play with something about relationships, love, or how we meet.

Hilary Galanoy - They speak to us. We've been in that situation. We've been in a *When Harry Met Sally* situation. We've all had a friend of the opposite sex. So it's when we can identify with it and I think we really have to like the characters and root for them. If you can see yourself in the characters on screen, then you are going to be more invested in them and root for them to end up together. So make them very human and relatable on some level. And it's not that they can't be larger than life, but I think if you don't root for your characters in your romantic comedy, it's over before it's even left the gate.

Q: How do you create characters that get sparks flying?

Hilary Galanoy - Casting. I'm joking a bit, but casting is huge. Liz and I are known for witty banter. We really work hard to have it be elevated. We spend time to make sure we have callbacks or themes in the banter or dialogue. We try to emulate that screwball comedy in dialogue, not completely because that's not in fashion anymore, but we love that *His Girl Friday* kind of banter.

Elizabeth Hackett - In a rom-com, comedy comes from conflict. So you want two characters who have some opposing conflict. They teach in drama school that drama is conflict. And it's true. When people are reading a script and saying it's not funny enough, what they are really saying is there's not enough conflict there to get comedy from. An old boss of ours told us something that is true: You want to torture your main characters so that you feel that this romance is earned at the end. You know they are going to get together, but there is the fun of watching them go through it and having to work for it.

Q: What distinguishes a rom-com from a standard comedy?

Hilary Galanoy - In a rom-com the romance is central. You have to find the romantic moments, too, which we haven't really touched upon. It's very important to have moments that are swoon-worthy for your audience. They are not just here to laugh. They are here for that relationship. So we always dig deep to find them. Sometimes, they are obvious, "Oh no, we are trapped in this elevator together." The stolen glances. The romantic comedies we write are pretty PG-rated. There's not a lot of hooking up or anything. You want those moments so that when you get that kiss it's so satisfying. It's a focus in a romantic comedy that is not like any other comedy.

Q: Can rom-coms be too cheesy?

Hilary Galanoy - Absolutely! But you know what? It works! So from our movie *Falling Inn Love,* there's this line that Liz wrote and it's genius. The two leads are redoing this fireplace and she wants to rip it out and he wants to keep it. It was a little conflict they had. It's her place and he's the contractor. And he says, "It's a beaut. We can't rip it out." It's set in New Zealand and they say "beaut" instead of "beautiful." When they are done redoing it, she says, "You're right. It is a beaut." And he's looking at her and says, "She sure is." Our actor did not want to say that line. But people quoted it on Twitter, they loved it so much! Knowing your audience, that's where it's at. We knew that was going to work and it did. So yes, you can be cheesy and it can work.

Elizabeth Hackett - Yeah, there really is a spectrum. There are the Hallmark people and there are the people who want the more gentle rom-com. I'm the person who saw *Bridget Jones' Diary* in the theater three times.

Hilary Galanoy - And there's a show that I'm a fan of and you, Liz, are even a bigger fan - *Bridgerton*. There's not a lot of comedy in it, so for me, it probably veered into the "too cheesy" territory five times per episode.

Elizabeth Hackett - That's more squarely in the romance genre. Hilary and I both love *While You Were Sleeping*. We grew up on 80s rom-coms where there was as much "com" as "rom." I like that the streamers are actually making those again. It's back to those things that we paid money to see in the theater.

Q: Can you put the kiss anywhere in a rom-com?

Elizabeth Hackett - It depends. The old rule of thumb with these kinds of rom-coms was only one kiss, but places are playing around with formulas and expectations.

Hilary Galanoy - It depends on what streamer or studio or channel you are making it for, but also what division. We work at a division at Netflix where the movies should be family-friendly. A mom and her fourteen-year-old daughter can watch it together, so we stay in a PG-13 arena. There are romantic comedies on Netflix that go into more R-rated territory. *Palm Springs,* which was at Hulu, which considers itself a more edgy streamer, made an R-rated movie. They slept together and they swear. But in the ones that we write for Netflix, we have more than one kiss. We have two kisses. One usually at about mid-movie and we have a kiss at the end. But if you have only one kiss or it's a more chaste romantic comedy - that kiss is your last thing. Literally. Sometimes, it's the kiss and you're out. *My Best Friend's Bouquet*, which we had on Hallmark, they admit they are in love, they kiss and the credits roll. It should be everything. It should be extremely satisfying. It should almost feel like a cheer moment when they finally kiss. That is the three-point basketball shot that wins the game.

Q: What are the forces of antagonism in rom-coms?

Elizabeth Hackett - There's usually a gentle villain. There's someone who is an antagonist, but not someone who is going to pull back the shower curtain and be there with a knife.

Hilary Galanoy - It's not so much that they are a direct villain as they are an obstacle for our two romantic leads getting together. We just finished a movie where there's no ex-boyfriend or ex-girlfriend complicating matters. A love triangle is a very common trope in romantic comedies. Instead, we had the heroine's ex-boss be the character who disrupts the new situation our heroine is trying to navigate, which drives our two main characters apart. So sometimes it's just a third-party force that derails the romance. You definitely need obstacles on the road to true love and happiness.

Elizabeth Hackett - Sometimes, the obstacles are within themselves - not opening themselves up to love, not being able to take that leap.

Hilary Galanoy - It's one of the few genres of movies where you don't have to have a real obvious antagonist. The protagonists can be their own antagonists. We tried to write a *Romancing the Stone* situation and in that case, the situation is the antagonist. Two people who can't stand each other trying to survive out in the wilderness.

Q: Should the characters in a rom-com be formulaic? Such as, the best friend?

Hilary Galanoy - I don't think you have to have the standard characters. In one of our movies, instead of her best friend, it's her Dad. She lives in her father's guest house and he is her best friend. It's really fun to write that. So many times in movies, people don't have parents or siblings. And you're often very close to them. Nothing was weirder to me than in the *Sex And The City* movie, where Sarah Jessica Parker's character, Carrie Bradshaw, is getting married and her parents aren't there. Does she not have parents? Very weird. And you need those characters because your lead character needs someone to talk to. We have to hear what's going on with them. With *Love, Guaranteed,* the lead character, Nick is a physical therapist and it's one of his patients with whom he's grown very close. It's fun to branch out the best friend character and not make it so obvious.

Elizabeth Hackett - In *Pillow Talk*, Doris Day's best friend is Thelma Ritter, who is her hungover maid who shows up every day. All of her confidences that she says come out while she's making a hangover cure for this woman. It's about finding those little memorable characters that make it feel fresh.

Hilary Galanoy - It's also about making it realistic to life. We often put siblings or parents in our movies because people have siblings and parents.

Q: Have rom-coms changed in any way?

Hilary Galanoy - The one thing we really like is there's a lot more diversity and inclusiveness now across all platforms. We wrote something for Hallmark and we had someone in a wheelchair. People are so much more open to LGBTQ storylines now. It's nice to be able to have more diversity. Definitely, the rom-coms of old were two white people.

Elizabeth Hackett - Yes, there are updates and modernizations, but I think at the same time there is a comfort food factor. These are the movies you watch when you are home, sick. There is an audience for that. So how do you take the same chicken soup and make it different, fresh, and interesting? People just want to escape sometimes, especially during the pandemic. They wanted to see a movie where people weren't wearing masks and who fell in love under normal circumstances. There's something to be said for feeling good.

Q: Are there similar rules in both rom-coms and Christmas movies?

Hilary Galanoy - Christmas movies are a little more formulaic because you want to hit a certain number of Christmas beats. At Hallmark, you want a lot of Christmas. They are not going away. They are so popular. Hallmark makes about forty of them a year. Lifetime makes thirty original Christmas movies a year. And it's not just Hallmark Channel, there's Hallmark's Movies and Mysteries Channel.

Christmas movie ideas are easy to find. We have a folder of them because whenever you read a heartwarming Christmas story, you just put it in there. *Fir Crazy,* our first Christmas movie, came from an article from the L.A. Times about New York City tree lots. Because they are on sidewalks, they can't close overnight. Someone has to be there and they live in a little trailer. The article was very funny because it talked about drunk people at 4 a.m. wanting to buy a Christmas tree. And you don't need a permit to sell Christmas trees in NYC, you just need the permission of the store you're selling in front of. We said that's an awesome arena for a Christmas movie and it just blossomed from there.

I just saw an article that was Thanksgiving-oriented about an older woman who texted who she thought was her grandson and it turned out to be another kid. She's white, he's Black, and they are from totally different worlds otherwise and she invited him for Thanksgiving dinner. And now for the past five years, he brings his girlfriend and they have Thanksgiving dinner together. That's a Hallmark Thanksgiving movie!

Elizabeth Hackett - The only problem with Hallmark Christmas movies is that there is someone there who is a genius with a spreadsheet and knows what idea was done in 2014 on the third day of programming. They know every idea they've ever done. There's no way we writers could keep track of something like that. So you think you have a hot original idea when in fact, they already have that idea in development or they just did it last season.

Hilary Galanoy - I really hope the person who takes care of that spreadsheet is someone who doesn't celebrate because I could see it being too much.

Elizabeth Hackett - That would make a good Christmas movie. The person who keeps track of Christmas movies and has grown to hate them!

Q: Do Hallmark Christmas movies usually have female protagonists?

Julie Sherman Wolfe - Generally, yes, but it's become more equal in the last couple of years. I try to put something in every movie that would make someone's husband or boyfriend or significant other look up from their phone and start watching! And while the key demo is women, I know plenty of men who love Hallmark movies. I want them to feel represented, too. In one movie, I had a whole bunch of hockey in it. I've heard from fans, "My husband actually liked this one. And he never watches these movies." When my husband and teenage son both tell me they love one of my movies, I know I succeeded in finding that balance.

Q: How do you approach villains/antagonists in Christmas movies?

Julie Sherman Wolfe - One thing I'm glad Hallmark's starting to get away from is the trope of "a guy who's a big-city lawyer who doesn't understand small towns or love." Or "a guy who's the evil real estate broker who's in town to build a mall on top of the community center." Or he's the reason our female lead can't keep her shop open. I'm guilty of all of these, by the way! I prefer to find the antagonist within a character's internal struggles. Christmas just heightens what they're already wrestling with in their own lives.

In *Dickens of a Holiday,* the male lead is an action star who isn't being taken seriously for dramatic roles. He takes the role of Scrooge in *A Christmas Carol* back in his hometown, to prove to himself, and others, that he can do it. It's all about his insecurities. Meanwhile, the female lead, who grew up in the same town, and who at high school was the Most Likely To Do Everything, went to New York to make it big on Broadway but didn't. She's a little jealous of this guy who she turned down dating in high school and who then went out to L.A. and became this big, famous star. So the antagonist for her is not knowing what she's meant to do with her life. It's internal for both of them - and when they meet, everything comes to the surface. Ultimately, they help each other realize the path they're meant to take. We all know they'll end up together and the fun is not knowing how. That's my job.

Q: How much are you thinking about theme in a Christmas movie?

Julie Sherman Wolfe - To me, and to the network, the most important aspect of the theme is that it's clear-cut and something with which people can identify: redemption, second chances, overcoming fears, or finding your confidence. A common theme in our Christmas movies is a character who has trouble opening their heart again after a tragedy. My job is to find a way for them to take that journey in hopefully, an original way and yes, that can be a challenge!

During the holidays, people tend to watch our movies while doing other things like wrapping presents, baking, scrolling their social media. I cannot get my son to watch TV without looking at his phone! So as much as I'd love to think people are captivated by my words and paying full attention, I know that's likely not the case. That's why we keep the theming simple, so even if the viewer misses something, they're still fully engaged with the story.

Q: How much Christmas do you have to cram into a Christmas movie?

Julie Sherman Wolfe - A lot! I will tell you, as much Christmas as I think I put into a script, the first note every single time is: There is not enough Christmas! There has to be Christmas in every shot. Wall to wall. At all times. In every conceivable way. If there's a page where Christmas isn't mentioned, you're getting a note: "More Christmas!"

The absolute hardest part when writing Hallmark Christmas movies is thinking up new activities for your characters to do that hasn't already been done to death. There are only so many ways to have a snowball fight. You have to have the scene where they trim the tree. You have to have something involving snow in some way which is not easy in July when it's 100 degrees in Vancouver! I don't know if you saw *A Clusterfunk Christmas*, but it seemed like all the jokes were written specifically for Hallmark Channel Christmas movie writers. There was no coffee in the entire town. Only cocoa, eggnog, or cider. They even nailed one of our Unspoken Hallmark Christmas Movie Rules: If you're having coffee, it better have Christmas-y toppings like a peppermint stick or green and red sprinkles. If not, forget it.

Q: Would a Hallmark Christmas movie set in Miami with no snow ever happen?

Julie Sherman Wolfe - I'm working on a movie about a woman from Miami who moves to New England and who doesn't know how to "do winter." But it's not for Christmas. People want to see the romantic, idealized vision of Christmas. There's this romantic notion of what Christmas looks like, and to be honest, a big reason why my husband and I didn't like Los Angeles was the lack of seasons and the vibe of Christmas or winter. It could easily be 90 degrees on Christmas Day in L.A. Once we moved to Connecticut, I put up all my holiday lights that I had in California, and went totally overboard. We had the gaudiest house in the neighborhood. What I figured out is, there's no need to overcompensate for the lack of a Christmas vibe here. People just put up nice, minimal, classy lights. There are no leaves on the trees. There's already snow on the ground. It feels like winter because it IS winter. It feels like Christmas! There's no song that goes, "I'm dreaming of an unseasonably warm Christmas." That being said, most of my Christmas writing happens in the summer, so I close the windows, turn on the Bing Crosby, and pretend it's December!

Q: Are there other "must haves" in a Christmas movie?

Julie Sherman Wolfe - There are entire podcasts dedicated to the many beloved tropes in a Hallmark Christmas movie, which admittedly show up a lot. The town tree lighting, Santa, caroling of course, gently falling snow, hot cocoa walk-and-talks, ugly sweaters and baking. Always baking! Trying to find an original way into a baking scene is probably the most challenging part of writing one of these!

Q: How is social media used with Hallmark movies?

Julie Sherman Wolfe - It's not mandatory, but a lot of us like to live tweet during the premiere. The actors do, too. It's a window behind the scenes. I'll talk about who a certain character is named after, or tell the real story behind one of the scenes. I was, for a while, writing in all these Easter eggs, like putting a reference to ranch dressing in all my movies just to see how many I could do in a row! Hallmark likes live tweeting because we're engaging with the viewers, and they can see the side-conversations going on with the cast, like where I'm sending fire emojis when they killed it during a scene! So during the premiere, I follow the hashtag for the movie, and I can see the audience's reaction in real-time. You know, the "Oh, no she didn't" moments. That's always fun. Sometimes, someone calls out a mistake or a plot hole, and my response is usually something to the effect of, "It was in there, but it got cut."

I really try not to read the Facebook comments, or reviews. I can read a hundred "loved it" comments, but just one "hated it" negates them all! So I avoid it altogether. I do try to write the best script I possibly can, but someone is always going to hate it, no matter what. I can never predict the viewers' reactions. I've had a couple of movies that didn't turn out how I wanted, and I thought for sure no one was going to like them either, but they loved them! Sometimes, I think, "This is the best thing I've ever written," and people are like, "Meh."

Q: Can Hallmark Christmas movies be too cheesy?

Julie Sherman Wolfe - I try to avoid cheesy dialogue at all costs, but sometimes it's unavoidable. I'll try and take what could be an overpowering cheese and make it more of a mild provolone. My main goal, in all my dialogue, is that no one can guess the next line. Most of the cheese comes at the big moment right before our leads are about to kiss. So that's where I try to surprise the viewers with unexpected dialogue - nothing that can be checked off a box in Hallmark Channel Bingo.

Q: What is Hallmark Channel Bingo?

Julie Sherman Wolfe - All the tropes of a Hallmark Channel movie will go on a bingo card and you mark them off when they turn up! Like "dead mother," "snowball fight," "struggling business," "hot cocoa cart." I have two pet peeves that belong on a bingo card. One is, "Guy sips cocoa. Gets whipped cream on his nose. Girl coyly wipes it off." My pleas to avoid this trope usually falls on deaf ears. It drives me crazy. And... here's my big one... empty coffee cups! It kills me. They walk around with them and fling them around; there's clearly nothing inside them. You carry a cup like that in real life, you're basically seconds away from a trip to the E.R. with third-degree burns. Just put some water in the cups. I beg you.

CHAPTER REVIEW: ROMANTIC COMEDY & CHRISTMAS MOVIES

- Romantic comedies have certain formulas and tropes. How you play around with them is what makes them different and fun.

- Having a premise or exploring a concept that is familiar to the human dating/relationship experience helps make a romantic comedy stand out.

- If a romantic comedy is not funny, it's usually because there's not enough conflict between the main characters.

- It may seem obvious, but romantic comedies need swoon worthy romance. Otherwise, they are just comedies. Conversely, romantic comedies need laugh out loud comedy or they are just romances.

- Where you put "the kiss" is really important. It can affect your whole structure.

- Villains in romantic comedies are usually obstacles to the romantic leads getting together.

- Modern romantic comedies are much more inclusive, which opens up the possibilities for situations and storytelling.

- Christmas movies have similar expectations as romantic comedies, except that you have to put a lot of Christmas elements into them. We mean it. A lot. Like on every page. There's never too much.

- Christmas movies tend to have female protagonists, but they are really more evenly divided between the two leads.

- People tend to do other things while watching Christmas movies like wrapping presents, so the plots and themes shouldn't be too complicated.

- Christmas movies have a strong and vibrant fan base to the point where you may find yourself live tweeting with them during a broadcast. Or you may see games like Hallmark Channel Bingo being played on your show.

CHAPTER 18

DRAMA & ADAPTATION

It's difficult to find a way to discuss drama as its own entity, since all genres contain it in some amount in order to keep their plots driving forward. In fact, you can find discussions about these kinds of films and shows throughout this book. So to give these projects their due, we've decided to look at them in the context of their most common form, as work based on intellectual property is still the preferred form of project.

Q: Is having a strong, dark theme important in a drama?

Deborah Haywood - I think so. That's why we watch films, isn't it? To go through somebody else's shoes. My thing is to try and find out who is the person behind the label. Who is the person behind the school slag? Who is behind the deformed, simple woman on the street? Who's the person behind the school bully? Kind of have a peep behind their mask because I think we do dismiss people. We know who that is but I don't think we know who that is. Everyone has rich, interior lives. They are not who we think they are. That draws me. Also, slightly not talked about stuff fascinates me.

Danny Strong - I don't know if I fully agree with that. I think you can have a very hopeful theme in a very dark drama. I think you can have a very intense drama, but have a very inspiring theme to it at the end of the day. A dark theme? I don't think of it in those terms. For me, I want the theme to be something human, global, and significant. If I am going to spend two to five years working on a piece, I want it to have something significant to say, thematically.

Barbara Stepansky - The nature of drama is that at some point you need to dig into something emotionally dangerous to the hero. It doesn't always have to be murder and bloodshed. We've all seen wonderful, deep dramas about the strength of the human spirit overcoming the odds. Those tend to win Oscars.

Q: How important is it to be authentic to a historical piece, both in plot and character?

Marsha Greene - That's the hardest part. In *The Porter*, we were doing a fictionalized drama about this period in time and this movement. Even though there were many real porters whose lives we could have picked, we very consciously knew we would have to stick to what really happened. So we purposely created fictionalized characters. In the case of Zeke, the porter, he's an amalgamation of a bunch of different porters who we read about. In our show, we had two bigger roles that were real people. Not everything was documented, but now you are bringing real people into a fictionalized world, so we were wanting to make sure that we were sticking to what was true to who they were and what we believed would be real. So, A. Philip Randolph, if he's on the train smuggling, well, no, that is a fabrication. But he could come here and have this kind of conversation with our main character, Zeke. This is probably what his advice would have been based on what we know about his philosophies of labor relations. With Marcus Garvey, we knew the historical facts of things that happened. We had his speech; the real words that he had said. We weren't taking liberties there except that he has a conversation with the fictional woman we created.

Right from the beginning, we changed certain things about the timeline. In the actual history of the porters, there are three different railways: the private, the public, and another one. Right away, we said there aren't going to be three railways. There's going to be one. Nobody is going to understand what is happening. So things that like were easy decisions for me, personally. In that case, I think about myself watching having to follow along.

Then, there were things that were aesthetic decisions. Our directors were also producers. There were things that they were more visually interested in that didn't quite fit into the time period. So because we had taken some liberties as writers, we were able to say, "Well, maybe this isn't exactly the same roof that was on the Chicago station, but it's beautiful, so let's just go with it." That's why we have a fictional show in order to allow for that. The story we are telling, ultimately for us, was about these four dreamers who, against all odds, are chasing their dreams. The odds might be people, circumstances, sexism, the 1920s, or whatever, but they are fighters and dreamers. Knowing that was our goal, we were inspired by the history, but we were really trying to get people to come out of it with a feeling of hope and this Black ambition that happened all these years ago which informed the lives that we live right now.

Q: What is your thought process for developing teen characters in teen drama?

Lauren Iungerich - I'm no longer a teenager. I'm not even twenty. This is my own point of view. But I think the teen experience is the same. The only thing that has changed is that teens have different sensitivities and different technology. The teen experience is the same - first love, finding yourself, your identity - all of that stuff. I can sense memory back to that time and really understand it. Why I think I have been successful in the teen space is that I don't write teenagers down. I don't write them soft. I write them as adults, but as adults who are discovering things that I already know. That's why the stories land and resonate because I am writing about what these teenagers are experiencing, except that I am not writing from the perspective of soft teenagers. They feel incredibly grounded and real. I am keeping my adult head on as I am activating those characters. They just don't know everything yet. What I try to do is allow my characters to make really bad mistakes, but I also give them opportunities to redeem themselves, as I would like teenagers to think that their mistakes can be redeemed. I feel, right now, that so much feels that it can't be redeemed and I want to send messages of redemption.

Q: Is there a difference in how you write on a soap like *EastEnders* versus some other kind of TV drama series?

Tony Jordan - Soaps are different because you will give them so much material. So for your thirty minutes of *EastEnders*, you get three or four page outlines of what happens in each episode. Who's in it? What are the story arcs? What is the cliffhanger? What are the sets? It's almost like a jigsaw puzzle. Someone has given you a bag of bits and can you put that in the right order? With your own shows, you aren't given anything. You are not spoon-fed characters or story.

Structurally, there's a difference in times. Thirty minutes is different from sixty minutes. The fundamentals still apply - be aware of your audience. Give yourself the freedom to be creative. Try not to operate in a self-induced box or have parameters that stunt creativity.

Q: How faithful to the truth are you on a biopic?

Moisés Zamora - On *Selena: The Series*, we worked really closely with Selena's estate on all of that. They are very protective of the Selena brand, which I get. And they are very protective of their own brand and the messages they wanted to convey with this story. At first, it was a drama, but I knew this was an inspirational story so there was always that tone, even to some degree, of wholesome and familiar. Everyone could come and watch. We never really deviated too much from it. The only things the family was totally against was that through the years, the media had a lot of gossip and other crazy stuff. They wanted us to stay away from those storylines. They even went as far as not allowing us to portray them as Jehovah's Witnesses. They just didn't want whatever gets associated with religion as part of their story. To me, it talks about those values, but it was okay not having it. It didn't take away from showing their hard work and the values they operated from.

Q: What mistakes could be avoided by drama writers?

Deborah Haywood - When they are writing something from the outside in rather than from the inside out. I think we can smell it and taste it. We're not drawn to it.

Tony Jordan - I think there's only one thing to get wrong, really, and that is to not see your audience. Read the room for fuck's sake! Just understand what an audience is looking for. I know some writers, some of my peers from back in the day, they are so fucking self-indulgent when they write. They don't give a shit about the audience. They don't even think about them. They are just doing their own stuff. Basically, they end up with a collection of images that they think look quite cool because they are trying to be Quentin Tarantino or something. Why don't you try to tell a story? The best of my peers and those whom I admire are writers that always see their audience. Always aware when they are telling a story. It's the difference between being in the pub and you have two different mates and they are both telling a story in different ways. One of them is so fucking up himself, he tells you the story exactly the way he's rehearsed it because he thinks it's fucking brilliant. It's the best story he's ever heard. Everybody gets bored halfway through it and he's probably told the same story four times. You try to tell him you've heard it and he still powers through. He's that annoying twat. And then, you get the other one and he's telling a story and he's looking into your eyes. He sees that you are maybe getting a little bit tired of this. So he speeds up and gets to the punch line quicker. Or he adjusts his pace. Or you'll be loving it and having the time of your life and he'll elongate it. Suddenly, the story doubles in size. You find it yourself. You look around and the room is on the edge of their seat. They are laughing and they're engaged. You embellish! The smallest detail takes an hour. You and your audience are sharing a moment. If you're the first person who is disappearing up their own ass, then that is what you can do wrong.

Q: What do you take into account when you look at an IP?

Alex Litvak - The challenge with IP is that it's a little bit of a blessing and a curse. The blessing is that there is the illusion of a built-in audience. People will show up because it's *The Art of War*. "I've heard of that." Or *Three Musketeers* or *Predators* or *Treasure Island*. The curse is I have seen a bunch of *Three Musketeers*. I have seen a bunch of *Treasure Islands*. The challenge with *The Art of War*, was how do you come up with a story that speaks to Sun Tzu and his teachings and has a coherent plot around it? That was incredibly challenging. But the biggest challenge with IP is: how do you satisfy expectations? Deliver me what I love from all those books, but don't give me the same freaking thing I've seen or read over and over again. So don't reinvent the wheel, just put a fresh tire on it. This is where I feel you need to be both incredibly referential and incredibly irreverent. You need to satisfy the fans while subverting their expectations. And if you've never heard of *Three Musketeers* or *Treasure Island*, you need to draw in new fans who are not familiar with the property and have them say, "Oh, that was a cool story." Marvel does a great job of it, where the fans love it, but people who have never heard of it, love it, too. My philosophy is to be incredibly true to the spirit of the original, but come up with a bunch of stuff that makes it fresh and exciting.

Scott Beck - *The Boogeyman*, which is our Stephen King adaptation from his collection *Night Shift*, was a story that stuck in our heads for a long time. It's the story of this troubled man who comes into a psychiatrist's office and says, "I've killed all my kids. The Boogeyman killed them." It's this infestation of the Boogeyman into someone's life. It's a one-scene short story. What was exciting was taking that jumping off point and figuring out what the adaptation could be while keeping the tone of Stephen King, which has been very well defined over the last several decades. It's very different from trying to adapt a 900-page Stephen King novel which has the full structure but it allowed us a chance to impart what we are dealing with, personally. That was the sweet spot for us for that adaptation.

We have done other adaptations. There's a much larger story base that you have to stay loyal to and that can be a curse and a blessing. It gives you the story down to a "T" sometimes, but it also means you are just regurgitating things in a screenplay versus having the flexibility to go off into different alleys.

Bryan Woods - One thing we try to do with adaptations is to go through the material and underline everything that we love about it. We really focus on those feelings and emotions that we felt when reading it for the first time. You do your best to try and stay in touch with what captured your imagination and what you found really exciting. Underline them - constantly go back over them. Scott and I regurgitate them to each other. That's the North Star that you are always chasing.

Barbara Stepansky - I feel that half the battle is won when the character is complex and feels watchable with their goals and dreams relatable. We watch TV for the characters and to see what they'll do next. Sometimes, an IP will come along that simply feels more like a film as the story is very self-contained and doesn't warrant more than two hours. In a way, once you read an IP and start to discuss it, the material itself will tell you what it wants to be.

Q: How faithful are you to the original material?

Deborah Haywood - The film I'm currently adapting is inspired by a book. I have to look at the book and think: How do I personally connect with this? What have I struggled with? I write down all the bits that speak to me, personally. I take the essence and the characters, all the ones that I connect with. If you try and write the book into a film, it's not going to work.

Moisés Zamora - You really have to be passionate about the story that you are telling. And then you combine it with the global commercial appeal of that story; what people want to see and experience. For *Selena*, it was so meaningful to do that particular piece because that family resembles my family. Our family did struggle at the beginning. We did clean houses. We did sleep on floors. We were a very close, tight-knit family. We are going to work hard and we are going to do this together. My parents were very career oriented; be a doctor, be a lawyer. They absolutely pushed us for education, not artistic professions. Those are hobbies. What I really loved about the Quintanilla's, especially the dad who was a musician himself and who was projecting his own ambitions and dreams, is that he saw something artistic in his children and then took it all the way.

When I met the producers, they had a six-episode limited series in mind. No. That would be just the first part. That's when the Dad and the kids are in the struggle and she becomes a woman, falls in love and finds her own stardom. She becomes a superstar and has to manage that. There's a three-part epic journey that we have to follow. How do you get to become someone like Selena? It's by going from city to city all over the country in a bus. Two countries! That's why everyone was surprised when she passed and so many fans came out to show their respect. It's almost like a sleeping giant was awakened. Where did all of these fans come from? Why is her death such a big deal? I wanted to take the time to show why it was a big deal because it shows that while she was talented, it was the hard work she put in that made her so successful. The discipline. The stardom that she achieved was not overnight. It took fifteen years. And for any artists who are struggling to accomplish something, like myself... oh, Selena did it in fifteen, I've got five more years to go! Ha! Then I'll be a household name!

Danny Strong - The point of an adaptation isn't how well you adapt the source material.

The source material is there to help you write a great movie or play. You take from it what is there, but you are not beholden to it unless you are adapting *Harry Potter* or *The Hunger Games.* Those are so popular that the fans will be really turned off if you veer off from them. But those are rare, and I worked on one of them, *The Hunger Games*. The films are very close to the books. That was smart because the books are great and that's what the fans want to see. But on the whole, when people ask about adaptations, they think that your fidelity or allegiance to the source material is important to the process, but it's not. You are making something else. You are making a movie or a TV show; a scripted drama. Your job is to turn it into movie form with actors talking. I let go of the source material. It isn't my North Star unless it is so good that I don't have to make it up. Which, by the way, great! Less work for me! But on the whole, I am just trying to make this work as best as I can in what it is.

However, with *Dopesick*, producer John Goldwyn came to me with the idea of doing a show on the opioid crisis. Multiple articles and books had been written about it at that point. I did some research and came up with what would be the show. And I sold the show to 20th Century Fox. Another studio, Fox 21, which is under the same parent company, Disney, didn't know that I had sold this show to 20th and they went off and bought the book to *Dopesick* in a bidding war. I read about it on *Deadline*. I was stunned and very confused, but they were in a lot of trouble because I had a pitch ready to go. They've just bought source material. Source material can take six months, a year, or two years to find a writer to adapt it. It just takes a while to read a book and come up with a take. It's a slow process; I know because I'm a producer myself. I go through this process myself where I try to find writers to adapt things for my company. So they asked me if I would team up on *Dopesick* with the author, Beth Macy and producer Warren Littlefield, who's a legend in the business. I had a meeting with them and I adored her book. I agreed to team up, but I told them what I was doing. One element of it certainly represented the spirit of her book which were the victims. She really took to my version and said that she would love to be a part of it. So we all teamed up. She was in the writers room, which was really important to her and I really loved having an expert on the opioid crisis in the writers room. But the show isn't really an adaptation of *Dopesick,* the book. The spirit of it is certainly in the show and the prosecutor storyline is covered in the book.

I read an interview recently with a really wonderful novelist, Dennis Lehane, who wrote *Mystic River* and a lot of other great books. He has since become a successful TV writer, himself. But before, he wrote these incredible novels that were adapted and he said as long as they embrace the theme or the core idea or spirit of the book, that's all he cared about. He understood that they are going to veer off and do other things to make it work.

I remember when I was younger there was always this discussion about whether the author was happy with the movie. Or do they feel that they ruined their book? The author would always be enraged, but you don't hear that much anymore. I think that authors just accept that once they have accepted the money, which it seems they want, it's just going to become something else. And that doesn't hurt their book one bit. It's always going to exist in that art form. As long as they aren't adapting it, they aren't responsible for the movie. Nor are they given blame or credit if it does poorly or succeeds. They may get some credit for writing a terrific book. Unless, as I said, it's something like *Harry Potter* or *The Hunger Games,* where the author is so famous and is so close to the fans that you don't want to alienate the author. If they come out and say that they hate the movie, you could really surprise your audience by turning fans of the book off.

Alex Litvak - I will say this about *The Three Musketeers,* if you love the movie, great. If you hate the movie, that's fine, too. There are things about the movie that I don't like and there are things that I wish were on the screen, but it is absolutely true to the intention of what I was trying to do. It was a script that existed before I came along, by a very well known and talented writer. It was a wonderful rendition of *The Three Musketeers,* but it didn't break any new ground. It felt very true to, not just the spirit of the book, but the letter of the book. So how was I to turn it on its ear? How do you write something that the kid in me who read that book cover to cover a zillion times says, "That's *The Three Musketeers* that I know and love, but it's not *The Three Musketeers* that I've read a zillion times."

That's where we came up with the idea of airships and that the Musketeers were an elite group of the French Secret Service. We started talking about period James Bond and Jules Verne. And while some of it was executed great and some of it we missed the mark, that was very much the intention of trying to find a fresh gear. I did a *Treasure Island* in space and that never saw the light of day, but the spirit of it; completely Stevenson. Long John Silver, for whatever reason, has always been one of my favorite childhood heroes. It's all about the friendship between him and Jim, but there's a whole new adventure there that has nothing to do with the book. I worked on *He-Man* for a number of years but how do you take something that people know and love, but the whole property is cheesy as fuck? It's a freaking cartoon, so where do you find the dimensions of these characters? You have to respect the spirit of the book, not the letter of the book. You have to service the fans, but at the same time surprise the fans.

Josh Olson - With *A History of Violence*, I was ruthless. I read the book when it came out and I really loved the title and liked the set up. But I remember reading it thinking, "If I had come up with this, I would have done this and I would have done that." And that's how I ended up getting the job. I was just starting out as a studio screenwriter. Cale Boyter, an exec at New Line, brought me in to pitch and made it clear that they were talking to a bunch of A-list writers. "You're not going to get the job, but I want you to come in and have the people here get to know you so we can put you up for other jobs that you can get." This was license to me to just pitch them what I would have written. It turned out they had exactly the same feeling about the book that I did. Five or six of these big writers came in and tried to do the book faithfully, but the guy who came in and said, "Ehhh, this is what I'd do," is the one that got the job. However, I've also adapted stuff where I've been incredibly faithful.

Michael Brandt - We were not faithful in *Wanted* at all. This is no disrespect to the creators, but the graphic novel starts with the idea of a disaffected employee who doesn't know who his father is. He finds out that he's got the bloodline of this amazing assassin in him. Then a woman shows up who wants to teach him about who he really is. That was in the first comic. After that, it becomes this superhero thing that goes into space with crazy monsters. I wanted to keep it way more grounded. Yes, we bend physics, but that comes from what these special people can do, not that they live in a fantastical world.

The graphic novel went into a fantastical world, which I personally had no interest in doing. That's just not my thing. So Derek Haas and I took the kernel of who the main character was, who he could be, who the woman was, and the concept of his father, and manufactured the rest. The curving bullets and other visuals - we created that along with the director, Timor Bekmambetov. That was the movie we wanted to write.

However, with *Arthur the King,* I felt very strongly that I had to be faithful. It's a real story about a real guy who is still alive. Thankfully, there wasn't a lot of re-imagining that needed to happen. Instead of the main character being Swedish, we made him American because Mark Wahlberg was going to play him. We changed who the team members were who were with him because there were some issues with some of the team members that we just couldn't get around. We changed the location of where the race took place. But ultimately, the major beats of the movie all really happened. The real guy, Mikael Lindnord, became a big part of my writing the script; talking to him about what he was going through. I felt very strongly about remaining faithful to his story.

Barbara Stepansky - I'm always trying to be faithful to the spirit of the original material. A one-to-one adaptation is never really possible because film and TV is a visual medium and you have to keep the plot moving forward to keep your audience engaged.

Bryan Woods - I don't think you have to be necessarily faithful at all. Novels, very often, are pieces of writing that exist as writing. It's the form of the written word and turning the page that makes it so singular and special. Those, very often, don't translate to movies. My favorite movies, on the flip side of the coin, are those that are uniquely cinematic. You couldn't tell the stories in any other genre. It wouldn't work. It's not why we go to the movies. There have been a lot of great adaptations that deviate from the source material.

Paul King - Famous source material is a funny poisoned chalice in a way. It's great from a commercial point of view. Paddington is a much-loved character and there's a brand. There's an awareness. You put Paddington on a poster and people recognize him and they say, "Oh, they've made a film about Paddington," rather than, "Who the hell is this and why should I care?"

But you have to be aware that he's been very special to different generations in different incarnations and there's this "please don't destroy my childhood" attitude, which is slightly unnerving if you are on the receiving end of it.

With *Paddington* itself, there's kind of an opening narrative that makes sense and then after that, the stories are stand alone short stories. So there wasn't a three-act structure that you could follow. It was more a tone and a spirit and that opening. I really loved *Paddington*, and I didn't really want to mess with that anyway. It wasn't like I was going to make this sow's ear into a silk purse. I loved that beginning and it really spoke to something inside me, so it was about figuring out why it worked the way it did and trying to capture that emotional resonance.

It took a long time to get it right. We were making the film for about five years. It was a long write and there were several very different versions of the script. Every time that I inched closer, it was because I would go, "Why is this image of a bear on a platform resonant?" That gives you some tentpole moments or a flag in the sandy beach of uncertainty. Here's a homeless bear. There's a homeless bear with a home. You can then very slowly start to chart out a story based on that image that has universal appeal. Children feel very safe in their homes and are scared of losing it. Okay, that's a good thing to dig into. That might make the audience come on board and root for him and feel with him despite him not being human.

Finding the right story model is useful, but models can also be dangerous because you're looking at stories, normally stories you love, and they might not work for you. There's the "weird visitor comes to stay with a family" genre of films like *E.T.* or *Whistle Down the Wind* where you normally tell it from the point of view of the family. Here's a slightly dysfunctional family. Here comes an outsider. Lo and behold, they are healed. That was very tempting for *Paddington* but ultimately it didn't feel right. I'm not sure why. Maybe because the books were written more from his point of view. Maybe I just liked the idea of going on holiday to Peru! Maybe because I related more to the outsider than the family. I just had to find what resonated with me.

I think if you can keep the spirit, tone, and comedy, you will be okay and probably have a lot of license, but personally I hated the idea of writing something which contradicted the stories. I'm not sure kids think in terms of different approaches to the same narrative. They think in terms of the character being a real person. So I didn't want to make anything which would make a child being read the books go "That's not what really happened."

Then, I found this really useful thing. I think it was at the beginning of the fourth or fifth chapter of the first book, where Bond says, "Before he knew it, Paddington had become a member of the household." And I thought ah, there's a window there. That's a tentpole. If I only go up to that point, then I can do whatever I want in here and I won't spoil any of the stories. You have not messed with the canon.

The family were, in many ways, harder to write than Paddington because maybe there was a little less to go on in the books. I remember talking to Michael Bond, the author of *Paddington*, and asking him what they would be like. He said, "Well, I vaguely had my parents in mind." I said, "Well, what would your parents have done if they found a bear at Paddington Station?" He said, "Well, my mother would have wanted to give him a bath and my father would have wanted to get the paperwork right." There you go! That sounds like a double act to me. That's just brilliant and sounds like a marriage.

Q: Many adaptations can be completely different from an author's work, what was your feedback?

Paul King - I was totally, totally terrified throughout the making of *Paddington* about what Michael Bond would think, what the producers would think, what audiences would think, about whether I would ever get to make another film. It ended up getting a really good response, but the omens were so bad. There were all these vicious articles coming out about it from the moment it was announced and all through it being made, willing its failure and wishing it had never been made. Then we released this first picture of Paddington and I was deep in the edit, and he looked a little bit blank-eyed and so there was a meme of horror-Paddington. That was funny in a way but also terrible, certainly not quite the response you'd hope for.

Then we replaced Colin Firth who we had announced as the voice of Paddington. Colin always suspected that he wasn't sure that he was the right choice for this. But he's Colin Firth! He's really funny and really talented! Of course he'll be great! But then once we started recording, we realized that he was right. He was too old and stiff upper class. He just didn't seem like a playful bear cub. So we amicably parted ways, but it was presented in the papers as, "Colin Firth quits *Paddington* because it's so irredeemably bad!"

And then there was this thing where it was rated a PG like many a children's film but then it became this newspaper story because the BBFC put it out as Parental Guidance, Sexual Content. There is zero sexual content in *Paddington* beyond the moment where Hugh Bonneville is in a dress and Simon Farnaby flirts with him. But then *The Daily Mail* said something like, "*Paddington*, this car wreck of a movie is meant to be pure filth." People still hadn't seen it! I was just hiding under the carpet because I lack confidence at the best of times and was convinced we were doomed.

But I somehow managed to survive all this and then, finally, the day came when the great Michael Bond was going to watch it. He had been reading all of this terrible advance publicity and must have been wondering what the hell was going on. What have you done to my bear? Why is he in a sex movie? Why do all the actors hate it? It was essentially impossible to show him the film before it was done because the bear is not there. You have to wait until the very end to see it, and by that point, it's too late to do anything about it.

So a few days before the release, he went to a screening room in London. I was supposed to watch it with him but I was too scared to go in. I just walked around the block for two hours because he's eighty-five and it took him a while to get up the stairs and have a wee before he went in. I was just waiting and waiting and waiting. Finally, Rosie, who is one of our producers phoned and said that he loved it. I doubled over in the street and went, "Ohhhhhhhhhhhh! God." I suddenly realized that was all I was really scared about. That I'd have disappointed him, that I'd have let him down, that this beautiful creation he'd been working on for sixty years would have been soiled by me. And once he said he liked it, I could finally relax. My wife said that that night was the first time I had slept well in three years.

Scott Lobdell - I remember there were times when I was on a plane chatting and people would ask me what I do. I would say that I write the *X-men*. "Oh. My. God. I love the *X-men*!" Then they ask if I pick out the voices. I'd say I don't write the animated show, I write the comic books that they are based on. "They still put out comic books? The *X-men* is a comic book?" Similarly, I always said that if everyone who read an *X-men* comic book ran out and bought, at the time, a $7, even a $20 movie ticket, Fox would have been bankrupt. Most people know the *X-men* as a movie franchise. Most people who grew up in the mid to late 90's know it as an animated TV show. I wouldn't be surprised if you asked people coming out of the movie what they thought of the old animations, they would have no idea they existed. Have many ever read an *X-men* comic book? No. If you only go after fans, you're doomed. That's why it takes $10,000 to put together a comic book and $100,000,000 to put together a movie, because you are going after a larger audience.

Barbara Stepansky - I do care that the author is happy, as it's their brainchild. Everything else is gravy.

Q: What is it like when your shows are adapted in different countries?

Ron Leshem - The writer and director, Karen Margalit of *The A Word,* fought for every word in the Greek and the Korean versions. I admire that because she wants it to be perfect, but for me, when we had *The Gordin Cell* in Korea, for example, I just wanted to travel and meet the local creators and actors and see how they would do something completely different. Sometimes, they would take our dialogue and start fighting with knives - something cultural that I would never understand. I think this was the most beautiful thing about what we did when we filmed *No Man's Land* for Hulu and Arte. We had filmmakers from ten different countries. I am always more interested in the Korean version than the American version. This is new on the television side where we have festivals and all meet. I now know the Australian executives and creatives, the Japanese, the Swedish, and the South African executives of the show - and suddenly, we are a community. I enjoy this more than anything.

Q: How does a writers room work when doing an adaptation?

Barbara Stepansky - On *Outlander,* we are adapting beloved material and the books are very long; there's a lot of story and characters. So the first thing we all do is read the books. Then we identify the big tentpole events of each book. Then for a few months, we break story and finally the specific episodes. We set an overall arc for the season and for the characters. On *Totenfrau*, again, as an adaptation, you identify the bits that are really working and that you can't do without. Sometimes, certain things work in novels, but not on the screen. We found a lot of that with *Totenfrau*. The writer's style could get away with a lot of logistical inconsistencies. There was some rethinking involved, and after breaking the season for a couple of weeks, we were off to write beat sheets and get into the actual writing of the script. We had fewer writers, only four, and fewer episodes. The genre was different, of course. *Outlander* is a historical romantic drama. *Totenfrau*, which translated means, "Woman of the Dead," is a dark thriller.

Q: What tips would you give on writing sequels?

Michael Brandt - The key for the sequel to *The Fast and The Furious* was coming up with something completely different but had the spirit of the first one. At the end of the first movie, people were spread to the wind, so the good thing about that was we could kind of do whatever we wanted. At that point, there was no indication that Vin Diesel wasn't going to be in the second one, so the first couple of drafts of the script included his character. But L.A. street racing had been covered, so we looked at Miami. It's a different visual look and it's a cool place. Then the idea of new characters was kind of obvious. A lot of it was driven by business choices. The studio had some things like, "We're not using this person this time, and we'd love you to get Ludicrous in." Okay, so let's find a place for Ludicrous. A lot of stuff is given to you in a sequel and you have to figure out how to make it work.

Ultimately, when the deal with Vin couldn't be made, that was kind of a scramble. We had been warned Vin's deal might not go through, so we were prepared for it. We had ideas for a new character, how to bring him in, and how that might work without changing everything else at the eleventh hour. We wrote a few new scenes, and the bulk of the movie stayed the same.

When you're doing a sequel, obviously, the studio and the major players are going to be involved. You need to listen to what the studio is telling you, and sometimes, even what they're not telling you. Sometimes, they're telling you things that may or may not be true, but you have to be ready for everything that could possibly happen. Even in the case that one of the two biggest stars of the first movie is not going to be in it. So listen to what they say and be ready for everything, as you never know what's going to change.

Alex Litvak - Understand what made the original work then try to replicate it - ideally with some upgrades and new ideas. It's a delicate balance of servicing what the core audience expects from the sequel while giving them something that widens the scope or tweaks the formula. Think of it as not reinventing the wheel but putting a fresh tire on it.

Q: Any tips on writing a remake?

Michael Brandt - Why make a remake is the first thing you have to answer. *3:10 to Yuma* was an easy one in the sense of, originally, it was a short story by Elmore Leonard, which was essentially two guys sitting in a hotel room bartering over the price of a man. That is the crux of all the versions of the movie because that's the theme. It all leads to that, no matter if he makes the train or not. The original film is really a two-act play that was made for TV. It didn't have the scope of a feature film, in my opinion. It felt that it was missing a second act. There was the opening act; the stuff on the ranch. There are the problems of what Dan Evans is up against. There's the capture of Ben Wade, and then there is, "what are we going to do with them?" In the original, it cut to the hotel room and then we get them on the train. So it really didn't have a second act other than the conversation in the hotel room.

It felt like it was ripe for a remake, too, because there was such a great strong theme with two great protagonists. If done right, you're gonna like them both. This goes back to what makes a great antagonist. He's just as smart, if not, smarter than our main guy. He has stakes, but they are different. There were other things, too. It seemed obvious that getting him on the train was overlooked completely in the first one. There was also no son in the first one or in the short story. Given that, I started to think about how you make a second act that is more than just a road movie; how do you up the stakes in that? That, ultimately, led to why the movie had more modern themes.

It came organically, in an almost silly way. After Michael Jordan's, "I want to be like Mike," Nike campaign in the 90s, Charles Barkley did a commercial just looking at the camera saying, "I'm not a role model. Parents, you're the role model. Don't make me a role model, But buy my shoes." That, to me, became the theme of our version. So when I spoke to the director, James Mangold, I told him that I thought that commercial was our second act. We put a son in this film who thinks his dad is lame. Today, a son who thinks Allen Iverson is his hero when his father just goes to work... what parent can combat that? How can you get your kids to listen to you when Allen Iverson is there telling them something else? Your kid buys his sweat gear and wants to be him. So Ben Wade can be an NBA star. Let Dan's son have heard about the notorious Ben Wade. He thinks his Dad is lame because he's not fighting for the family farm. All of a sudden, Allen Iverson shows up in their kitchen, and the kid is enamored. "I want to be like him. I don't want to be like my dad, who lost his leg in the war and can't pay the water rights to keep the farm going and lets them burn down the barn." So that brought the modern theme to it; let's treat Ben Wade like a pro athlete. That organically made the second act relevant because it led to the son showing up in the second act having snuck away from home and joining them on the road. The meat of it is the son listening to these men, one of them whom he doesn't respect who happens to be his father, and the other, whom he does respect, is a killer. How do they react to things on the road? Put it through the son's eyes in that part of it. When we figured that out, there was a reason to remake this movie. Now, there's a whole middle that's an important piece of the story that bleeds into the third act, which we set up in the first act.

Knowing why to remake a movie is the most important thing. The only reason is to make it different. Of course, we're all competitive, we want it to be better. But how do we tell the story differently? What different points of view can we put on this that makes it worthy of remaking? The "why we make it" has to be answered first.

The only reason that Derek Haas and I got hired to write *Yuma* was that we had done *2 Fast 2 Furious* and it had made a lot of money. James Mangold had gone to the studio at the time, which was Sony, saying he wanted to remake it. Part of them saying he could remake it was that they didn't want an old dusty Western. They wanted something that felt a little more modern. That led to us getting a phone call asking if we'd be interested in writing a Western and working with Jim. I think Jim knew it wasn't going to get made unless he worked with someone who'd made a movie that did well in the summer. Ironically, I didn't want to do the *Fast and the Furious* movie. I literally said to my agent, "Do I have to watch the first one?" I didn't view myself as the summer car racing dude. I always viewed myself as the guy who would write the remake of *3:10 to Yuma*, but I wouldn't have been able to have done, were it not for having a summer hit.

Q: What adapted screenplays would you recommend?

Barbara Stepansky - What isn't an adaptation screenplay these days? Adapting IP, books, graphic novels, short stories, podcasts, even older movies seems to be the only material that makes it to production now. There are so many great ones around, but stand-outs to me in recent history have been *Hidden Figures*, adapted from Margot Lee Shetterly's non-fiction book and the TV Series *Archive 81,* adapted from the podcast by the same name. Just beautiful work.

CHAPTER REVIEW: DRAMA & ADAPTATION

- Themes don't necessarily have to be dark, but they should be global, universal, or significant.

- You can take some creative license with historical events to simplify or condense them in order for the story to work better. This is harder to do with people who are still living.

- Writing for teenagers works best if they are grounded. They just don't know how life completely works yet. They can make mistakes, even bad ones, but allow them the opportunity to redeem themselves.

- Writing a story from the outside in, as well as not understanding what the audience wants, can be big mistakes in writing drama (or any story).

- The hardest part of adaptation is finding a fresh take on the material, especially when it's well known. Leaning into what created an emotional reaction in you when you read it, is the best way to go.

- If you adhere to the spirit and tone of the material, you should be OK.

- If you find yourself working on a sequel, the approach is similar to an adaptation. Use the spirit and tone of the original as your guide.

- If you are working on a remake, the key question is: Why does it need to be remade? What is it about the original that would resonate with a modern audience? How can you make it better?

CHAPTER 19

ANIMATION & FAMILY

Parents are always desperate for ways to entertain their children, and these entities often fit the bill. However, writing for the younger ones poses some interesting problems. How do you keep a child's attention? How do you make it entertaining for adults watching with them? How do songs affect the screenplay? Some of the top animation and family writers provide insight into how they make shows that get watched over and over again. And over and over and over…

Q: Are there any big dos or don'ts when writing in a family-friendly genre?

Paul King - I never felt like, "Oh, don't do this. It's a family movie." Obviously, you are not going to swear or spray brain matter over the camera, but I never wanted to do that, so it wasn't really a problem. My hero references were Chaplin and Pixar and Jeunet. I think Pixar had, in comparatively recent years, opened the way to such complex, emotionally nuanced storytelling for family audiences, that it felt like the challenge was to get anywhere near that level of emotional engagement, rather than trying not to upset the kiddy-winks. It was more like, how can we make them weep?

My tonal palette was pretty clear from the start. I felt if I could mix *Amelie* with Pixar and Chaplin, I could make a really good film that I would like to go and see. We didn't try to do jokes that were just for the kids. I like slapstick, anyway, so I only tried to make myself laugh with that side of things. There are definitely jokes that adults will get that kids won't. *The Winter's Tale* stage direction joke is not going to be loved by the under sevens. But I love Chaplin as much as anyone and I don't need to be seven to laugh at somebody covered in Sellotape. I just tried to make it funny and hoped for the best.

Dave Reynolds - If you are working for a studio, language is going to be pretty straightforward. When we were doing *Tarzan*, Turk, the ape had to go save Tarzan. She was whining about something and Tantor, the elephant grabs her by the scruff of the neck and says, "I'm tired of your emotional constipation! Our friend needs us!" He throws her on his back and says, "So sit down and shut up!" The studio comes back to us saying that we can't say "shut up." Kids will just start repeating it, "Shut up, shut up, shut up." So, we needed an alternate line to drop in there, the only problem was the scene was already animated. We came up with "pipe down." But that was after a page of alts lines, "stop it," "quiet down," "not now," etc.

It shows you how kids are influenced by everything they see and hear. Case in point, many years ago I went to a high school reunion in Chicago and someone asked me if I worked on *Mulan*. I told him I did, and he shakes his head. He tells me he was watching his daughter one afternoon and when he thought it was too quiet in the house, he went looking for her. When he enters the kitchen, he sees a big clump of hair on the floor. His daughter then walks in with half her hair cut off, saying, "Look, Daddy. I'm Mulan." In the movie, Mulan cuts her hair with a sword to secretly join the army. His wife was not happy!

Q: Is there any difference between writing animation vs. live action?

Becca Topol - When it comes to writing in both live-action and animation, good storytelling is key. That part does not change and the actual writing is not that different. Animation scripts do seem to have a lot of sound effects such as when a character gets hit and goes flying, you might write "OOMPF!" You also won't see a ton of animation where the characters are giving long soliloquies or sitting at table and having a twenty minute conversation. You'll want action and movement or a fantastical way of demonstrating how the character feels to illustrate the depth of expression.

With live action, if I say I want to put a whole scene on a yacht and then I'm told by Production that we can't afford a yacht, then I put it somewhere else. With animation, Production may tell me, for example, the character can't fall into a tree because the trees aren't rigged to move. Or, say, for example, you want to do a gag with a character racing down the street who collides with a dog walker who has multiple dogs on leashes. This can get very complex from an animation perspective, so I may need to change the gag. You can let your imagination run wild when it comes to animation. You are literally making up worlds and settings that exist in your mind.

Meg LeFauve - At the core base of it, there is no difference because you are always digging towards, as we say on my podcast, the lava. We are always digging towards, what director Andrew Stanton (*WALL-E*, *Finding Nemo*) says, *"Is it true?"* You are always digging into the human condition. You are not worried about whether it speaks to children or adults because if it's the truth, it will speak to everybody. You are digging into your own life experience and whoever the filmmaker you are working with, wants to say.

The difference is the question of why it needs to be animated. When I first started, it dawned on me that animators don't want to animate just two people talking. That's just lips moving. Animation is a very active tool. You can expand access to where you can go and what you can do. Nowadays, you can do it too with a live-action movie with a $200 million budget with all those visual effects. But there are many more metaphors that you can grab onto in animation.

Dave Reynolds - As a writer, you are always tweaking the lines. If I am doing something where we are recording a celebrity voice actor, I know that we are going to get that person three or four more times, at least. In that time, the story or their character could change many times, so you have to re-record the same lines saying, "You know that thing we did the first time, what if we did it more like this?" That's one way. The other way is in the recording sessions where some directors have been very nice and let me sit in to write alternative lines on the fly. So I'll hear an actor say something and I think, what if they said it like a question instead of a statement? That changes the whole dynamic. And everything can be tweaked with this new point of view.

When Indiana Jones steps on screen you're immediately trying to figure out who he is. Hat, gun, whip. And he's passionate about archeology. You think to yourself, what do you do in archeology that you need a whip and a gun for? He steps on screen and we see all those layers. He's been doing this for the last twenty years. His character is fully formed.

In animation, we spend a lot of time in the story room trying to figure out who these characters are from the ground up. We knew when we were doing *Emperor's New Groove*, that Eartha Kitt who played Yzma was evil and a diva. David Spade was the spoiled brat character. That was about it. Then we had to take those two characters and plunk them right in the middle of a Chuck Jones comedy. Make it a *Bugs Bunny* fast-paced thing, but like those cartoons, this was going to be character-based. If you break down Bugs Bunny's character, you'll see that he is always true to who he is. If he's trying to do a prank or something he shouldn't be doing, his character never wavers.

Q: How does writing animation affect how you describe items in your script?

Becca Topol - The wonderful thing about animation is that there's a lot of room for what's in your head. You can make up any world, but you have to be aware that certain things can be very expensive. However, once you've created a show, the budget will dictate the number of sets, characters and props in each episode. For instance, even something simple as going through a tunnel onto a bridge. We may have a bridge already that's been built and established, but no tunnel. Are we really going to make a tunnel for just one scene? You might ask, why do characters typically wear the same outfit in every episode of a TV series? The answer is because each new outfit is considered a new character. And that effects the budget.

Q: Can you rewrite jokes so often that you lose what's funny?

David Reynolds - There's a joke fatigue that happens on animated movies that is common because everybody wants to be smart. "Here comes the joke about the thing." Do you have anything better? Do you remember the first time you saw that joke? You have to sometimes call people on that. You have to remember the initial time that you saw it or heard it for the first time. That is how the audience is going to hear it. If you have time and it's not animated yet, you can write alternate jokes and test them out. Different screenings. You can get a feeling for it. But nineteen out of twenty times, that first joke was the joke. Unless something has happened in the story, then you can readjust. Many times, we would pull in assistants or people who haven't heard the joke and they laugh. Okay, got it.

I remember the opening weekend of *Finding Nemo*, there was this one joke that we were all worried about. It was at the end when Nemo meets Dory for the first time. Dory is swimming around and she's lost; she can't find Marlin. Nemo sees her and goes to help her and says that she can't find someone. He says his name is Nemo and she goes, "Nemo! That's a nice name. Anyway..." She's completely forgotten. But we thought, we can't do that because she's been looking for him for the whole movie. I went to a screening of regular people, and they loved it. Then, we came to that moment and the test screener in me is wondering if we'd earned that moment. But they all laughed. So you have to trust your instincts. But you also have to be open to bringing in someone from the outside and without tipping them off, ask them to watch or read it. Does it make sense? Does it make sense for what we are trying to do? Does the joke dilute the point of the scene, even if it's really funny?

Q: What is the process of development with Disney Animation?

Becca Topol - It depends on the project. For *Mira, Royal Detective,* Disney had an original idea that involved a detective series. They brought me in and it was a bake-off: there were a number of people pitching. I pitched a take, and they liked it. It was a very long process of doing a treatment first, then outline and then writing the TV pilot. Disney has a very extensive process of testing their projects before deciding to make them. So there would be a storybook test. They present the story and characters to an audience of parents and kids to see what they think before they greenlight a show.

As Mira is Disney's first South Asian protagonist and based on Indian culture and customs, they brought in Disney India very early on to look at everything and give their feedback. At that point, it had just been me writing and developing the show. Disney picked the production company Wild Canary to work on the storybook test. Then it was greenlit, and the team was assembled.

Dave Reynolds - In the old days at Disney - the mid-1990s to mid-2000s - you could come in and pitch a story or a concept that could be very broad. If they liked it, they knew that a creative team behind it would be able to, hopefully, figure it out. The development process would involve our team coming back and presenting the execs with something a little more concrete each time. These days, every studio wants a full script and some development art before they say yes to an idea. I get it. These films are not cheap to make.

Back when we were working on *New Groove*, I was in a story room with the director, Mark Dindal, and about a half dozen storyboard artists. We started thinking about tone. How fast-paced or funny it should be. Then everyone in the room starts pitching ideas of what it could be like. A lot of these people can draw so fast. They are holding up pictures, "Is this it? Is this it? Is this it?" During this process, which may seem like a lot of goofing around, we were getting a lot of wrong answers, but from those wrong answers, you start to figure out the idea. What if it's this thing? That's too much. Or that's too weird. One time, Chris Williams, now a brilliant animation director, pitched a really funny joke that ended with a shot of the Space Shuttle taking off. Mark and I thought that it didn't fit in the story we were building and had to cut it. Chris laughed and said, "You've got a guy who turns into a talking llama. And this is too weird?" But in the world we were creating, it was.

We were lucky on *Emperor's New Groove* because we had David Spade and he could do super sarcastic, super funny stuff. And we had Eartha Kitt who was a diva in real life. This is not me being snippy; she would tell us she was a diva. When you met her, she was the focus of the room. She would say, "Well, when Orson Wells and I were dating…" Okay, here we go. But, when she would record, she became that character. You just had to steer her in the right direction. Anytime we told her that something has to be done with a flourish, she said, "Of course, darling, my life is all about the flourish!"

Q: Is a writers room different when it comes to an animated show?

Becca Topol - So much has changed over the years in terms of the size of writers rooms for live-action and animated shows. For limited series, you might have the creator and two other writers. Some animated shows are written entirely by freelancers with the head writer, or story editor, editing the scripts as they come in. I'm currently a producer and story editor on a new Marvel show which consists of myself, the executive producer, who is a writer EP, then a team of staff writers, and a script coordinator.

The process typically in animation is to come up with what's known as the "springboard." This is the idea for the episode which is then submitted to the network. For *Mira, Royal Detective,* the room would brainstorm different ideas for episodes. What kind of mystery would be good for this show? For example, a chicken is accused of stealing a pocket watch from one of the kids in town because the watch ends up in the chicken's coop. The chicken has some anger management issues, so he's really pissed off, but he can't explain what happened because he can't communicate with the other characters. Mira comes in and says, "Wait, we can't accuse him until we know the facts." Part of what I wanted in the show was the idea that everyone deserves a fair hearing; don't rush to judgment. So Mira's sidekicks, the two mongooses, basically appointed themselves the chicken's defenders as Mira went around and figured out what happened. And, indeed, he is proven innocent. In the room, I'm very specific with the writers saying our stories need to have a good mystery character, action, and theme. Theme is very important, especially when you are dealing with family shows because you've got to know the "why" for your audience to care. That's true with any writing.

The writers go off and write their scripts and the scripts go through extensive rewrites once the network gives notes. The production team will give notes as well. The good thing about animation is you have opportunities at various stages to change dialogue in the scenes.

Q: What makes a great protagonist in a family film?

Paul King - I think the most important thing is that the audience can see themselves reflected in the protagonist. Paddington might be a bear from Darkest Peru, but he feels lost and alone in a big, scary new world - and that's something everyone can relate to. He does his best to fit in, but often messes up, which everyone can relate to, too. I suspect your protagonist can be anything at all so long as their emotions resonate with the audience. I think there's also an element of wish fulfilment which works especially well in family films. I remember watching *Star Wars* every Christmas as a child and I never really paid any attention to the plot. I still couldn't tell you exactly what happens. But I remember wanting to be in that world, fight with lightsabers and go into hyperspace. I think the same thing applies with the *Harry Potter* films. I couldn't tell you exactly what happens in any of them, but I just love being in that world. If a protagonist lives in an exciting world, or turns a mundane world into an exciting place, then you're onto something. I remember wishing E.T. had come to visit me instead of Eliot, and I always wanted kids to wish they had a Paddington bear.

Dave Reynolds - Right at the beginning of your film, something has to happen right away where the main character through thought or action has to state their purpose. For example, they're in a line at a cafe and people keep stepping in front of them, then they get to the counter and order a coffee, only to be told that they are out of coffee. The world is pushing against this character and we the audience want to see how he/she responds to obstacles in the way of their goal.

In the opening scenes of *Raiders of the Los Ark*, Indy had his hand on the gold idol and then Beloc takes it from him. Just by looking at Beloc, you know that he's your bad guy, wearing a white suit in the jungle. He's not going to do anything to get himself dirty. Then, here's our guy, Indy, covered in dust and spider webs. He's the good guy. Then his guide on the way back double-crosses him for the whip. Then the boulder comes. It just keeps coming. He's running through the jungle to start the plane. Swinging out on a vine to get there. He's a superhero without superpowers. You're saying to yourself, this is our hero and I'm all in! And then when he climbs in the plane, there's a huge snake and he's afraid of snakes! After all of that, he's afraid of something. Everything is seeded in there: who the bad guy is, what he's doing, what our hero is afraid of, etc. Then later he gets sealed in a tomb filled with snakes! A perfect callback to what you thought was a comedic moment early in the movie. It all works because it goes directly to his character.

Q: What makes a great villain in a family film?

Paul King - In the first *Paddington*, I wanted several different layers of opposition. Here's a bear in London. Henry, whom I want people to like by the end, doesn't want him in his house for good reason. He thinks he's a danger to his children, which he is. Then you have Mr. Curry, who is sort of a nimby and doesn't want him on his street. But I didn't think Mr. Curry gave you the stakes for a 90-minute movie. So I wanted a real villain and came up with Millicent. If Henry doesn't want Paddington in the house, and Mr. Curry doesn't want him in the neighborhood, then she doesn't want him to live. There are three antagonists, and three tiers of opposition, which gives you a lot to play with.

That idea of dramatic scale was a big issue for us because the *Paddington* stories are generally very sweet and simple with comparatively low stakes. They are bedtime stories; not life and death. But because our movie was going to be longer, and because it was very expensive - the first one was $35 million - it had to appeal to a wider audience than preschoolers. So to make sure it wasn't toddler fare, there was a lot of talk about getting the stakes up, which we did with Millicent. The challenge then was to make sure that she sat tonally alongside the rest of the *Paddington* world, and that was a real challenge.

When we got to the second film, I didn't want to write another antagonist who just wanted to kill Paddington from the outset. I didn't like the idea of that character. Who are these people that wake up and just want to kill bears? It's fair enough to think there might be one Millicent out there, but I hope London isn't full of them. So we wanted to create a villain who wasn't a villain to begin with at all.

One of the things that we tried to do with the second film is to create this narrative snowball thing. It starts with Paddington simply trying to get a present for his Aunt Lucy. But before you know it, he's been sent to jail, there is a prison break and chase sequence, and a train crashing into the water. It was about continually upping the stakes without feeling we had jumped into a different movie. Somehow that just felt very Paddingtonian, because he's always getting into trouble, despite the best of intentions.

When we started talking about the villain, we felt we should try to do the same thing. They start like any of our community characters, with his own vanity and stupidity, then we can push him and he will become this narcissistic, murderous rogue. I think everyone loves Phoenix. You don't get to the end of the film and want him to get his comeuppance at all. He's a joy. There's a lesson there that I'm not sure the villain has to be that bad. He can be funny and let the plot push him to these ludicrous ends.

Dave Reynolds - Well, the prototype in animation is that they have to be kind of over-the-top. Whatever their silly thing is, they want it in the worst way. As we saw in *The Lion King* when Scar took over, it wasn't working out well for him. The pridelands deserted, barren. Then you realize that he never really thought about what it took to be a leader, he just wanted to be better than his brother. That his wanting to be king was more sibling rivalry than wanting power. It then becomes a personal story. "I'm second born and you are the golden child."

I like when villains get their comeuppance, and they always have this insane over-the-top reasoning for what they are doing. I'm talking about animation villains here. While Scar was a pretty serious version of a villain, Yzma in *The Emperor's New Groove* was just an evil diva. One of the things we did was saddle her with Kronk. She hates that she has to depend on him. He's lovable, nice, honest and he likes animals. Not the usual qualities in an evil sidekick. I wrote him in such an anti-evil way that we wanted Yzma to be thinking "Can't you just be evil for two seconds?"

When we were presenting Kronk as Yzma's sidekick to the studio executives, we showed the scene where we push in on Yzma as Kuzco says she's, "living proof that dinosaurs once ruled the Earth." He then says that she has a right hand man, Kronk, who promptly hits himself in the head and he falls off the stage. The execs liked the sequence but said, "We don't need that Kronk character. He's not adding anything."

In our heads, we knew that we wanted Patrick Warburton to be the voice of Kronk. The studio was trying to get the cost down and they didn't want to animate another character. But to his credit, Tom Schumacher, the president of Feature Animation at Disney said, "Okay, Dave. Write a scene that shows us why we should keep this character." Our director, Mark Dindal, settled on the dinner party scene where Yzma and Kronk try and poison Kuzco, as our test.

So that night I'm at home, squirreled away in my cubbyhole office, staring at the keyboard. How do I introduce Kronk's character? I had one shot at this. I decided to just start the scene and see where he would come in. And that's what I did. Yzma, like a Norma Desmond diva, throws open the curtain, looks at Kronk and says, "Is everything ready for tonight?" Meaning, are we ready to poison him? Having seen the drawings and having Patrick Warburton's voice in my head, I immediately write Kronk, saying, "Well, I thought we would start with a soup and a light salad and start with that." Yzma blurts, "Not the dinner! The... *you* know?" I start laughing and realize he's only worried about the dinner! I wrote the whole scene in fifteen minutes. I just put Kronk and his unique POV in the middle of a traditional scene where a villain is trying to poison her rival. The structure of the scene never wavered and Kronk's voice just jumped off the page.

Chris Williams storyboarded it and a few days later we presented it to Tom and his boss, Peter Schneider. The second Kronk said, "soup and light salad," everyone started laughing. At the end of the pitch, Tom says, "Okay, Dave. You've got your guy." Once we had Kronk, we could start building on his character in the story. It's funny, you can write and write for months and come up empty and sometimes you get lucky and your best character walks through the door carrying spinach puffs.

Q: What makes a good villain in a children's animated show?

Becca Topol - In *Mira, Royal Detective*, which is aimed at younger viewers from two to seven years old, the villains are sort of misguided thieves. There is a lot of Mira helping people in the town. Finding simple things like a pocket watch. Or a kid loses his pocket watch and blames the chicken. Or we've found a puppy, but there's only a part of their collar. Who does this puppy belong to? We have mysteries and things to figure out. There's goop coming out of every fountain in town. Who did it? It was the Prince who was doing a sculpture down in his private art studio. Then there are brother and sister villains who are always using disguises and they are pretty much thieves. They just want to be rich. They steal the queen's crown on the train right off her head. The lights go off in the train and when they come on, the crown is gone. Then they start stealing things from a lot of the people on the train. Stuff like that. And then Mira ends up catching them, but they are in disguise so she has to figure out who they are. So there's a little bit of a *Scooby Doo* element.

In *Elena of Avalor*, which is aimed at children aged eight to twelve, we had a very clear villain and that was a big part of the storyline. She had co-conspirators. There was a lot of fantasy in that show. So the fantasy in the way that the villain was using magic was also key. With *Mira*, there is no magic and you are not going to have serial killers or murders!

Q: How soon do the storyboard artists, animators, and the director get involved?

Becca Topol - From the outline of the story, it's the art director who starts designing sets, characters and props. A lot of visual research went into *Mira, Royal Detective*. For example, we had one episode which was inspired by the snake boat races in Kerala. Our art director, Dorothea, researched the snake boats and designed them to fit our show.

With the boards, there are script-driven shows and there are board-driven shows. With board-driven shows, like *Phineas and Ferb*, a lot of the writing happens in the board phase. But with the script-driven shows, the writing department locks the script earlier in the process. Once the directors have worked with board artists, they may come back and say, "We really think we need a line here. We have action happening and we need a line of dialogue to fill it." So there is a lot of back-and-forth that happens between the writing and production departments at the point of the animatics. They might also have ideas to punch the action or the comedy.

Dave Reynolds - Animation is a slow building lane and every once in a while, you have to wipe it off and rebuild. It is such an iterative process that you are just constantly just tearing things down. A horse can turn into a camel before it ends up being a llama.

Q: Are writers brought in to do punch-up work on animated shows?

Dave Reynolds - It can be a good idea to bring in other writers because when you are not fully immersed in a subject, you bring an outsider's point of view. For example, in *Tarzan* there's a sequence where the elephant and the ape, who are friends with Tarzan, come in and see the human camp. They brought me in for that sequence as they couldn't crack it. I suggested, "What if seeing human things was like a horror movie to them?" They see all of these strange and frightening objects that shouldn't be in the jungle. Show them in whip pans, one to the next, building the tension. Mike Surrey, who was an animator and who was storyboarding it, started laughing. What if we pop to a grandfather clock? Then, I suggested, "What if they cut to a tea set? Wait, what if it's Mrs. Potts and Chip from *Beauty and the Beast*?" So the whip pans escalate in scariness with the third cut being Mrs. Potts and Chip. The two characters recoil with horror. That was one of the bigger surprise laughs when it was screened in-house at Disney.

A lot of times writers get into a rut. They research and research and rewrite and rewrite. If you go to a writers room, the other writers can offer suggestions, but you've probably already thought of them. They've all lived it for so long. They need someone else to come in and say, "Hey, have you ever thought about doing it this way?" If you're an open writer you say, "Well, what would that do?" Now, here's the beauty. You always have that first draft to go back to if you stray too far afield. But for now, put it aside. Let's work on this new angle. Sometimes, a new angle on a script can be very slight. It could be flipping character. Or editing. What if we jump from here to there? That's another version of a pitch from me to another writer. You can suggest an edit. You say, the main part of this section is seeing our guys on the island, right? Maybe we don't need all this stuff in between. We just see them on a boat and then one character says, "Uh oh. Is that a huge wave coming our way?" And then we're on the island. We don't care how they get to the island unless something happens in there that's important to the story.

Q: As the writer/creator, how much control do you have over the way a show looks?

Becca Topol - Being a producer on the show means you are weighing in on everything. You weigh in on designs. I spent seven years developing *Mira, Royal Detective* so I had a lot of ideas about how it should look and the inspiration for the characters. Disney also weighs in heavily. It's a collaboration between the creative team and the executive team at Disney.

Q: Does Disney have a set of rules about what you can and cannot do with your story?

Becca Topol - Disney works very closely with an education department and an S&P (standards and practices) department. One of the big concerns is modeling. They don't want imitable behavior. They don't want characters putting bags over people's heads. If they're targeting a younger audience, they won't want a character to pick food off the ground and eat it. So they check the story idea, but you get to a point when you have a sense of it. Be kind to animals. Treat animals well. When you're writing a script, you're keeping all these concerns in the back of your head while also being as creative as possible. Some of it is that I have a kid myself and I have to think what would I want my child to see when she's that age. In the case of *Mira, Royal Detective*, there's a pretty wide range for that show because a lot of young kids like it as there's a lot of music. But because of the music, it is skewed older. Around eight to ten years old. So part of it was to make mysteries that were not too obvious. I really set up quite a challenge to make this show!

Q: Does each show or film have to have a moral or a theme?

Dave Reynolds - I think most do. *Finding Nemo* is obviously all about family and learning to trust that a child needs to go out in the world. There's the scene at the beginning of that movie where they have the house on the reef right before the barracuda attack. Originally, it was written that Coral, Marlin's wife, found the house, which is an anemone, and Marlin was super nervous about it. "It's too close to the open water." Coral excitedly says, "No, they can see a whale go by!" She was happy. I took a pass at it and Andrew Stanton pitched the idea, 'What if Marlin was the one who found the house?' I'm from Chicago and there's this way of talking there like, "Hey, did your man deliver or did your man deliver, huh?" And then, "A lot of other fish had their eye on this place." He's so proud being the father. He wants only the best for his kids. Then, when the barracuda attack happens, it goes directly to his character. "This is all my fault." If it was the other way, it would still work, but now it informs how his character will react going forward. Marlin's character now lives with the idea: What if you do something for a right reason and it turns out to be the worst result? Now, he won't let Nemo out of his sight.

Sometimes an ad-lib can add to character. We were on the recording stage with Albert Brooks recording the scene where Marlin picks up Nemo as an egg. Before this, we were recording all of the funny stuff about Marlin naming half of his kids Marlin, Jr., etc. Next, we recorded Marlin finding the lone surviving egg. He picks it up and speaks to it. So we are all standing there, director Andrew Stanton, co-writer Bob Peterson, myself and Albert. The four of us, in front of an open mic. Andrew says, "What would you say to your baby?" Albert says, "There, there…" During this I suggest, "Daddy's got you." Albert says it and we all knew how strong that was. Because that was the first time that Marlin truly realized that he's a Dad to this one tiny egg. That all goes back to character. What has just happened to Marlin and what will happen going forward. The world is burning around you and you are just trying to calm a baby. You become a different person.

Becca Topol - Themes are important in any film or TV show. I find that the ones that have strong themes will stick with me more. For animated shows for kids, there are lessons or themes about teamwork, not judging a book by its cover, giving people the benefit of the doubt, valuing friendship. I think touching upon universal themes makes strong, inspiring storytelling. Kids are smart, so you also don't want to dumb things down. It can't be too preachy. In my R-rated material, emotional complexity is a given, but for the kid/family audience, you want to keep the story and character arcs at a level that kids can relate to and follow.

Q: How do you walk the line between kid jokes and adult jokes?

Becca Topol - That's the fun part! It's really fun to have jokes that work on different levels. There's nothing better than being a mom and really enjoying what my kid is watching.

Dave Reynolds - When *Finding Nemo* came out, Andrew Stanton said, "I do my movies for ages six and up. I know people think these are kid movies, but if I'm trying to tell a compelling story, I can't cater to four-year-olds. These are not Saturday morning cartoons." So the angler fish or the shark might eat these little fish. That's real and if we have that drama, then when they don't get eaten, you're exhilarated. They've escaped death! It's real. You can't do a story about two little fish in the ocean and nothing happens to them. We know kids will watch this, but we are not writing a children's movie.

When we were doing *Emperor's New Groove*, Mark Dindal and I both had kids. He said that if we are going to do comedy, I want it to be like the old Chuck Jones/Bugs Bunny shorts. Kids love them, parents love them. There are jokes and inferences that work on both levels. He said, "If this movie is going to be on a DVD in the back of my car for a road trip for five hours, I can't hate it!"

All comedy comes back to character. The Kuzco character was such a jerk that I said that any time they fall or hit a wall, it's Kuzco who should get the worst of it. He's such a spoiled brat but he's also getting his ass kicked all the time. That was intentional. There was a scene where he and Pacha are going across a rope bridge. A board breaks and Pacha falls through, dangling over a river below. Kuzco jumps over him and continues to the other side. He refuses to help Pacha. It was important to me that he got across to the other side and was safe. Then I wrote him coming back to insult Pacha one more time - this is when he falls through the bridge. Being that kind of jerk was more to his character. Because you're always thinking of your character, constantly rebuilding it. What if he did this? What if he did that? You're what if-ing everything.

Q: On a show like *Mira, Royal Detective*, how much Indian culture do you bring into the show?

Becca Topol - A lot. I worked with a team of really great South Asian writers and a lot of the stories would come from their personal experiences and their culture. One example is a writer wanted to do a mystery around Rangoli, which is very specific to South Asian culture. Rangoli is an art of decoration drawn on the floor or the entrances of homes. It's thought to bring good luck, and to welcome guests. So we had a mystery of someone going around and messing up the Rangoli. It turned out that one of the characters invented this crazy vacuum cleaner that's out of control.

Q: How does the inclusion of songs affect the writing?

Becca Topol - Each episode has two, eleven-minute episodes and one of those episodes has a song. That's fairly standard if you have a musical show. We did some specials that had two songs in them because they were twenty-two minutes long - so one full episode. And then we did one that was a music episode that had four songs. So the music is a really big part of it and there, again, we worked with a really great team. And consultants worked with them - really talented individuals. Matt Tischler and Jeannie Lurie wrote the songs and did a brilliant job. In terms of the scripts, we thought carefully about how the songs move the story forward and/or reveal something special about the characters.

Dave Reynolds - What the directors, Tony Bancroft and Barry Cook, of *Mulan* did, was to lay out the story and the songwriters went off and pulled out moments. You would work with the song team or composer and show them how it flows. That becomes sort of surgical. If it's an "I want" song where Ariel wants to be on land, or a 'where are we now' song, or a 'villain's motto' where they say what they want; you just pepper it in. As a writer, the songs help you sometimes. It's covering space. It's collapsing story for you. It can reduce the elements for what you don't have to do. Sometimes, they work for you and sometimes they introduce characters. Usually, they collapse story. You can introduce characters who weren't in the beginning of the song but are now at the end of the song, or it's a new development, then you walk into this thing where - new guy, who are you? Then that jumps them into the next scene.

When I saw the rough cut of the sequence with the song *I'll Make a Man Out of You*, the slam cut from this upbeat musical number into the devastation of what the villain has done, was incredibly powerful. It was so upbeat and then wham! We're back into our story and the villain means business. It was really great. There were no Mushu lines, no jokes. Just silence. Every character on screen was devastated and so were we as the audience. That was amazing storytelling.

Q: How do the voice actors impact animated shows and films?

Becca Topol - Voice actors bring so much to animated shows and films and the best material can come out of collaborating with them. We have a great cast on *Mira* with Jameela Jamil, Kal Penn, and Abu Utkarsh Ambudkar. There's a lot of improv-ing that happens in the booth which can end up changing what's on the page. Luckily it's not airing in two weeks like live action. It takes a year or so from the time you write the script to it being finished.

Dave Reynolds - When you hear your voice actors for the first time, it's the second time these come alive. Up to this point, the voices have been in your head. Andrew Stanton originally had Dory from *Finding Nemo* as a male character. Then he heard Ellen DeGeneres do stand up where she was forgetting in the middle of a sentence. And he said, "That's her. That's Dory." He wrote a year's worth of drafts and then brought me and Bob Peterson in and we worked with him for the next three years. Around that time, Albert Brooks was touring Pixar and he was interested in *Nemo* because he had little boys at the time. They asked him to read some lines that a fish might say. He riffed for ten minutes and as you could imagine, it was incredibly funny. We found our Marlin.

But later when Andrew and I were working on his character, a thought occurred to me, Albert is insanely funny but Marlin can't be. His son has just been kidnapped. We realized we'd have to tell one of the funniest minds in the world to play it straight. But Albert's an incredible filmmaker in his own right and he knew what was best for this story. We quickly figured out the Marlin/Dory dynamic. It was as if you're a passenger in a car and the driver of the car can't quite remember where they're going. That's where the comedy comes from, how Marlin reacts to all of Dory's sidetracking. When Marlin is in the submarine and Ellen says look, 'es-ca-pe' for escape. "Wait, you can read?" "Oh, yeah, I can read!" "Ah! The whole time?!" They're both staying within character while reacting to the situation.

Sometimes, ad-libbing with comedians in recording sessions, leads to script changes. When we were recording the scene where Marlin drops Nemo off at school, Andrew had written that other dads ask Marlin to tell a joke because he's a clownfish. Marlin says he knows one joke and he starts telling one about a sea anemone and a sea cucumber. The dads all glaze over as he tells it. As we are recording it, I pitch: "What if he deconstructs the joke?" Albert laughs and says, "I can do that." So he leaps behind the microphone and now he's this guy who thinks he's telling a joke, but he keeps pulling it apart. Because Albert's mind is so fantastic, we were covering our mouths to keep us from laughing. Albert is looking at us trying not to laugh and it's feeding him and he keeps going. We ended up using about thirty seconds of it in the movie. But more importantly we realized that he created a running joke, of Marlin trying to tell a joke, throughout the movie. It wasn't there minutes earlier, now it's a reoccurring bit in the movie, all because of improv with our voice actor. You never know when or where these unexpected gems are coming from, you just have to be open and ready if it does.

Q: What is hard for you when writing a family film?

Paul King - The first *Paddington*, even though I had support from the production company, I essentially wrote on my own. The second one, I wrote with Simon Farnaby. I wrote *Wonka* with Simon, too. It's much more fun being with Simon because he's really funny. He's also a really great comic actor, so it's incredibly useful to hear all the lines delivered by a really funny person. When the actual movie actors are finally reading them, I have to bite my tongue because occasionally I want to say, "Just read it like Simon. You're ruining it." We spend at least 80% of our time wrestling with plot. Maybe it just doesn't come naturally to us and there are some people who can make good stories without thinking, but I suspect plotting a movie is like engineering an airliner. It's not something that you can be instinctively good at. I never believe everyone has a story in them, or a novel in them. They might have an idea, but writing a story is a craft. It's like saying I have a Fabergé Egg in me. I can't just lay it. I need to learn how to make it.

Q: What are the challenges of writing animation?

Dave Reynolds - Once something is animated, it costs a lot of money to make any changes to it. When we were finishing up *The Emperor's New Groove*, I thought up a really funny transition scene that Mark Dindal and I thought was better than what we had animated. I pitched it in a meeting and Tom Schumacher, who was running the company at the time, turned to someone and asked how much it would cost. He hears a figure, turns back to me and says, "Dave, is that joke worth $400,000?" I said, "To me it is." He looks at me, and says "It's not to us."

The most intense version of that was *Toy Story 2*. The main creative heads at Pixar had been working on *A Bug's Life* which was a bear because it was so ambitious story-wise. Now, it's September of 1998 and *Toy Story 2* is going to be released the following November. I'm invited to see a rough print of the film. Some of it was storyboards, and some of it was finished animation. I hadn't seen it in a while and Andrew Stanton asks my opinion. I said that it was funny and it works. He asked me what scene I liked best. I said the scene where the toys have to cross the street with orange cones on. That was unexpected and hilarious. And he nods and sighs, "We have to make the whole movie that good."

So it was all hands on deck as we proceeded to rework over 70% of the movie one year before it was to be released. I was flown up to Pixar and put in a room where Andrew Stanton would pitch me a sequence he was redoing. For the next hour I said, "What if you did this? Or that?" Over and over. Then someone would knock on the door and tell me they need me down the hall. I would walk in to see Bob Peterson reworking the sequence where Woody's being repaired. And I would say, "What if you did this? Or that?" I was shuttled from room to room just pitching ideas for three days. I was there to reload their story ammunition. When I saw the movie a year later, I was blown away. Every scene was as good, if not better than that original scene with the orange cones.

On *The Emperor's New Groove,* because we took the release date of the first version of the movie that was shelved, we only had eighteen months to complete the film. So from start to finish, we had to write, storyboard and record all at the same time. After a month or so, as we were working on the first act, they told us, "We have 300 animators who are sitting at empty desks right now. We need a big scene with a lot going on to feed the beast." So we came up with a sequence where the main characters were tied to a log and falling in the river. There were water effects, a lot of stuff. We wrote that, boarded it and everyone was like, "Yes! This is great!" We shipped it off to animation, feeding the beast. A few months later, we're writing and recording voices, and I came up with a new idea when they are on the road. What if instead of them tied to a log in the river, they blah, blah, blah? Mark loved it, yes! Let's do that. We tell the producers to throw out the log/river scene as we now have a new scene. They said, "We're going to stop you right there. That log scene has been animated and it's going to be in the movie. We don't have the time or money to change it." We turned around and ripped up the pages. As a writer, you never stop thinking story. You are always trying to make it better. Sometimes, they will tell you, "That's enough. We're good."

CHAPTER REVIEW: ANIMATION & FAMILY

- You need to have content that can work for both adults and kids.

- Clearly, bad language and overly violent scenes will not be acceptable. You don't want children imitating bad or undesirable behavior or thinking that it's normal.

- You can let your imagination run wild with animated stories, but remember that someone has to actually animate it. Just like in live action, complicated scenes can blow your budget and time allowed. However, what's complicated varies from live action to animation.

- During the voice recording of animated projects, you have a lot more opportunity to try different takes of lines than you would in live action.

- As crazy as your ideas can be in animation, they still have to make sense with your world and story.

- The general concerns for character building are the same in animated or family friendly stories. State who the protagonist is and what they want early on.

- Antagonists can't be too complicated for young children, so you may need a few of them to explore different aspects of your topic.

- The age of your audience matters greatly to the level of villainy you can show.

- You don't have to dumb down your story too much because it's for children. Nor make it too preachy. Just make sure it's something they can relate to.

- Songs help collapse story. They can do a lot of the character building, world building, "where are we now" and introduce new developments in the story.

- Improv-ing with voice actors can generate loads of great ideas for plot, character, and jokes.

- It's very expensive to re-draw an animated sequence, so once something is drawn, it's locked unless the whole thing is a complete disaster. You will have to save that better idea for another sequence or story.

CHAPTER 20

THE BUSINESS

―――――

While this book primarily concerns itself with the craft of writing, we would be remiss not to ask our panelists for their thoughts on the actual industry itself. From looking for representation to working with producers and financiers to work/life issues to the skills necessary to make it as a screenwriter, this chapter provides some tips for having a long career in screenwriting.

Q: What should an aspiring writer be looking for when seeking representation?

Marsha Greene - Someone who believes in you and understands you and with whom you can be honest. All the people that I know who chase agents because they want to be with a particular agency, I feel like it never works out. You want to be with the agency that wants to be in the business of you. Not that you want to be in the business of them. They need to understand your voice and the kind of work you want to do. You are not going to be successful if they are sending you out on jobs that you are not right for. They need to understand what you write and what you bring to the table, so they know how to market you to people. You don't want them just throwing your name into a hat for a job. That's not a good strategy. That is not what you want.

My agent is a very blunt, straightforward person. What I like about that is it makes me feel that I can be straightforward. That's important because sometimes we don't have the same opinion. Sometimes, he thinks I should do something and I don't want to do it. I need to feel free to be honest. And it's important to feel like you are being heard. We have worked together for many years so he knows me very well. He can pretty much predict what I will say in any situation. But in the beginning, you are learning. The best scenario is that it feels like a relationship, not they are working for you, even though they are, but more that it's a relationship where there is respect and trust. They are going out there speaking for you, so you have to make sure they are representing you in the right way.

Josh Olson - After *History of Violence*, my agent had just retired so I was bouncing around a couple of places looking for new representation. Agents would say, "This is where you need to be." But I didn't really want to be that. *History* was such a weird film because it was a genre film, which I love writing, but it was, and I hate this term, elevated. So there was this sense that I could write "serious stuff" but also mainstream action movies. I'm not either of those things, though. I've been struggling for decades to figure out what I am. I know what I like and I know what I like to write.

Shortly after *History,* I was offered a massive franchise film for an ungodly amount of money. In retrospect, if I had done it and pulled it off, we'd be doing this interview in my private jet right now! But I had no feeling for it, whatsoever. Okay, you spend six months of your career getting paid, but it will ruin your career if you fuck it up. I will be the guy who screwed that up and I didn't want that to happen. And then the next day, I get a call asking if I wanted to write a *Batman* cartoon for $1,200. Yes, I do! I've always wanted to write a *Batman* cartoon! So my advice would be find someone who wants to do what you want to do.

Scott Beck - Before we had representation, Bryan and I would think, "OK, who is Chris McQuarrie's agent?" Or, "Who is Steven Spielberg's agent?" That is definitely not the goal you should be setting for yourself. The first person we signed with was just a junior manager at the time. He was still learning the ropes and had worked in the industry for a couple of years. He certainly didn't have a huge client base. What was great about that was that he was just a couple years older than us and we could rise together. We loved his personality. He was very authentic. You know by the word representation, they will be representing you any time that they are reaching out to other people. We did meet with other agents and managers who would be kicking their feet up on the table or drinking Red Bull, which didn't give us confidence on how we wanted to be put out into the world. Finding someone who you connect with as a human being, who has authenticity and a genuine love of movies, not someone who just wants a quick spec sale, will really help you out. Finding someone at your level is vital. The agents and managers that are at the highest levels are representing clients that are doing so well for themselves that you will find yourself at the bottom of the roster.

Mohamad El Masri - I've had my best experiences when I find people who share my passions, enthusiasm and tastes. Reps are collaborators. These relationships can last longer than a lot of friendships, and often become friendships in of themselves. My reps are passionate and authentic, with tireless work ethics and are very good at what they do; I trust them implicitly. As a result they elevate me and my work. My goal is to elevate them as well. Hustle is a two way street. Finding that is not easy, but, again, I've found the people who find me are often a reflection of the person I want to be. And vice versa.

Q: Have you ever had to go through credit arbitration?

Scott Lobdell - Yes. The original script of *Man of the House* was about a rough and tumble Texas Ranger who has to travel with a group of cheerleaders who have witnessed a murder. He has to protect them and get them across state lines to testify like *Midnight Run* - a buddy comedy road movie. When Tommy Lee Jones came on as a producer, he said that he had done *The Fugitive* so many times, he wanted to keep the movie in one place in Texas and so suggested that his character could move in with the girls instead. At 35,000 feet, it's the same story.

When it came time for arbitration, they send you all the drafts of the script. There were twelve writers in total who worked on the project. You then have to write your arbitration letter to say I deserve this credit because this is my writing here and here in the movie. So to be thorough, you have to read all the drafts and what I discovered right away was that although they bought my original script about a bunch of cheerleaders who witness a murder, they were mortified by it. So they stripped out everything about cheerleading, except for that initial thing being that they're cheerleaders.

In the final version of our original script, they rescued Tommy Lee Jones' daughter by using their cheerleading abilities that were shown earlier. They get her off the train so Tommy Lee can stop the bad guy. And in all the following drafts, they did everything they could to get rid of that core idea. Then, finally, the last writers came on and said, we should follow that *Midnight Run* buddy comedy idea that if you have a tough person and a comedic person, at some point the comedic person's skills have to help the tough guy. So the writers said to the studio, "Hear us out. Why not, at the end, have the girls use their cheerleading skills to

WGA CREDIT ARBITRATION

Screenwriters get work based on their credits, but often more than one writer will contribute material to the final film or episode. So how do you figure out who gets what credit? If you're working under the auspices of the Writers Guild of America (WGA), there is a process called Credit Arbitration that sorts this out.

Before a movie or episode is released, the WGA recieves the final shooting script, which then goes to all participating writers. If a screenwriter feels that they are not being credited properly, or at all, they notify the WGA. They, and all other participating writers, deliver a written statement as to why they deserve a certain credit. Then a three person panel of WGA members review all the drafts of the project and compare them to the final shooting draft. The main thing panel members are looking for is the amount each participating writer contributed to the final script.

From this, each panel member makes a decision as to who gets what credit such as Written By, Story By, Screen Story by, Screenplay by, Adaption by, Narration Written by, Based on Characters Written by. All panel members and all writers involved in the process are anonymous so as to eliminate bias.

As of the printing of this book, original writers of a screenplay need to show they contributed at least 33% of the final shooting script. Subsequent writers need to show that they contributed at least 50% of the original work and at least 33% of any non-original work that goes into the final shooting script.

Credits usually matter to profit sharing percentages. If you are required to share a credit with another writer, then those points would be split accordingly.

An automatic arbitration will trigger if a production executive is proposed for a writing credit, three writers are suggested for "Written By" or "Screenplay by" credit, a "Screenplay Story by" and/or an "Adaptation by" credit is proposed. A director could be considered a "production executive."

Screenwriters should know that not only writers can receive credit. Production executives can apply for this, as well, but this is a general term for non-writers and most often applies to directors or producers who have contributed literary work to the project.

This information was taken from the WGA's Screen Credits Manual. You can download it at https://www.wga.org/contracts/credits/manuals/screen-credits-manual.

save the daughter? Then Tommy Lee can come in and shoot the bad guy." The studio said, "What a great idea! So glad we paid you to fix this script!"

To me, going through all these drafts was like reading six different adaptations of your work and when you got to the last adaptation, you discover they went back to your original idea. Yet those writers got the screenwriting credit and I got the story credit. There were so many scenes like when they are on the run and they go into a 7-11 and he has to get tampons for the girls, which is a comedic scene. In the finished version, he's moved in with them so he has to go to the store while they stay home and safe. So it's the same scene but done in a supermarket, instead. So yes, this is the movie that I wrote, but it's also been adapted.

Eli Craig - I haven't been through this, as it's more typical of someone who isn't directing their own stuff, but it does get kind of nasty. Some of these projects will go through six or eight writers. I have written drafts of things that have gone out and I'm not credited. Oh, well, whatever. What's weird is that you're all buddies until there's money on the table and everyone starts brawling over it. In a way, it's a creative suck. It sucks the creative life out of you, so I try not to spend too much time thinking about the money. I just do it and move on and not think about how I got screwed out of this or that.

That's the other thing, you're going out there and throwing your ideas out on the table. Then you see your ideas come out from the production company a few years later. Or similar enough. What are you going to do? Are you going to be that guy that runs out there saying, "That was my idea!"

We're all in this creative soup and we're all born of the same age. There are so many zeitgeists and things that I'm always surprised at how many of my ideas I have thought of or even written, pop out a year later from someone else. Wow! That was the movie I thought of. You just have to admire the good execution. It's why I won't hear random pitches anymore. I know the Duffer Brothers got sued over *Stranger Things* because somebody pitched a project to them that was remotely similar. But the Duffer Brothers went out and made *Stranger Things*. You can't take that away from them. I don't care if you had an idea about a being from another dimension. People think an idea makes a movie. No. It's execution. Execution in both screenwriting and on screen makes a movie. And it is hard work, so hats off to the people that do it. I don't get hung up on ideas. Great ideas are a dime a dozen.

Scott Beck - It happens. We've had other writers come on after us and we've come on after other writers. To be honest, it's been a fairly pleasant experience. We feel we want to make it that way. I feel like this business is too hard and it can pit a lot of people against each other. But when you think of the process of rewriting, for us, especially when we have been the second writers on, it's always like, how can we honor the work that has come before us? We do whatever we can to address the notes, but not reconstruct it so entirely. So often that process from the studio is like, "This is the first draft of the script." We want to know what the purest version of the story was because usually it gets distorted when studios bring in another writer after another writer after another writer. When we have been through that process it has been really enjoyable and not as difficult as sometimes you read in the trades.

Bryan Woods - I think it's helpful to reach out to the original writers or the writers that you are working off. We try to do that in order to get inside their head, and so they know we are playing in their sandbox. It's really their piece that we are trying to make fire on all cylinders, not just addressing the ridiculous wants that the studio has. Just being respectful. Writers aren't always treated the best in the film business. It's a concept to us that doesn't really make a lot of sense. It's evolved to this place where writers have to fight for their place at the table. It shouldn't be like that. Television has made a great argument for those things changing, with the respect that writers often get in that field. Writers have to be good to each other because no one else is.

Scott Beck - Not to get too boring on specifics, but we've been in arbitrations just due to technicalities because we're executive producers. If you have an executive producer credit then you've triggered an arbitration. In those instances, the Writers Guild does their process. They read all the drafts and they make the credit determination. The credit determination more often than not in our experience is exactly what was originally proposed by the studio. In our experience, it's worked itself out pretty seamlessly. I know that's not always the case and we have friends that have been in other situations.

Q: When do you get informed by the WGA that you are in arbitration?

Barbara Stepansky - In the post process when they're going through the credits. The WGA informs you what the credits are going to be. You can either say, great, done, or you have one week to put in your protest. It's all through the union. I didn't feel that there were enough changes done to warrant two credits. It was the first time for me where the other writer agreed. She was like, "Yep, it's all yours." They didn't even want to go through the process.

Q: Is there any difference between working with a streamer vs. a network or studio?

Tony Jordan - British broadcasters and commissioners would tell you that they are all completely different. Different values and different things. Essentially, they are guardians of what they perceive to be the content. They are all inevitably lead by an ethos. BBC Drama under Polly Hill and Ben Stephenson is a completely different beast to BBC Drama under Piers Wenger. We can all pretend that it was all the same because it was the BBC, but it's not true. It was completely different. Not better or worse, just different. For example, Polly Hill bought *Death in Paradise* in ten minutes. She recognized that it was perfect for the channel at that time. I don't think Piers would have ever commissioned it. That's just the truth. That doesn't make him a better commissioner or worse commissioner. It just makes him a different commissioner. Ultimately, you are pitching to individual commissioners.

Briana Belser - Netflix has a certain algorithm. They have a churn and they know you are going to binge. When a Netflix show premieres, you know all ten episodes are going to drop. They have numbers where they know at minute XYZ of this episode, audience members fall off, so here's what we're aiming for. We have data-driven metrics, "Your script can be this length." They would tell you, "You have this many pages." And if it was over that, they would say, "Please cut those pages." Broadcast is paid for by advertisers. There will be this many commercial breaks and the story you get to tell between those breaks, we call

WRITING STEP TERMS

When you enter into an agreement to write a screenplay, there are stages to the process called steps. These correspond to the various iterations of the project you do. You will often get paid a fee upon commencing a step and then another upon completing a step. Some of these are specified by union agreements, while others are more informal terms used to communicate the work needed. You can get more information on these and the minimum union prices at your country's writers guild. Here is a link to the WGA in the USA, as an example: https://www.wga.org/contracts/contracts/schedule-of-minimums.

Most screenwriting agreements allow for three steps: First Draft, Second Draft, and Polish. However, financiers are often under no obligation to use all these steps and may fire a writer after any one of the steps in order to bring on someone new or to kill the project. However, unused steps are still contractually valid and therefore writers can be brought back to complete them, if needed.

Treatment: A prose version of your story with all the plot points and characters worked out. This is a contracted step by most unions.

First Draft: The first completed version of your screenplay. That doesn't necessarily mean the first completed pass. If working with a producer, you will go back and forth with them many times until you both feel the script is where it needs to be to give to a financier. A balance must be struck between the goodwill of working with the producer to get the project right and being taken advantage of by doing loads of free writing. Remember, you don't get paid until the draft is complete. You will need to consider this issue throughout every stage of the project. This is usually a contracted step.

Second Draft: The second completed version of your screenplay that incorporates notes from the financier. This is also a contracted step.

Polish Draft: This step refers to smaller changes to the characters, action, and dialogue. This can be contractual or informal.

Page One Rewrite: When you are told to throw out most, if not all, of a previous draft and start over in a fresh direction. This is an informal term.

Specialty Pass: A process that enhances something specific in a script. Example: a Comedy Pass to punch up the jokes and gags to make them funnier. A writer brought in to do a specialty pass would receive an agreement with many of the steps listed above. This is an informal term.

DEVELOPMENT HELL/TURNAROUND

Once you decide to work with a producer or financier on your project, you enter the development process where the work is tailored to the producer/financier's liking. Many good projects get stuck here for long periods of time known as Development Hell. Here are some of the reasons for this.

- Sometimes, the people who bought your project get fired or move on to other jobs. The new executives may decide to shelve your project because it doesn't interest them or they wish to distance themselves from their predecessors.

- Projects may be bought as favors to producers to give them something of their own to work on while they work on other things for the studio. This pacification means some projects were never intended to see the light of day.

- The subject matter of your script is at the mercy of world events. A story about terrorist bombings immediately after 9/11 will have difficulty getting made.

- Financiers will often require a star actor or a big time director to commit to the project in order to feel secure financially. Those people have busy schedules, so you may have to wait a long time until they read it and give you an answer.

- Related to the above, projects with big name talent will have priority over those that don't.

- Faulty communication of creative ideas can hinder progress. Sometimes, executives' notes want something, but can't state it in a way the screenwriter can understand. Likewise, a screenwriter may not have the skillset to do what an executive wants. This can result in a cycle of frustrating rewrites.

- Financiers are businesses that are taxed. In order to offset those taxes, they will purposely leave projects in development in order to take business losses and expenses against them.

- If you weren't paid for your work, one way out of development hell is for you to stop working with your collaborator. You still own the script and all the changes made.

- If you were paid for your script and any work done on it, another way out of development hell is via turnaround. If a financier doesn't want to proceed with the project, they can release it back to you. Often this happens by letting options expire. However, they own all drafts and the changes made for which you were paid. You can get those back, too, but you would have to reimburse them what they paid you plus interest. Costly!

- Sometimes, people just fall out of love with your project and let it languish.

acts. And you will adhere to the act structure. So by the end of Act 1 on a legal show, we better know what the case is and what we're doing. By the end of Act 2, we better be into the case. By the end of Act 3, there needs to be a twist. By the end of Act 4, we should think it's all going to shit and by the end of Act 5, we should be happy it didn't go to shit. It was so explicit, as to the beats that we needed to hit - and merciless. The story better fit. Make it fit. Streamline it. Beef it up. Whatever. That sort of structuring came from the higher-ups and from the truth and reality of the legal system.

Also budget makes a difference. Broadcast receives so much money from advertisers and that enables more production sets. They are ready to bank and ball out on these actors, sets, and wardrobe. The budget for streamers is like, "Here's your main, here are your standing sets. You have X amount of episodes to go somewhere that we have not already built. Scatter it wherever you would like. Make sure you come in on budget."

Josh Greenberg - I have been on a couple of network shows where there has been product placement. They want us to integrate an Amazon Alexa into a story. So you have to do it in a way that's as organic as possible. It's pretty rare, but I suspect that with corporate synergy, it's going to become more and more common. Sometimes it's really egregious and silly when a character says, "Hey, I just ran to this store to get these Twizzlers. You know, they come in two delicious flavors." What?! Why are you saying that?

Q: How hands-on are the streamers and networks on their respective series or films?

Briana Belser - They all demand a story area, an outline, and a script. You have a first draft, a second draft, and then every day you may be releasing different revisions of a shooting draft. In terms of hands-on-ness, you are getting notes and calls on every piece of paper you hand in. Seeking approvals from them for the people that you cast. There's something nice about that It feels collaborative. For me, I'm not a showrunner - one day hopefully - but what I like about that, is that CBS made it very plain what would and what would not go on the network. The clarity was helpful for me. I could go, "Okay, let me try this. Oh, too far? Let me dial that back." Those parameters were really helpful and freed me from having to worry about it. If I bumped up against something, they would let me know at the story area stage. That's super helpful because you don't get down the rabbit hole. When you write your own feature, you might get to write a whole thing, but it has not fulfilled the XYZ mandate, which immediately cuts you out of the market for certain people.

Josh Greenberg - Streamers and networks are very, very involved. I say that with some degree of love for them because that is a timeless quality of TV writing; network executives who are overseeing a show love to get involved, even though they are not writing it. They love to give thoughts and tips and they are paying for the show, so it's not like you can ignore what they say. And you may have heard this expression before, and I love it, "You are looking for the note behind the note." Sometimes what an executive is articulating is not clear. They are not able to say what they mean, but the fact that they are pointing it out tells you that there is something wrong, and we need to examine it.

Carolina Rivera - My experience of the streamers is that they are very respectful of the creator. Very respectful of what you are trying to tell. But they do have some limits like you can go to forty-eight minutes or forty-nine, but no further.

Q: Do podcasts offer a new avenue for screenwriters?

Josh Olson - I did an audio drama podcast called *Bronzeville*. Two seasons. I wrote every word of sixteen episodes about the numbers racket in Chicago in the 40s starring Laurence Fishburne and Lorenz Tate. The most work I've ever done. 600 pages over three months, delivering a script a week. It was an incredibly satisfying experience. I've always wanted to work with Laurence Fishburne; he's one of my favorite actors and he did not disappoint. You can't believe the talent that came through. You know if you are going to play a character in three or four episodes of a TV show, that's three or four months of your life. But you come in on an audio drama and it's maybe two days and bang out your scenes. No hair. No makeup. No waiting for the crew. It was terrifying for me because it's a different medium. As a screenwriter, you learn to run as far away from exposition as you can. You have no visuals, but you can't write "Hey, look at that woman over there, lying on the ground with the knife in her back and all that blood." And that scared the shit out of me. However, other things could be easy. If we needed to change location we could do it in the blink of an eye. I remember doing that once in the middle of the recording when the actors said "They shouldn't be in the church, they should be in the pool hall." Alright, cut, take two. Now you're in a pool hall. Go! Imagine Spielberg realizes it shouldn't be World War 2, it should be World War 1!

Making *Bronzeville* cost maybe twice of what it would just for me to write a TV pilot, but most TV pilots end up sitting on a shelf. Why not throw your money into this so you have something you can actually go out and sell. So since then, Steve Bing, Victoria Pearlman and Mick Jagger, and I created Rainy Day Podcasts, which has a first-look deal with Warner Bros. Digital Networks.

Q: How has being a producer or a production executive helped you as a screenwriter?

Tony Jordan - I think it's harmed my writing more than helped it, if I'm honest. For two reasons. One, it's sucked time away from my writing. It sounds like I'm saying this and it's boo hoo, poor me. I'm not saying that at all. I have the best time in the world. I love working on other people's material. I love being part of things and making telly up. But talking as a writer, and even from just running a production company which I don't do much these days, and just in case my two joint MDs read this and say, "You fucking don't do anything" … it sucks your time. And not just writing time, physical headspace. If you've got someone else's whole show in your head, there's less space in there for your own stuff. So that's just a time thing. The other thing is that I find myself self editing. When I was just a writer and I didn't have to worry about the other stuff, I'd be writing, "Fifteen helicopters come flying over the road and a dinosaur eats one of the helicopters!" And now, the childish writer inside of me goes, "Fifteen no, fourteen, no, ten, no…there's a helicopter, no, there's a bloke on a bike coming over the hill with a toy dinosaur in the basket." A different part of

> ## COPYRIGHTING YOUR SCREENPLAY
>
> You can't copyright an idea, but you can copyright something written. But how do you prove that you wrote it and at what time? The best protection you can get is by officially copyrighting your work. This gives an official chain of title and gives you protection should a lawsuit be filed contesting ownership. You can't go back and register after the lawsuit has been filed.
>
> In the USA, that means contacting the US Copyright Office (www.copyright.gov), filling out a form, and paying a nominal fee (around $35 if you do it online at the printing of this book). In the United Kingdom, you get copyrighted automatically just by making something. You can learn more at www.gov.uk/copyright. Check with your home country to find out what protections you can get.
>
> Another option you have is to register your screenplay with the Writers Guild of America West. For a small fee, you get a certificate that verifies that you wrote a screenplay on a certain day but it doesn't give you an official chain of title. At the very least, it may give you some peace of mind. These days, however, emailing and texting scripts back and forth produces timestamps, which may make registration outdated.
>
> In either case, seek advice from an intellectual property lawyer from your home country to find out the best course of action.

my brain kicks in and interferes with the creative process. To be honest, when I notice I am doing it, I stop and try to overcome that particular hurdle. I just worry about the ones I miss. I always pick up the big ones. My writer's brain and my producer's brain start rolling around on the floor. A kind of weird, middle-aged man fighting thing. Like that *Bridget Jones* fight. I see that fight and I have to decide who wins. I'm always on the side of the writer fighter. If he wants his fifty-nine helicopters, let him have his fifty-nine helicopters! Then I write it in and we might lose it down the road. But I might miss ten little ones. There might have been a few Earl Grey teas that have been switched for PG Tips. So for those two reasons, time and self-editing, those are the pitfalls of being both.

Meg LeFauve - Having been an executive helps the understanding of the specifics of how the business works. It's a business and an art. It helps me understand the pieces that come together to form a movie. The script is a huge piece of it, but it is not the end of it. I understand what directors need, which gets funneled into the script because it's going to get directed. I understand what actors need, which gets funneled into the script because it's going to be acted. If you are in animation, you have to understand what animators need. You have to understand why it has to be animated. All of those things, having sat on the other side of the couch, certainly helps.

It certainly helps that I was a teacher. If you're doing animation, it's a very collaborative art. The same with television. If you're a screenwriter, you're going to be collaborating with producers, directors, and studio executives and you do need to know how to ask the right questions; to be able to dig down into something. To be able to make people feel

OPTIONS & SHOPPING AGREEMENTS

If someone (a producer, usually) wants the right to make your script into a film or series, there are two main paths for that to happen: Options and Shopping Agreements.

Option

This agreement gives the producer the exclusive right to alter your script, sell it to a financier, and convert it into a film or series program. For this, they will pay you a negotiated amount of money for a certain period of time called a "term". Usually, this is eighteen (18) months and the producer has the right to extend the agreement for an additional eighteen months for another amount of money. When the option expires, a new agreement must be drawn up or extended.

Should the producer get a financier to make the film, the screenwriter will have a "production bonus" or "production fee," which is a line item amount in the production budget. A portion, if not all of the money paid in the option period, will be deducted from this larger amount and the screenwriter gets the balance usually on the first day of principal photography. The screenwriter will get some profit sharing (backend points) in the film, though these are usually on net receipts.

Shopping Agreement

Producers working with lesser known writers or less commercial material often don't want to go through the optioning process because they aren't sure they can make a sale and don't want to pay the writer option fees. They may offer a shopping agreement, which is a shorter term, non-exclusive arrangement between the producer and writer.

The pros of the Shopping Agreement is that the script is tied up for around 6-9 months. The screenwriter can sell it to anyone else as it's non-exclusive. If the project does get set up, the screenwriter (or their agent or lawyer) will negotiate their fee and backend points directly with the financier (some may see this as a con.)

The cons of the shopping agreement are that you aren't getting any money for your work. In addition, scripts typically only get one read per financier, so if the producer gets a few, it may ruin the desire of others who wish to pay you as they have less places to go to.

As always, you should consult with an experienced entertainment attorney before entering into either of these agreements.

safe, excited, and impassioned. You also have to be able to say the hard thing at the right moment. I learned a lot of these things from teaching.

Q: How is it working in Hollywood?

Ron Leshem - In a weird way, I sometimes feel that Hollywood is becoming more conservative than it was in the 1980s and almost, in a sense, the 1950s. This might be out of trying to do good and fix the broken world. When you sit in an executive's office, the didactic of what you are not allowed to let a character do, is a lot. You want to defend minorities. We need to avoid making a character look too bad to the public. Your whole dialogue is political.

Many streamers tell you that they greenlight a project based on a one-liner because they don't have time to read scripts. So the one-liner has to be very sharp. Is she going to be number one in chess or not? I know what the story is about and I can make a decision. Every day is a struggle to convince people in what you believe in. It took six and a half years to convince people about *Euphoria*. They told me that it wouldn't work. Then when it does work, it becomes the most watched show at HBO since *Game of Thrones*. The entire profession is a struggle.

Karen Walton - To be clear, my own Hollywood experience is very limited compared with most of my peers from Canada who work and live there. I mostly just visit, and occasionally work with Americans. It is fun, especially if you are not from America. When working in film, I was being driven crazy in the Hollywood system because development seemed an industry unto itself. I would be in drafts for years and years on one project, unable to take on much else, but equally unable to move anything forward. It was never shooting and I write to shoot. Writing for its own sake, or I should say, writing for a pay check as the endgame is not for me; it's not why I write.

But in television, it's faster and the path is clearer: it's conceive, execute, shoot, post - broadcast or stream - go-go-go. I write, we shoot, next challenge please! There's no stasis, no creative drag on the momentum for the writer - personally, that's ideal for me. So moving to television made financial and creative sense for me - in both systems, Canadian or Hollywood. No surprise that you see a lot of brilliant independent filmmakers of my generation who also made the switch to TV. Most of us trained in film, and learned TV to survive. Not necessarily exclusively, just to do what we love doing - making things people see - and making a living to boot!

If you are very lucky, you can do all this grand stuff with amazing people for a couple of decades. But as you are getting on, your priorities in life are bound to change. After doing this go-go-go for twenty years non-stop and speaking only for myself, now in middle age and as a woman who enjoys so many freedoms most of the world never gets to enjoy, I went, "I'd actually like the freedoms that I am allegedly now able to enjoy!" At some point I realized that's what I wanted. I wanted weekends, I wanted to decide where a concept could really go, and I missed the film writing lifestyle - which for me was a room of one's own, a room of one that cool collaborators can visit, but never feel stuck in. Still collaborating, but also growing new stories, new teams, new creative ideas and ways forward. I wanted to stop feeling like I was just working to work. I do want to write and to make my own things, again. So sooner or later, many lucky working writers do get to this point. We ask, what's it all about? And I find myself with my colleagues, certainly those who are my age and experience-level here, all asking, "Do you have an exit strategy?" or "What is it you'd *really* like to be doing?" Tick tock! So, I took the off-ramp, at least regarding Hollywood careers and lifestyles; and regarding most "for-hire" writing, staff writing at this stage in my career in Canada. Every career is different. I am Canadian and I always intended to love to live and work in my own country and collab with other countries' industries and cultures. I have been very fortunate to be able to do that. It's a 'sacrifice money and glam gigs' choice; a personal choice. It's not a choice for every writer. But I love it.

Eli Craig - Working as an actor and a director, you are exposed. People are most likely going to see the work that you do. It's how you make a living. You have to act or direct something to get paid. But as a writer, the ratio is much, much less of what you write to what actually gets seen. *Tucker and Dale* got made after three years of really struggling to get it financed. Now, I would say the ratio is about ten to one. I've written twenty scripts for two movies. You don't always know why something doesn't go forward. You just don't have them advocating any more for a certain project, and you have to move on. But sometimes they come back around. I have a project I wrote three years ago that people are now saying, hey, this script is really good. Maybe we should make this!

Q: Do awards and accolades actually help your career?

Josh Olson - Definitely! That's probably why I still have one. It's nice to have the asterisk. It's given me freedom that I am sure I have misused in many ways. A few years into that process, it hit me that it was something that I never cared about. And I didn't come here to Hollywood with dreams of making giant movies. I wrote the stuff I wanted to write and I love movies. I was working on a sequel to a giant film, but I wasn't really enjoying it. I made the decision that I wasn't going to pursue that stuff anymore and try to only work on stuff that moved me personally. There has to be something that makes me want to work on it regardless of whether I am getting paid. It's been a weird and bumpy road, but it's been paying off and it's how I get to do something like *Bronzeville*. I think a lot of people are like, "It's nice to have a little side project, but that side project is more writing than you've done in the last five years combined in a three-month period with minimal money." For me, it was a fantastic challenge and I have a comfortable enough cushion where I can afford to do that. The same thing with my podcasts, they're fun! The instant they are not fun I will stop doing them.

Q: How has the industry responded to calls for diversity and inclusion?

Carolina Rivera - I was part of over 200 LatinX creatives that wrote an open letter to the industry asking for more representation in both those areas. I've seen change. I was working on *Jane the Virgin* for the six years it lasted and then I went to *Roswell, NM* and I feel it's been changing, more in the US than in Latin American countries. I think Hollywood is very conscious about it now. It's crazy that back then people said they couldn't find LatinX writers or creatives. What? There's a whole LatinX committee in the Writer's Guild of America. That's where you go. All the networks and studios are signatories, so that's where you go when you want to find LatinX writers: The Writer's Guild. Just ask for the LatinX Committee. You can go down the roster and find them. You can see what their positions are, if they are staff writers or Co-EPs. Of course, there are less LatinX EPs and Co-EPs because there has been less opportunity in Hollywood for those writers to work in writers rooms. But there's no pretext to find the writers. You have a huge guild.

But it has changed a lot. A lot of productions are aware of it and are anxious to hire, not only women but minorities. You have to have a percentage of minorities in the rooms. It's just funny that women are considered a minority when we are the majority of the population in the world. So crazy. It's good in a way because we have to be hired, but some of my friends are like, "I'm just the minority in the room. Nobody cares what I say." I don't think it's a war that's been won. There are a lot of battles still to do. And in Latin American countries, especially, because women are not expected to work. Even less so in entertainment where the hours are crazy. But we're fighting the fight and now more than ever, things are opening up in Latin America and the US. When you are fighting the fight, you get some wins but you still have to keep fighting.

Marsha Greene - When I started out, the only other Black people other than myself, were those who worked in the craft truck. Without fail. Sometimes, there would be one camera guy. One grip. I've seen such a huge change since. People call me a lot now because I've had all these years of experience and there aren't that many Black showrunners. There aren't enough Black writers who work enough to get to the level of showrunner. I got there before the movement happened, so I end up doing a fair amount of mentoring. There are so many organizations who are doing so much more than I ever could and trying to work with them. So I have noticed a change, even in terms of crew. People are just aware and conscious that we have to change that. Before, people weren't invested in the change and now I feel people across the board are invested in the change. It's not you alone trying to get one person a job; bringing one person a long where we were slowly making our way through the change. On *The Porter*, every department is going to have a person of color. Some of those people, it was their first job. Great! Now they have their first job and they've met all these other people who can recommend them. That kind of big commitment from everyone on that show is what is going to make real change.

With CBC here in Canada, if you have an indigenous story, you must have an indigenous writer. That is an actual rule where the other is an accepted practice for everybody else. It's challenging. I support this very much, but I think there are two problems. One, I had a friend who got hired as a writer, but not really as a writer. It became clear to her in the course of doing this that she was like the Black consultant. They hired her, but not to write for all the characters. They had a Black character and so now she would be the person who writes for that character or says what is right or wrong just for that character. That is a problem. Also, only if there is an indigenous character, will an indigenous writer get hired. So it's like, we don't need you. We just need to check that box. That's very dangerous. You just want to have writers in the room. You can hire an indigenous writer and then you have the possibility of doing an indigenous story. And they could also just write a story.

The second problem is that it's good for people to create those standards, but then we need to invest in preparing those writers to be in those roles. So if you want to tell a

Black story and want a Black showrunner, there are only two Black showrunners to go to. If they're not available to do it, then what? What I find, is there are all these grassroots organizations that are trying to create all these programs, but the people at the top could be doing more. Investing more in the talent that they need to make their shows. I realize it's my personal taste, but to get authentic storytelling, it comes from personal experience. You are not going to have it if you don't live in those worlds. So it's good to have these standards and now I think we have to think more broadly about representation and not be so specific. How do we get more exposure and have more stories available to us?

Ben Philippe - I think it really depends on the showrunner and the network. I think John Hoffman, the showrunner on *Only Murders in the Building,* is so amazing at empowering people to bring in new perspectives and new stories. We still fall short. I am not going to say it is the most diverse show. It's two white rich men on the Upper West Side who are just rich enough to be bored and go through their neighbor's apartment. I think that the diversity we see on the screen is occasionally ahead of the diversity we see behind the scenes. We are catching up to it. It's always strange. When you are making TV in conditions like COVID, the money argument can be, "Well, we tried, but at the end of the day, we have to go with the person who was best suited for the job that was available right now. We can't spend months and months searching for a supporting actor who is going to be a person of color or with a disability." No. If you want to find these people, you will find them.

I know I have been lucky. I can't stress that enough. All of my shows have been inclusive environments. I was on a show for five weeks before jumping into Season 3 of *Only Murders*, called *Straight Man*, which is an adaptation of a Richard Russo book that stars Bob Odenkirk on AMC. It's the midlife crisis of a straight, white professor who kind of has an affair with a student. It was written in the 90s, so it's not the most progressive book, but the room? Incredibly diverse. It's mostly young women and we were mostly invited to bring our own perspectives. The fact that I am a college professor was also part of the discourse. I think a lot of effort is being made to bring people in to make things even, while knowing that they are not there yet. And they might never be because TV is a tradition. The way writers rooms have run for the past sixty years is not going to radically alter overnight inside the same industry. For some showrunners, the philosophy can be "This is a creative space and I want to be comfortable here."

I'm adapting my pilot so I get to pick my writers. I am going to pick my six favorite working writers. All of those people are the exact ethnicity, gender, and background as me and we all went to the same college and have the exact same sensibilities. I don't believe it's insidious. In fact, it's eerily logical. I'm just lucky that the rooms I've been in have always consciously resisted this impulse.

When I first started to write on *Only Murders in the Building* and on other shows, I was shocked by the amount of time we spent blue-skying. Blue-skying is the term used for the first few weeks of the room when you are talking about what the show could be about. You are not breaking story yet. I think the teacher in me wanted to say, "Okay, it's 10 a.m. on Monday. Let's start carding up Episode 1 and talk about Act 1, 2, and 3." But no, it was about getting comfortable talking around each other and talking about these characters. Who do you see as this young woman who lives in this building that she can't afford and is interested in solving murders? What is her background? Just making suggestions about these characters in the broader sense is incredibly helpful because these are the moments when you unlock specificities for characters.

For *Interview with the Vampire*, we spent a whole day talking about Louis and Lestat and coming to the conclusion that Louis is a closeted Black man and that Lestat is a pansexual white man. We made the distinction that one of them is only attracted to men and the other has lived centuries and has affairs with women. How would their lives together reflect that? That was really important for the characters. It really instructed us to when things really get bad in their marriage and Lestat is going off into the world. Of course he makes a girlfriend who is a woman - someone that Louis doesn't have access to. We also discussed that they are an interracial couple. Louis is very unhappy when he realizes that he's never going to die and his mortal family is aging. They want nothing to do with him because he's a demon. "We are all sixty, why do you look like you are thirty?" He's incredibly depressed and Lestat wants to cheer up his partner, so he makes him a vampire daughter. He picks a little Black girl. Louis gets very angry because it's one of his people who has been cursed to this horrible life that he doesn't want anymore. When Claudia, the daughter, and Louis, the protagonist, turn on Lestat, he's like, "Well, I'm in a house with two Black people who both think I am the villain. I can't do anything right." Those are all fascinating dynamics to talk about that trickle down into the show, in a direct, textual, scene to scene way.

There's not a lot of disability representation. I know we are in a period where people occasionally roll their eyes at the amount of diversity, but when you are in a writers room, it's often not. I don't say this to criticize the show, and I know that John always gets the best people for *Only Murders in the Building*, but our room is on the lower side of diversity. When you are a minority in the room, how much can you push back on those elements of representation? In *Only Murders*, John is so good about having us talk this out. A couple of doctors move in the building. It's just a couple so they can be anything, They can be two women with adopted children. They can be non-binary people. But this is an industry where, for a lot of people, a doctor and his spouse is a white man and his wife and their two children.

Q: Has it got better in Hollywood in the post-*#MeToo* movement?

Meg LeFauve - I do believe that anybody should be allowed to write anything. I should be able to write the next *Gladiator* movie. People from outside of America can write classic American Westerns. I also believe that women's stories have been told by men for so many thousands of years that I would like women to have many more chances and to tell our own stories and points of view on being a woman.

Karen Walton - I can't speak personally to the climate in Hollywood, as I don't work there often, or live there. From the outside looking in, I don't think anything has changed necessarily - I would not assume it has, systemically.

In Canada, the same people who have always gotten away with terrorizing or excluding and undermining women and marginalizing people on the job, seem to have gotten away with it, at least in terms of past behavior. They continue to work. Continue to profit first and most often, in terms of opportunities. They continue to be celebrated. Our #MeToo moments were not about justice, but they were, I think, successful in mass education and empowerment, for those who truly do pay for the price for lasting trauma they sustain at work. It drives me crazy that people call it a movement. What's the movement? That white guys are now aware that they shouldn't get caught cornering or demeaning women anymore at work?

What I hope it is, is an evolution. And that those coming up after us are better aware and equipped to confront predators and abusers in our industries. And that our systems stop blaming victims for speaking out, and stop rewarding people who destroy other human beings' lives and livelihoods for doing that. Because the world in general has not stopped producing predators, we have to make sure that what we have learned, remains top of mind, that it is an ongoing action for which we are all responsible. All the time.

Marsha Greene - In terms of #MeToo, it put all this aggression and behavior in context. Of course, it has to do with women, but this abusive nature in the name of genius, in general, has been much more scrutinized in light of that movement more than it ever was before. It was so excused before. I was fortunate to never have to deal with any sexual harassment related to work, but I feel like I've seen the shift in the culture, overall. People are like, "It's not cool."

Lauren Iungerich - The #MeToo movement was incredible and brought to light so much bad behavior. What was once an industry that turned a blind eye - now everyone has their eyes open. But it had some rough ramifications, too. Namely, watching some good men go down for things that were mere infractions of character, not criminal behavior. I also now see more men afraid to hire women for fear of being accused of any wrong doing. But the worst outcome has been watching women continue to tear each other down out of fear that there are not enough seats at the table for all of them. In some ways, the working world got better, and in other ways - it got worse. It's still incredibly hard to be a woman navigating for an equal place in this business.

Q: Is there any pressure on being the first Latin American woman with a deal with Netflix?

Carolina Rivera - It's more like a privilege. With my track record, *The War Next Door, Daughter* and *Against the Ropes*, we have 52% of women working behind the scenes. In Latin America, that's not the case. It's very hard for women to prove themselves in the industry and have an opportunity, so that's my quest. I'm very privileged to take that position.

Q: As a creator and showrunner, how do you juggle working and having a young family?

Barbara Stepansky - It's challenging. I couldn't do any of it without the help of my husband and a nanny. When I'm in the writers room or supervising set, I'm simply not around and they take the brunt of childcare. When I'm just writing in my home office, my days become more flexible, but I still need the hours to complete my pages. And then I will often be present in body but not in spirit because my mind is still trying to figure out a scene or a plot turn or dialogue lines and I keep jotting down thoughts on my phone. I just have a hard time "switching off." I want to be present for my family but I also want to keep writing. Some days I manage to balance just fine, others feel like lost battles.

Lauren Iungerich - I am really lucky as I have a great husband who is my producing partner and my music supervisor. We're always working together. If I am directing, he will go home early from set. And sometimes, if I am not directing, I leave early and he stays. So the juggle with the kids is a real thing. We have an incredible nanny who is like family. I'm really lucky. It's such a question because I didn't have children to watch them be raised by other people. I had children be part of their life and have them add to mine. I also wanted to ensure that I was a whole person living my dream. I didn't want to forgo having a career by having children. So with that, you invite someone else into your life to help you raise your children. There are times when the nanny sees my children more than I do. My children really love her and I am so grateful that they have someone else that they love and who loves them as much as we do. It was not how I was raised. I was raised where my mom went to work and was home at six. I would get home from school and be by myself until then. It's a different time now. I am really grateful that I am able to live and do my work, be a woman and have children. I am married to a total feminist who is supportive of all of that. But we have to create boundaries for our family time. During the pandemic, I didn't work on weekends. I stopped thinking that I had to do things then. It's going to get done when it gets done. That's the way I work now. I've finally carved the space I need to do what I need to do and know that it doesn't all have to get done before I spend time with my family.

Q: How have the streamers changed the industry?

Karen Walton - The endgames have changed. The audiences have changed, grown, diversified; they are more options savvy, get to choose more of what they want to watch, more of the real entire world's stories to watch, what they get to try out, when they watch it, how they watch it - or not. Yes, you want someone to go watch your big pricey movie packed with famous celebrities, but you need to consider a blockbuster that folks will watch in their living rooms. It's not always the cinema, the night-out, or the "Must See TV" appointment viewing anymore. How stories can find audiences, and presumptions about those audiences, have changed. If the world has come to terms with anything else during the pandemic, it's the idea that all the way around the planet every human being has been aware of one thing that we all have in common, at least right now, which is: Tomorrow might not be the same as today. We haven't had that one common global experience, as a species, in a long time. I find it all fascinating. I was alive for the home video debates, so change to industry structures do not alarm or frustrate me. They excite me.

Alex Livak - The magic of movies is universal. I grew up in Russia in the former Soviet Union. Movies, particularly American movies were a way to escape my reality. I empathize with those characters even though I knew nothing of what life was like in America. With truly great stories, it doesn't matter where you are in the world because the human experience is fundamentally universal. There's more that unites us than divides us. One of the tragedies of the Russian invasion of Ukraine is that before, everyone was looking to go into that part of the world to explore stories. After *Squid Game*, everyone was like, "We want another *Squid Game*." The Korean market is very well traveled, very well mined. What about Russia? It's a big movie market. There's so much opportunity there. Netflix was in the early stages of making a Netflix Russia, which for me was great because there are so few writers in Hollywood that have a Russian background. Now, five things I was working on? Gone.

Marsha Greene - It's interesting because we had a traditional broadcaster in the CBC and then we had BET+ for *The Porter*. They have different rules. They have different wants. Tonally, we had to make sure the show fitted those two things. On a practical level, one is going to have commercials and one is not. One, the episodes will all come out the same time and you can go from one to the next, and the other, you are going to have to wait a week to see the next episode. You have to think about the storytelling in that way. When you do a direct pick-up from scene to scene with a commercial, it works. When there isn't a commercial, it's weird.

We also didn't have a simultaneous launch. We launched in Canada first and went week to week until it finished and then it launched in the U.S. and went all at once. I think we would have loved to have it launch simultaneously because it would have been a big splash all at once, but we knew that with a streamer, often their goal is to put it all out at once and then they are promoting in this very specific and online way. The traditional broadcasters are promoting it in a completely different way. So I do think it changes the way we tell stories a little bit. It changes the way we market it more. The other thing I would say is that in Canada, the streamers are so huge that they are close to putting traditional broadcasters out of business. That changes a lot for us as professionals because it's harder for cable to compete. I still have cable. I'm holding on!

Ron Leshem - One of the things that happens in our time now is that you have 550 scripted series a year in the U.S. It becomes really hard to try something new or say something new. The number one problem in the TV industry I think, is that there are not enough executives. There hasn't been a new generation of executives that can handle so much capacity. In previous decades, someone at that point in their career would be moving from the mailroom at WME (William Morris Endeavor) to being an assistant to an agent. He is now a development executive at a streamer with the need and ability to greenlight stories for development. He doesn't have the experience to read, or the confidence to read, but he also doesn't have the time to read. The executives are reading mostly all the scripts that are in production or development and giving notes. So reading new stories is almost impossible.

It has created two things in the U.S. industry. First, it's created the lack of confidence and the need to create some mechanism to bring in a lot of MBA and Harvard Business School executives to try and create an algorithm for what works. And then every senior executive, the President of a network, has created "mandates" of what they are looking for each year. "We want to have a new *NCIS* with a female character and this and that." When you look at the mandates, almost all of the networks would look the same. They'd have slight differences, like AMC is dependent on commercials so it needs the DNA of *The Walking Dead*. The problem is that you are predicting based on what people are watching today on what will work two years in the future. That's ridiculous. The other side of it is that the industry is going to create 400 shows that look exactly the same with the same mechanisms. Eventually, the one show that will be outstanding and break the chain will be the one that didn't go by the rules. It will be the show that went against all the rules. It wasn't based on the mandates and now it's unique.

The first mega-hit of Netflix was *Stranger Things*. *Stranger Things* got a pass from all twenty buyers that they went to and they all said the same thing: you can't do a show from the point of view of the kids. You have to have this about the FBI. So everyone said "no" to it. Eventually, Netflix did say "yes," and it turned out to be the most watched show ever because it was different.

I come from Israel and much of my work is still in Israel. Israel is tiny. It's like a small town in the U.S. I ask executives how come Israel is creating so much drama TV. The number one reason TV executives in L.A. will tell me is that they feel the Israeli audience is the most neurotic audience in the world. It gets bored very easily, so you have to be edgy, but at the same time, you must be mainstream. It's such a tiny community, so if the show is just a niche, it won't make sense financially. It has to have 30% ratings or 20% ratings. It must be a campfire - an edgy, mainstream. At the same time, you are working in such a mess because Israel is such a mess. The industry is a mess, so you are breaking all the rules. You are breaking everything and thinking outside of the box.

The other thing is that Israel fell in love with the idea of globalization in this industry. The U.K. has a very unique thing - a bold and successful story. The U.S. creates shows for Americans, by Americans, speaking American English on American soil. Then someone sells this to 200 territories. Right now, there are too many American stories that feel the same. Now, the American audience wants to fly somewhere else. So now the American audience will not only accept an American story abroad - an American in Paris or Argentina, which had never been the case in the past, but Americans want to see foreigners on their televisions. So if you look over the next five years, the stories are going to be more global. This is what makes it fresh as a story.

Eli Craig - There are all these weird algorithms now with the streamers which is an added difference. "This title doesn't work," they say. Or, after all the executives had agreed on a route I was going to take on a project, they then come back to me saying, "The algorithm doesn't love that idea, do I have a spin on the idea that the algorithm might like?" To be honest, I'm not sure how these things work - are there hashtags that they put into the algorithm? What do they feed into it to get a response? Then, on the other side, as a viewer, Netflix's rating system was changed to an algorithm system, so it now suggests movies for you to watch based on what your previous watch experience was. So when my film *Little Evil* was at Netflix, they told me 25 million people watched it in the first month. If that many people saw the film in the theater, that would be a huge box office hit. But people have told me that they accidentally stumbled upon *Little Evil* or had to seek it out, as horror comedy wasn't something that they usually watched. For me, personally, I want to see things that I wouldn't necessarily watch. I don't want to have content forced upon me that's so similar to the last thing I watched. I want to see things that other people have liked. It's definitely a changing landscape and throughout my career, all the changes seem to happen so fast. If you are a creator you have to stay agile enough to stay in the game.

Q: Do you think because of big-budget Hollywood films, a lot of originality has disappeared?

Bill Nicholson - There seems to be fewer big budget Hollywood films these days. There used to be the very big budget tentpole movies and then a middle band they called dramas. That middle band has disappeared. There were a lot of indies in that area, but also the studios got into that area. The budget range of sort of $7 million to $20 million. That has now become very, very difficult. Where there is huge originality, is on the small screen. That is the exciting area. All the time I am seeing new stuff come out that is so fresh. Unlike the boilerplate entertainment that we've had. I don't think there's any threat to originality, I just think you have to figure out where your film belongs.

Q: What skills are important to have in this business?

Mohamad El Masri - In my experience, a vital thing people are looking for is enthusiasm and a sense of self. I've noticed that wearing your enthusiasm on your sleeve and being yourself is something people find infectious and gravitate towards - and by extension, toward your work. Creative voice is important, but carrying yourself well seems to have been most useful to me. How are you in meetings or in phone calls? Do you listen well? Do others feel heard by you? Social IQ has probably been the most helpful thing in my career. I've realized that people ultimately want to feel inspired and excited after a conversation with you - and they want to know you are a good person with values and integrity. Of course, the work has to be a reflection of your sensibilities - voice matters. But your presence and approach with others is the most important thing. Work ethic matters, in that context, of course; realizing that everyone involved in a creative or business conversation, no matter what they do, have goals and dreams as strong and passionate as yours. Everyone's on a journey of their own. The goal is to find a like-minded tribe, with a creative voice that rhymes with yours, who want to take one together.

Marsha Greene - Well, being a joy to be around isn't really a skill. It's more of a trait. What's difficult as a writer in a room or as a writer at the beginning of your career, is the feedback - the negative feedback; how hard that is. You have to be open to that feedback but make sure it doesn't crush you, it doesn't stop you. You have to keep going. That doesn't mean it can't affect you. You just can't let it stop you. That's a trait that you learn over time. By the time you are showrunner, you realize that ideas or lines that you don't say "yes" to, has nothing to do with what you think the writer's talent level is. You just have your own idea of what you want it to be. People have their own personal tastes. There's no right or wrong. It's just right or wrong for the show you're on.

Karen Walton - The skills to have in this business? Life experience and resilience.

CHAPTER REVIEW: BUSINESS

- Choose a representative that understands and believes in you.

- If you are working under a WGA contact, you can use credit arbitration if you feel you are not being credited properly.

- Streamers, TV networks, and studios tend to be hands-on with their projects. The notes they provide are not meant to be meddling, but rather efforts to make the project better.

- It's possible to use your writing skills for newer mediums like podcast stories to help move your career along.

- Working as a production or studio executive gives you an idea of how other entities like actors, crew and financiers will view your story. This can be helpful such as making sure your characters are rich and interesting for casting purposes, but it can also hinder you if you're constantly letting money rule your creative decisions.

- The entertainment industry is getting better at including minorities and women in the creative processes of content, but there's still a long way to go to achieve equality.

- Streamers have fundamentally changed the entertainment landscape in the way content is released and consumed. And with so much more of it, it seems that more executives are needed to manage it all. But should all of them have MBAs?

- Enthusiasm for the business is one of the most important traits to have to be successful. Other important ones are resilience and being able to work with different groups of people.

CHAPTER 21

PERSPECTIVE

———

Screenwriting can be wonderful and maddening for a myriad of reasons - lots of lows and highs. So we've asked all of our panelists that very question to find out how they celebrate the best moments and get through the worst.

Q: What are the lowlights and highlights of screenwriting?

Becca Topol - Oh, God. So many! It can be challenging, rewarding, and also at times, very difficult. I love the process of writing which is creating. I used to be terrified of starting a new project as the blank page can be so intimidating. But now, I allow myself more space and freedom in terms of figuring out where a story goes and where my deeper self wants a story to go. It's great to be in production on a show, and so fulfilling to see your material get made but it can be very challenging to work on very fast deadlines, especially when you're a perfectionist. I've learned that it's important to trust in the process and the team.

Hilary Galanoy - I would say the lowlights are the long, soul-crushing periods of unemployment. Both Liz and I worked as development executives and my first boss told me, "If you're looking for job security, don't be writer."

As for the high, there's nothing like seeing one of our movies being made. One of the most joyful moments that I will ever have in my life is when we get to go to a premiere or a screening or some of our friends are gathered here to watch on TV. It's so fun to watch with family and friends and hear people laugh out loud at something you wrote. That's pretty awesome. That I brought joy to people.

Elizabeth Hackett - I had an acting teacher who said, "An actor's breakfast is rejection." That's a really depressing thing to say to a sixteen-year-old, but it's good to arm someone to go out into the world. There are low periods. There is rejection. There are periods where you feel out of ideas. It feels really slow. Things move at a glacial pace in the film industry - until they don't. But then there's this moment where you've had this crazy idea and suddenly, it's a movie. And you're watching it. And people are in it. You only get what you give. You have to be constantly generating stuff. Hustling and all of that. But it is rewarding to see your ideas come to life.

Paul King - The lowlights have definitely been the times when I've been stuck. That's really hard. When you've gotten yourself into a corner and don't know how to get out of it. I do feel that painfully. I think that's why I prefer writing with someone else because when you are stuck and sitting in a room on your own, it's just lonely and awful.

I don't think I would write on my own again. I only got through the first *Paddington* because I had so much help from David Heyman and Rosie Alison at Heyday who are very experienced and hugely attentive. They kept bringing in other people who I could talk to and who could help me. I find it easier to think when I am talking than when I am staring at a screen.

It's also very difficult when something you've made isn't liked. *Bunny and the Bull* actually did okay critically, but a lot of people didn't like it, and that was no fun at all. It takes so long to make a film. You've had to pour your heart and soul into it and act like it's the most important thing in the world for so long - and before you know it, it can seem like it's actually become the most important thing in the world.

There are all those over-the-top metaphors that say making a movie is like having a child. Of course, it's not really like having a child at all; it's just a job. But the emotions that come with it are not as far away from those you get having a child as they should be. You've cared for your movie, and grown it and nurtured it, and if it dies, it does bring on a weird sort of grief.

The highlights, and my favorite part of the process, is that you can sort of get it perfect on the page. The scene is just the right shape. It's funny and it's touching. It turns all the corners it should, at the right time. I suppose a script can be sort of the Platonic ideal and you say, "Oh, this is just gorgeous." When you come to film it, I have that dread in the back of my head that there is this perfect version of the scene that you are trying to capture. Sometimes, you get it and sometimes you fall woefully short and there's not a lot you can do about it. You had your shot, you blew it and it's too expensive to go back and try again. It's lovely when you feel it's all working on the page and we laugh a lot and that's good fun.

Briana Belser - Lowlights. It's solitary. Your butt hurts. Solitary and sedentary are the two lows. The highlights? When it has been so well written that someone can skim the story and fully get it. Just from a skim, you have taken them on the emotional journey that you have architected. That is so worth it. I have a tear-jerker script where I cried the whole time when I wrote that thing. And I have had one or two calls with people who had just finished it and were in tears. They were like, "I had to call right now. I know our meeting is tomorrow, but I had to call right now."

It's so rewarding when you nail it. When you sit at a table read and hear a joke that you wrote but up to that point it's not been performed aloud, and the whole room cracks up because it landed. Really what I am getting at, is that I told the story and those characters came alive on the page. You didn't have to see anything. You didn't have to hear anything. You spent ninety minutes of your day with them and they moved you. And they left you with something you have to think through and work through and that's why I'm here.

Barbara Stepansky - Lowlights, writing on my own. I miss the interaction in a writers room of putting out an idea and somebody else jumping in. Highlights, when you write and you feel like you're "channeling" story and character and the script is talking to you rather than forcing words onto the page.

Julie Sherman Wolfe - The highlight is seeing your work on screen, and knowing that you're bringing a little joy, or a couple hours of happily ever after, to people in a world where that's not always easy to find. The absolute high point of my career was when my movie *A Holiday Spectacular* premiered at Radio City Music Hall. It was the first movie to premiere there in forty years, and it was unheard of for a basic cable movie. Something I never thought I'd experience in my life. Also of course, being on set is always wonderful, and a big highlight of every movie. If I can't be there, I love watching audition videos from casting. It's the first time I've seen any of the dialogue on its feet and there's no better feeling when you realize it works.

Another crazy highlight is that I created an event called Avon Winterfest in one of my movies. I literally did it as a diabolical plan to have the powers that be in my hometown of Avon see the movie and say, "Hey, why don't we have something like that? Let's do it!" Then a local charity decided they wanted to make it happen! There was a beer garden, ice skating, caroling, Santa, and yes - lots and lots of hot cocoa. They screened the movie outdoors as a drive-in movie with people snuggled up in their cars with the sound coming through the radio. Everyone kept saying it was just like a Hallmark movie. So mission accomplished!

As for the lowlights - getting fired from a show is always a blow. You go right to, "I guess that's it. I'm never working again." But I really do think everything happens for a reason. Getting canned gave me the time to write my first romantic comedy feature script which sold to Disney. Which led to another sale at Paramount, which led to my first Movie of the Week with Lifetime, which led to Hallmark. I wouldn't change a thing. Another lowlight was when I had a viewing party for the premiere of one of my movies, and I didn't realize until the moment it aired, that the director had completely rewritten the script during production. It was disconcerting, and very embarrassing, because it wasn't good. And that's putting it mildly. And yes, my name's still on it.

Emma Ko - The highlights - it's a job where you get to tell stories. You get to collaborate with brilliant, funny, smart, creative people. Ultimately, your work ends up on a screen. And if you're incredibly lucky, changing hearts and minds and making people laugh or cry or think differently. I mean, there's no better job. And all of this comes from the kernel in a screenwriter's mind. How do I tell this story? The lowlights are: it's lonely, competitive, full of rejection and has quite a lot of dubious people working in it.

Scott Lobdell - A big highlight was that Stan Lee and I were best friends for fifteen years, which was great considering I started out as a fan. At one point, he said to me, "I don't know how you do it with all these notes. It would drive me crazy because I could never deal with the studio notes and the producer notes." I told him that the first draft is art and everything after that is commerce. That's why I always feel it's important to write the draft that I want, then send it out and get it sold. And then everything after that, especially if they pay you, is theirs. Here's an example. I sold *Happy Death Day* to Universal and Rogue Pictures. It was written almost exactly like what you saw. There were changes, but it was essentially the same story. After we sold it and everything was signed, the two producers and the development executive at Rogue Pictures said they had a few notes. They said, "You do all this stuff where she wakes up and she talks about getting drunk with her friends. And she sleeps with this guy and this and this and this. But you're telling, you're not showing. What we want is instead of her waking up on page 1, we should have her wake up on page 20. That's where the movie starts. Every screenwriter knows that."

So they wanted the first twenty pages to be set up; showing her being rude to her roommate and not talking to her father. The father comes to her sorority house, but she tells her sorority friends to send him away. And that way, when she gets the phone call, we know she doesn't want to talk to the father. But I was like, "That's not what this movie is. This movie is a house of cards and if you start pulling cards at random, you're not going to have a movie." But they were insistent, and the rule is, the first draft is art, everything after is commerce. So I wrote it in a way that if that is the movie they wanted to see, this would be that. I turned it in and the producers were thrilled and the development executive was thrilled. They said that would send it up to the head of the studio and have a call with that person a few days later. That day comes and we're all on the phone. The head of the studio says, "What the fuck did I just read? I bought this dark, edgy, funny horror movie and now I feel like I'm reading *Melrose Place* or something. Why do I care about this one and she almost slept with that one? Why is all of this in here?" And the development executive said, "Scott, I apologize. This is all on us." She explained to the studio head "He was insisting this was not the direction to go. We pushed him in that direction and now we will bring him back." The studio head was fine with that. That's the thing, once it's theirs, they get to do what they want. I could say that I'm not going to do it, but they would say, "Okay, here's your two steps. See you later." Lowlight.

As for highlights, the worst day of writing is still better than the best day of work! I have not had a job in thirty-six years now. If I had to get a job tomorrow, they would look at my resume and see a huge gap. It's still better than the break room! It's still better than the manager being in a bad mood that day. People reporting you to the manager because their food got cold even though you didn't cook the food. And I think what will always be a highlight for me, is that I created a comic book called *Generation X* for Marvel Comics, which was a spin off of the *X-Men*. They did it as a Fox movie with Finola Hughes and Matt Frewer. At one point Jubilation Lee is introduced to... Angelo Espinoza! There is nothing more thrilling than seeing what started out as a blank sheet of paper and seeing it embodied by actors.

Another highlight was the premiere of *Happy Death Day* at Universal Studios. Afterward, there was a party and as I was leaving, I stopped because all the young actors and the crew people were all dancing away on the dance floor, having a great time. All of this was happening because I turned off my phone and unplugged my internet and I wrote *Happy Death Day*. And that only happened because I met a producer who said, "Of all the ideas you've pitched me, Scott, this is the one you should write." It's weird to know that it all starts from a blank page or a thought.

Carolina Rivera - The highlights are: you can be the god of your world. You have amazing power. Even in the pandemic when you couldn't go anywhere, you could go anywhere in your mind. I could be in a room for twenty hours and not care. I was not there. That's a highlight. Also, for me, filmmaking is a collaborative thing and being able to work with all this talent - that's a highlight, too. You work with the directors and the other writers, it's great. Especially, in the U.S. where you're also the producer.

Lowlights. In Mexico, most writers don't have the power to decide anything. You are very secluded from production. Nobody wants a writer on set. Nobody cares about what writers think and nobody includes them in the decision making. That is something we have been fighting because we are the creators of the worlds and the stories. We have to be able to have a say in the process.

Moisés Zamora - The highlights are two. The happy writing process of being able to create worlds and put everything together, I think it's just wonderful to be in that place. And, two, the end product. When you see Regina King performing your dialogue in a scene, it's just an incredible experience.

The lows. There are a lot of lows. You are going to get 99% rejected. Sometimes, not getting a no is also a low. Being a screenwriter is a lot of rejection. So build a community and do a lot of things that are not screenwriting in order to alleviate that. Also, working on something so hard for so long and not having it made because the budget wasn't there or the guy, and it's usually a guy, making that decision didn't connect with the piece. There goes a lot of time, effort and sweat.

When I talk with emerging writers and they say it's their calling and their purpose and they want to be in this business with the ups and downs, I tell them to go for it. But what we do is volatile. We're contractual. It was eight months before I started making money again from show to show. If you're wealthy and you don't have to worry about that, then by all means. That was not my case. It's a really weird and anxious place to be, but it's also very rewarding. I find other ways to fulfill my writing needs other than screenwriting. You will find a lot of writers do that, too, in order to fight the lows.

Deborah Haywood - The lowlights are following paths that I shouldn't have followed because people told me I should follow them. *Pin Cushion*, I took it to Binger Filmlab in Amsterdam and they said it was too plot-y. They didn't understand it. It doesn't have to have story. It can just be about character or feeling or whatever. So I went off and I wrote something that is great for character, but it wasn't a page turner. Then I applied to iFeatures and they were looking for something more "bums on seats." So I tried to make it all teenage exciting, but it wasn't. It went away from the tone to a more like, trashy humorous tone. Both times I felt like I was betraying myself. It wasn't until Lizzie Francke said come to the BFI and write it, but first go away, and think about what you really want to write. That's when I went back to the original tone and fairy tale. Thank God she said that because I think I was chasing it from the wrong way.

The highlights. I think just learning. Learning a bit of craft that's going to help me down the line. When you get notes from people and they say they've really connected with it. Or they felt like that. That's a highlight. Just getting any kind of commission is a highlight, isn't it? I never ever thought I would end up doing this. I was pregnant at sixteen. I failed to get into the biscuit factory. I've got no qualifications. So to think that I could get any kind of commission, that's like the biggest highlight. Somebody said to me, "It's easy getting into the industry. The hardest part is staying in it." So hopefully at the end of my career, I can look back and say these are the highlights. It's a bit of a retrospective thing, isn't it? I'm still learning everything.

Alex Litvak - The low point of writing is writing. I always say there are two stages in the life of a screenwriter. It's either shit or THE shit. Invariably, in the course of any project, I go, "I don't know why I am wasting my time. It's not good and nobody will care." Then invariably, there's a point on the same project where I go, "Oh my, God. Steven Spielberg is going to be on his knees begging me to direct this." The truth is somewhere in the middle, so you have to just stay the course and you can't let the bad days get you down or get high on your own supply. You have to keep running the marathon and that's the hardest part. You have to finish. I wrote twenty pages of the script! Good for you, where's the other 100? If it's not done, you've got nothing. And then you get into your rewriting, which is how do you deal with preserving the good that is there while making it better.

Another low point is the version of writer's block where you have a scene and you don't know how to get from point A to point B. And many times I highly advocate walking away. Like when you are looking for your keys and you don't know where they are. Walk out of the room and come back in an hour or tomorrow and you will find the keys. Writing partnerships are great or if you are writing solo, it's good to have people you can talk to because invariably you can talk it out. I'm working on one thing with a writing partner. She called me and said she was stuck on something and then I was able to solve it in five seconds. It was simply because she was in it for an hour and she was pitching it to me and I said, why don't we try this and great, it was solved.

The high moments are when you finish a great scene. It's a sense of accomplishment. At the end of the day, you cannot seek validation from people. Yes, it's nice to get paid and it's nice when your stuff gets made. But at the end of the day, you have to find validation in telling a good story. That was me on that page. I created something that was good and entertaining and it would not exist if I did not put my blood, sweat and tears into it. Everyone wants to get paid and get stuff made. But I can tell you that stuff gets made for a million reasons that have nothing to do with you. The things of mine that got made, versus the things that didn't, was because it was the right moment at the right time.

Karen Walton - Lowlights. I would call the creative or career phase I was in most recently, recovery. It took me years to realize that I was injured, as an artist. I was tired. If I were a dancer I would have that thing where I couldn't dance anymore. Or a singer who suddenly couldn't sing. I lost my voice. I felt I lost my passion. I wasn't convinced anymore that the way I tell stories, or the stories I wanted to tell were necessary, or had value. All I had learned about the job was turning me off the job. So lowlights were saying yes to some of the wrong people or the wrong projects for the wrong reasons: gigs that would drag on, were abusive or fucked-up in whatever way, trying to deliver while wondering if you can afford it - emotionally and financially. And ultimately, being convinced I would always only be writing in service of some white guy's vision. My generation of women who write were always told how lucky we were just to be there, no matter the working environment - you were working! "Suck it up!" We were made to feel that any sort of real issue was our problem, a personality flaw. It took a very long time for me to understand that the issues in screenwriting and the industry I was encountering, weren't my own personal failings. They were my own values colliding with reality, and what I was internalizing was just toxic crap nobody deserves. If I had known that sooner, who knows what I might have accomplished.

However, I have the great privilege of a place in a profession, a career in creative work. This is extraordinary. I know lots of people feel they are totally deserving and entitled, not me. I'm lucky to live where I live and get to be a working screenwriter. I know some people feel totally entitled and deserving in my profession, that their own ideas or "talent" is all it takes, and should therefore be seen and rewarded. I don't think so. I got to learn on the job, and evolve as a human being because I was included as a screenwriter, a voice, one perspective. I didn't start writing until I was thirty years old. I learned a lot of unfortunate things, bad habits and for a long time, I internalized systemic BS. I also got to make my own mistakes. And then I got to learn how to change things for all of us, or at least try.

As to highlights - once I went to a salon and my name was called out for my appointment. A lady with her toes in a bath and her hair in curlers goes, "You're not Karen Walton?!" It wasn't the fact of being recognized, it was the fact that she was a teenager who saw a character and a story that you told which then changed how she felt about herself. I love that. Did I think that would ever happen? I don't remember writing *Ginger Snaps*, saying, "I am going to change the world for a group of teenagers in Minnesota at a slumber party ten years from now!" I'm thinking: does this suck? But it's seeing people talk about stories that matter to them - that's why I write.

Marsha Greene - A definite lowlight is working in a room where the vibe is not good. I think of the writers room as my happy place. I was once in a room where it was just a bad vibe. The show and the company - it was really quite contentious. Having to go there every day and deal with that energy was like - I can't do it. I once took a job just for the money. I was working on *The Porter* thinking it was going to get greenlit the following year so I just needed a little bit of money to keep me going; a short job. It was a lowlight because in the end, I didn't think I was right for the show. I had a lot of trouble writing the script. I really struggled. I couldn't find myself in the work. Not only did I feel bad for myself, I felt bad for the showrunners who obviously were going to have to rewrite it. I was never going to do that again. It felt like a good reason at the time, but now I realize it wasn't. The other thing that was a struggle for me, was that writing had always been my outlet and now it had become my job and that changes your relationship to it. There are these moments, of course, where you are coming up with stories and it's fun, but, ultimately, it's your livelihood. I had to get new hobbies. So I made that writing gig decision as a business decision, but it wasn't the right choice for me as an artist. Those are the growing pains you go through.

Highlight. Every 'first' was a huge highlight. I remember getting my first script. I was walking down the street in the Fall and I couldn't believe after all this time, it's really going to happen. I remember it airing for the first time. That was the first time I got a half-script. Then the next season, I got a full script. My own name, alone. Then, the first time I was nominated for a Canadian Screen Award. So many highs.

The Porter being greenlit was such a highlight. Partially, because we had worked on it for many years. We were poised to pitch it and then the pandemic hit. Once again, it was going to set *The Porter* back for more years. So when we found out it was greenlit, it was such a thrill. I was losing hope that we were ever going to make the show.

The reason it was so momentous for me is because it was a crux in time when I had a good job and I made this decision to leave it all behind and become a screenwriter. I felt confident in the decision because I knew if I didn't do so, I would always wonder, what would have happened if I didn't try? I had been writing my whole life, but never thought I could make it a job. And along the whole way, when you tell people what you're doing, people are telling you it's a crazy dream. When I quit my job and told my boss that I was going to become a screenwriter, he said, "You have to be a very good writer for that." Then he said, "I know two people who work in TV. One produces a fishing show and the other produces a fishing show." Basically, these two people who had their pipe dreams, failed. When I told my boyfriend, he said, "There comes an age when you have to give up these dreams. You are foolishly giving up on our real life to chase this thing." When I told a work colleague, "I am doing this, but I want to be a writer." She'd say to me, "Oh yeah, I wanted that too once upon a time." You're constantly getting these messages: you're dreaming; it's not real; it's not going to happen. So when I gave up my successful career, I had a lot of doubts. I was so broke and applying for assistant jobs or writing jobs and not getting them. I'd often think, "What have I done?" I remember filling out a form and I had to list my accomplishments. I had won an English award when I was in Grade 8. I had won an essay competition at university. I was thinking, "Am I done?" Are all my accomplishments from when I was a child?

One of the things that attracted me to screenwriting was that there seemed to be a lifetime of things to strive for. You never feel like you've conquered it. There's always another thing to do. I've written a show, there's another one I can do. I've been nominated for a CSA, but I haven't been nominated for a Writers Guild Award. Or an Emmy. Being able to pitch to Netflix, Apple and Hulu. Everything feels like such a high and such an accomplishment. It feels so rare, as we know from all the other people in world who've not been able to achieve their dreams.

Dan Mazer - The highlight of screenwriting, the honest answer, is somebody giving you a call to say that they have bought your pitch. That's it. That's fantastic! That's great. From that moment on, it's pretty miserable. You are sitting on your own in a coffee shop or in your office for days on end trying to work out if it's good and driving yourself crazy and being paranoid about whether you've shat the bed and your career is over. That is until the next time you sell a pitch. The phone calls are the highlight. We've bought your pitch; we've been greenlit; those are the highlights because those are the times you interact with any other human being and feel that the thing that you've invented in your head is real. Before that, it's just a bunch of pretend people on a page and it could be something or nothing. You could spend two years on something that just disappears into the ether, or it could be a film that gets nominated for an Oscar. It's only the phone calls that distinguish that because the process remains the same, regardless. Those to me are the highlights.

The lowlights. Sometimes, it's depressing to see what some people have done with your ideas, which is why I wanted to become a director. You have conjured this world and these characters in your mind and in reality the execution is nothing like you imagined. Sometimes, it's better, but it tends to be worse, in my experience. It's the old joke about the actress who tried to sleep with the writer to get on in Hollywood. As a writer, you don't really get involved in any of the fun parts of filmmaking. Frankly, it's fun to be on set with all the glamorous actors, the private jets, and the executives. As the writer, you sort of hand it over and you are forgotten about. That can be quite hard. I went to the Oscars for the first time when *Borat* was nominated for Best Screenplay. You are very aware of your place in the hierarchy, which is being shouted out to get out of the way of real stars. You think this is the pinnacle of your career. You are on the red carpet and Wesley Snipes is behind you and the only thing anyone is shouting at you is, "Get out of the way! Get out of the way!" I remember going in the limo, you drive up and there are banks of crowds and you have to wind down your window to have your identity checked or whatever. I remember being so excited at arriving at the Oscars in my limo, winding down the window and having 3,000 people collectively groan. "Oh, it's the writer." So if you are looking for external validation and celebration, then writing is not the job for you.

It's weird. There's no sort of parameter in the actual process of writing of good or bad or success. If you're a trader, you do a deal. If you're a builder, you finish a house. If you're a plumber, you fix a toilet. You've come out of your day with something tangible. I can come out of my day thinking that I've written a good scene, but I can't tell anybody about that.

Nobody sees that. It's a very solitary craft, which suits some people and on some days, I like it. But it can be a bit depressing.

Jed Mercurio - I think the lowlights are, firstly, not getting your work produced. Rejection, in other words. Then the other lowlight is when your work is produced, but in a way that you are not happy. I think lots of writers have had both of those experiences. I think the first one of outright rejection is something that we all have to deal with and we all have to recover from. It happens to every writer, no matter how successful. It happens to me, week in, week out. It happens now at the point I am in my career, and it happened early in my career. You can set aside how successful you appear to be. Often, the decision is made purely on the needs of the network or the studio and it's got nothing to do with the quality of your work.

The other one is much harder to deal with because it can be quite an insidious process where you are embarking on a project in good faith and, for whatever reason, it's going in the wrong direction. Steps aren't being taken to firstly recognize that, and secondly, to redirect the project towards what it should be doing. There are a lot of writers who can be quite traumatized by that. That's probably the lowest of the low.

The highlights are abundant if you are lucky enough and privileged enough to have your work produced and for it to connect with an audience. That's an incredibly fulfilling experience. So being part of successful shows, being part of projects that are well regarded, is very uplifting for writers.

Josh Greenberg - Highlights. For someone who hadn't done multi-cam and then got to experience it, feeling the energy from a big crowd of people laughing at your jokes being said by an actor, is the coolest thing ever. I mean, talk about immediate gratification. When you write a movie, you write some dialogue and it could be a decade later that an actor says it. When you are doing a multi-camera, I've had times where a joke isn't working and right on the spot you think of an alt, "What if a character says this?" Then you run over to the actor and you say, "Okay, you are going to say this line." Then they do the scene and you have 200 people roaring with laughter. There is no greater feeling. Then you get to drive home feeling all good about yourself. I even think that translates to when you are writing alone. If I am writing a scene by myself and I come up with a satisfying scene or turn, that is really a great feeling. That is a real high.

In terms of the lowlights, it's really struggling with how to make the story work. You can feel that there's a lot of potential to make the story work, but we just can't quite figure it out. That is just so damn frustrating. But the nice thing is that it usually gets resolved. Someone says something and it all starts to come together. It's a short-lived frustration. Every show that I've been on has those moments; really gratifying joy where you're really proud of something that you've done and frustration at not being able to crack an idea or story.

Meg LeFauve - Highlights has been working at Pixar with all these incredibly creative people who so deeply care about storytelling. Of course, the cherry on that cake has been *Inside Out* because of the effect it's had on people. I met a woman once who said to me, "You really made my job so much easier." I thought maybe she worked with kids. I've heard it's helped non-verbal autistic people and their therapists. This woman said, "I work for the city of Los Angeles and when there's a trauma with children involved, I am immediately able to connect with them because we talk about your characters and how they are feeling." Who needs anything else to happen in their lives? Who needs awards or anything? I was part of something that is helping people communicate with each other; connect with each other; and support each other. That is what storytelling is all about.

Lowlights, it's hard. Art is hard. Art is fire. Art is opening yourself up and being vulnerable. Art is failure. Is it a lowlight? Yes, nobody wants to fail. Nobody wants something to not work out. To not have it be what it could have been. For it not to get made. But that is art and you don't get the other half of it without that. Even in the low, you are learning something that you can bring back to your next story.

Bill Nicholson - The lowlights are when it doesn't happen; when it fizzles out. The whole thing collapses. In the olden days, you could do several drafts on a Hollywood picture and then everyone would just go silent. You would find out after a while that some other writer is writing it. Nobody ever tells you, and that's really hard. They don't like bad news calls. They like good news calls. 50% of the screenplays I've worked on have never been made. But then I've got twenty-one films that are written by me, that have been made. That's a decent amount. However, I'm very grateful because in my life, the film world has been well paid and there are very few creative arenas that have actually got any money in them.

Also, if you write a film and the director screws up, then that's bad. If a film does well, then everyone congratulates the director, yet it is the writer who creates the whole story, all the characters, and all the scenes. Having said that, brilliant directors do things that are beyond anything that I have done. Ridley Scott for instance, with *Gladiator*. I saw what he did with what I had written and it was amazing. You do need a great director, the right cast, a great cinematographer, and a great designer. And, of course, you need great music. It has to have a fantastic track.

Jennifer Raite - With the lowlights, there's a lot of heartbreak. You have to care so much about every individual project because they require so much individual energy. You have to be the champion of your own project. You are its parent. You are its life force that's not going to come from anywhere else. Eventually, there may be producers buoying that with you, who care almost as fundamentally as much as you do. But it's coming from you! So when those things don't work out, it's devastating in a way that only other writers will understand. We had something that we really loved, not go. And a couple of Chris' writer friends wrote him this beautiful caring note and gave him a gift. Only these people understand. There is a mourning, as much as there is a love, a birth, and an energy that all of these things create. When they don't happen, which is often, you have to go through that emotional turmoil every time. It's wonderful and horrible.

Highlights? Making our film, *The Aviary*, is a pinnacle so far. We got to make the movie with Jessica Rhoades who we met at Blumhouse. She's the producer we have worked with the longest and who was the champion of our first project when we were literally no-one. Having this creative shorthand with her and her producing partner and having so much of it build from the creative core of the four of us. And having so much creative freedom and support, even within the constraints of a low budget film, and getting to carry something all the way to its completion. That's one of the ones that we didn't have to bury. It gets to live forever.

This straddles a highlight and career advice: when you find those people who get what you are doing and who want to work with you, and you feel that they are easy to fold into your world - hang onto them! If you were to ask our reps, they would tell you they want you to be as diversified as possible; work with lots of different people. Expand. There are a lot of good reasons to do that, but when you find people who will go into battle with you; don't let them go.

Chris Cullari - There was a project, I can't say what it was, but it had the exact same title, the exact same concept as our film. This person had been in our brains. I don't think it was stolen, but it was a really crushing lesson in somebody got there first. And a really crushing lesson in your idea wasn't as cool as you thought it was. We asked our agent if our script had been sent out somewhere, and there was just no way it could have happened. We don't know the person. I doubt they ever read our material. Someone else had it and they beat us to it.

But the highlight reel is incredible. Making our own movie. Writing *12 Deadly Days*. Getting to work with Ed Sanchez who directed *The Blair Witch Project* and Joe Lynch on that show. Getting one of the *Blair Witch* stars, Josh Leonard, to be in *The Blair Witch* director's episode and see them have a little on set reunion. Getting the stamp of approval from John Carpenter. He read one of our pilots, liked it and had a meeting with us. He said, "You guys are really good at this. What else do you want to do?"

Eli Craig - I've had a lot of lowlights. One of the funniest that laid out the business for me was early on when I was acting in these terrible movies like *Carrie 2*. I got a job in a Clint Eastwood movie, *Space Cowboys*. The role was playing Tommy Lee Jones as a young guy. I thought this was cool, I'll be an actor. So I went to the audition and I will talk like Tommy Lee Jones. I get the part. I didn't even think I sounded like Tommy Lee Jones, but I am going to give it my best. So I'm playing alongside this actor who is playing Clint Eastwood as a young guy. We can't believe it! We're flying jet airplanes. We're in a Clint Eastwood movie. In the meantime, I'm writing this script that gets set up at Tom Cruise's company. I'm killing it, I think. Then, the Tom Cruise script gets dumped. They make it as a documentary. The Clint Eastwood movie comes out and my voice gets completely dubbed over by the real Tommy Lee Jones. All my friends were wondering what I did for that role. Did I smoke twenty packs of cigarettes a day? You sound just like Tommy Lee Jones! And then I realized that this isn't going to be that easy. Nobody told me I was going to be dubbed over. They just did it. So I went back to the drawing board and started writing comedy.

As to highlights, three years after coming up with the idea of *Tucker and Dale* at USC Film School, I am at the film's opening at Sundance at the Library, with about 1,200 people! Nobody had seen the film. We had just finished it three days before. We were scrambling to get it finished. And it opened with so much laughter. I couldn't believe how well it did. And, of course, there were no buyers. Everyone was like, "Cool movie, dude!" It took us nine months to sell this movie. It was 2010, so it was a bad year for film. It didn't actually get released until the end of 2011. It was released in six theaters and three people saw it. Then it went to Netflix and then everyone saw it. A lot of people pirated it. It had a real indie following that I didn't even know about. I was writing and getting jobs, but it wasn't until four years later that people started saying, "Dude, I saw *Tucker and Dale*! That was incredible!" Really? You saw it? Where? One of the few movies in history that found an audience three to five years after it was made. Of course, I would have rather it hit right away. I'm not going to lie. But it was better than it just disappearing. Alan Tudyk, who played Tucker, texted me after it opened, "Dude, what happened? Did we even open this weekend?" That was a high and a low. There are so many highs and lows and I think, as a writer, you have to accept that it's an up and down lifestyle.

The final thing I would say about writing is setting up your life so that you can be okay with you writing. Most of the time, it feels so self-indulgent, like you're wasting time. Especially when you're starting. You're just this guy in a room writing. It feels like you are not doing anything. That's why I'm a director, too. I'm a do-er. Sometimes, I would rather go outside and dig up a garden. Look! I dug a trench. Congratulations! I did something! But to go to work and write on a page and maybe nothing will happen and get your family to support that through the ups and down and not give up on that, that's by far the hardest part. I think the only thing that makes a writer a writer, is that they get up and write. They don't procrastinate too much doing all the things that can take up your day and with all the things that can make you feel like you are doing things in life. Our society is made for people to go to work and toiling doing stuff that they probably don't really love. At the end of the week, they probably feel like they did something. At the end of the week of writing, you just throw away all your pages and feel miserable.

Ron Leshem - Lowlights. I got used to everyone saying "no" and sometimes in a humiliating way. The hardest part is when you always feel disappointed. Not when you bring a pitch and they say it's not good enough. Or a pilot. That happens daily. But when you go into production and your rewrites are not good enough. Or you are late with rewrites. When you go to bed knowing that everyone is disappointed, not in your talent, it's just that everyone is always angry at you. So there are lots of moments where you feel frustrated. We all have had ideas that we thought would be the next big thing and before you were able to create it, someone else did. Many times you hear about people stealing ideas from their partners. Not that they are thrown out of the project, but that someone else chooses the tone or you get minimized.

I guess the highlights will usually be one of two scenarios. A show that gets a life out of the screen and becomes 360 degrees of deep emotional engagement. We had that not only with *Euphoria*, but also with *Valley of Tears*, *Incitement* and *Beaufort* for example, where Wikipedia's official statistics, for over two months, showed that true stories from the show constantly occupied at least one of the five top most searched pages in Israel. The other scenario is when I take a fifteen or twenty four-hour flight to the other side of the universe just to meet local audiences who watch our stories, and give different interpretations to it.

Lauren Iungerich - The lowlights are going totally unseen and dealing with the uncreative side of the business. It can be a tough environment. But as for highlights, after the first season of *Awkward* came out, my highlight was seeing how many people loved the show; their connection to it. There was a kid, who has since become my penpal, who Facebook friended me telling me that he loved the show and that I got him through high school. I love being a storyteller. I love finding the story, making the story work, but connecting to a human being who really needs your work and who tells you that it got them through something - that's a highlight.

Tony Jordan - Lowlights, that's real easy - Fade In and Fade Out. Fade In and you've got that pain waiting for you. That self doubt. That loathing. Again, go back to William Goldman who said, "Screenwriting is easy. Just stare at a blank piece of paper until your forehead bleeds." Fade In and Fade Out. That's the joy and the ecstasy and everything else.

Highlights are when you write something, everybody loves it, it's a hit - a sensation. It's like you've become a good writer overnight. I've had shows that have bombed. That's no fun. All of those things are true, but if you boil it down to its essence - Fade In - it's not really a low point. Maybe that's the high point. Depends on how you view things. Fade In can be a high point where you love what you do and can't wait to get stuck in and Fade Out is your lowest point because you've finished and the journey's over. Or you could do it the other way around, which is Fade In, "Fucking hell, I feel so unprepared! I feel inadequate! I don't think I have enough talent to do this!" And Fade Out, "Wow, how on Earth did I manage to get to this point? I love it and I'm happy with what I've written."

Michael Brandt - The highlight is always when I'm alone and it is personal. It's never been the red carpet. It's never been seeing an audience react. Those are good, but they are always so far removed from the time that I wrote the show or movie. The highlight is when you've finished a scene and you think it worked. That's what I wanted to do, no matter whether someone else gets it or not. I got there and it was better than I thought it was going to be. It's not ego. It's an accomplishment. If you're writing because you want to see your movie on the big screen and see people stand up and applaud, you are going to be disappointed. It's not that it's not going to happen, but if it does, it's gonna happen two years after you were working on it. When I wrote *Arthur the King*, I wrote it and COVID happened. People aren't going to see it until at least four years after I started writing it. What I do know is that there were moments when I was sitting alone and I was writing stuff I really liked; that I actually got moved by. That is why I do it.

I could see receiving notes that are harsh, as a lowlight. But, that's not as bad as writing something that you know isn't good; that you know doesn't work. I'm bulletproof to notes. Not that I won't do them, but I've already accomplished my highlights and lowlights when I was by myself writing. All of the notes stuff is just business. The studio wants this. The director needs this. This is the new actor. This needs to be a woman. Now, you're doing the business of it. I take that business back to my little hive and I'm alone again where I try to accomplish the highlights and avoid the lowlights again. It all happens there, for me. That is why I want to be a writer. That is my reason to be. Like being in the flow and the characters speaks to you and they take over - that's why you do it.

Scott Beck - We tried to make our first film with a budget of $1.5 million. It played in ten theaters across the nation. It played in Los Angeles, and Bryan and I made a pact. It only played for a week, but on the last night, we are going to go to the very last show. We know nobody else is going to be there and it will be a swan song of sorts. It's the script that we wrote, worked on for years, it's on the screen, nobody is going to be there. We go to the theater and we go to buy tickets and the person at the counter looks at us kind of confused and says, "No, the last screening of that film we canceled. We had to make room for the new *Fast and the Furious*." It was this realization where you can be on your dream of selling your scripts, getting the movie made, and getting it on the screen but that still doesn't make it bulletproof to making it to the very last night. There was a poignancy to that, which was a low, but was also a high, meaning it kicks you in the teeth, but you realize how lucky you are to be working in this industry. To get something made and to celebrate it with somebody else. It was bizarre because we were sitting at a diner commiserating when we should be watching the movie, but this is about the journey. It's not about the end goal. We should be celebrating small moments throughout our career. That is something we have taken to heart since that moment. Did you get a good day's worth of writing in? Did you write two pages when you set out to write one? That is all you need sometimes and you don't need an Academy Award to solidify what you have achieved.

Bryan Woods - *A Quiet Place* was the other end of the spectrum where people did go see it. The critics did like it. It was the mirror opposite of what happened on our first film. It didn't change that the writing is the fun part. You would rather it be successful than not be successful, but it doesn't change the fact that the most fun part about being a filmmaker is using your imagination, creating work, and working with friends and collaborators that you love. It was full circle confirmation on why we do what we do.

Ben Philippe - I love this job. It's not a job I thought I would have for a very long time. I was an economics major in college, but pretty soon I found out I liked film and writing. I took a risk and majored in that. I was afraid I wouldn't find a job and I didn't for a long time. I was cleaning houses. Working as a freelance paralegal. It takes longer to break in than most careers. I went to Columbia University and got my MFA at the University of Texas - Austin, moved to New York and found myself still at square one. Okay, maybe square four by then but still no clue what to do next. If you want to be a doctor, you go to medical school, then you get an internship. It's structured in a way. But when you are a writer, no two writers have the same career. Some writers are like, "My parents are producers so they got me a writer's assistant position and then I worked my way up from there." Some are geniuses who sold shows early and started at showrunner. There is no map. That can be scary. My students ask me how to start as a TV writer and I always say, "I don't know…by continuing to scratch until the door gives way and you hopefully have some fingers left!" I did the thing of moving to Los Angeles and I moved back after four months. I was exhausted and broke and didn't know how to drive and didn't have connections. In a way, the BlueCat Screenwriting Competition was a way to get validation that I was good at this and I could take meetings.

I would say my lowlight would be my early 20s. The first six years of doing this is not a linear path. I wrote books and was teaching writing before I was an actual working writer. That's already very strange. It's exhausting to break in. That's a universal thing. I was entering contests and not getting to the semi-finals of some. It feels a little random and it takes longer than you think. To be a staff writer on a show, you might get it at 24, you might be in your early 30s, you might get it in your early 40s.

My highlight? Everything else. I love this job. Even when I'm fighting over the most simple story points, which I've done on *Only Murders in the Building* with Stephen Marley. We were on Zoom screaming at each other for seventy-four minutes about whether there should be a peephole or a crease in the door. I remember screaming like this was the most important thing in the world. Eventually, Stephen won out and I remember thinking I didn't want to ever write again. Of course, now Stephen and I are trying to develop our own show. That argument was actually a highlight for me, a seventy-four minute fight about a door crease versus a peephole. It's one of my favorite memories. I wish we'd recorded it.

Dave Reynolds - Every writer can have lowlights of a script being bought and not being made. I had a script that sold to Fox and they said it was going to be a tentpole for them. Then after I did a year's worth of rewriting on it, Fox was swallowed up by Disney and my script, like a lot of Fox projects was buried under the rubble. So that wasn't great.

Getting my first TV job was great and that was a crazy two years. I'm still jittery after that some twenty-eight years later! Working on *Finding Nemo* as you can imagine was great. *Emperor's New Groove* was so crazy and fun because it was created literally from the ashes. I love that it's become a cult movie and it's still really popular. I get kids in universities or colleges come up to me talking about that movie. A marketing person once said if you want to see how successful your animated movie is, check out how many tattoos there are of your characters. So, go ahead and Google, "*The Emperor's New Groove* tattoos" and watch out! It's crazy. Validation truly does come in many forms.

CHAPTER REVIEW: PERSPECTIVE

- Every writer has highs and lows in the entertainment business.

- Writing is solitary, so if that bothers you, consider directing, too. Or go into series writing where you could end up in a writers room.

- Notes and other feedback can be harsh, so try to remember that they are there to help make the project better. It's not personal.

- Projects can seem like they are going to get made and then fizzle out. Conversely, dead projects can sometimes come back to life. You need to keep an even keel.

- Getting your project made is exciting and seeing your name in the credits never gets old.

- A writing career is a marathon not a sprint. Perseverance is key.

- No matter what, keep writing!

CHAPTER 22

INSPIRATION

───────

We hope that you've found the perspectives and tips our contributors gave to be useful and motivational as you pursue your own writing path. But what inspires them? In this final chapter, we put that question to them, as well as any final advice they may want to share.

Q: Who inspires you as a screenwriter?

Paul King - Dead people, mostly! In terms of the writing, most of my touchstones tend to be older films. I don't think this is just because they don't make them like that anymore - although they don't. This is embarrassing, but I find contemporary films harder to watch because I am so anxious about the practicalities of it. Oh, there's that costume designer or that DP that I would like to work with. They got this or that and they have X or Y funding. The business of making it, changes my enjoyment of it. Who did that set extension? Oh, it was Framestore. I must try to work with them. I can shut all that noise off because I am not jealous of anyone in a Frank Capra film. They are all dead. I can't use the costume designer. I can't get Jimmy Stuart to be in the film. I don't have to worry about whether he said something embarrassing on Twitter. It's more relaxing and I can just enjoy it.

Danny Strong - My biggest influence is Arthur Miller, the playwright. Playwrights, in general, like Edward Albee, Ibsen, Chekov - I think the amount of emotion and depth they create on stage is very impressive. I love the films of Sydney Pollack and Sydney Lumet, even though they are directors. There is a tone and an energy to those pieces that inspire me quite a bit.

Becca Topol - There are so many great writers! I read a lot of fiction. I'm mesmerized by the work of Elif Batuman and Annie Ernaux. In terms of screenwriters, I am a huge fan of Amy Poehler, Tina Fey, Issa Rae, and Michaela Coel. They are all strong storytellers who have a unique point of view. I find Issa and Michaela particularly inspiring for the work they have done and am so grateful their voices are out in the world.

Julie Sherman Wolfe - I know this is a total cliché for a romantic comedy writer, but number one is Nora Ephron. Obviously, I love all the chaste rom-coms of the past such as *Pillow Talk, Singin' in the Rain,* and *Roman Holiday.* They had to create sexual tension with nothing more than subtext and innuendo, and it took skills! I worked at a movie theater in the 80s when *When Harry Met Sally* came out. I saw it probably thirty times! That's when I knew that was the kind of writing I wanted to do and that I could do. Nancy Meyers and Carrie Fisher belong in that group, too. But that being said, my favorite snarky, quippy, sarcastic writer, in all forms, not just screenwriting, is Dorothy Parker. Her writing took no prisoners, made no apologies, and she basically created the concept of a writers room with the Algonquin Round Table. She's my, "If you could have dinner with anyone from any time in history" answer.

Alex Litvak - There are two screenwriters that I credit with me having a career: William Goldman and Shane Black. I highly recommend them. It may not be your cup of tea, but you should check them out because they are great storytellers. These guys have a way of telling a story where you are instantly glued. Instantly, you are on the edge of your seat. I always think of Shane Black and Bill Goldman as your favorite uncle coming over for dinner and saying, "Listen, kid. I'm going to tell you a story. And you are going to pay attention. It's going to be fun and exciting and you are going to be in it for the ride." They just own you. So much of the personality of the storytelling is coming through. The classic example I always give is when you read a traditional script and it reads:

> INT. JOHN'S APARTMENT - NIGHT
> John's alone. There's a knock on the door. He opens it and there's Jane.

That's how a classic writer would write it. Here's how Shane Black or Bill Goldman would write it...

> INT. JOHN'S APARTMENT - NIGHT
> A shit hole. Actually, that would be a compliment. John is alone. Another
> TV dinner night. A knock at the door. He opens it. There's Jane. She could stop traffic. Air traffic.

It's the same thing you are going to see in the shot, but somehow it's told with such gusto, and some snap, crackle and pop, you can't help but go, "Yeah, tell me more."

My favorite Bill Goldman scripts are *The Princess Bride* and *Butch Cassidy and The Sundance Kid*. There are so many quotable lines and tremendous performances and great directing. To me, those movies are a celebration of writing. If you look at the scripts for these movies, and I know we have the hindsight of all those actors, so much of it is in the writing.

I was taking a writing class in college and it was for a short film. I turned in the first draft and the teacher said that it read like a short story. At that time, my background was in journalism and short creative stories. I had never done screenwriting. He told me that I should check out of the library a copy of a script for a movie that I'd seen so I could understand how the images get translated into words. My script had a little bit of action, so one of the scripts I looked at was *Lethal Weapon*. There was so much there!

There's also, within a slightly different genre and book writing, Stephen King. Some great stories, some not so great stories, but always told incredibly well. He has a tremendous collection of essays called *On Writing*, which I very much recommend. Bill Goldman has *Adventures In The Screen Trade*, which I read at the beginning of my writing decades ago. There's Donald Westlake who as Richard Stark writes the *Parker* series, which ironically is possibly going to be made at Amazon with Shane Black. Razor sharp. Everything is so muscular and taut. There's a show I'm doing, which is very much influenced by the writings of Richard Stark. And a British writer who I'm a tremendous fan of - Joe Ambercrombie. After finishing the *Song of Ice and Fire* series, I was trying to find something else in the fantasy space. Tolkien was a huge inspiration for me as a kid, but I didn't want to do the orcs and goblins. I stumbled upon Joe Ambercrombie and I am a die-hard fan. I love what he does. He takes these genres be it a Western or a heist movie and sets them in this fantasy world. His last trilogy was taking Victor Hugo's *Les Mes* and mixing it with Charles Dickens' *Tale of Two Cities*. Tremendous writer. If he ever reads this book, just know that I am devotee! And by the way, in audiobooks, there's this guy called Steven Pacey who is a master!

Mohamad El Masri - Right now, Sally Rooney is redefining my idea of what's possible. She's remarkable. Sally has become the voice of millennial angst and agita. She's the Irish Mishima or Murakami. Her ability to capture generational tension, anxiety, and stunted growth with grounded, human, intimate, and compassionate characters is story craft working at its highest level.

The chief study in Sally's work is to realize that her small stories, which are rooted in rich and messy relationships, are actually imbued with a lot of really big, profound social ideas and commentary. It's a great study in how to do that through character and emotional psychology. *Normal People,* both the book and the series adaptation, is some of the best dramatic writing of the last ten years. *Beautiful World Where Are You,* which is also being adapted to screen, is a great study in structure and character. Sally's work is just incredibly fresh and exciting, but also what she's saying about the world around her is essential. It's writing at its absolute best and most inventive.

Barbara Stepansky - I'm a fan of the auteurs. Many of the writers that I admire happen to also be directors because I feel that it is a unified vision that you see on the screen that is so beautiful. So Jane Campion, Alfonso Cuarón, and Billy Ray. I'm reading *Overlord* by Billy Ray right now because I watched *Overlord* in the theaters and loved it and then his name shows up in the end credits and I'm like, of course! I was very lucky enough to talk to him early in my career. Probably my all-time favorite writer.

Josh Olson - For me, I get so much more out of studying films, and then, I read the script. The script always feels like it's the unfinished version, because it is. I will learn more about how they made it work on screen. There are so many filmmakers whose work I love; whose influence I bring into my work. I like something that's carefully constructed and thoughtfully designed. There was a movie that I saw as a kid which was more of a learning experience than I thought at the time called *Charlie Varrick*, written by Howard Rodman and directed by Don Siegel, right after *Dirty Harry*, starring Walter Matthau.

Back in the day, my dad and I would go see a movie and if it was sold out, you would go in next door to another movie even if it had started forty five minutes ago. When it was done, you'd stay for the beginning because they started again right after. So we walked into the middle of *Charlie Varrick* which is this clockwork precision thriller. I remember watching the beginning after I'd seen the ending, and marveling as a kid thinking, "They plan this stuff!"

If you are watching the film for the first time, you don't get that it's important that he takes his wife's ring when she dies at the beginning. But at the end, boy is it important. I saw *The Sting* the same way. I love that if you were paying even more careful attention than you are, you would be able to see the ending coming a mile away, and yet nobody does. They are telling you literally everything you need to know to see the ending and you're not going to figure it out. Wow, that's so cool! I love that.

Meg LeFauve - I love the magazine journal, *The Sun*. Not in terms of looking for specific stories, but in the amount of truth-telling going on in the articles and short stories. It always is a great touchstone for me. This is what it's about. This kind of truth-telling. The amount of reflection on the human condition. I read that magazine every month and it reinvigorates me. Also, helping other people with their stories, really helps me stay connected to the fact that I am a story junkie. I do love helping other people dig into things and watching their head crack open when they say, "Oh, my God! That's what I'm doing!" To help bring that into consciousness, just by asking questions. I'm not a miracle worker. Ask questions and they all of a sudden understand what they are trying to do. That inspires me.

Scott Beck - M. Night Shyamalan. We have read all the scripts of his that we can get our hands on. We love his ability to get back on the horse and write again and also try to provoke an audience. *The Sixth Sense*, *Unbreakable*, *The Village*, and *Signs* are all movies that hit us and were incredibly influential when we were teenagers at the time. They taught us what our interests were; what movies could be. How you can make something commercial, but peel back the layers to have interesting characters and themes. Also, seeing Shyamalan's evolution, even in times when you watch some of his films and it doesn't feel like the purest sense of him, but in one scene you see what he was scratching at. The career chapter that he's at now, he's writing these smaller films and I think it's getting back to the roots of what his filmmaking was. That tenacity is inspiring from his stories, but also from a career perspective. You are not done until you say you're done for yourself. There's always a way through tenacity where you can find your voice again and make movies that connect with an audience.

Bryan Woods - We're fans of everybody's work whether they are successful or not. We are students and are always trying to read scripts from The Black List that comes out of Hollywood every year. We are always studying and learning. A collection of filmmakers that we really admired when we were younger were the writers who really split their guts on the page like Cameron Crowe who did *Almost Famous*, *Vanilla Sky*, and *Say Anything*. Or a writer like Sophia Coppola who did *Lost in Translation* and *Marie Antoinette*. When I think of those writers, what links them is that I don't feel like I have to meet them in person to know who they are. I know exactly who they are through their work. They are just so honest. They tell the truth. They put their feelings and their heart on the page. I know their voices through their writing and that's really inspiring.

Briana Belser - I love the Nolans, Chris and Jonathan. I think they are so heady and people who are like, "Look audience, you are either going to keep up or you are not." I can't speak for *Tenet* because even I was like, "What the fuck is going on?" But the really early stuff and *Westworld,* Season 1? They take for granted that the audience is smart enough to keep up. They challenge intangible, abstracted concepts with real world characters. The notion of memory and time and space, I think that stuff is fun to think about and anyone when they've had enough drinks can philosophize. They take you on this whirlwind of a journey and I love that.

Also, there is Michael Dante DiMartino and Bryan Konietzko, who did *Avatar: The Last Airbender,* which is my favorite show in the entire world. Mike and Bryan are such nerds. You know they love that Eastern culture they use for inspiration. They love anime. They love animation. That passion and then the stories that they took those characters on, are timeless. I have rewatched that show infinite times and it holds up. There are characters that are disabled, there are female characters, they were this, they were that. They were ostracized. They were scarred before those were tenants of storytelling from a political correct standpoint. I love that and I think it's so valuable. It reminds me of why I would watch and read and consume those stories and feel powerful afterwards.

I love N. K. Jemisin. She is a fantastic fantasy writer. Why I love her is because she takes me on a journey. and she takes for granted that I am smart enough to keep up. She is not holding my hand through the story. Her stories almost always have this sexiness and this creepiness that always leaves me prickly. Oh, my God! They are going to kiss! Oh, my God! Someone's going to die! There's something so fun about the slow rumbling that she has. Her twists are twisty and breakneck, and her world building is fantastic. The other thing is she's a Black woman and there's this narrative we have about representation. I need to see myself and yadda yadda. I think that's valuable. I am not dismissing that. What do I take from her because of that background? She tells stories that I don't think always aligned with the hallmarks of stereotypical Black American myth. But she takes them and makes me care and it reminds me that we are nuances, we are whole and we're not a monolith. I haven't walked those walks and journeys even though she and I are part of the same culture and yet it still matters. That makes me think that even when I write something that someone else will never know about - if it is well written, they will have an emotional investment. So I love that.

I also love J. K. Rowling. She was funny and silly and even as I look back as an adult, some of the names are ridiculous. Her asides to the audience are snarky and they are funny and fun and those books came out when I was four, five, six, seven, eight. I grew up as the same age as those characters. It was the first time meeting characters that I didn't want to let go of. It was the first time my mom took me to midnight book premieres. J. K. Rowling's ability to keep storytelling fun and to talk to me as a child without talking down to me and to empower me was so awesome.

Moisés Zamora - The most recent thing that inspired me is the George Saunders book, *A Swim in the Pond in the Rain*. He has a creative writing class. He deconstructs the master Russian short storytellers in a way that it's so universal that you could use the same creative approach to story in film and TV. In fact, he uses a lot of cinema references to make his points. It's so exciting! It just makes you fall in love with story, period. You could have a narration or a piece of writing, but what makes it a story - a memorable story, that those Russian short story tellers, those masters of the form, were able to achieve? He gives it in a tiny little bottle. It's just so exciting to discover as a storyteller. And I have implemented some of that learning into some of my recent work.

Carolina Rivera - I have this movie that I love because of what it made me feel - *Magnolia*. The Paul Thomas Anderson movie with Tom Cruise. I love that movie and I can't explain it. I just feel the feels. When you are exposed to something you can't analyze it because you are feeling everything. All the stories were connected by guilt. I guess I was feeling very guilty back then. Guilt is something in my life because I am a Mexican woman with a

Catholic upbringing. So I connected with that feeling very strongly. Also, another one that I really love is a Mexican movie called *Y Tu Mamá También*. I loved everything that was hidden. I loved the way the characters related to each other in an innocent way, and yet with what was going on underneath.

Like my voice, though, the movies I like are different in various phases of my life. What I like now is not what I was into twenty years ago. Recently, I loved *Belfast*. I was amazed by the acting and the aesthetics. It's so intimate and relevant with all the immigration and the violence. And it's told in such an intimate way. When you can't be home anymore for different reasons. I feel for a lot of people. Even for myself, with the President we have. A very concrete example is that we were trying to buy a house here in Mexico, but we don't know what the situation is going to be in a few years. We don't feel safe. We feel the President is gearing toward being a dictator just like Venezuela, so we're not going to buy a house because we don't know if we are going to go somewhere else. I don't know if I am going to last here. I can't tell my kids to buy a house here or put down your roots here. I don't what's going to happen. So I connected to that message in *Belfast*, which is so intimate. It's one of my favorite movies now because I'm living it. You don't have to feel bad if your favorite movie isn't your favorite movie anymore because things change and you change.

Scott Lobdell - One thing I would recommend is *Inherit the Wind* with Spencer Tracey and Frederick Marsh. Since YouTube was invented, I find myself at least three times a year watching the courtroom scenes from that movie because they are so fantastically written and well-acted.

When I was eight-years-old and moved into a new house, I went downstairs to get a drink of water at what must have been one in the morning and realized that no one else was awake in the whole house. So I went into the living room and I turned on the TV very low. There was this black and a white movie about these two old women who had murdered someone and their new tenant is having tea with them. They are talking and the two women are casually chatting at the table while the guy is at the window box unaware he is sitting above the dead body - and he is clearly next! I was like, "Oh my god! That is horrifying!" So I turned off the TV and ran upstairs and under my covers. For years, people would always ask me what was the scariest movie that I ever saw. I would say, I don't know the name of it, I just remembered that snippet. It wasn't until my mid-20s that I learned the movie was *Arsenic and Old Lace*, which is a comedy starring Cary Grant! That really taught me a lesson about context being so important. If you don't have the proper context, the setup for laughs is similar to the setup for scares.

Marsha Greene - I'm inspired by Michaela Coel. I thought *I May Destroy You* was a literal masterpiece. It's not just that it's so raw, but it was also so fresh. She took a subject matter that was so personal and found a way to make it funny, tragic, and interesting. And, to approach it in a totally different way, a topic that had been very much spoken about. I was amazed by her work.

Prior to seeing *I May Destroy You*, I saw *Fleabag* and thought this was literal perfection. I have no notes. The third person who came to my mind was Issa Rae because she has had such an amazing trajectory from this person who created this web series to having her show and becoming the showrunner. Not only creating other shows but creating other opportunities for other people. She is like a mogul. I also admire Shonda Rhymes because she's kind of like a badass bitch. She is just so unique. I think she is just such an empire. I admire empires, I don't know if I want to be one. I think I am more like Michaela Coel who doesn't feel like an empire, but rather an entity onto herself; a writer with a very distinct POV.

What inspires me most is when I watch stories that I feel are really specific and unique. If there's nothing like it on TV, that will draw me in. When Issa Rae did *Insecure*, there was nothing like that on TV. The things they were saying were so true. I would have friends that watch it and say, "That is so real about Black women." When I was making *The Porter*, I must have brought up *I May Destroy You* a thousand times, which was funny because one of the actors from *I May Destroy You* was in our show. Weird coincidence!

I like writers who take their personal life and experiences and turn that into story. When I am in a room and a writer is willing to share and be vulnerable in that way, I really like that. I try to be that way, but it's hard. I admire it and in some ways, it's what I look for. I feel that is the precursor to the kind of work that I am attracted to that feels really grounded and real, specific, and authentic. I have done work that is more high-concept, in a way, but my dream and the next thing that I will write will be smaller and more personal.

Deborah Haywood - I'm inspired by Sarah Polley, the Canadian director. She makes films that I really connect with. She made a documentary, as well and that was really revealing. She finds a way to tell really honest stories.

Ron Leshem - I go running everyday and I listen to podcasts. I listen to writers, actors or directors and I learn a lot. *Euphoria* was inspired by *Trainspotting* and *Kids* and Gus Van Sant. The toxic freedom. But the thing that made me want to be a writer was the South American writer, Gabriel García Márquez's *100 Years of Solitude*. Another one is the Italian writer, Elsa Morante, who wrote *History*. The film about Che Guevara, *The Motorcycle Diaries*, I loved. And the Brazilian film, *City of God*. I wanted to work with Walter Salles who directed *Motorcycle Diaries* and produced *City of God*. And now I am working with him!

Bill Nicholson - The things that inspire me are the things that do something that I thought couldn't be done. In the last Oscar batch, *Drive My Car* pleases a person like me especially because there are whole long sequences of people talking. But he's so worked the characters, you're there for it. It's the opposite of something where you think the technical prowess of the director is so startling you're in awe of it. It's something very plain, very simple but very powerful and very long. A lot of people find it quite a boring film. I did not. I found it inspirational. Because I thought, why am I so engaged in this? I would be working out what he had done, how he had made me want to stay with these people through this crisis.

As I start a film, I'm usually able to predict how the whole story will go, which annoys my family like anything. I'll say, 'You'll see, she'll end up doing this...' So I love watching something where I simply cannot predict what the hell is going to happen. Particularly if their twists work. It's no good having things happen at random, that's like a dream. If you tell someone a dream, it's completely boring, i.e. "...then the elephant exploded and two knights in armor came through the door..." It should be incredibly exciting but it isn't because there's no cost to anything, no rules, no sense of why - so it's incredibly boring. You can't do films like that. You have to have the emotional logic. And when you do have the emotional logic and it suddenly goes bing! You think, wow that was clever. In *Watchmen*, Damon Lindelof has an entire twenty-minute long sequence in a sixty- minute episode and he doesn't explain who these people are or what they want - it's completely bonkers! But then you think, I'm going to trust this guy and we're going to find out, and we do.

Dan Mazer - As a writer, you would be surprised at the amount of writers who haven't really read any scripts. Go and seek out the scripts of your favorite films and see it laid out on the page. See how it's crafted. See the rhythms of it. You will focus on different things and notice different things about the script that you will about the film. *When Harry Met Sally* is my favorite film of all time and it was so enlightening and educational to read that script. So find scripts of the movies that you love and compare and contrast the two.

As for writers that I love, Nora Ephron, I think is fantastic. She has that combination of hilarity, relatability and authenticity, so that things are simultaneously brilliantly funny, but heartbreakingly real.

Lauren Iungerich - I still live in the world of Cameron Crowe and James Brooks. They are both my heroes. John Hughes, too. The person I feel most close to are Cameron Crowe in his romance and James Brooks in his heart and humanity. *Broadcast News* and *Terms of Endearment* are my two favorite movies. I still go back to them and hold my heart watching them. I love Nora Ephron. I sort of have a classic sensibility in what I am interested in and what I don't see enough of and want to see more of. As a contemporary, Noah Hawley, I am so impressed with him. I love his work. He's someone I really look up to.

Jed Mercurio - I tend to look at the real world for inspiration. I'm not necessarily looking at fictional works as a roadmap as to go about creating a work of fiction. I'm looking at the real world and taking some of that as the way into the story. And then, with each particular project, there will be separate influences. There will be models for how it was done well; models for how it was done in a way that didn't work for me as a viewer. Those are quite specific. There are no general influences on my work.

Eli Craig - I think my inspiration is something new that I find funny. It makes me smile. I do watch a lot of movies, but I don't specifically watch movies for inspiration. I try to find something that makes me smile and then as I begin to work on something, there's a deeper theme to it that gets me really excited. I will spend a lot of time writing about theme, initially. It's sort of ridiculous that I do. With *Little Evil*, this is about step-parenting. Love your kids, really. *Tucker and Dale* is about a classist system that doesn't let the underdog thrive. Then I will get really excited about it, as if it's deep, then I will laugh at my highfalutin idea and sort of start making fun or satirizing it. Although my kids watch all the Marvel movies and are plugged into pop culture, I am definitely not tempted to stay plugged into pop culture. I try to do things that make my day more enjoyable. Writing is hard and it's not always fun, so I like having those days where you are literally smiling and laughing and getting a kick out of what you are writing.

Hilary Galanoy - Even though some of his work is now viewed as problematic, and rightly so, John Hughes inspired me. I will always remember going to a midnight show of *The Breakfast Club* as a teen and how I felt: like I wanted to grow up and make movies like that. Funny, touching, relatable... even though it was also pure fantasy. RIP John Hughes!

Emma Ko - I remember reading Shane Black's script for *Lethal Weapon* and being really blown away by the chances he took. I remember reading later that it was the first time someone had put things in like, "They drive up to a house in the Hills. The kind of house I would want to live in if this script sells." I remember reading that and just being blown away by the slickness. I thought it was a fantastic script to read. Probably a little dated now. But at the time, it's slick. It's action packed. I think reading any and all the scripts you can, good and bad, is a great idea.

Because of the show I'm working on, I've been reading a lot of sitcoms. There's a show on Apple called *Mythic Quest,* which is based in gaming, so it's a similar template of an entertainment world. I studied it quite a lot and I ended up finding a draft of the script that was online. It was very well written and funny. What was interesting though, was that a lot was cut out of that pilot episode and dispersed throughout the rest of the series. One single thing was left - a spade, which became the theme of the whole plot. I actually think *Mythic Quest* is the perfect pilot. It's got everything. Reading that draft, which was missing two of the main characters, spoke to me on many levels. But it still wasn't good enough. It was interesting to see how far they had to travel to get to what I think is the perfect pilot episode with the addition of two new characters - including the nemesis. It's the understanding that your job is never done and you have to be open to changing 90% to get to the 1% that makes it the best. In terms of reading for better understanding, read as many scripts as possible. But certainly, understanding where earlier drafts ultimately end up gives writers hope, especially when they are dreading writing another draft.

Tony Jordan - If I look back and think about the one writer who gave me the stuff that I needed when I was writing, I would say it would have to be William Goldman and for a couple of reasons. His movies, obviously, *All The President's Men*, *Butch Cassidy*, all those films that I remember being completely immersed in. And also the fact that he could be two kinds or writer. He could write *All The President's Men* and he could write *Butch Cassidy*. Because people are so quick to pigeon-hole you as a writer... 'so you're a real drama writer', or, 'your stuff is darker or it's this or light.' I've wanted to do everything. I've done comedy, deep drama, religious stuff. William Goldman taught me that you could have that breadth. You were allowed to be a different writer on different days.

The second reason is that quite soon after I started writing, I read his book, *Adventures in the Screen Trade* and that taught me everything I needed to know about surviving in the business. If for no other reason that he makes a point of reminding you on every page that in the industry in which we work, nobody knows anything. Everybody is making up everything as we go along. That was such a truth for me. That allowed me to understand that no matter what room I was in, whether it was in London or Los Angeles or Paris, whatever commissioner I was sat in front of, they didn't know anything more about anything than I did. That empowers you. Needless to say, there's a host of writers who I admire and am in awe of but if there was one writer to read up about, it would be William Goldman. Go read *Adventures in the Screen Trade*.

Josh Greenberg - I love classic film. That's what I always dreamed of doing. So I always tell people that the weirdest film that had the biggest influence on me was *Clue*. So profoundly. That is when I first understood how comedy dialogue worked; this very fast-paced screwball tone. That really affected me deeply. Eventually, I got to meet the guy who wrote that - this writer/director named Jonathan Lynn. I was just blubbering to him how much I loved it. There are so many older figures that inspired me like Peter Sellers. I can watch a Peter Sellers film today and it's still fresh and funny and that is so inspiring. Really good comedy does not age. The same with the Zucker brothers and *Airplane*. It's really timeless.

Michael Brandt - I feel like I'm inspired by competition. Take *Finding Nemo*, for instance. It's not a movie I'd ever write, but I'm so inspired by the perfection of the storytelling. *The Professional* is a perfect movie. The beats of that movie, the heart of the movie, the action of the movie, how it services the heart of the movie - I think is a perfect piece of filmmaking. We all saw *Pulp Fiction* and *Reservoir Dogs* and took our shots at the way Tarantino wrote with the cultural references. But nobody can do it like him, so don't try. Just hold that in awe.

In truth, though, I am more inspired by singer/songwriters than I am by movie and television writers. It's the use of words that singer/songwriters use; the way a character can be encompassed in three minutes and you can understand and feel like you know that character even though you don't necessarily know what's going to happen. That inspires me. When I write, I listen a lot to James McMurtry, a singer/songwriter from Texas. His father is Larry McMurtry who wrote *Lonesome Dove* and *The Last Picture Show*. James tells stories about individuals in ways that I find so fascinating. I love listening to singers who tell stories about people. Or the way a lyric can turn a word or phrase succinctly and I like having characters do that. I like having characters recall something from the beginning or the end of a scene, or use the same phrase but differently. It's a way of enhancing their intelligence level. That's what a singer would do with a turn of phrase in lyrics. That just sticks to my bones.

Elizabeth Hackett - I'm a huge Billy Wilder fan. I love that while *The Apartment* was released in 1960, I still say lines of dialogue like "That's the way it crumbles, cookie-wise" in everyday life. He created real life people with that extra twist of wit we all wish we had in reality. His characters say the lines we think of only hours after an argument has finished.

Ben Philippe - The shows inspire me. I learned English by watching *Seinfeld* and *Gilmore Girls*. My parents were going through a divorce; I had a TV in my room. My native tongue is Creole French because I was raised in Montreal. I would come home and watch those shows. I wasn't really popular. I would watch TV from 4 p.m. to 11:30 p.m. *Mad Men* has the single best episode of TV I've ever seen, *The Suitcase*. Peggy and Don Draper alone in their office. There's something fascinating about a show like *Game of Thrones* which has so many viewers. This is ridiculous! It's wizards and dragons! And yet, I am riveted on the edge of my seat, so there has to be something there.

Right now, my favorite shows are *Succession* and *Dave*. It's the rapper, Lil Dicky who makes a half-hour comedy based on his life trying to be the greatest rapper in the world. The poster for Season 1 is him peeking out of his own underwear. I remember seeing it on a billboard thinking you could not pay me to watch this show. Then, someone I trust told me it was really good. I watched one episode and now it's one of my favorite shows on TV. It's so sharply written. I think it's so specific. I love *Girls*. I know Lena Dunham is a controversial creator. And, as a teacher, that led to a lot of people writing boring pilots about their roommates or the person they have a crush on. A whole wave of that. But I think it has a specificity. I respond to anything that is really specific. Shonda Rhymes is the obvious answer. She has made such an extraordinary powerhouse career. I do think network is harder than streaming because it's twenty-two episodes that you are shooting. You are at the whim of actors who have built an entire thirteen-season story around Derek and Meredith's love story and marriage in *Grey's Anatomy*, and all of a sudden, the actor playing Derek doesn't want to do it anymore. What do you do? The only narrative answer is often: We have to kill you. If you have a show built on the relationship of two characters and one retires and the other is still there, how do you write that in? Sometimes she gets texts from her best friend who no longer exists in this world. Keeping the engine of that show going for nearly twenty years is such a phenomenal feat.

Dave Reynolds - I've just watched the last season of *Derry Girls*. I would love to meet Lisa McGee. She is insane in the best possible way. The plates that she could spin and how they intersect. One character would say something over here and then comment on something over here while doing a third thing. It's the best thing you are going to see. Mindy Kaling is someone else. She has a show called *Never Have I Ever*. On the surface, it seems like one of those teen series about a girl who wants to date the hunky guy. It's so layered and smart. And, of course, there's Tina Fey. No one is faster and funnier. Of course, there are many more great writers, but those three are the gold standards.

There was a great show in the UK called *Detectorists*. The premise of the show centers on two main characters who love to search fields for treasure with metal detectors. That's it. And it's brilliant. Mark Dindal and I were hooked on it because it was all about these characters and their lives. They would find a button and they would go in and they would say, "This button is nothing." Mackenzie Crook from *The Office* created that show. And Toby Jones is in it. It's absolutely seamless how beautiful it is. Mark and I would talk to each other and wonder how we could write that. It's so specific. You couldn't even pitch it to anybody. Two guys in the middle of the country with their metal detecting wands who are trying to find treasure. I mean, what are we rooting for? You can imagine all the studio notes that you might get! It is so fantastic and we couldn't wait for each episode!

Q: What advice can you give screenwriters reading this book?

Mohamad El Masri - This business is collaborative. Social IQ is huge. Work with people. Listen. Know how to quarterback creative conversations and hear stakeholder needs and concerns, and know how to creatively problem solve and contribute. And remember, this business is a marathon, not a sprint. Hills. Valleys. Either way, run your race.

Scott Beck - Make sure you celebrate the small victories. Don't wait for the one big parade lap. It is a hard career. It's mostly failure. To be able to celebrate those things is as worthy as anything. Honestly, those are the most important moments. The other thing is that as a writer, it costs you nothing to write. You can create your own opportunities, you can create your own careers. I can't tell you how many times we have sat on airplanes flying to Ireland or somewhere and knowing that the reason we are on this plane is because we started writing words in Final Draft. It's a weird feeling, but it's a reminder that it can take you places. It can take you places in your imagination and it can take you places physically - literally around the world. There's an excitement in that. It allows you to have new experiences and broaden your life. There's nothing more important as a writer than also having life experience which gives you things to write about. So understanding the power of that is really something we try to remember.

Emma Ko - Buy a little notebook and a pen, and write down everything that comes to you. Write snippets of conversation that you hear. Any idea that comes into your head and just keep writing, writing, writing. The work that it takes to sit down with a fresh script and write it, is quartered, halved, three quartered, whatever. If you have a whole load of notebooks of your voice and your stories. All these little scenes that you can pepper in because you are already coming from a place where you have done an observation and you know where you are going. A notebook where you are writing stuff down means that you've done the work one month, one year, one week, ten years before. So while you're struggling to think what's this scene that is going to bring me to the next thing? Oh, my God, that time on the bus when those two women were having that conversation would be perfect! You've already done the work rather than having to think of something new and fresh. So have a little book with you at all times and write in it. Fill it with ideas. Sometimes, I just write down a quote and maybe put in brackets that it's for this project or that one. It means that you have a reference book at all times that is full of your words and thoughts.

Moisés Zamora - You are not born with talent. You are born with a brain. Talent is grown. Cultivate your talent, your craft. You will be a genius. Genius is only achievable through hard work and cultivating your craft.

Bill Nicholson - Screenwriting doesn't have to be perfect. Don't agonize. Once you've thought your way through it and planned, get down and write. It's not going to be perfect. That can be sorted later. Be prepared to be rough and ready because once you start agonizing, and hugging it to your chest, honing it and honing it, you'll start caring about every phrase and turn, and when the criticism comes in, it will kill you. Think of it as something you knock out quickly and roughly and then gradually polish it and turn it into something beautiful. By then, the other people involved, are with you, as well. They all think they're writing it. So when you deliver a script, they think that it is some incredibly raw ingredient begging to be cooked. You think it's the final product. And you're both right, really. They don't want to be given a script where you say, "Do not touch a single pause in this. Do exactly what I tell you." That is not the way the film world works. So given that, you might as well give them something rough. Rough and fast. Listen to what they say, do more, do it together.

Barbara Stepansky - Please live a lot of life. Travel, get your heart broken, make mistakes, make tough choices, be in the world. You can't write without having had as much life experience as possible, regardless of genre. Then read. Books, newspapers, screenplays, whatever you can get your hands on. Read scripts of your favorite movies, figure out what you admire about the storytelling, style and characters. Then write. Badly at first, until your voice emerges. Finally, persevere. The only way to fail is to stop.

Jed Mercurio - Write a lot. Having ideas and working up ideas is great and part of your development. But it's only when you get into the drafting process that you start encountering the details of story progression, genre expectations, logic problems, plausibility issues, character diversity and so on. All those issue that are so important to the overall quality of a script. All writers are solving the same kinds of problems over and over again. The problems that I encounter as a writer are the same problems that writers in other genres encounter; the same problems that brand new writers encounter when they are writing their first short story. The more experience you develop at solving those problems, the better equipped you are at solving them in the future.

Eli Craig - Keep going and know that the mantra is: be grateful, be playful and just keep swimming. You have to treat your entire life as a joyful game. You have to take your work seriously, but you have to not fall into capitalist ideals right away, of success and failure. I remember when I was starting out, friends of mine asked me what I was doing. It's almost embarrassing to say that you're a writer. What do you do? Well, I write. Even when you are getting paid and getting paid by a studio, it still looks like you aren't doing much. You have to put all of that aside and look at a script from the point of view that even if you get to the end of it and it's not sold, you're learning something from it. You're growing as a person and someday, maybe it will sell. Maybe you will have a lot of stuff to call back on when you get that success? Success happens in this business in big waves and sometimes you don't even know when it's happening. Is this a moment? Am I having a moment now? All of a sudden I have all this work. Then the wave crashes and it's gone. I've been in this business for a while and I feel like there's this wave crashing over me where I have all these things happening and then they all go away and the tide goes out. It's just you sitting there with a few scripts in your lap. Then, you can have a meeting and it all comes back.

So if you love writing, just keep doing it. Keats created the phrase "negative capability" to describe how a writer is someone who pursues artistic beauty even when it leads them to confusion or uncertainty. My take on that is that a writer is someone who can live with hating themselves. At least part of the time. The other part of the time has to be raising your arms to the sky, saying, "I did that!" Or just riding the roller coaster and embracing life.

Dan Mazer - Be different. Do something you feel has never been seen before or done before. There's no reason I should be a film writer apart from the fact twenty-five years ago, Sacha Baron Cohen and I, came up with something that felt unique and different and that was *Ali G*. And then that got us into *Borat*. That elevated and isolated us and just drew attention to us because it was different. If you write a great script, it might feel as if it's generic and it's been seen before. There are people who have been in the business for twenty years with a reputation who will write that generic script and it will get read and seen before yours because they have a body of work that goes with that generic script that will elevate it above your version of it - even if your version is better.

So the benefit of being unknown is that you can surprise people and come out with something that hasn't ever been seen before. Pushing yourself to be as different and possibly as extreme, but definitely as fresh as possible, is the biggest advice I would give.

Lauren Iungerich - Write for yourself. Do not write for what you think other people want or what you think other people want from you. Be the biggest fan of what you are writing.

Write the thing that you are a fan of. That has been the secret to my success. I write a show that I want to watch.

Bill Nicholson - Be true to your own instincts about the characters and the story, but recognize that criticisms are probably going to help you. So feed those criticisms back into those instincts rather than contort yourself to fit the criticisms. Make them fit you, rather than somehow making yourself be something you are not.

I think fear of failure is a big problem. If you can, as a new screenwriter, be prepared to have your script not accepted. It could be a brilliant script. It doesn't mean you failed, but it feels like it. I maintained a day job for seventeen years before I could feel secure. So keep the day job. Having a day job is really good. That's how you learn stuff. If you go straight from school to a writer in a garage, then what the hell do you know? And you need to know stuff. Writers need to know stuff. That's where it comes from. But if you keep the day job, when do you write? I did my writing early in the morning. Then I went into my day job about half past nine. I had done three hours by then. I did that for a long time. But I loved it. I felt like fate cannot harm me. I've done my day's work by the time I got into my real job.

Marsha Greene - Understand that as a writer you are creating art, but your producer or network are selling a product. It's really important to understand that distinction. They are not an art gallery. That is not to say you have to turn your art into a product. It's about helping them understand why your art is valuable. Getting them onboard with understanding that your art is something that needs to be marketed and given to the masses. You need to approach it in that way and not from that of an artist. When you are pitching, having a notes meeting, or having business interactions, you need to be thinking about the business. That is more effective and productive. That has really helped me along the way. Also, don't take things personally.

Ron Leshem - Never stop learning. You could learn for fifteen years and you still won't know the profession as well as you need to.

Elizabeth Hackett - My first boss in Hollywood once said, "If writing is really want you want to do, just don't quit. So many people quit. It's a hard, unfair way to make a living, but if you don't quit you're already ahead of the game." It's a roller coaster of a career. You have good years and lean years and years where you take on a side hustle because you've got bills to pay and no writing gigs on the horizon. The beauty of it is, you're always one script away from a comeback. In your most down moment, you can write a new feature or TV spec that puts your name back in the conversation. In that sense, you have control of your career. Whether someone buys it for $750,000 or options it for scale price five years later or it merely serves as a coaster for your coffee cup, none of it can happen if you never write the script.

Tony Jordan - The thing that freaks me out the most is when I go and do festivals or talk to new writers and they come up to me at the end of the talk and they say, "I want to be a writer." I have to stop and ask what's going on in their life that's stopping them. Are you locked in a room with no pens? I don't think people can stop you from doing that. I think it's a basic fundamental right. "I want to be a writer and write scripts." Well, why are you talking to me? Why aren't you at home writing scripts? That's not the real question. The real question is, "How can I make money and make it my job?" That's a whole other thing. I don't know. That's career advice. A writer writes.

One hundred percent I believe that if you write from your heart and you write the story you want to tell and, this is a big one, underline it a hundred times, you are talented as a writer. If you can suck people into your story, then I believe people will find you. There are so few brilliant writers around. Everybody is looking for them all the time, I swear to you. You will be found. You have to be talented. You can still write and not be talented, but you might not make any money. You would be doing it just for you and that's fine, too. That goes for everything. You can't be a plumber if you don't have a gift for plumbing. If everywhere you leave after you're done is fucking wet, no one is going to pay you. It's just common sense.

If you're a comedian and you're doing gig after gig and no one laughs, go back to your bedroom mirror. You can still do it. No one's stopping you.

So just write your scripts. Try to get people to read them. Do what everybody does. Some people blame it on that no one is giving them the job as a writer. They deserve it and they can't get a foot on that ladder because of some hideous conspiracy against them. The truth is that it's possible you don't have it. Maybe people have read your scripts. Maybe your friends and family are telling you you're the next Dickens. You know, maybe they just love you and maybe you're not. The only way to truly find out is to keep writing and getting other people to read your scripts. Listen to them and if there is a flaw in your writing, try to find out what it is.

Carolina Rivera - First of all, not to censor yourself. Telling stories make you feel vulnerable, and nobody wants to feel rejected or judged, or many times, as a woman, you feel you don´t deserve to tell certain kind of stories. But you have to put yourself out there, to be able to succeed. No one is going to read you if you put your stories inside a drawer! The rule is: write, believe in yourself and show your stuff to people.

Josh Greenberg - If you are writing something of your own, make it truthful. That is what great comedy stems from. As a quick side note, I've been really obsessed with this show, *The Bear*. It's just amazing. It's a dramedy about this chef in Chicago. I don't have any connection to this world. I don't understand the world of a chef. That's not where I live. These aren't the people that I know. But it's written from such a specific point of view, that I feel like I can relate to it. I think that's sort of the key. I think the biggest pitfall is trying to write something that you think will be commercially successful or viable. That never works. It might be corny to say, but write something to please yourself and it will please other people.

Chris Cullari - Just read as many scripts as you can. I feel I've learned as much from non-horror scripts as from horror scripts. At the end of the day when we are writing, there's very little formula application. There are certain gut checks we will do such as looking at page 10, page 30 to make sure you're advancing your story. We've been doing this for a while, but I'm still learning this. So much of it is internalizing the rhythms of what you like and then having a gut check. Jen and I feel our way through a script. We feel our way through as if it's a movie. You have to feed all that stuff in. You just need to read and read and read. Then there are certain scripts that you can go to that are sort of manuals on how to execute this sequence on the page.

Danny Strong - Swing for the fences. The more ambitious a piece is, the better it will be. Don't follow what you think an audience wants. Write what you think is great, and the audience will follow you.

Meg LeFauve - You are not alone and keep writing. You need to reach out and have support and learn your craft from other people. It can be isolating if you are a feature writer, so how are you going to stay connected? But you have to keep writing. I understand that the story in your head is so much better than what it comes out as on the page, but that's for everybody. That's the process. You do have to write to learn your craft and find your voice. What you are learning from all these seminars doesn't matter if you don't actually put it into your writing. I understand that the writing can feel like fire, but you have to keep writing.

Michael Brandt - It's too long. Whatever you wrote is too long. Every script is too long. Every scene is too long. I promise you, it's too long. Let the audience fill in some of the blanks. It's okay for readers to be confused for a bit. I have no advice on how to make something good, but I promise you, if you make it shorter, it will be better.

Ben Philippe - I'll tell you advice given to me by a visiting professor at my MFA program: nobody cares if you write. There is no one waiting at their computer for your script. And, for a lot of the people who are going to read your script, it's going to be work in the slush pile. A lot of these people are going to be agents trying to find people to represent, so you are creating work for people. The very least you can do is make that work interesting. Period. That's the bottom line. Whether it's vampires or murder mysteries or memoirs or novels, you have to keep it interesting.

Sometimes, you see writers of color online doing full Twitter threads of: The industry doesn't represent us. The industry is bad. There are not enough diverse voices. Okay, but what was the last thing you wrote? Are you writing right now? If you only have one pilot on your desktop, that's not enough. So start the second one. The first great one will nudge an inch of a door somewhere, I promise. Start the third one. Eventually, it all works out. There's only one surefire way I know how to fail at becoming a working writer, which is to give up. So don't give up.

I know so many people who were driven after their MFAs. They needed to make it by age twenty-five. Okay, now you're twenty-six. What changed? Yes, in submitting scripts and manuscripts, rejection hurts as a creative person. "I worked so hard on this." And you get, "Sorry, we are going to pass on this adaptation, Ben." That's a bummer. I don't chase too many bummers. I prefer to focus on one or two projects at once and just put all of myself into it. If it doesn't work, I'll be sad, but I will keep going. Even if you only produce one script every five years, that's fine. Or if you produce seven scripts a month, also fine. Although I might doubt their quality, but I could be very wrong. Just keep going.

SCREENWRITERS ADVICE

Becca Topol - Trust yourself and the process. Write and re-write and re-write. It's very important not to be overly consumed with selling your work to the point you ignore the importance of always creating new things. Push yourself out of your comfort zone. Be disciplined. If you don't have deadlines already, make deadlines for yourself. Find a fellow writer and have regular check-in meetings to hold yourself accountable. And have fun! Explore!

Dave Reynolds - You have to keep writing. Write as much as you can. The worst thing that writers do is pre-edit in your head. You are at your keyboard and you think, what if this happened? No, that can't happen because of this. The clock is ticking. You then might decide to play online games. No, you have to push through the pre-edit and get things down fat. Get them down wrong. Andrew Stanton used to say, "Be wrong as fast as possible." If it's on the page, you can always fix it. Judd Apatow used to call it a vomit draft - everything comes out.

In a perfect world, you need six to eight hours a day to do a good day's worth of writing. Most people can't do that. So you need to create a writing bubble for at least one hour. You just turn on Do Not Disturb and be loyal to that bubble. Don't worry that it's not enough time. A lot can be done in an hour. Just think back to high school when you forgot about a paper that was due. You did it then.

A great writer, John August, does this thing on Twitter that he calls a "Writing Sprint." He will say, "OK, everybody at 10 o'clock…go!" … And you just write until 11 o'clock. You turn off your phones and you just go. At the end of it, he says, "OK, how did we do?" It forces you to focus. When you finish that hour, you've magically written. It might not all be usable but some of it may be great or it may lead you to something great. How cool is that?

And lastly, as you head out into the business of writing, it will seem like everyone wants to say "no" to you. They all want to shoot a hole in your stuff. You have to develop Teflon skin. You have to say to yourself, the reason I am telling you this story is because it is compelling or funny. You have to believe in it. Enough people are going to tell you that it's not good, that "this part stinks and your third act doesn't make sense." At Pixar, you couldn't just say, "That doesn't work," in the room. You'd have to say what you think doesn't work and why. You also had to give an example of what might work in its place. You had to back it up. Also try to find people to give you positive, constructive notes. We all need someone to tell you if your idea makes sense. You might get that little nugget, that keeps you going or turns you in the right direction. Remember that you're not going to knock out a great script or story in the first pass. Or the second. The third pass was good but you'll get it on the next one… and try to always remember why you started it and what the driving force is of your main character.

Paul King - Find the films you love and watch them obsessively. Work out how they work. Pull them to pieces and chart all the character flows and the plot development and see what you can learn. I think that is the golden rule - to learn from the people that you admire. If I can do it, anyone can.

CHAPTER REVIEW: INSPIRATION

We've gathered the recommendations of the interviewees in this book into this list. It's a combination of screenwriters, authors, playwrights, songwriters, and magazines that you will, hopefully, find as inspiring as they did.

Scott Beck - M. Night Shyamalan/*The Sixth Sense, Unbreakable, The Village, Signs.*

Briana Belser - Christopher & Jonathan Nolan/*Batman, Westworld*; Michael Dante DiMartino & Bryan Konietzko/*Avatar: The Last Airbender*; N.K. Jemisin (author); J.K. Rowling/*Harry Potter* series.

Michael Brandt - Dave Reynolds/*Finding Nemo*; Luc Besson/*The Professional*; Quentin Tarantino/*Pulp Fiction, Reservoir Dogs*; James McMurtry (singer-songwriter).

Chris Cullari - John Carpenter & Debra Hill/*Halloween*; Simon Pegg & Edgar Wright/*Shaun of the Dead*; Dan O'Bannon/*Alien*; Brian Duffield/*The Babysitter*; Chris Carter/*The X-Files* pilot.

Mohamad El Masri - Sally Rooney/*Normal People, Beautiful World Where You Are* (author).

Hilary Galanoy - John Hughes/*The Breakfast Club.*

Marsha Greene - Michaela Coel/*I May Destroy You*; Phoebe Waller-Bridge/*Fleabag*; Issa Rae/*Insecure*; Shonda Rhymes/*Grey's Anatomy.*

Josh Greenberg - Jonathan Lynn/*Clue*; Zucker Brothers/*Airplane.*

Elizabeth Hackett - Billy Wilder/*The Apartment.*

Deborah Haywood - Sarah Polley/*Women Talking, Take This Waltz.*

Tony Jordan - William Goldman/*All the President's Men, Butch Cassidy and the Sundance Kid, Adventures in the Screen Trade.*

Emma Ko - Shane Black/*Lethal Weapon*; Rob McElhenney/*Mythic Quest.*

Meg LeFauve - *The Sun* magazine for inspiration: www.thesunmagazine.org/.

Ron Leshem - John Hodge/*Trainspotting*; Harmony Korine*Kids*; Gus Van Sant films; Gabriel García Márquez/*100 Years in Solitude*; Elsa Morante/*History*; Jose Rivera/*The Motorcycle Diaries*, Braulio Mantovani *City of God.*

Alex Litvak - Shane Black/*Lethal Weapon*; William Goldman/*The Princess Bride, Butch Cassidy and the Sundance Kid*; Stephen King/*It, Christine;* Donald Westlake/*Parker* Series; Joe Abercrombie.

Scott Lobdell - Jerome Lawrence, Robert E. Lee (play), Nedrick Young, Harold Jacob Smith (screenplay)/*Inherit the Wind;* Julius J. Epstein & Philip G. Epstein/*Arsenic and Old Lace.*

Dan Mazer - Nora Ephron/*When Harry Met Sally.*

Jed Mercurio - looks to the real world for stories.

Bill Nicholson - Ryûsuke Mamaguchi, Takamasa Oê/*Drive My Car*; Damon Lindelof/*Watchmen.*

Josh Olson - Howard Rodman/*Charlie Varrick;* David S. Ward/*The Sting*

Ben Philippe - Jerry Seinfeld & Larry David/*Seinfeld*; Amy Sherman Palladino/*Gilmore Girls*; Matthew Weiner/*Mad Men*; Lil Dicky; Jesse Armstrong/*Succession*; Lena Dunham/*Girls*; Shonda Rhymes/*Grey's Anatomy;* David Benioff & D.B. Weiss/*Game of Thrones*

Jennifer Raite - Bryan Fuller/*Hannibal* (TV series).

Dave Reynolds - *Derry Girls*/Lisa McGee; Mindy Kaling/*Never Have I Ever*, *The Detectorists*/Mackenzie Crook.

Carolina Rivera - Paul Thomas Anderson/*Magnolia*, Kenneth Branaugh/*Belfast*.

Julie Sherman Wolfe - Stanley Shapiro, Maurice Richlin, Russell Rouse/ *Pillow Talk*; Betty Comden & Adolph Green/*Singin' in the Rain*; Dalton Trumbo, Ian McLellan Hunter, John Dighton/*Roman Holiday*; Nora Ephron/*When Harry Met Sally*; Nancy Meyers/*What Women Want, Father of the Bride, Something's Gotta Give, Private Benjamin*, Carrie Fisher, Dorothy Parker.

Barbara Stepansky - Jane Campion/*The Piano, Top of the Lake*; Alfonso Cuarón/*Gravity, Roma, Y Tu Mamá También*, Billy Ray/*Overlord.*

Danny Strong: Arthur Miller/*Death of a Salesman, A View From the Bridge, The Crucible*; Anton Chekov's short stories; Sydney Pollack, Sydney Lumet.

Becca Topol: Elif Batuman (author); Annie Ernaux (author); Amy Poehler/*Parks and Rec*, Tina Fey/*30 Rock, Mean Girls*; Issa Rae/*Insecure*; Michaela Coel/*I May Destroy You, Chewing Gum.*

Bryan Woods - Cameron Crowe/*Almost Famous, Vanilla Sky, Say Anything*, Sophia Coppola/*Lost In Translation, Marie Antoinette.*

Moisés Zamora - George Saunders/*A Swim in the Pond in the Rain*, Russian shorts storytellers (Anton Chekov, Ivan Krylov, Fyodor Dostoyevsky,etc.)

WRITING EXERCISES & REFERENCES

We hope that all the advice that our writers have given to this point will give you lots of inspiration. However, some people get their creative juices flowing via practical experience. Due to this, we've included a few exercises in this section that touch upon many of the aspects of screenwriting, such as plot, character and motivation. Why not give them a go?

IDEA GENERATION EXERCISE

This is a classic writing exercise that helps get your creative juices flowing. It can be done alone or in a group setting. This should train you to free-think and get faster at generating concepts when brainstorming. Have fun!

- Choose a location of any kind (castle, spaceship, swamp, etc.) and build a story from that place. You can choose any genre or time period. It doesn't have to be very detailed, maybe a paragraph in length. What characters are in it? What are their goals? How does the location help dictate the story?

- Repeat the exercise, but by choosing a character (warrior, secretary, baker, etc.) You can either continue the story or start fresh. Who are they? What are their external and internal motivations (what do they want/need)? Where do they live?

- Do the same process with an object (apple, boulder, etc.). Consider how the object affects the plot and characters. You can continue the story, or start fresh.

- Do the same process with an action (swimming, kissing, etc.). Is your character doing this action or are they witnessing it? How does it affect the plot? You can continue the story, or start fresh.

- Now choose a line of dialogue ("You said to go up!") Who says it and how? How does it affect the character? How does it affect the plot? You can continue the story, or start fresh.

LATERAL THINKING EXERCISE

Lateral thinking is an important skill to master, especially when generating new ideas.

This exercise works on the principle that stories often come from kernels of ideas tangentially related to the final form. An image of an apple can get one thinking about trees, worms, snakes, fruit, the color red, etc. From there, you might think about roots, decay, danger, sex, or blood, respectively. It could lead you to a character, a location, a theme - anything, really.

To do this, find an image of any kind (photo, artwork, cartoon, etc.) or a phrase (line of poetry, famous saying, graffiti, etc), and start thinking outwards as to what it means or represents to you. What do you feel? What does it inspire? Start building a story based on that and keep exploring!

RISING CONFLICT EXERCISE

There's a classic acting exercise where one actor asks another to do something and the other refuses to do it. They repeat this again and again, raising the intensity of the ask and refusal each time. The fun is in how many rounds they can go through before they resort to screaming at each other.

Writers can adopt this by putting two characters through the same process. How much tension can you squeeze out of them before they come to blows?

CHARACTER DIARY EXERCISE

If you're having trouble getting inside the head of your characters, consider writing a diary from each of their point of view. They can discuss the plot points that have happened, are happening, will happen, or how they feel about their relationship with other characters in the story. This can be helpful before and after major plot points such as the inciting incident, midpoint, or the end of Act 2, as their internal struggles can inform their external actions. Using expressive words to identify their emotions, such as excited, vindicated, furious, or remorseful, will help you create their dialogue.

By the way, this doesn't have to be written. If you think better by hearing and exploring out loud, fire up your acting skills and turn this into a video diary.

OBSTACLE EXERCISE

Drama comes from characters attempting to overcome problems. To sharpen your conflict creation skills, have two characters move through any kind of space and encounter some kind of obstacle. This can be another character, something from nature - any antagonistic force.

How do your characters try to get around the problem? Do they work together? Does one take more charge than the other? Are they in constant opposition? Is there something more sinister afoot? Does the obstacle have more problems than originally thought? You see the true colors of people when they are in trouble.

DROP IT/PICK IT UP EXERCISE

Create a scene with two characters. One of them drops something and the other picks it up. You can choose any pair of characters, genre, time period, or location, but you have a two-page limit to the scene. Can you get all of these elements out and tell a full story in that time? It's harder than it seems!

MISSING SCENE EXERCISE

Have you ever wished there was an extra scene in a sequence that would help the plot or character development? Have you ever wondered what happened to a character when they left a scene and weren't followed? Write a "missing" scene from one of your favorite movies or series that does one of these two things. It can help you understand your character's motivations in greater depth, which may inform a previous or upcoming scene. It can also suggest new plot possibilities or illuminate holes.

VILLAIN INVERSION EXERCISE

When discussing villains in our Character chapter, Scott Lobdell stated that he would love to write a version of the action film *Die Hard* told from the villain's (Hans Gruber) point of view. This would give one of the most iconic characters in cinema a whole new perspective. You could explore in greater depth why Hans is doing the heist, both internally and externally. Perhaps you see him assemble his team - each with their own specialty. John McClane now becomes his main antagonistic force, screwing up his well-thought-out plan.

For this exercise, pick your favorite film or series villain and tell the story from their point of view. Consider how they got into the situation and what they hope to get out of it. Who are their allies? Who are their enemies? Can you make them empathetic? Can you turn some of entertainment's most beloved heroes into baddies? If you're interested in writing anti-heroes, or if you want to see if one of your villains is working properly, this exercise is for you.

REFERENCES

Gerrig, Richard. "Experiencing Narrative Worlds: On the Psychological Activities of Reading." New Haven: Yale UP, 1993. 1-25.

Green, M. C., & Brock, T. C. "The role of transportation in the persuasiveness of public narratives. Journal of Personality and Social Psychology", 79(5), 701–721. 2000.

Writers Guild of America. "Screen Credit Manual." November, 11, 2018. PDF.

INDEX

SYMBOLS

2 Fast 2 Furious 272
3:10 to Yuma 271, 272
12 Deadly Days 175, 326
20th Century Fox 265
21st Century Screenplay 64, 67
24 233, 329
30 Rock 240, 350
100 Years of Solitude 338
1899 72, 113, 167, 169, 171
#MeToo 307, 308

A

Aaron Sorkin 17, 66, 111
Abi Morgan 86
A Bug's Life 289
Abu Utkarsh Ambudkar 287
Academy Award 329
A Christmas Carol 254
A Clusterfunk Christmas 255
Act 1 57, 61, 63, 64, 65, 69, 71, 72, 85, 198, 203, 299, 306
Act 2 56, 63, 64, 69, 70, 71, 72, 198, 299, 353
Act 3 44, 63, 64, 69, 70, 71, 72, 181, 198, 299
action sequence 127, 202
adaptation 47, 50, 118, 171, 172, 215, 220, 263, 264, 265, 267, 270, 272, 273, 295, 306, 334, 347
Adaption by 294
ad-lib 38, 238, 239, 246, 285
Adrian Brody 200
Adult comedies 243
Adventures in the Screen Trade 67, 340, 349
AFI 140
Against the Ropes 235, 308
agent 26, 28, 29, 42, 50, 142, 173, 176, 187, 239, 272, 292, 293, 302, 310, 326
agents 25, 133, 140, 142, 159, 292, 293, 347
A History of Violence 54, 116, 184, 266
A Holiday Spectacular 317

Airplane 58, 341, 349
Alan Rickman 100
Alan Tudyk 327
Albert Brooks 285, 288
Alejandro Iñárritu 96
Alfonso Cuarón 334, 350
Alfre Woodard 117
Algonquin Round Table 333
algorithms 25, 311
Alice in Wonderland 226
Alien 208, 219, 220, 349
aliens 25, 29, 218, 221
Ali G 70, 243, 344
Ali G Indahouse 243
Allen Ginsberg 16
Allen Iverson 271, 272
all is lost 63, 198, 200
All The President's Men 340
Almost Famous 335, 350
Al Pacino 98
alts 151, 238, 246, 276
Amazon 49, 231, 299, 333
Amblin' Entertainment 42
AMC 143, 171, 306, 310
Amelie 276
American Crime 101, 162, 186
American Horror Story 214
American Pie 243
Andrew Stanton 277, 285, 286, 288, 289, 348
animated 242, 269, 276, 277, 278, 280, 283, 284, 285, 287, 289, 290, 301, 330
animation 30, 80, 275, 277, 278, 279, 280, 282, 289, 290, 301, 336
Annie Ernaux 332, 350
Annmarie Morais 169, 170
anthology 215
anti-hero 100, 101
anti-heroes 97, 101, 354
A. Philip Randolph 261
Apple 151, 187, 323, 340
A Quiet Place 29, 149, 208, 211, 213, 216, 218, 219, 329
arbitration 293, 294, 296, 313
arc 34, 44, 50, 69, 72, 87, 91, 92, 99, 117, 150, 158, 165, 232, 234, 248, 270

archetype 89
Archive 81 272
Ari Aster 212
Aristotle 69
Arsenic and Old Lace 337, 350
Arthur Miller 100, 332, 350
Arthur the King 61, 267, 328
A story 19, 56, 78, 188, 204, 298
A Swim in the Pond in the Rain 336, 350
Austin Film Festival 141, 142
automatic arbitration 294
Avatar: The Last Airbender 336, 349
Awkward 121, 327
Azteca 230

B

baby writers 125
backend points 302
Back to the Future 219
Bad Robot 143
bake-offs 42
Barbarian 210
Barry Cook 287
Based on Characters Written by 294
Batman 98, 293, 349
BBC 25, 26, 65, 136, 187, 296
BBC Drama 296
BBC Maestro 65
BBC Three 187
BBFC 269
beats 45, 46, 54, 58, 61, 71, 80, 92, 110, 127, 168, 197, 211, 253, 267, 299, 341
Beat sheet 76
Beaufort 191, 327
Beautiful World Where Are You 334
Beauty and the Beast 284
Begbie 102
Belfast 337, 350
Benjamin Bratt 113
Ben Smith 73
Ben Stephenson 296
Ben Wade 271, 272
best friend 186, 234, 252, 342
BET+ 310
Beth Macy 265
bible 50, 58, 177, 230
Big 94, 95, 103, 141, 232
Big Brother 94
Billions 115

Billy Mernit 140
Billy Ray 334, 350
Binger Filmlab 320
Black Eyed Kids 216
Black Panther 56, 103
Black Swan 58, 184
Blair Witch 106, 326
Blake Snyder 54, 61, 63, 68
blind deal 191
BlueCat 140, 142, 329
BlueCat Screenplay Contest 140
blueprint 77, 79, 80, 113, 120, 213
blue sky 168
Blue-skying 306
Blumhouse 175, 216, 325
board-driven 283
Bob Beresford 193
Bob Odenkirk 306
Bob Peterson 285, 288, 289
Bob Weinstein 124
Bohemian Rhapsody 125
Bond villains 102
Borat 18, 98, 242, 244, 245, 323, 344
brainstorming 17, 155, 163, 178, 352
Braveheart 200
Break into 2 63
Break into 3 63
breakout room 163
Brian Duffield 219, 349
Bridesmaids 58
Bridgerton 251
Bridget Jones 251, 301
Bridget Jones' Diary 251
Broadcast News 339
Bronzeville 300, 304
Bruce Lee 29
Brüno 18, 98
Bryan Fuller 219
Bryan Konietzko 336, 349
budget 100, 166, 176, 177, 178, 182, 194, 195, 199, 200, 205, 277, 278, 290, 299, 302, 312, 320, 325, 328
Bug 211
Bugs Bunny 278, 286
Bunny and the Bull 317
Bunny Folger 73, 168
Buster Keaton 242
Butch Cassidy and The Sundance Kid 333
button 22, 76, 149, 342

C

CAA 44, 142
Cale Boyter 266
Cameron Crowe 335, 339, 350
Carol 28, 254
Carrie 2 326
Carrie Bradshaw 252
Carrie Fisher 332, 350
Cary Grant 337
Casino Royale 127
catalyst 54, 55, 61, 63, 64
Catholic 230, 337
Catholicism 234
CBBC 115, 169
CBC 305, 310
Chad Stahelski 127
Channel 4 25, 136, 187
Channel Zero 214
Chaplin 276
character 16, 19, 20, 21, 23, 24, 25, 26, 28, 34, 36, 38, 46, 49, 50, 52, 54, 55, 56, 57, 58, 59, 61, 62, 63, 64, 65, 66, 67, 68, 69, 70, 73, 74, 75, 76, 77, 78, 79, 81, 84, 85, 86, 87, 88, 89, 90, 91, 92, 93, 94, 95, 96, 98, 99, 100, 103, 104, 106, 107, 110, 111, 113, 114, 115, 116, 117, 118, 119, 120, 121, 122, 124, 127, 148, 150, 151, 155, 158, 165, 166, 167, 168, 169, 170, 175, 188, 189, 190, 197, 200, 201, 203, 204, 205, 208, 209, 211, 212, 213, 214, 217, 219, 221, 224, 225, 226, 230, 232, 236, 239, 240, 241, 242, 243, 244, 245, 248, 252, 254, 256, 260, 261, 264, 266, 267, 268, 270, 271, 277, 278, 279, 280, 281, 282, 283, 284, 285, 286, 287, 288, 290, 293, 299, 300, 303, 305, 308, 310, 317, 320, 322, 324, 334, 341, 342, 344, 348, 351, 352, 353, 354
character arc 150
character arcs 64, 70, 88, 158, 165, 167, 286
character breakdowns 50, 90, 91
character-driven 88
Charles Barkley 271
Charles Dickens 334
Charlie Varrick 334, 350
Chekov 101, 332, 350
Chicago Fire 79
Chicago PD 118
Chip 284
Chris McQuarrie 293
Christmas 18, 247, 253, 254, 255, 256, 257, 280
Christmas movies 253, 254, 255, 256, 257
Chris Vogler 55
Chris Williams 279
Chuck Jones 278, 286
Chucky 214
Cinemax 127
Citizen Kane 25
City of God 338, 349
classic structure 69
cliffhanger 60, 64, 70, 72, 76, 81, 232, 236, 262
climax 64
Clint Eastwood 326
Closed World 6, 56
Clue 341, 349
Cobra Kai 225
Cocktail Party Pitch 35
Co-Executive Producer 177
Colin Firth 268, 269
Columbia University 329
comedies 18, 23, 30, 64, 104, 219, 227, 243, 244, 245, 248, 249, 250, 251, 252, 257
comedy 18, 20, 23, 29, 30, 38, 45, 46, 49, 52, 57, 60, 65, 80, 87, 99, 100, 115, 119, 122, 126, 135, 163, 166, 171, 178, 187, 190, 198, 210, 219, 223, 224, 225, 226, 227, 228, 232, 238, 239, 240, 241, 242, 243, 244, 245, 246, 248, 249, 250, 251, 257, 268, 278, 283, 286, 288, 293, 294, 311, 318, 326, 332, 337, 340, 341, 346
comic book 39, 224, 269, 319
commercial 17, 62, 64, 68, 70, 71, 72, 75, 191, 211, 212, 213, 215, 264, 267, 271, 297, 302, 310, 335
Commissioner 25
Conan O'Brien 21, 22
conflict 70, 74, 92, 93, 94, 95, 100, 101, 111, 115, 118, 153, 154, 211, 234, 240, 244, 250, 257, 353
contrived 188
Coppola 88, 210, 335, 350
Co-Producer 177
copyright 39, 301
Coronation Street 91

Cotswolds 60
Coverfly 141
COVID 42, 43, 49, 142, 166, 306, 328
credit arbitration 293, 313
credit determination 296
critical mass 65

D

Damon Lindelof 339, 350
Dan Evans 271
Danny Boyle 215
Dark 97, 168, 215
dark thriller 270
Darth Vader 98, 105
Daughter From Another Mother 99, 234, 235
Dave 21, 22, 25, 30, 75, 80, 119, 192, 242, 276, 277, 279, 282, 283, 284, 285, 286, 287, 289, 341, 342, 349, 350
David Cronenberg 116, 184
David Giler 220
David Heyman 316
David Mamet 110
David Spade 278, 279
Deadline 128, 265
Death in Paradise 143, 296
Dennis Lehane 265
Derek Haas 112, 181, 266, 272
Derivative 188
Derry Girls 342, 350
Detectorists 342, 350
development 24, 36, 50, 54, 55, 63, 76, 81, 107, 137, 166, 167, 188, 189, 193, 240, 249, 253, 279, 287, 298, 303, 310, 316, 318, 319, 344, 348, 354
Diana Gaboldon 173
Diane Keaton 118
Dickens of a Holiday 254
Dick Fosbury 70
Dick Wolf 78, 79
Die Hard 93, 94, 100, 103, 124, 126, 248, 354
Dimension Films 124
director 27, 29, 44, 50, 62, 78, 80, 81, 96, 113, 118, 119, 120, 127, 129, 130, 151, 174, 175, 176, 178, 179, 180, 181, 184, 189, 191, 193, 194, 211, 212, 216, 217, 226, 240, 266, 270, 271, 277, 279, 282, 283, 285, 294, 298, 304, 318, 323, 325, 326, 327, 328, 338, 341
Dirty Harry 334
disability representation 307
Disney 22, 24, 30, 68, 69, 136, 143, 192, 265, 279, 282, 284, 285, 318, 330
Disney Animation 30, 279
disruption 61
diversity 29, 68, 252, 253, 304, 306, 307, 344
Django Unchained 69
Doctor Who 125
Donald Westlake 333, 350
Don Draper 341
Don Siegel 334
Dopesick 26, 72, 87, 88, 175, 176, 265
Doris Day 252
Dorothy Parker 333, 350
Dory 278, 288
Doug Liman 198
drama 29, 38, 64, 65, 68, 72, 87, 92, 93, 95, 100, 101, 102, 107, 118, 140, 164, 188, 208, 210, 229, 232, 236, 241, 243, 245, 250, 259, 260, 261, 262, 265, 270, 273, 286, 300, 311, 340
dramedy 232, 346
Drive My Car 338, 350
Driving Miss Daisy 98
Duffer Brothers 295
Dumb and Dumber 18, 114
Dustin Hoffman 121

E

Eartha Kitt 278, 279
Eastenders 19, 60, 134, 165, 262
Easter egg 74
Eavesdrop 117
Ed Sanchez 326
Edward Albee 332
Elena of Avalor 283
Elevator Pitch 35
Elif Batuman 332, 350
Ellen DeGeneres 288
Elmore Leonard 271
Elsa Morante 338, 349
emerging writers 26, 320
Emily Blunt 216
Emmy 323

Emperor's New Groove 80, 278, 279, 282, 286, 289, 330
England 20, 38, 255
episodes 22, 24, 27, 44, 50, 57, 59, 64, 70, 72, 88, 125, 163, 164, 165, 166, 167, 168, 169, 170, 172, 173, 175, 176, 181, 182, 197, 215, 221, 231, 270, 280, 287, 297, 299, 300, 310, 342
ER 114, 160
Eric Killmonger 103
Erin Brockovich 124
E.T. 42, 268, 280
Euphoria 17, 28, 106, 303, 327, 338
Event Horizon 215
Everybody Loves Raymond 66, 240, 244
Evil Dead 18, 30
Executive Producer 175, 177, 238, 280, 296
Executive Story Producer 176
Experiencing Narrative Worlds 355
Exposition 95, 120, 121, 300
External motivation 85

F

Falling Inn Love 179, 250
family-friendly 251, 276
Family Guy 165, 241
family movie 276
Farrelly brothers 243
Fast and the Furious 172, 199, 272, 328
feature film 8, 15, 26, 27, 56, 58, 63, 64, 73, 78, 143, 197, 214, 237, 271
features 26, 71, 77, 78, 81, 174, 204, 217, 245
filmmaker 8, 29, 112, 277, 288, 329
Final Draft 77, 116, 128, 141, 144, 151, 343
Finale 64
financiers 20, 24, 41, 51, 155, 182, 199, 223, 228, 291, 297, 313
Finding Nemo 277, 278, 285, 286, 288, 330, 341, 349
Fir Crazy 253
first draft 57, 80, 119, 124, 129, 150, 153, 166, 191, 284, 295, 299, 318, 319, 333
First Draft 297
first-look deal 300
five act structure 69
flashback 64, 72, 73
flashforwards 81
flat character 87
Fleabag 337, 349
Flint 22
Forces of Antagonism 68
Fosbury Flop 70
Fox 21 265
Francis Ford Coppola 210
Frank Capra 240, 332
Frank Gallagher 103
Frank Hannah 185
Frasier 66, 244
Fred Cuny 96
Freddie Mercury 90, 125
Freddy Krueger 102
Frederick Marsh 337
free-think 352
Friday the 13th 214
Friends 18, 66, 115, 244
FX 161
Fyodor Dostoyevsky 350

G

Gabriel García Márquez 338, 349
Game of Thrones 84, 303, 341
Gary Ross 95
general meeting 35, 42, 49, 142
genre 15, 18, 20, 23, 25, 28, 29, 30, 31, 34, 36, 45, 52, 60, 63, 68, 75, 94, 98, 101, 111, 141, 171, 188, 189, 190, 196, 197, 201, 202, 208, 209, 210, 214, 215, 216, 219, 227, 232, 237, 240, 242, 247, 249, 251, 267, 268, 270, 276, 292, 333, 344, 352, 354
genre expectations 197, 344
George Lucas 217
George Saunders 336, 350
Get Out 210, 225
Ghostbusters 227
Gilmore Girls 115, 350
Ginger Snaps 322
Gladiator 96, 307, 325
globalization 311
Gone Girl 220
Goonies 227
Goosebumps 215, 216
Gore Verbinski 198
Grace and Frankie 165
graphic novel 39, 266

greenlit 279, 322, 323
Grey's Anatomy 169, 342, 349
Groundhog Day 18, 249
Gus Van Sant 338

H

Hallmark 50, 85, 164, 180, 192, 249, 251, 252, 253, 254, 255, 256, 257, 318
Hallmark Channel Bingo 256, 257
Halloween 208, 209, 214, 225, 349
Hannibal 214, 219, 350
Hans Gruber 103, 105, 354
Happy Death Day 18, 224, 226, 318, 319
Harrison Ford 96
Harry Potter and The Prisoner of Azkaban 95
Haunt 209
Haunting of Hill House 214
HBO 165, 303
HBOMax 231
Heat 98
heist movie 202, 334
Hello, Mrs. Chan 29
He-Man 266
hero 18, 22, 25, 55, 62, 88, 89, 92, 93, 94, 96, 97, 98, 100, 101, 103, 105, 106, 127, 196, 198, 200, 208, 209, 239, 260, 271, 276, 281
heroine 94, 196, 252
Hidden Figures 272
high concept 20
Hill Street Blues 78
His Girl Friday 250
History 54, 116, 184, 266, 292, 338, 349
Hitchcock 58, 212
Hollywood 25, 28, 29, 35, 38, 67, 86, 128, 140, 144, 159, 185, 187, 192, 197, 209, 248, 303, 304, 305, 307, 310, 312, 323, 325, 335
Homeland 28
Honeymoon 211
horror 18, 23, 28, 30, 46, 52, 54, 55, 60, 70, 93, 101, 102, 106, 185, 207, 208, 209, 210, 211, 212, 214, 215, 216, 217, 218, 219, 220, 221, 223, 224, 225, 226, 227, 228, 268, 284, 311, 319, 346
Horror-comedy 210
Howard Rodman 334, 350
Hugh Bonneville 118, 269
Hugh Grant 90

I

Ibsen 332
I Give It A Year 18, 19
Imagen 230
I May Destroy You 337, 338, 349, 350
imitable behavior 285
immersive storytelling 43
improvisation 119, 238
Incitement 106, 327
Inciting Incident 61, 63
inclusiveness 252
index cards 148, 168
indigenous story 305
Inglorious Bastards 66
Insecure 338, 349, 350
Inside Out 324
Intellectual Property 39
Internal motivation 85
In the Room Pitch 35
IP 6, 17, 39, 40, 57, 61, 81, 85, 263, 264, 272
Iron Man 56, 96
Issa Rae 332, 337, 338, 349, 350
It Follows 210
ITV 25, 26

J

Jack Nicholson 239
Jacob's Ladder 226
Jameela Jamil 287
James Bond 102, 127, 266
James Brooks 339
James Cameron 91
James Mangold 271, 272
James McMurtry 341, 349
Jane Austen 111
Jane Campion 334, 350
Jane the Virgin 232, 304
Jantje Friese 72, 167, 171
Jason Blum 216
Javier Bardem 102
Jaws 97, 185, 211, 214
Jean Claude Van Damme 203
Jeannie Lurie 287
Jennie Urman 232
Jessica Rhoades 325
Jess Rosenthal 142, 143

Jeunet 276
Jill Chamberlain 68
Jodie Foster 62
Joe Ambercrombie 333, 334
Joe Lynch 326
Johnathan Demme 210
John August 128, 348
John Brancato 54, 92
John Carpenter 226, 326, 349
John Goldwyn 265
John Grisham 80
John Hoffman 72, 143, 165, 306
John Hughes 339
John Krasinski 216
John McClane 94, 124, 354
John McLaughlin 58, 184
John Ridley 101, 162, 163, 186
John Singleton 161
John Truby 67, 71
Joker 98, 102, 105
Jonathan Lynn 341, 349
Jordan Peele 225
Joseph Campbell 55, 61, 63, 67, 68
journalist 21, 191
Judd Apatow 348
Judy Bloom 233
Jules Verne 266
jump scare 212
junior manager 293
Justified 215

K

Kal Penn 287
Karen Margalit 270
Kiefer Sutherland 233
Kill Bill 203
King of Queens 89
kiss 192, 232, 250, 251, 256, 257, 336
Kristen Bell 95
Kuzco 282, 286

L

Larry McMurtry 341
Late Night with Conan O'Brien 21, 30, 80
Latin America 55, 305, 308
LatinX 304, 305
Laurence Fishburne 300
Law and Order 78, 204
Lee Jessup 144

Lena Dunham 342, 350
LeStat 118, 225
Lethal Weapon 93, 333, 340, 349, 350
LGBTQ 253
Lifetime 22, 193, 253, 318
Lil Dicky 341
limited series 26, 27, 56, 72, 264, 280
Linda Aronson 64, 67
Linda Seger 71
Lisa McGee 342, 350
Little Evil 227, 311, 339
live-action 277, 280
live tweet 256
Lizzie Francke 320
logline 20, 40, 44, 61, 76, 143, 184
Lonesome Dove 341
Long John Silver 266
Looking 165, 216
Lord of the Rings 84
Lorenz Tate 300
Lost in Translation 335
Love, Guaranteed 252
love interest 89
low concept 20
Lucha Libre 235
Lucy V. Hay 68
Ludicrous 270
Luke Skywalker 98

M

Mackenzie Crook 342, 350
Madeline George 168
Mad Men 17, 341, 350
Magneto 101
Magnolia 336, 350
manager 26, 140, 144, 161, 173, 293, 319
managers 133, 159, 182, 293
Manchester By The Sea 20
Mandy 211
Manhattan Murder Mystery 118
Man of The House 58
Marathon Man 121
Marcus Garvey 261
Margot Lee Shetterly 272
Marie Antoinette 335, 350
Mark Dindal 80, 279, 282, 286, 289, 342
Mark Wahlberg 267
Marlin 278, 285, 288
Martha Marcy May Marlene 209
Martin Campbell 127

Martin Short 118, 169, 172, 243
Marvel 56, 96, 101, 103, 105, 263, 280, 319, 339
Marvel Cinematic Universe 56
Mary Kills People 116, 117, 173, 178
Matt Tischler 287
MCU 56
meet cute 248
Melanie Green 43
Mel Brooks 58
melodrama 232
Mentor 55
Michaela Coel 332, 337, 338, 349, 350
Michael Bond 137, 268, 269
Michael Dante DiMartino 336, 349
Michael Hauge 68
Michael Jordan 271
Michael Myers 106, 214
Michael Stuhlberg 87
Mickey Rourke 112
Mick Jagger 300
Midnight Run 293, 294
midpoint 62, 63, 69, 72, 85, 198, 353
Mikael Lindnord 267
Mike Pence 242
Mike Surrey 284
Mindy Kaling 342, 350
Minnie Driver 187
Mira, Royal Detective 22, 279, 280, 283, 284, 285, 286
Mishima 334
M. Night Shyamalan 335, 349
Modern Family 135, 165, 241
monomyth 55, 67
Monopoly 218
monster 55, 85, 93, 211, 221
Mr. and Mrs. Smith 29
Mr. Curry 60, 281
Mr. Smith Goes to Washington 240
Mrs. Potts 284
Mulan 276, 287
multi-camera 73, 114, 324
Murakami 334
Mushu 287
My Best Friend's Bouquet 251
My Best Friend's Wedding 248
My Name is Earl 114
Mysteries Channel 253
Mystic River 265
myth 55, 88, 336
Mythic Quest 340

N

Nancy Meyers 248, 332, 350
Narration Written by 294
narrative transport 43
National Lampoon's Vacation 93
NBC 136, 142
NCIS 310
Nemo 277, 278, 285, 286, 288, 330, 341, 349
Netflix 25, 51, 72, 104, 113, 136, 137, 148, 160, 165, 219, 227, 231, 233, 234, 239, 249, 251, 296, 297, 308, 310, 311, 323, 326
network 41, 50, 64, 70, 76, 78, 86, 144, 158, 167, 171, 177, 178, 184, 187, 191, 192, 204, 211, 215, 219, 220, 230, 249, 254, 280, 296, 299, 306, 310, 324, 342, 345
Never Have I Ever 342, 350
New Line 266
Nic Cage 211
Nicholls Fellowship 140
Night Shift 263
N. K. Jemisin 336
Noah Hawley 339
No Country for Old Men 102
No Man's Land 23, 270
non-binary 307
Non-Stop 60
Nope 126, 210
Nora Ephron 332, 339, 349
Norma Bailey 178
Norma Desmond 282
Normal People 334, 349
notes 24, 42, 49, 50, 54, 58, 112, 117, 148, 149, 150, 152, 160, 164, 165, 174, 181, 183, 184, 185, 186, 187, 189, 190, 191, 192, 193, 194, 211, 216, 217, 238, 280, 295, 297, 298, 299, 310, 313, 318, 320, 328, 337, 342, 345, 348
No Time to Die 102

O

obstacle 34, 96, 97, 140, 160, 232, 252, 353
obstacles 56, 63, 83, 86, 87, 96, 98, 189, 203, 231, 232, 233, 252, 257, 281
Ocean's Eleven 202

Oldboy 203
one-note 107, 221
one-pager 50, 76
Only Murders in the Building 72, 73, 165, 168, 170, 173, 238, 241, 306, 307, 329
On My Block 88
onomatopoeia 214
on-the-nose 111, 112, 117
On Writing 68, 333
Open World 6, 56
Open writing assignments 42
Option 302
Orphan Black 167
Oscar 186, 248, 323, 338
Outlander 168, 172, 173, 176, 270
outlines 46, 50, 54, 71, 76, 110, 148, 262
Overlord 334, 350
Overwritten 188

P

Pacha 286
pacing 54, 73, 76, 212
Paddington 24, 25, 30, 60, 79, 89, 90, 118, 137, 198, 240, 267, 268, 269, 280, 281, 288, 316
Paddington 2 30, 60, 90, 240
page one rewrite 193, 297
Palm Springs 249, 251
pandemic 42, 44, 148, 253, 309, 319, 322
Parker 252, 333, 350
parkour 127
Patricia Highsmith 28
Patrick Warburton 282
Patton Oswalt 89
Paul Thomas Anderson 336, 350
Paul Warnick 49
payoffs 54, 219
Peaky Blinders 98
period films 210
Peter Schneider 283
Peter Sellers 341
Phineas and Ferb 283
Piers Wenger 296
pigeonholed 28, 29
Pillow Talk 252, 332
pilot 17, 24, 44, 60, 79, 130, 142, 143, 144, 165, 167, 169, 173, 191, 214, 219, 226, 238, 241, 279, 300, 306, 327, 340, 347, 349

pilots 24, 54, 79, 142, 171, 300, 326, 342
pilot script 24, 219
Pilot Season 167
Pin Cushion 102, 320
pitch 33, 34, 35, 36, 37, 38, 39, 41, 42, 43, 44, 45, 47, 48, 50, 51, 52, 59, 62, 76, 91, 148, 153, 162, 166, 167, 169, 177, 184, 191, 215, 225, 227, 265, 266, 279, 283, 284, 288, 289, 322, 323, 327, 342
Pitch Decks 51
pitching 24, 35, 38, 41, 42, 43, 44, 45, 46, 47, 48, 51, 52, 66, 68, 80, 96, 167, 174, 179, 191, 249, 279, 289, 296, 321, 345
Pixar 30, 62, 80, 276, 288, 289, 324, 348
plausibility 344
Pleasantville 95
plot-driven 88
Plot Point 1 63
Plot Point 2 63, 69
podcast 127, 169, 272, 277, 300, 313
podcasts 119, 256, 272, 300, 304, 338
point of view 24, 38, 74, 93, 106, 107, 137, 159, 175, 177, 187, 197, 261, 267, 268, 277, 284, 311, 332, 344, 346, 353, 354
Polish Draft 297
Polly Hill 296
Predator 200
Predators 200, 263
Prime Minister Rabin 106
Producer 7, 169, 176, 177
production bonus 302
production fee 302
protagonist 23, 62, 87, 89, 94, 95, 96, 97, 98, 99, 100, 102, 103, 105, 121, 137, 189, 201, 202, 203, 204, 205, 279, 280, 290, 307
protagonists 63, 88, 98, 99, 102, 104, 203, 234, 252, 254, 257, 271
Pulp Fiction 341, 349
punch line 116, 232, 263
punch-up 239, 284

Q

Queer as Folk 125, 165
Quentin Tarantino 203, 262, 349

R

Raiders of the Lost Ark 200
Rainy Day Podcasts 300
Raising Hope 170
Ramen Girl 22
read-through 242
Rear Window 22, 23
recording sessions 277, 288
Red Planet 25, 143
Red Planet Prize 143
Regina King 320
rejection 59, 316, 318, 320, 324, 347
representation 24, 137, 140, 141, 142, 182, 291, 292, 293, 304, 306, 307, 336
research 21, 22, 23, 57, 65, 77, 90, 101, 107, 193, 249, 265, 283, 284
Reservoir Dogs 341, 349
rewrites 27, 50, 104, 148, 177, 180, 191, 194, 280, 298, 327
rewriting 27, 57, 86, 119, 120, 180, 183, 184, 186, 191, 193, 194, 295, 321, 330
Rhett Reese 49
Richard Donner 227
Richard Pryor 58
Richard Russo 306
Richard Sackler 87
Richard Stark 333
Ridley Scott 208, 325
Roadmap Writers 24, 128, 136, 141
Robert DeNiro 98
Robert Eggers 210
Robert McKee 8, 68, 70, 71, 125
Robert Patrick 203
Robert Rodriquez 112
Robert Smigel 21, 22, 119
Robert Thorogood 143
Roger Kumble 179
Rolin Jones 171
romance 17, 25, 46, 225, 248, 250, 251, 252, 257, 339
Romancing the Stone 252
Roman Holiday 332, 350
romantic comedies 23, 30, 248, 249, 250, 251, 252, 257
rom-coms 248, 250, 251, 252, 253, 332
Rose Matafeo 187
Rosie Alison 316
Roswell, NM 304
Royal Tenenbaums 226
R-rated comedy 243
Russell T. Davis 125
Ryan Coogler 103
Ryan Reynolds 26

S

Sacha Baron Cohen 70, 242, 344
Sally Hawkins 118
Sally Rooney 334
Sam Raimi 212
Sarah Jessica Parker 252
Sarah Polley 338, 349
Saturday Night Live 245
Save the Cat 54, 63, 69, 128
Save the Cat Beat Sheet 63
Say Anything 335, 350
Scary Tales to Tell in the Dark 215
sci-fi 24, 25, 50, 93, 207, 208, 215, 217, 219, 221
Scooby Doo 283
Scream 225, 227
Screenplay by 64, 294
Screen Story by 294
screenwriter 8, 18, 20, 26, 27, 29, 58, 68, 95, 103, 134, 135, 144, 211, 237, 266, 291, 294, 298, 300, 301, 302, 318, 320, 321, 322, 332, 345
screwball comedy 250
Script Anatomy 144
script-driven 283
Script-ment 76
Scrooge 254
Seabiscuit 95
Second City 119
Seinfeld 341, 350
Selena 113, 118, 160, 163, 172, 262, 264
Selena Gomez 118, 172
sequel 30, 242, 270, 271, 273, 304
set piece 27, 129, 185, 190, 197, 198, 199, 200, 201, 205, 245
setups 219
Sex And The City 50, 252
sexual harassment 308
Shadow 55
Shakespeare 17, 39
Shameless 103, 160
Shane Black 333, 340, 349, 350
Shang-Chi 101
Shaun of the Dead 46, 219, 349

Shonda Rhymes 338, 342, 349, 350
Shopping Agreement 302
Shorts 26, 27, 141
showrunner 21, 48, 50, 58, 72, 78, 113, 117, 138, 143, 144, 145, 157, 158, 159, 160, 161, 162, 163, 164, 165, 166, 167, 169, 170, 171, 172, 174, 175, 176, 177, 178, 179, 181, 182, 299, 305, 306, 308, 312, 329, 338
Showtime 127
Shudder 215
Signs 335, 349
Simon Farnaby 30, 90, 240, 269, 288
Simon Kinberg 29
single-camera 72, 73, 114, 126
sitcom 29, 63, 72, 76, 89, 107, 114, 115, 125, 164, 187, 244, 245
slug lines 58
SNL 22
Snowfall 161
Snow White 24
soap 215, 230, 262
Social IQ 312, 342
Something's Gotta Give 248, 249, 350
Song of Ice and Fire 334
Sophia Coppola 335, 350
source material 240, 264, 265, 267
Space Cowboys 326
spec 24, 55, 79, 135, 143, 144, 148, 161, 174, 293
Specialty Pass 297
Spencer Tracey 337
Spiderman 30, 61
Spider-Man 98
Spotlight 189
Squid Game 113, 310
staff writer 21, 143, 159, 162, 165, 166, 171, 173, 174, 176, 329
Stan Lee 97, 318
Stanley Kubrick 239
Star 25, 101, 113, 163, 199, 217, 264, 265, 280
Starstruck 187
Star Wars 25, 199, 217, 280
step 22, 27, 28, 86, 110, 124, 151, 153, 175, 176, 189, 193, 202, 212, 243, 297, 339
Stephen King 68, 263, 333, 350
Stephen Mangan 86
Stephen Marley 329
Steve Bing 300

Steve Martin 119, 143, 169, 172, 225, 238
Steven Spielberg 42, 194, 217, 293, 320
Stock, Aitken, and Waterman 125
Story By 294
Story Editor 176, 177, 181
Story Producer 176
Straight Man 306
Strangers On A Train 28
Stranger Things 137, 295, 311
streamers 28, 163, 231, 248, 251, 299, 300, 303, 309, 310, 311
structure 17, 30, 34, 50, 53, 54, 56, 58, 62, 63, 64, 65, 66, 67, 68, 69, 70, 71, 72, 73, 74, 76, 77, 81, 90, 115, 119, 144, 145, 150, 151, 191, 200, 211, 214, 219, 227, 235, 239, 249, 257, 263, 267, 282, 299, 334
studio executives 34, 160, 227, 240, 282, 301
stunt coordinator 127, 129, 181, 200
Subtext 112
subvert 70, 105, 201, 202
Succession 101, 341
Sugar In My Veins 140
Sundance 136, 326, 333, 349, 350
Sunshine 215
Sun Tzu 263
superhero 96, 266, 281
Superman 98
supernatural 55, 208, 209
Supervising Producer 169, 177
Supporting characters 100
Syd Field 8, 61, 63, 68, 71
Syd Field Paradigm 63, 68
Sydney Lumet 332, 350

Sydney Pollack 332, 350

T

table read 49, 114, 179, 317
taboo 215, 216
Tale of Two Cities 334
Tara Armstrong 173
Tarantino 69, 124, 203, 262, 341, 349
Tarzan 276, 284
Tassie Cameron 173
T'Chala 103
Ted Danson 95
TED Talks 39
teen characters 261

telenovela 229, 230, 231, 232, 233, 236
Telenovelas 5, 230, 231, 236
Televisa 230
Tenet 335
tentpoles 58
Terminator 54, 203
Terminator 2 203
Terminator 3: Rise of the Machines 54
Terms of Endearment 339
Thanos 101, 103, 105
The Anatomy of Story 67
The Avengers 94
The Aviary 209, 211, 325
The A Word 270
The Babysitter 219, 349
The Bear 346
The Black List 7, 128, 136, 143, 335
The Blair Witch Project 326
The Boogeyman 263
The Conversation 88
The Cooler 185
The Descent 46
The Emperor's New Groove 80, 282, 289, 330
The Evil Dead 18
The Fast and the Furious 172
The Fugitive 293
The Game 54
The Good Place 95
The Gordin Cell 270
The Guerrilla Film Makers Handbook. 67
The Hangover 20, 46
The Hero's Journey 6, 23, 55, 61, 68
The Hit Factory 125
The Hollywood Standard 67, 144
The House of Leaves 106
The Humans 210
The Hunger Games 95, 265
The Jerk 225
The Last Picture Show 341
The Lion King 282
Thelma Ritter 252
The Lone Ranger 198
The Martian 29
theme 23, 34, 44, 50, 52, 74, 75, 87, 93, 101, 107, 163, 209, 254, 260, 265, 271, 272, 280, 285, 339, 340, 352
themes 17, 18, 35, 41, 51, 74, 97, 100, 104, 115, 171, 209, 249, 250, 257, 271, 285, 286, 335
The Motorcycle Diaries 338, 349

The New Yorker 28
The Notebook 26
The Office 342
The Omen 227
The Porter 23, 59, 116, 117, 169, 170, 173, 260, 305, 310, 322, 338
The Princess Bride 333
The Professional 341, 349
The Red and the White 203
There's Something About Mary 58
The Simpsons 172
The Sixth Sense 335, 349
The Sleepover 215, 216
The Sopranos 100
The Strangers 106, 219
The Sun 335, 349
The Talented Mr. Ripley 28
The Tao of Pong 41
The Texas Chainsaw Massacre 18
The Three Musketeers 199, 200, 266
The Ultimatum 93
The Village 335, 349
The Walking Dead 214, 310
The War Next Door 234, 235, 308
The Winter's Tale 276
The Wrestler 112
The Writer's Journey 55, 68
The X-Files 214, 219, 349
This Is Us 26, 142, 143
three act structure 63, 64, 69, 70, 81
thriller 27, 29, 45, 71, 94, 190, 196, 197, 201, 202, 203, 204, 205, 225, 270, 334
ticking clock 21, 93, 201
Tim Allen 238
Tim Kono 73, 169
Timothy Brock 43
Timur Bekmambetov 129
Tina Fey 332, 342, 350
Tom Cruise 210, 326, 336
Tommy Lee Jones 293, 326
Tommy Shelby 98
Tom Schumacher 282, 289
tone 23, 40, 44, 46, 50, 51, 52, 63, 68, 112, 118, 119, 120, 137, 144, 150, 158, 159, 162, 171, 176, 177, 180, 190, 193, 200, 202, 213, 220, 226, 240, 241, 246, 262, 267, 268, 273, 279, 320, 327, 332, 341
Tone shift 189
Tony Bancroft 287

INDEX

Torchwood 125
Totenfrau 270
Toy Story 2 289
Trainspotting 102, 338
Treasure Island 263, 266
treatment 54, 57, 58, 76, 239, 279, 297
tribalism 35
Trick 'r Treat 215
Trigger Warning 92
trope 248, 249, 252, 254, 257
Tucker and Dale 18, 35, 46, 114, 225, 304, 326, 339
turnaround 298
TV series 26, 39, 57, 64, 86, 138, 214, 233, 350
twist 60, 168, 172, 202, 299
Tzvetan Todorov 61

U

UCLA 136, 140, 144
Ukraine 309
Uma Thurman 203
Unbreakable 335, 349
unemployment 316
Universal Studios 30, 200, 319
University of Texas - Austin 329
Us 26, 142, 143, 225
USC Film School 326
US Copyright Office 301

V

Valley of Tears 17, 327
Vanilla Sky 335, 350
Victoria Pearlman 300
Video Village 181
Viggo Mortensen 116
villain 62, 87, 94, 95, 97, 98, 99, 101, 102, 103, 104, 105, 106, 116, 127, 196, 203, 204, 209, 214, 231, 232, 236, 251, 252, 281, 282, 283, 287, 307, 354
villains 25, 85, 95, 98, 101, 102, 103, 104, 105, 106, 209, 214, 215, 231, 254, 282, 283, 354
villain's motto 287
Vince Gilligan 220
Vin Diesel 270
VO 121
voice 24, 28, 41, 42, 43, 57, 68, 86, 90, 114, 115, 121, 126, 133, 134, 135, 137, 138, 150, 166, 171, 175, 182, 240, 268, 277, 282, 287, 288, 290, 292, 312, 321, 326, 334, 335, 337, 343, 347
voice over 121

W

WALL-E 217, 277
Walter Hill 220
Walter Matthau 334
Walter Salles 338
Wanted 129, 181, 266
Warner Bros. Digital Networks 300
Warner Brothers 44, 226
War of the Roses 225
Warren Littlefield 265
Watchmen 339
Wesley Snipes 323
Westworld 335, 349
WGA 7, 163, 294, 296, 297, 313
What We Do in the Shadows 241, 243
When Harry Met Sally 46, 249, 250, 332, 339, 350
While You Were Sleeping 251
Whistle Down the Wind 268
Will & Grace 172
William Goldman 66, 67, 328, 340, 349, 350
William Hurt 116
William Morris Endeavor 310
Windsor Gardens 60
WME 310
Wonka 288
Woody Allen 118
Working Girl 248
Working Title 70
world-building 20, 207, 218
Writer Duet 149
Writers Assistant 176, 177
writer's block 56, 79, 80, 321
writers rooms 42, 77, 162, 163, 164, 178, 236, 280, 305, 306
Writing and Selling Drama Screenplays 68
Writing Sprint 348
Written By 294
Wrong Turn 18

X

X-men 269

Y

Yana Gorskaya 241
Y Tu Mamá También 337
Yzma 278, 282

Z

zombie 29, 46
Zombieland 49, 227
Zoom 34, 37, 41, 42, 43, 44, 45, 46, 48, 49, 142, 143, 165, 166, 173, 329
Zucker brothers 341